Economics and Economic Change
Microeconomics

D1735154

The Open University course DD202 team

Paul Anand, Reader in Economics

Suma Athreye, Deputy Course Team Chair and Senior Lecturer in Economics

Brenda Barnett, Course Secretary

Penny Bennett, Project Leader

Pam Berry, Compositor

Karen Bridge, Software Designer

Michael Brogan, Course Manager

Vivienne Brown, Professor of Intellectual History

Stephen Clift, Editor

Lene Connolly, Print Buyer

Neil Costello, Associate Director, SQW

Sarah Crompton, Graphic Designer

Graham Dawson, Course Team Chair and Senior Lecturer in Economics

Sue Dobson, Cartoonist

Christopher Downs, Software Course Team Chair and Senior Lecturer in Economics, University College, Chichester

Wilf Eynon, Audio Visual

Ian Fribbance, Staff Tutor

Phil Gauron, Series Producer, BBC

Janis Gilbert, Graphic Artist

Richard Golden, Production and Presentation Administrator

Mark Goodwin, Editor

Celia Hart, Picture Researcher

Martin Higginson, Staff Tutor

Susan Himmelweit, Professor of Economics

Steve Hoy, Producer, BBC

Andrew Law, BBC

Damian Lewis, Software Developer, BBC

Avis Lexton, Secretary

Maureen Mackintosh, Professor of Economics

Ione Mako, BBC

Paul Manners, BBC

Mariana Mazzucato, Professor of Economics

Vicki McCulloch, Graphic Designer

Judith Mehta, Lecturer in Economics

David Morris, Software Developer

Jonathan Owen, Graphic Artist

Anne Paynter, Course Secretary

Carlton Reeve, BBC

Roberto Simonetti, Senior Lecturer in Economics

Hedley Stone, Staff Tutor

Andrew Trigg, Senior Lecturer in Economics

Chris Wooldridge, Editor

Tutor consultants

Michelle Jenkins

Maureen Le Roi

Alistair Young

External authors

Nick Crafts, Professor of Economic History, London School of Economics and Political Science

Guiseppe Fontana, Lecturer in Economics, University of Leeds

Francis Green, Professor of Economics, University of Kent at Canterbury

Diane Perrons, Senior Lecturer in Economics, London School of Economics and Political Science

Malcolm Sawyer, Professor of Economics, University of Leeds

David Spencer, Lecturer in Economics, University of Leeds

Andrew Stevenson, Honorary Senior Research Fellow, Department of Economics, University of Glasgow

Anthony J. Venables, Professor of Economics, London School of Economics and Political Science

External assessor

John Vint, Professor of Economics, Manchester Metropolitan University

External consultant

Dr Terry O'Shaughnessy, Tutor and Fellow in Economics, St Anne's College, Oxford

Economics and Economic Change

Microeconomics

Second edition

Edited by
**Graham Dawson, Maureen Mackintosh
and Paul Anand**

An imprint of **Pearson Education**

Harlow, England • London • New York • Boston • San Francisco • Toronto • Sydney • Singapore • Hong Kong
Tokyo • Seoul • Taipei • New Delhi • Cape Town • Madrid • Mexico City • Amsterdam • Munich • Paris • Milan

Pearson Education Limited
Edinburgh Gate
Harlow
Essex CM20 2JE
England

and Associated Companies throughout the world

Visit us on the World Wide Web at:
www.pearsoned.co.uk

The Open University
Walton Hall
Milton Keynes
MK7 6AA
www.open.ac.uk

First published 2006

ISBN-13: 978-0-273-69371-0
ISBN-10: 0-273-69371-9

British Library Cataloguing-in-Publication Data
A catalogue record for this book is available from the British Library

Library of Congress Cataloging-in-Publication Data
A catalog record for this book is available from the Library of Congress

10 9 8 7 6 5 4 3 2 1
09 08 07 06 05

Typeset in 10/12pt Minion by 35
Printed and bound in Great Britain by Ashford Colour Press, Hampshire

The publisher's policy is to use paper manufactured from sustainable forests.

Contents

Preface

Economics and Economic Change is a new introductory economics text intended mainly for students on courses which are components of multi- and inter-disciplinary degree programmes as distinct from more traditional single honours economics degrees. These degree programmes include business studies, social sciences, social policy and public policy. The book contains the core teaching of an Open University course of the same title, which consists of *Microeconomics* and *Macroeconomics*. More and more students in higher education are studying independently, in part because part-time and distance provision are expanding and in part because large classes create difficulties in providing adequate individual attention for full-time students. Economics principles texts can be hard going for students without the support of seminars and discussion. In contrast, *Economics and Economic Change* mixes critical debate, ethical reflection and discussion of current economic issues with the exposition of theoretical analysis. Together with the interactive style of teaching drawn from The Open University's long experience of open supported distance education, the text offers, we believe, an engaging introduction to an important social science for full-time and part-time students alike.

Economics and Economic Change is one of a 'new generation' of economics courses that reflects the economic and social impact of information and communication technologies. While the text teaches students how to analyse the effects of new technologies on the economy, the accompanying CD-ROM enables students to see themselves as taking part in the economic processes they are learning to understand. In presenting a range of teaching materials in this way – real-world case studies, 'test your understanding' quizzes, a statistical package and 'virtual tutorials' on diagrammatic analysis – *Economics and Economic Change* 'enacts' the changes that are taking place and enables students to develop ICT skills.

This book is based upon an Open University course and is therefore a product of collective working. The course team, listed on p.ii, includes both Open University academics and outside contributors. The academic editors are grateful to our external contributing authors for giving the considerable time this enterprise requires. We would particularly like to thank Malcolm Sawyer for his collaboration in planning and editing *Macroeconomics*.

An Open University course team also includes many essential contributors besides academic authors. The academic editors of this book are very appreciative of the outstanding professional effort and expertise contributed by the course manager and project leader, the secretarial staff, the publishing editors, the designers and artists, the software designers and the BBC producers. The external assessor for the course as a whole, John Vint, has been a source of wise advice on structure, content and the accessibility of the course. Finally, the members of our panel of Open University tutors have put a great deal of effort into trying to ensure that the course content is appropriate for students and have always contributed to the conviviality of course team meetings.

Finally, Justinia Seaman, her colleagues at Pearson Education and their reviewers have contributed much valuable advice about turning an Open University course text into an introductory economics textbook for all students who approach economics as a social science or through business studies.

July 2005

Introduction

Graham Dawson

As a child in Birkenhead, I was regularly taken to visit my great aunt Adelaide. For her, the problem was how to occupy the seven-year-old boy while she and my mother brought each other up to date on news and gossip from their branches of the family. (It seemed to be part of my younger sister's early socialization that she was expected to sit in on the exchange.) The solution lay in a large glass-fronted bookcase. The only book I still remember was a very old one called *The Romance of Business*. Within its dark-blue cloth covers I discovered biographies of major nineteenth-century industrialists and entrepreneurs and indeed the 'life stories' of the firms they created. As far as I can recall, Mr Bryant and Mr May got together to manufacture safety matches, Jesse Boot started out with a stall in Nottingham market and our local hero (albeit born in Bolton) Mr Lever established Port Sunlight as the supplier of the nation's soap.

These narratives gave me an early inkling of two ideas, which I think I understand a little more clearly now. First, there was a sense of the risks these businessmen had taken in being so innovative, bringing new products to market with no certainty that they would 'catch on' with people. The book's title did not lie; there was adventure and glamour about their economic exploits, creating industrial empires and family fortunes out of what proved to be good ideas. Second, in making their own way in the world, they transformed it. Soap and safety matches are now so ubiquitous that we do not give them a second thought, but there was a time when they were innovative 'high-tech' products, perhaps encountering consumer resistance before transforming the daily habits of the population.

Thanks to my great aunt 'Addie', I received an early introduction to the importance of innovation and to the idea of economic change. Economics came later. As an undergraduate I discovered that the standard methods of analysing the activities of firms involved diagrams, tables of statistical data and a rather formal and abstract way with verbal explanation. It was much more like physics than a biography. Nevertheless, the models of consumer demand, perfect competition and monopoly, once applied to the real world of buying and selling, of production and trade, were just as illuminating as the old blue book, although the light they cast was more austere.

Economics and Economic Change is an attempt to bring you both the romance and the physics of economic life, to reflect the rapid pace of economic change and to capture the enduring structures that shape it. However, there is another dimension of economic change that the course addresses: the moral or ethical dimension. Economic change is not only beneficial, liberating and exciting in its impact on the lives of the people who shape it and are in turn shaped by it. There are casualties as well as victorious generals. Indeed, the military metaphor is appropriate, because economic change has been and continues to be at the heart of a struggle between social classes, ethnic groups and nations that sometimes bursts out into violent conflict. On a less spectacular level, economic change brings with it for many people dislocation and upheaval, the loss of traditional livelihoods and accustomed ways of life and the reality of material deprivation and hardship. Throughout the course there is an engagement with the implications, both beneficial and damaging, of economic change for people's lives and for their well-being.

As the title suggests, *Economics and Economic Change* combines an exploration of some major aspects of economic change in the international and national economies with an introduction to economic theory. You will, therefore, find two 'storylines' interwoven throughout the text. One is about economic change: what is innovation, how does economic change occur and what are the most important economic problems that arise? The other storyline is about economic analysis: the exposition of economic ideas and economic debates. Describing the two main strands of the text in this way acknowledges that they are closely related. We need economic concepts and ideas in order to understand economic change and to identify and analyse economic problems. But changing economic events also feed back upon and influence the ideas and preoccupations of economists.

In emphasizing the interaction of ideas and events, this book – like all texts in social science – is very much a child of its time and place. Written in Britain, in the West, and from within the Anglo-American tradition in economics, the text reflects a number of early twenty-first century uncertainties. This is perhaps most evident in the themes we have chosen for the 'economic change' strand. Among the contemporary economic issues the book explores are the following: Are we living through a new Industrial Revolution, led by information and communication technologies? Why is the intensity of work effort increasing? What should be done about increasing inequalities in some economies, including inequality in access to adequate health care? Why have capitalist economies tended to go through booms and slumps, causing inflation and unemployment? What do we know about the economic outcomes of globalization? Is capitalism environmentally sustainable?

Models and voices

In the 'economics' strand, too, *Economics and Economic Change* reflects early twenty-first century questioning, for example of the benefits and limits of both markets and government and of the ways in which they complement each other. The 1990s saw the long US boom, heralded by some as the 'new economy' inaugurated by information technology and welcomed by some as the reward for political confidence in the benefits of the unfettered market. This context has strengthened a renewed interest among economists in innovation and the role it plays in industrial revolutions. It has also triggered an interest in economic institutions, reflected here in the discussions of market institutions and of the economics of policy and governance.

Over many years economics has been exploring the consequences of how markets go wrong, or 'fail' – a concern which has been rekindled by the failure of some Western market systems to re-employ all the unemployed. This text picks up this renewed concern with the imperfections of markets, treating markets that work imperfectly as the dominant case in analysing markets and the national economy.

There is a further sense in which the approach to economics in this text is clearly the product of its time. Economics is a social science, though one which makes considerable claims to precision and prediction. In broad terms, recent social science has been marked by a systematic focus on what might be summarized as standpoint and language. There has been intensive questioning of whether there is necessarily a diversity of understanding of the social world structured by the points of view of those undertaking the theorizing. Related to this, there has been a renewed awareness of the importance of language and metaphor in social science.

These concerns with language and method in social science have until recently largely passed economics by. However, the last few years have seen a new interest among economists in the rhetoric of the subject, in the basis of its claims to knowledge about economies, and in its fundamental assumptions. In this text we have tried to reflect some of these concerns in our approach to teaching economics.

One of the main ways in which economists seek to understand economies is by constructing economic 'models'. These models are rather formal statements of how different elements of the economy interact: what influences what and how. Economic models can be stated in words, visually in diagrams or by using mathematics. In an introductory text such as this, the main media are words and diagrams. Like all textbooks in economics, this book sets out to explain how economists construct models to try to understand how economies work.

Economics and Economic Change uses models drawn from some rather different theoretical perspectives. There is a pluralist feel to the text. It uses models that engage with the historical narrative of economic change, with the 'life cycles' of industries that follow, for example the car industry, from a 'new dawn' of innovation through maturity and into decline – and, in that particular case, renewal. This text also uses models that are expressed in geometrical diagrams and in equations to 'stop the action' and examine the properties of market structures, to investigate the balance of the forces of supply and demand at a particular moment.

This book is also a child of its time in reflecting contemporary engagement with ethical issues, with questions of right and wrong, and even with questions of what is ultimately good for people. Questions in ethics are on many people's minds, provoked by a range of issues from cloning and euthanasia through the responsibility for climate change and other environmental damage to the importance of trust and integrity in corporate life and the afflictions of sleaze, scandals and spin in political affairs. In this text we introduce ethical questions by thinking about well-being, or what is ultimately good for people, and how economic activity can contribute to it. We return to ethical issues at several points, for example when examining the ethics of the environment.

Another activity encompassed within 'economics' is the examination of economic data and the use of models and data together to explore economic change. This activity, its theory and practice, is the specialism of a branch of economics called econometrics. While this text does not teach econometrics, it recognizes that understanding economics requires some understanding of the excitements and difficulties of trying to confront models with data.

Finally, a word about styles of writing. Economists speak in many different 'voices', reflecting personalities, subject matter, aims and audiences. They write both to analyse and to persuade, and hence do both in a cool and abstract tone and in emotive prose. Economics makes strong claims to clarity and exactitude while being a highly political subject: the stuff of public debate.

Unusually, this text contains some of this flavour of many voices. It is written by a variety of different authors, all professional economists but with different specialisms and approaches to economics. The aim of the editors has been to ensure that the presentation of the theory and arguments proceeds logically through the text, but not to suppress differences in style and approach. Style and content are deeply interrelated, and we hope to provide a feel for the variety and range of what is called economics.

Using the text

This book has been developed from a distance-learning text and we have retained two key features of the original text: it was designed to be studied independently, and it is written in a style addressed to you, the student. We believe that there are significant advantages in retaining these features. Using a textbook is a solitary activity and it is important not to increase the sense of isolation by adopting the impersonal style that is familiar from so many texts. We hope that we can reward the interest in economic issues and events that sparked your interest in the subject by constantly emphasizing the application of theory to economic issues, not only through formal case studies but in the integration of real-world examples into the main text. The text is also designed to be studied in the order in which the material is presented. The presentation builds up logically from Chapter 1, with cross-referencing between chapters throughout.

The rest of this Introduction previews the first half of the book, *Microeconomics*. Chapter 1 considers four ways in which some social scientists have claimed that there might be a 'new economy' coming into being: the switch from manufacturing to services, globalization, new technology and flexible labour markets. The good and bad points of economic change, its benefits and costs, are discussed. For example, what does it mean for people trying desperately to balance the urgent demands of work and life? Chapter 2 takes one aspect of the debate concerning the new economy – innovation in the form of the introduction of information and communication technologies – and places it in the historical context of industrial revolutions. Is the new economy really new or 'just another' industrial revolution? This highlights the role of innovation in creating industries, a theme that is picked up in Chapter 3. The main focus is on firms and how the costs of producing output change as they increase the scale of production and introduce new technology into the production process. Chapter 3 also introduces the diagrammatic analysis of firms' costs and of consumer demand. These chapters introduce the range of activities that constitutes economics: formulating theories, modelling, debate and persuasion, analysis of data, understanding the behaviour of economic institutions such as companies and households, and analysing economic processes. These chapters seek to show how all of these economic techniques can be used to build up a rich understanding of innovation and economic change.

This approach is taken up and developed by Chapters 4, 5 and 6, which explore the behaviour of firms within markets and the different forms that competition can take, such as competition on price as well as competition through innovation. Theory is combined with practical case studies and examples. Chapter 4 is built around a case study of Microsoft, the US software company that was accused by the US authorities of misusing its power to block competition. UK and EU legislation also seek to curb the power of large companies because it may be used to harm the interests of consumers, for example by charging prices that are 'too high'. The role of large companies, or monopolies, in innovation, in bringing new products to consumers, is also analysed. However, not every market is marked by product innovation, rapid technical change and monopoly power. Think of buying fresh fruit and vegetables in the sort of market that takes place in many towns on 'market day'. Or think of buying second-hand goods, anything from a house or a car to a baby buggy or guitar, through the classified ads in a local newspaper. Chapter 5 examines markets where competition among a large number of sellers provides one way of securing for consumers the lowest possible prices. Markets of this sort have been seen by some politicians and economists as an ideal way of organizing economic life, as 'free markets', and their role as a benchmark in economic theory will be further discussed in Chapter 8. Chapter 6 analyses competition in markets with a few firms, each of which takes its rivals' behaviour into account in determining its own competitive strategy. In this situation competition can be understood as a war, involving alliances and collusion as well as supermarket 'price wars'. A new technique, game theory, is introduced to model firms' decision-making in markets where we might imagine each firm trying to guess what its competitors are going to do.

Microeconomics concludes with four chapters that are more directly about people rather than firms, markets and industries. Chapters 7, 8, 9 and 10 explore issues to do with the well-being of the people who make economies work, as producers and consumers. Do flexible labour markets provide good jobs? Why is the intensity of work effort increasing? How do material wealth, happiness and sustainability measure up as different interpretations of well-being? How is the role of government in furthering people's well-being changing? Do governments still have the will to redistribute income and wealth for the sake of reducing inequality? What can governments do to secure equal access to adequate health care?

Chapter 7 analyses the distinctive features of the labour market, paying particular attention to differences in skill, minimum wage legislation and trade unions. This provides the background for a discussion of issues of special contemporary relevance, including the flexible labour market and increasing work intensity. Chapter 8 introduces the ethical dimension of economic analysis. The national income accounts, which measure the value of the output of goods and services available for consumption, are explained and their limitations as an estimate of people's well-being exposed. This chapter also examines the underlying theory that equates well-being with the satisfaction we enjoy as consumers. Alternative concepts and measures of well-being are explored. These include 'green' national income intended to measure environmental damage and repair, the claim that people have rights to essential goods, and psychological approaches to well-being as happiness. Chapter 9 turns to the contributions that governments and, in particular, welfare states make to well-being. The chapter outlines the standard economic arguments for government intervention in markets that left to themselves, or only minimally regulated, would 'fail', that is, fail to ensure that people are as well off as they might be. The examples discussed are wide ranging, from environmental degradation to unemployment benefits. The chapter also introduces techniques for measuring the degree of inequality in the distribution of income among a national population. Chapter 10 applies these techniques to the measurement of an especially important aspect of inequality: inequality in access to appropriate and effective health care. The chapter also analyses the ways in which market failure would occur if the finance of health care and its delivery were to be left to lightly regulated markets. One response to health-care market failure is the UK National Health Service and the chapter includes a case study of NHS reform.

Throughout the text, we have used two conventions to assist your studying:

Questions

You should stop and try to find answers to these before reading the commentary that follows in the text. They are designed to help you find out how well you have understood the preceding material, and to get you to pause and think for yourself.

Exercises

The exercises allow you to test your understanding of concepts and techniques by applying and practising them. The answers are at the back of the book. You should not give in to the temptation to skip these, since they are an important part of the teaching. Sometimes you will only understand the following section if you have worked through an earlier exercise.

Questions for discussion and review

At the end of each chapter you will find a number of questions of different kinds that together give you an opportunity to review and test your understanding of the contents of the chapter and to develop answers to essay questions of the sort you are likely to encounter in formal examinations. You might think of these questions as a bank of resources to draw upon as you prepare term-time assignments and end-of-course examinations.

These questions come from three sources. Some are printed from the 'test yourself' quizzes at the end of each Part of the text on the CD-ROM. Some are from the end-of-course examinations for each year since the Open University course DD202 Economics and Economic Change was launched in 2003. And the rest are taken from the continuous assessment component of the OU course. All the questions have therefore been 'tried and tested' by hundreds of Open University students. We hope that you find them helpful and appropriately challenging in your own studies.

Welcome to *Economics and Economic Change*. We hope that you enjoy this invitation to what we regard as the fascinating subject of economics.

Microeconomics

Living and working in the 'new economy'

Diane Perrons and Graham Dawson

Concepts

- the switch from manufacturing to services
- globalization
- information and communication technologies (ICT)
- the weightless economy

Objectives

After studying this chapter you should be able to:

- appreciate different understandings of the new economy
- understand claims about the benefits and costs of the new economy.

1.1 Introduction

10 p.m. Friday evening

Sunil, in India, has just received an email from Claire in Brighton, England, who runs a micro enterprise from her front room, clarifying details of some programming she has just subcontracted.

Tom is at a wine bar celebrating news of a £1 million investment of venture capital in his company.

Stephen has just begun the night shift in a call centre.

Joyce has just left her cleaning job, one of three jobs she currently holds. She is also a part-time office administrator and runs her own small enterprise designing and selling cushions.

These people reflect the varied dimensions of what it has become fashionable to call the 'new economy'. In emailing Sunil, Claire is using the Internet to run an enterprise from her own home. Tom represents one of the successes of the new economy and illustrates how some dot.com companies attract the interest of venture capitalists, financial institutions that invest in new enterprises. Stephen demonstrates how routine jobs underpin the workings of the new economy and Joyce illustrates how workers lower down the employment hierarchy often have to become entrepreneurial and construct their own work patterns in order to survive. The examples also illustrate how jobs are more likely to be in the service

3

sector rather than manufacturing, as likely to be done by women as men and how the working day has lengthened, all characteristics of the new economy.

These are real examples but are they typical? Recently, academics from a range of disciplines and journalists have used the term 'new economy', but their understandings of it differ. This chapter considers some of these different understandings. What is the role of information and communication technologies (ICT) thought to be in the new economy? Section 1.2 suggests that they are a major feature of the economic changes currently taking place but globalization and the shift from manufacturing to services are also important. Should we welcome the new economy for the opportunities it brings or feel threatened by its disruption of ways of economic and social life to which we are accustomed? Section 1.3 discusses the benefits and problems of the new economy and examines the possibility that the opportunities and threats embodied in the new economy are two sides of the same coin.

This chapter examines a debate about the new economy; it does not investigate the new economy directly or take it for granted that there ever was such a thing. The important point is that the debate highlights some of the causes and effects of economic change, a central theme of this book.

1.2 Understanding the new economy

Reflecting upon the economic activities mentioned in '10 p.m. Friday evening' suggests three possible ways of understanding what is actually happening to the economy, how it is changing. First, it is widely believed that we live in an increasingly globalized economy in the sense that economic activity in different countries is more interdependent and more integrated than it used to be. Second, this interdependence is connected to the fact that ICT plays a greater role in economic activity nowadays. For example, as Sunil in India and Claire in England demonstrate, the Internet brings people closer together in space and time and has created new ways of organizing business transactions. Third, the nature of work has changed, with new jobs in high-income countries tending to be in the service sector rather than in manufacturing. These changes – globalization, greater role of ICT and the shift from manufacturing to services in industrialized economies – have been linked together to characterize the new economy. In examining these changes we will discover that working patterns have also undergone significant change, adding a fourth dimension to the new economy. The typical worker is now as likely to be female as male and to work with a computer whether they are gas boiler engineers or travel agents. They are also much less likely to work a standard working week than even ten years ago. In Sections 1.2.1–1.2.3 we examine these three changes in turn and in Section 1.2.4 reflect on their implications for subsequent chapters.

■■■ 1.2.1 The shift from manufacturing to services in industrialized economies

There was a profound restructuring of economic activity in 'older' industrialized countries in the last quarter of the twentieth century from manufacturing to service activities. There are several reasons for this restructuring. First, the long-established industrialized countries such as Germany, the USA, Japan and the UK have faced increasingly intense competition as more countries have industrialized. Second, productivity, or output per worker, has increased in manufacturing industries, enabling the same output to be produced by a smaller number of employees. Third, many people in the richer countries already possess a wide range of the consumer goods that manufacturing industry supplies, but are short of time. So there has been a growth in personal consumer services, such as leisure, including holidays and fitness training.

Service sector work, however, is far more diverse than manufacturing, particularly in the USA and the UK. There are highly skilled and highly paid producer service jobs in information systems, marketing, design and finance, in which most workers are male and white. At the bottom of the hierarchy are people engaged in private consumer services, often in cleaning, catering, security, leisure and personal care work, who are low-paid, rarely earning more than the minimum wage in the UK. Many of these lower-status jobs, for example those referred to in '10 p.m. Friday evening', are directly related to the activities of the time-pressed high-status workers who rely heavily on marketed services.

This restructuring of economic activity from manufacturing to services in part contributes to rising wage inequality. In the period following the Second World War, manufacturing employment provided many working-class people, especially men, with an opportunity to earn regular and relatively high wages in industries such as cars and steel. Earnings were concentrated quite narrowly around a relatively high average wage and maintained through trade unions, which ensured that workers obtained a share of the benefits of productivity increases. Earnings in the service sector, by contrast, are characterized by a lower average wage and a higher dispersion, that is, a greater difference between higher and lower wages. There is also a much wider range of employment opportunities in service industries (Harrison and Bluestone, 1990). The restructuring of employment from manufacturing to services can in part explain the increases in earnings inequality in the UK and US economies.

The result of these changes is that a much smaller proportion of the population in the long-established industrialized economies are directly involved in the production of physical goods in either agriculture or industry. Restructuring, however, rarely takes place as smoothly as some economic models might predict. As the Cambridge (UK) economist Joan Robinson – one of the most important economic theorists of the twentieth century – once said, the real world is not made of plasticine, and neither people nor buildings can be instantly remoulded. Not all factories can be converted into telephone call centres, although this does happen, and people may be unwilling, unable or not given a chance to change their skills.

■■■ 1.2.2 Globalization

Economic globalization may be defined as the increasing interdependence and integration of economic activity in different countries (Thompson, 2000, p.92). Interdependence means that the production of goods in one country is affected by the production of goods in another. For example, the import of Japanese cars into the UK has affected the UK car industry by taking sales away from it. Integration is a closer relation than interdependence, implying that production processes in different countries are so closely co-ordinated that they are best understood as parts of a single complex production process. An example is the manufacture of Honda car engines in Swindon, UK, for installation into cars assembled elsewhere.

Economic globalization has been facilitated by the development of ICT. One outcome of ICT-assisted globalization is that some leading companies, especially in clothing and footwear, no longer play any direct role in manufacturing the goods they sell; Nike, for example, does not manufacture any shoes. Similarly, many of the well-known clothing labels do not manufacture their clothes because they can make more profit from branding and marketing products. Production takes place in a range of companies in both rich and poor countries, which are variously owned and often connected through complex subcontracting arrangements. Each firm seeks to minimize risk in the highly competitive and volatile global market. Underpinning these developments has been the evolution of ICT which, somewhat paradoxically, has facilitated the location of modern factories in poorer countries and the re-emergence of small-scale producers in richer ones.

In the case of clothing, some production takes place 'offshore' in low-wage countries, but some remains in rich countries. For example, Los Angeles, often thought to be the heart of the US new economy, has the highest number of manufacturing jobs in the USA: 663 400 in 1997, which is nearly 6000 more than Chicago and 200 000 more than the third largest manufacturing city, Detroit (Bonacich and Appelbaum, 2000, p.28). These jobs are found in both the new 'high-tech' manufacturing industries and also in the old-style garment industry where over 100 000 workers, many recent migrants, work in the growing number of sweatshops (Bonacich and Appelbaum, 2000).

One reason why sweatshops have re-emerged is the increased power of brand marketers and retailers. Their ability to subcontract production to offshore producers and small-scale local producers enables them to maximize flexibility and so minimize their own risk, which is especially important owing to the transient nature of fashion. It also means that they can absolve themselves of responsibility for the working conditions of producers, although by no means all do so. These conditions can be particularly desperate owing to the global nature of the competition. The corresponding downward pressure on wage costs is intensified by the uncertainty of fashion, leading to long working hours, largely by women, especially in the rush to meet deadlines, and low pay, both offshore and in local sweatshops. The wide choice we as consumers have between different fashion products is paid for by the working conditions of the people who make them.

At the same time the increased economic integration of different countries has increased labour mobility. Many economic migrants to 'older' industrial countries from low-income countries end up working in low-productivity manufacturing, for example as home-workers or as owners of or workers in sweatshops in the clothing industry or in the low-paid jobs expanding in the service sector. Indeed, one of the ironies of globalization is that while many women workers in Bangladesh are working outside the home for the first time in new clothing factories, their compatriots, who migrated to London, are more likely to find themselves working at home (Kabeer, 2000). Women and minority ethnic groups are often over-represented in all of these low-paid activities which are often characterized by part-time work with unsociable hours.

In other industries, such as cars, the shift in manufacturing from the UK and the rest of Europe, far from creating sweatshops, has raised incomes and living standards, for example in east Asia. The shift in manufacturing is by no means complete; cars are produced in large numbers in the UK and Europe, while also being made by a largely male workforce overseas.

■■■ 1.2.3   Information and communication technologies

The new economy is much more than a shift from manufacturing to services and the increased integration of economies on a global scale. It is also strongly linked to the development of ICT, which has facilitated the development of new processes and products, especially 'knowledge goods' which are described below.

The Internet has increased the 'connectivity' or interconnectedness between economies by making textual communication possible in real time as well as providing a new means of disseminating new products and services. For example, ideas can be transmitted across the globe far more quickly than ever before and product obsolescence is much faster. The speed-up in communications means that events in one part of the globe can very quickly affect the fortunes of people living thousands of miles away. For example, the financial crisis in south-east Asia in 1998 led to a worldwide restructuring of the microchip industry. This restructuring resulted in the closure of a firm in Sedgefield in north-east England, which in turn affected the incomes of bar workers and taxi drivers in and around that locality as well as those who were made redundant by the closure itself.

The Internet also allows organizations to take advantage of different time zones and different wage cost zones in order to make cost savings. For example, you may book airline tickets or make enquiries at any time, but if you do so at night your connection is likely to be routed to a different time zone. In this way, companies can provide a 24-hour service, without having to pay higher night-time wage rates. Small firms, micro enterprises and even sole traders as well as multinational organizations can subcontract work globally. As in '10 p.m. Friday evening' a worker in the new media sector in Brighton can subcontract work to a programmer in India whom she had 'met' through the Internet (Perrons, 2001).

In terms of changing patterns of work, the Internet has also facilitated the development of the 24-hour economy. Longer opening and operating hours require flexible working patterns, which in turn allow people to fit paid work around other activities, such as caring or education. But, at the same time, they disrupt collective norms and rhythms of work. As the working day becomes more flexible, many salaried workers are expected to work long hours to demonstrate commitment to their organization (Hochschild, 1997) and to match the working hours of different time zones. In this way, new, more flexible working patterns have complex and diverging implications for other aspects of life.

Knowledge has always been central to competitive economies, to production processes and to selling commodities, but in the new economy a lot more knowledge, intelligence and 'style' is embedded within existing products such as cars, cameras and washing machines. Cars, for example, may have electronic windows and automatic windscreen wipers and headlights, which are programmed to respond to rain and light conditions. More significantly, there has also been an expansion of goods consisting almost entirely of knowledge and for Quah (1996) this represents the hallmark of the new economy. Software is the classic example. The cost of producing the actual physical product – the game or software package – is minuscule. However, the research and development costs going into its production are massive. In other words, the cost of the first product is enormous but the costs of replicating it many times over are then comparatively small.

We will take a closer look at 'knowledge products' in Section 1.3.3 but now it is time to reflect briefly on the significance of the new economy for the economic analysis to be explored in Chapters 2–6.

■ ■ ■ 1.2.4 Looking ahead: understanding economic change

Section 1.2 has looked at different ways of understanding the new economy, of understanding what is actually happening.

Question	Look back over the different understandings of the new economy. Is there really a new economy, just one, or are there three 'new economies'?

There is no single obviously right way of answering this question. Three distinct processes seem to be going on: the switch from manufacturing to services, globalization and the development of ICT. Changes in working patterns seem to be associated with all three processes. Thinking about economic change in terms of the new economy may be helpful in organizing our inquiries. The academics and commentators whose different interpretations will be examined in Section 1.3 certainly think so. They tend to see themselves as interpreting the 'new economy', just as those whose work we referred to in this section see themselves as debating different understandings of the new economy. It is therefore convenient to continue to use this terminology. However, it is worth remembering that the term 'new economy' can be used to pick out any or all of the three changes that are taking place in economic activity. Some of the differences in interpretation may reflect the way in which economists are focusing on different aspects of the new economy – on new economies or simply on economic change.

Now that we are stepping back from the different understandings of the new economy to take, very briefly, a more detached look at them, it seems a good moment to broach another critical question.

Question	Is the 'new economy' really new? Or we might ask, *how* new is the 'new economy'?

There is no simple answer to this question either. It seems reasonably clear that the different changes described above are not all equally new. For example, the shift from manufacturing to services in industrialized economies has been researched and debated for 30 years, while the widespread use of the Internet by consumers is no more than five years old.

Focusing on one dimension of change, the development of undeniably new technologies, economists try to understand what is happening by asking whether a new industrial revolution is taking place. What parallels are there in the past for today's rapid technological change and what do such episodes tell us about contemporary economic change? The next chapter explores these questions through a comparison of the early stages of the US automobile industry and the personal computer industry. Both industries exhibit a common pattern of development or 'life cycle' and Chapter 3 looks more deeply into the economics of the technological innovations underlying them.

Chapters 3–6 take up the theme of innovation and examines the ways in which firms use innovation to compete for sales and profits. Firms also compete in other ways, for example by trying to match or even undercut the prevailing price at which the product is sold. In trying to understand the new economy, and how new it really is, economists therefore look closely at the behaviour of firms and the industries and markets to which they belong. They also debate these issues energetically, because there are different understandings of the behaviour of firms, industries and markets.

1.3 The benefits and costs of the new economy

As well as looking at the behaviour of firms and the industries and markets to which they belong, economists also engage in a different style of inquiry, thinking about what economic change means for the lives of the people involved. Once again there is a variety of interpretations and different ideas but this time they concern the desirability of economic change. What benefits does the 'new economy' bring and what costs, or negative effects, does it impose on people? In analysing these benefits and costs, different economists will be guided by different priorities and values. Some economists may place greater weight on material rewards as against health and happiness. Some may prioritize the well-being of workers over that of consumers. Others may assume that the interests of entrepreneurs are paramount and overlook the needs of people with caring responsibilities.

In the late 1990s some economists, especially in the USA, emphasized relationships between 'headline' economic indicators such as inflation, wages, productivity and growth (which are analysed in Chapters 11–20). For these economists, such as Alan Greenspan (1998), the Chairman of the Federal Reserve (the US central bank), what was new about the new economy was the almost unprecedented coexistence of economic growth and low inflation. The combination of 'tight' labour markets (where employers have difficulty in finding enough workers to fill all the job vacancies) and hence low unemployment with low pressure for wage rises was also unusual. The coexistence of these factors challenged the conventional economic theory that tight labour markets lead to wage rises and more generally that rapid growth – a boom – will lead to inflation and then to 'bust'. This view is encapsulated in the extract from *Business Week Online*:

The New Economy
It works in America. Will it go global?

It seems almost too good to be true. With the information technology sector leading the way, the US has enjoyed almost 4% growth since 1994. Unemployment has fallen from 6% to about 4%, and inflation just keeps getting lower and lower. Leaving out food and energy, consumer inflation in 1999 was only 1.9%, the smallest increase in 34 years.

This spectacular boom was not built on smoke and mirrors. Rather, it reflects a willingness to undertake massive risky investments in innovative information technology, combined with a decade of retooling US financial markets, governments, and corporations to cut costs and increase flexibility and efficiency. The result is the so-called New Economy: faster growth and lower inflation.

(*Business Week Online, 31 January 2000*)

In fact it *was* too good to be true. US economic growth slowed during 2001, the terrorist attacks on the World Trade Center on 11 September undermined consumer confidence and by the end of the year the US economy was in recession. This raises the question, 'was the spectacular boom built on smoke and mirrors after all?' In other words, was it a unique historical episode or is it reasonable to believe that the economy will be seen nevertheless to have undergone a lasting change?

There are understandings of the 'new economy' that emphasize longer-lasting changes in the nature and organization of firms and employment patterns. The development of information and computing technologies is emphasized because they can potentially revolutionize business organization and therefore have implications well beyond the high-technology sector itself. Changes in the composition of the workforce, such as the increasing participation of women and the development of new, more flexible patterns of employment, affect how people can manage their work/life balance. The role of the state in creating a deregulated environment, which promotes flexibility in financial markets and working practices, has also been emphasized. All of these changes are claimed to be deep-seated and widespread and therefore unlikely to be reversed, despite short-term ups and downs in the economy.

The benefits that are claimed for the new economy arise from the development of high-technology and knowledge which offer new products and processes and new forms of high-level employment as well as opportunities for entrepreneurs. These are some of the real changes that are thought to underlie the unprecedented levels of inflation-free growth in the late 1990s in the US economy as referred to in the extract (above) from *Business Week Online*.

By contrast, the negative aspects of the new economy are highlighted by writers such as Ulrich Beck (2000) and Richard Sennett (1998), who link rapid economic change with increasing inequality, risk and insecurity, family breakdowns, falling fertility and the fragmentation of communities.

Some economists link the positive and negative effects of the new economy. For example, Danny Quah (1996) argues that the positive and negative dimensions of the new economy are opposite sides of the same coin and form part of an emerging digital divide. That is, some of the essential characteristics of the knowledge-based economy which contribute to economic growth also increase economic inequality and put increasing pressure on balancing the claims of work and life.

▪▪▪ 1.3.1   The benefits of the new economy

The benefits claimed for the new economy are mainly concerned with technological change, productivity and economic growth. Manuel Castells (2001) argues that we have entered a new technological paradigm centred around microelectronics-based information/communication technologies. The development of the Internet, in particular, is said to have profound implications for the organization of economic activity and for increasing productivity.

The Internet provides a new communication medium between businesses and between businesses and consumers and facilitates new ways of organizing the production, distribution and exchange of existing goods and services. It can reduce transaction and search costs between buyers and suppliers in a wide range of areas and allows the development of new products and services. These developments arguably underlie the unprecedented growth in the US economy in the second half of the 1990s.

Internet business-to-consumer sales are expanding rapidly but nowhere do they account for even 1 per cent of retail sales – being highest in Sweden at 0.68 per cent followed by the USA (0.48 per cent) and the UK (0.37 per cent) (OECD, 2000). Evidence on the comparative costs of Internet sales is mixed. In principle, consumers can save on search and travel costs by comparing prices and purchasing directly from home. They have immediate access to world markets, which could stimulate competition and bring about increases in efficiency at a global level. Suppliers would also save on showrooms but their overall delivery costs could rise as distribution would switch from high- to low-density routes, that is instead of journeys from warehouses to shopping centres more diverse journeys from factories to residential areas would need to be made (OECD, 2000). This problem would not arise in the case of 'weightless' or digitized products, which can be distributed very cheaply and incur minimal storage and inventory costs.

A further potential efficiency gain for producers is that they can target their marketing much more effectively as it is easy for them to build up a profile of their clients, allowing a form of mass customization. Amazon.com, for example, recommends new purchases to clients by comparing their purchase records with other clients. A firm called Babycenter.com tailors their information to parents according to the stage of pregnancy or age of the children (Borenstein and Saloner, 2001). Thus, by using their electronic databases, constructed in part by the consumers, firms can provide individualized and what appear to be personalized services far more efficiently than by traditional face-to-face contact, as Reich, a former Secretary of Labour in the Clinton administration, notes:

> I'm all of four feet ten inches tall, with a waistline significantly larger than that of a ten-year-old boy, which means that if I'm to look even vaguely respectable, anything I wear has to be custom-tailored. It is a royal pain, and often I don't bother. But recently I discovered the Web site of a clothing manufacturer on which I can enter all my size specifications and select the shirts and trousers (along with fabrics and styles) I want. Within days the garments arrive at my front door. When I first ordered, I expected the tailor who received my improbable measurements to assume they were mistaken, and change them (this had happened before). But the shirt and trousers fit perfectly. And then it hit me: I wasn't dealing with a tailor. I was transacting with a computer that had no independent judgement.
>
> *(Reich, 2001, pp.11–12)*

Thus, there are some advantages for consumers, even though the technology potentially allows sophisticated forms of price discrimination as prices could in principle be varied according to the individual customer profile (OECD, 2000). Consumers can also organize auctions and exchange products on the Internet, as in the case of the Napster music system, which essentially allows users to download each other's CDs. At the time of writing the legality of this system is being challenged in the courts. Consumers and protesters, for example the anti-sweatshop movement, can also exchange knowledge about the actions of companies very quickly, thereby enabling more effective monitoring of the ethics of trade (Klein, 1999).

Companies involved in training, marketing and public relations have also begun to provide these services through the Internet. These activities have generated a range of new firms and new employment. The jobs include the computing technologies themselves (hardware and software) for managing web-based transactions and have created a whole new range of activities from web-based graphic design, web system/database management, video installations through to programming. Because many of these activities are at the boundaries of new technologies, it has led to the development of small firms and micro enterprises which fuelled the so-called dot.com boom of 1999–2000.

The Women's Unit of the UK government has argued that ICT represents 'one of the biggest opportunities for women in the twenty-first century to earn more, have more flexible working practices and adapt their current business or try a business start-up'. Thus, they maintain that 'self-employment and enterprise offer women a real alternative means of earning good income and achieving greater flexibility in their working lives' (Women's Unit, 2000). That is, given the way that contemporary technologies extend the range of working opportunities both temporally and spatially, they potentially provide a means of redressing current gender inequalities. 'Family friendly' working patterns, if not quantity of work, can be constructed by entrepreneurs, homeworkers and freelancers who can manage their own routines. In some ways they may realize the vision of the 'electronic cottage' (Toffler, 1980), although the problems of social isolation and family tensions also have to be recognized (Perrons, 2001). However, women also face constraints. In the UK, for example, they are under-represented on ICT courses, the proportion of women working in these areas has fallen and they have more problems obtaining access to capital. The limited evidence suggests that the gender balance has not changed.

One of the reasons why it might be difficult to establish statistical associations between productivity growth and ICT is that they are general purpose technologies so their effects are wide ranging (see Chapter 2). E-commerce can potentially increase efficiency, as discussed above, but the physical delivery of products, where necessary, remains a labour-intensive activity. Thus, it is very difficult to gather data that might adequately describe the complex and diverging nature of the new economy.

Changes in the organization of economic activity also lead to employment changes at both ends of the employment hierarchy. At the upper end, highly skilled specialists in computer programming, systems analysis and web design are employed in setting up systems to facilitate Internet transactions. At the lower end, people are employed in warehouses and call centres. So the high-technology side of the new economy remains dependent on some labour-intensive work in delivering products and in all forms of personal services. Aggregate statistics bury these divergent trends.

Even the OECD (2000) report effectively predicts an emerging duality in the workforce as well as the disappearance of some jobs altogether. It points out that:

> a retail sale via the Internet probably does not require the same intensity of sales staff, but it requires people with IT skills to develop and program software, operate and maintain computer servers and networks and people skilled in graphics design to keep the web site attractive *and others to dispatch orders* [emphasis added]. In addition, firms will implement modifications to their production processes in order to exploit the potential of B2B [business-to-business] and B2C [business-to-consumer] commerce over the Internet. Certain jobs, especially those characterized by the transfer of information from one party to another such as travel agents, insurance and stock brokers are likely to be redefined and become less common.
>
> *(OECD, 2000, p.208)*

■ ■ ■ 1.3.2 The downside of the new economy

During the US boom of the 1990s, some economists attributed the paradox of economic growth, rising productivity, but stable or only modestly rising wage costs, to the growing sense of insecurity in the labour force (Greenspan, 1998). Employment insecurity is also emphasized by sociologists such as Ulrich Beck (2000) and Richard Sennett (1998). This section outlines some of their arguments because they are central to those who take a critical view of the new economy. Their arguments also contain implications for the social sustainability of the new economy that is emerging in Europe and the USA.

Ulrich Beck, the German sociologist, argues in *The Brave New World of Work* (2000) that in the new economy work at all levels is characterized by insecurity and increasing inequality. Fernando Flores and John Gray (2000, p.24) speak of the 'death of the career' and argue that life-long identities are giving way to 'brief habits'. They suggest that 'the lives of wired people are more like collections of short stories than the narrative of a bourgeois novel'. These writers all suggest that work in the new economy is organized around projects and is therefore very fluid or changeable. This is especially so in the high-technology sector where teams of people with necessary skills are constructed for particular projects and then dissolved as the project is completed. People change – or are required to change – their employer and their geographical location frequently. Consequently, connections between individuals, firms and communities are fragile. If this view is correct, these processes could undermine the social sustainability of the new economy.

The empirical evidence for claims about increasing insecurity is, however, rather mixed. There is fairly strong evidence for a growing sense of insecurity but at the same time aggregate statistics on job duration indicate little change. In a five-country European study (Ireland, Norway, Portugal, Sweden and the UK) a survey of people between the ages of 18 and 30 perceived jobs to be episodic and insecure, even though those in work tended to work long hours (Lewis and Brannen, 2000).

There has been a considerable restructuring of economies and companies have also been downsizing, which may be responsible for the sense of insecurity and 'skill obsolescence'. In these circumstances employees may be willing to accept low wages in return for job security, possibly accounting for the coexistence of economic growth and moderate increases in wage costs. A study of people in low-paid work by the Institute for Public Policy Research (IPPR, 2000), a left-of-centre policy think-tank, found that the security of a full-time job and a long-term contract superseded all other 'quality of work' concerns for older workers who had experienced periods of unemployment, but was less important to younger respondents. An illustrative comment came from a male airport worker aged between 40 and 50 at Hounslow: 'I'm just happy to have work, to have some security and to be earning a living.' In the mid to late 1990s only a small proportion of new jobs coming onto the labour market in the UK were full time and permanent (Gregg and Wadsworth, 1999).

Data on employment duration, however, may not be an adequate measure of insecurity. People are sometimes more likely to stay with an employer if they are uncertain about their prospects of re-employment. By contrast, in the high-tech sector, short-term contracts may reflect employee strength rather than weakness. That is, what some workers might conceive as insecurity, an independent contractor might welcome as the freedom to move between contracts to build up their skill portfolio. Security can mean different things to people at different levels in the employment hierarchy and these different dimensions will be conflated in aggregate statistics for employment as a whole; thus, insecurity is difficult to test empirically.

A further downside of the new economy is the emerging duality in the labour force, referred to in the quotation from the OECD (2000) at the end of Section 1.3.1, and increasing income inequality. Middle-class well-educated men are over-represented in high-technology jobs in firms while women, including some who have arrived in the country only recently, are over-represented in the less highly rewarded jobs that provide services more directly for people, such as care work for children and the elderly. Boyd *et al.* (1995) have referred to this as a division between the high-tech and the high-touch occupations. Both types of work are very much part of the new economy and share characteristics of insecurity, but they are very different in nature and in financial reward.

The development of the personal care and personal services sector depends on whether people are willing to work for low wages. These jobs are typically labour intensive and the scope for productivity increases is limited. In some sectors, such as retail and call centres, students are employed, but this group rarely finds work in personal care attractive.

Employment in call centres is growing. Estimates suggest that there are (in 2001) the equivalent of about 400 000 full-time jobs in UK call centres – about 1.8 per cent of the workforce. Some estimates suggest that this figure will double in the next five years. But newer technologies, such as voice recognition software and direct use of the Internet by consumers, could also displace these workers. Call centres deal with telephone enquiries, usually about banking, ticket bookings and billing, but especially for services such as electricity, gas and telephone, or with mail order sales. The size of the workforce in call centres varies from 20 to over 300 people. Often they are completely separate from other activities of the firms to which they belong, which means that career opportunities are limited. Typically, there are four tiers, from an operator (the lowest level) to team leader, supervisor and manager. Promotion to supervisor can be rapid, partly because of the high level of turnover. Pay varies between different types of call centre and by the level of wages in the locality, but generally it is considerably above the minimum wage, though still well below average pay (Incomes Data Services, 2001). Thus, opportunities are limited within call centres and there are no career routes from call centres to the wider organizations whose calls are processed.

These jobs are important because they are the archetypal 'footloose' form of employment sought after, for example, by Local Economic Development Agencies in the UK, who emphasize that low pay is prevalent in their areas in order to attract companies. Even though these are part of the new economy, many old-style working practices remain. The employees are closely monitored, their conversations are constantly recorded and employees often work from scripts designed to keep the calls as short as possible. When they have finished one call, another call can be automatically directed to them.

▨ ▨ ■ 1.3.3 The weightless economy

In this subsection we want to look at one attempt to link some of the positive and negative aspects of the new economy. Danny Quah is an economist at the London School of Economics who has studied the new economy over a number of years. He refers to the new economy as the weightless or *dematerialized* economy and he examines its economic implications and also why it has a tendency to lead to increasing economy inequality.

According to the 'weightless economy' argument, the fact that current economic expansion has been inflation-free may be because it places less pressure on physical resources than earlier episodes of rapid industrial and technological change. One reason is that new materials and microcomputers have led to a reduction in the size and weight of goods. For example, we have as much computing power on our desk as would have filled several rooms in 1980. The argument is that without a huge increase in demand for resources such as raw materials, their prices have not increased dramatically.

However, it is perhaps the nature of 'knowledge goods' that has the most profound economic implications. Knowledge goods are infinitely expansible and non-rival, which means that their consumption by one individual does not reduce the amount available to another. Thus, as Quah illustrates, several people can be using the same word processing package but they cannot all eat the same chocolate biscuit (Quah, 1999). The weightless form of knowledge goods together with the Internet creates a disrespect for physical distance, and therefore potentially these products also have infinite global reach.

A whole new range of goods and services are made up of bits and bytes, rather than bricks or steel, and can be downloaded directly from the Internet. Computer software is one example, sometimes freely provided, and the practice is spreading to books and films. There are also entirely new products coming onto the market, such as interactive digital media. For example, the Channel 4 programme *Big Brother* was broadcast 24 hours a day on the Internet, and the pop group Gorillaz had a top ten hit record despite having only a virtual existence. Similarly, some computer games can be downloaded from or played directly on the Internet.

Quah points out that although not everyone would consider a Britney Spears recording a 'knowledge good', the fact that it can be directly downloaded from the Internet gives it the same economic properties of being replicable or infinitely expansible and non-rival. For Quah (2001) these properties represent the defining feature of the new economy: that an increasing range of goods and services, from business computer software to computer games and films, has become like knowledge.

Two main economic implications of knowledge goods and the weightless economy can be identified. First, weightlessness opens up the prospect of *sustainable* growth, insofar as it enables economies to grow without depleting stocks of natural resources. To the degree that the economy is weightless, 'international trade becomes not a matter of shipping wine and textiles from one country to the next, but of bouncing bits off satellites' (Quah,

1996, p.7). Critics of the weightless economy argument, such as Lutz (1999, p.231), observe that PCs and other hardware still have to be manufactured and transported all over the world, using up resources including oil. However, according to Quah (1999), consumer hardware accounted for only one-third of IT (information technology) and 'in the foreseeable future it will likely become a progressively smaller fraction of the total' (Quah, 1999, p.10). This issue will be taken up again in Chapter 20.

Second, in theory, knowledge goods create a more egalitarian world (Quah, 2001). Suppose that consumption does not reduce the amount of knowledge goods available for other consumers, that knowledge goods are sometimes freely provided and should have an infinite global reach, and that they are replicable at almost no cost. In principle, ensuring equal access to them should therefore be easier than ensuring equal provision of physical goods and resources. In reality, however, the opposite trends can be observed, with increasing inequalities on a global scale and also within countries. Furthermore, it is the economic properties of knowledge goods that paradoxically contribute towards increasing economic inequality.

For example, the existence of dematerialized products contributes to the 'superstar effect', which helps to explain increasing income polarization, particularly marked in the USA and the UK. Quah (1996) demonstrates this by asking why the income differential between opera singers is greater than that between workers in many other occupations, such as shoemakers.

In the case of opera, it makes little difference to the singer, in terms of the effort involved, whether they are singing to 2 or 200 000 people. Consumers, however, generally prefer to listen to more famous singers than ones of lesser renown even though they may be of minimal perceptible difference to the majority of listeners. The almost costless replication of products such as CDs means that market size is unlimited by conventional barriers such as distance.

Consequently, the market share taken by superstars is huge, limited mainly by competition from other superstars. Therefore, in these cases, 'the winner takes all', which explains why the gap between high and low incomes is greater for singers than it is for shoemakers. The spread of incomes is much wider for knowledge goods than for products where such dematerialized replication is not possible.

Quah (1996) points out that the income differential is not simply a question of differential returns being given to differential natural endowments. Whose voice is replicated or who becomes a superstar depends on the selection decisions made by companies and so superstars are to a considerable extent *made* rather than born. Given this recognition, the comparison with the shoemaker becomes slightly more questionable. Branding and style have also made some shoes much more 'desirable' than others, making the returns to the owners of popular brands (although not the shoemakers themselves) much more wealthy than those of similar products but with 'no logo' as Naomi Klein (1999) puts it.

One reason why people accept widening inequalities, Quah argues, is increasing social mobility. That is, the poor tolerate the rich because they can see a greater opportunity for becoming rich themselves. However, there are also specific features, including gender stereotyping, associated with the restructuring of economic activity and the work of lower-paid workers that make their chances of becoming rich through their current work remote.

▦ ▨ ▪ 1.3.4 Looking ahead: economic change and human well-being

There are different interpretations of the new economy and its impact on human well-being, on whether the changes sometimes labelled the 'new economy' are desirable or beneficial. It is time to review the benefits and costs of the new economy.

Question	What do you think are the main points for and against the new economy in its impact on human well-being? A list of points is all that is required, although you may want to add your own comments or responses.

This is our list. It is not definitive in any sense and there is no intention either to find 'matching' good and bad points or to place them in order of importance. The idea is simply to initiate discussion.

Arguments for the new economy	Arguments against the new economy
Faster growth and low inflation	Social isolation
Personalized services	Family tensions
Efficiency gains	Employment insecurity
Flexible working patterns	Flexible working patterns
Environmental sustainability	Social unsustainability
Access to knowledge from remote locations	Income inequality increasing

Our first impression is that positive things about the new economy seem to be mainly economic, while the negative aspects are largely social. This brings to mind a picture of economic change disrupting established patterns of social life. It also suggests that the greater material well-being that economic growth brings may be bought at the cost of increasing threats to health, happiness and security. The general principle that emerges from these thoughts is that human well-being has a number of different components or dimensions, social as well as economic, and psychological or spiritual as well as material. Sifting these different senses of well-being is one of the tasks of Chapters 7–10.

However, qualifications soon occur. There is, above all, the danger of excessive generalization, of assuming that everyone wants the same things. For example, the fragility of communities and the fluidity of relationships might suit some, perhaps many, people. Not everyone wants to live their lives within a set of permanent relationships or in what can easily be experienced as the stifling atmosphere of a close-knit community. This is why 'flexible working patterns' appears in both columns. For many women with caring responsibilities who have been denied access to good jobs by traditional assumptions about gender roles, flexibility increases opportunities for paid work. On the other hand, there are many middle-aged male workers, such as the airport worker from Hounslow, who would probably prefer a 'job for life'.

In this case it seems possible to identify groups of winners and losers systematically on the basis of employment status, gender, age and other social characteristics. This is not quite the same as recognizing differences in personal preferences, such as wanting to be left alone. Taking this thought further reveals some tensions within the more 'economic' positive aspects of the new economy. For example, personalized services through computer ordering is a benefit for consumers, which, in an overall assessment of the desirability of economic change, must be weighed against adverse effects on other economic groups such as increasing insecurity and lower wages for some workers.

Following this line of thought further raises questions about the efficiency gains from the widespread use of ICT: who benefits and who should benefit? To what extent do consumers benefit as efficiency gains bring lower costs that might be passed on as lower prices? Should more of the efficiency gains from ICT be passed on to consumers in this way? This issue is raised as early as the discussions of competition policy in Chapters 4–6.

The policy dilemma is how to ensure that enough of the cost reductions from ICT are passed on to consumers while allowing enough to be kept as profits to provide adequate incentive for firms to keep on innovating.

Increasing inequality introduces another dimension in our thinking about economic change and well-being. It might seem that we can simply say that this is just another situation of winners and losers. Increasing inequality of incomes is unfortunate if you work in personal care or a call centre but it is fine if you are an opera superstar. However, while some people might accept or even welcome inequality as the foundation of aspirations to material success that motivate many people's lives, others find it unacceptable, unfair or unjust. Among them are people whose views about income inequality are independent of their own income position, that is, independent of the outcome of economic activity for themselves. When people become interested in other people's well-being, they are engaging in ethical inquiry. Ethics is concerned with questions about what is good for people, about what the good life for a person is and about how we ought to live. This includes the issues of what economic and social arrangements are desirable and on what basis we should make such decisions. For example, is there a conflict between inequality and efficiency? Without some (how much?) inequality, would we lack adequate incentives to engage in economic activity to the best of our abilities? On the other hand, does a sense of social justice suggest that income inequality has gone too far, devaluing relatively low-paid but socially valuable work, such as jobs in the personal care sector?

Ethical questions such as these lie at the heart of Chapters 7–10, which explore key issues concerning the well-being of the people who make economies work as producers and consumers. Do flexible (or competitive) labour markets provide good jobs? Why is the intensity of work effort increasing? This part critically examines material wealth, happiness and human capabilities as different interpretations of well-being. How is the role of government in furthering people's well-being changing in the twenty-first century? What can be done to reduce inequalities, not only in income, but in health status and in access to health care?

1.4 Conclusion

Every era defines for itself its most pressing economic problems. They emerge from a complex public dialogue, involving ideas and experience, theories and political pressures. Economists influence and take part in that dialogue but they certainly do not control it. Are we living through a new industrial revolution powered by ICT? Should we be grateful to big companies such as Microsoft and Nike for their new products or try to curtail their power? Does more material well-being always make people happier? Do poor countries gain from international trade and globalization? Is continued economic growth environmentally sustainable? Assumptions about what is economically possible and desirable influence the answers that politicians and commentators as well as academics give to these questions. John Maynard Keynes, perhaps the twentieth century's most famous economist, wrote at the end of his best known book:

> the ideas of economists and political philosophers, both when they are right and when they are wrong, are more powerful than is commonly understood [. . .] Practical men [and women – *authors*], who believe themselves to be quite exempt from any intellectual influences, are usually the slaves of some defunct economist.
>
> *(Keynes, 1936, p.383)*

The tone may be rather self-congratulatory and reflects the sexist attitudes of the time, but the point has as much force now as in the 1930s. Economic issues change but economic ideas continue to matter.

The variety of understandings of the new economy and of interpretations of its desirability illustrate how economic theory is as much a debate as the public dialogue to which it contributes. The presentation of theory as debate carries the most general message of this chapter, namely that economic theory is not a fixed body of knowledge but, like all social sciences, an arena of research and dispute. Economists, like other social scientists, develop differing and distinctive ways of thinking about the world, or broad conceptualizations within which they work. These different visions of the world are influenced by the issues which economists regard as important. In other words, how economists think depends in part on what they think about.

Hence, as economies and economic issues change, so does economics. We hope you will enjoy your exploration of this endlessly debatable subject.

Questions for review and discussion

Question 1 The 'new economy' is differently understood by different economists, but over certain features there is broad agreement. Tick the letters corresponding to the three statements below that command this broad agreement:

A ❑ It is likely to be easier to find work in a call centre than in a car assembly plant.
B ❑ Productivity in manufacturing is likely to be low or falling.
C ❑ Incomes across occupations are likely to be tending towards greater equality.
D ❑ The rate of inflation is likely to be low or falling.
E ❑ Research and development costs are likely to be high as many new products incorporate a lot of 'knowledge'.

Work changes us as people

The workplace of people in professional, managerial and administrative jobs is being transformed. The routines of the traditional office are being replaced by working on the move, working at home and working in a new type of office.

These changes have profound implications for skills, managerial strategies and team working. They are changing the kind of people we are.

Work is now done electronically using mobile phones, email, laptops, PCs and similar devices. As long as we are in touch with the 'electronic envelope' we can work anywhere and at any time.

Although these developments may bring benefits, they also pose challenges.

Nick Jewson (Centre for Labour Market Studies, University of Leicester),
The Sunday Times (Appointments)

Question 2 Using evidence from the above extract, and from the course text, discuss the nature of the changes brought about by the 'new economy'. To what extent is it true to say that the benefits are largely economic, while the challenges are largely social?

2

Information technology: a new era?

Mariana Mazzucato

Concepts

- industrial revolution
- technological change
- productivity
- industry structure
- industry life cycle
- information technology
- new economy

Objectives

After studying this chapter you should be able to:

- understand the relationship between technological change and industrial revolutions
- appreciate the pervasive effect that new technologies can have on the economy and, in particular, on productivity
- understand how industry dynamics can be analysed using the 'industry life cycle' model
- use data and historical examples to support economic arguments.

2.1 Introduction

> Everything that can be invented has been invented.
>
> *(The Commissioner of the United States Office of Patents, **1899**, recommending that his office be abolished, quoted in* The Economist, *2000, p.5)*

> There is nothing now to be foreseen which can prevent the United States from enjoying an era of business prosperity which is entirely without equal in the pages of trade history.
>
> *(Sutliff, **1901**)*

The rise of information and communication technologies (ICT) – that is, computers, software, telecommunications and the Internet – and the large impact that these new technologies are having on the way that society functions, have prompted many to claim that we have entered a new era, often referred to as the 'Third Industrial Revolution', the 'information age' or the 'new economy'. Previous industrial revolutions were also linked to the rise of new technologies: the First Industrial Revolution, concentrated in Britain from around 1760 to 1850, introduced Cort's puddling and rolling process for making iron,

Crompton's mule for spinning cotton and the Watt steam engine; the Second Industrial Revolution, from around 1890 to 1930, witnessed the development of electricity, the internal-combustion engine, the railway and the chemical industry. In each of these cases, the new technologies allowed new industries to develop and economic growth to increase.

The concept of the 'new economy' is thus a claim that the emergence of new information technology (IT) was responsible for the economic prosperity (e.g. rising incomes, rising employment) experienced by most Western countries in the 1990s. This was the decade in which personal computers (PCs) were diffused throughout the economy, and the decade which saw the commercial rise of the World Wide Web. The PC reached a 50 per cent household penetration rate in the USA only in 1999, while before 1990 the Internet was used mainly by the US Defense Department, not for commercial purposes.

However, as the two introductory quotations indicate, proclamations that we have entered a 'new' era are not new. In fact, the advent of electricity, the internal-combustion engine and the radio telegraph witnessed similar proclamations about the future. They too emerged during periods of prosperity; for example, electricity and the automobile diffused through the economy during the prosperous and 'Roaring' 1920s. So how can we tell whether we are really entering a qualitatively new era or whether recent changes have simply been a quantitative extension of the past?

This chapter uses tools and frameworks from economics to study this question. It focuses on the historical and theoretical relationship between changes in technology, productivity and economic growth. The key driving force discussed will be *technological change*: that is, organizational and technical changes in the way that societies organize production and distribution. As in the previous chapter, the question is: what exactly is so *new* about the 'new economy'? But whereas in Chapter 1 the focus was on the effect of new technologies and work practices on the way that people live and work, here the focus is on the organization and evolution of firms and industries.

In each industrial revolution (including the current one), important *non-technological* factors have influenced industry dynamics and growth. Socio-political factors have been particularly prominent. For example, the rise of industrial trade unions in the Second Industrial Revolution greatly affected firm-level, industry-level and country-level growth. In this chapter, however, the analysis is limited to the role of technology.

We shall conduct our investigation by focusing on two related questions, neither of which has a clear-cut answer. The goal of the chapter is to help you to think about these questions using concepts and tools from economics.

First, after a brief overview of the concept of the industrial revolution, I shall ask whether the rise of IT has significantly affected economic growth, as new technologies did in previous eras. Focusing on the effect of technology on economy-wide growth implies that the perspective is a macroeconomic one. Macroeconomics looks at the functioning of the economy as a whole.

Second, I shall take a more microeconomic perspective. Microeconomics looks at the functioning of individual elements of the economy, whether they be consumers, firms, industries or markets. I shall ask whether the rise of new information technologies has fundamentally changed the way that individual firms and industries operate. To do this, I shall compare the patterns that characterized the early phase of a traditional industry with those that characterized the early phase of a relatively new industry. The traditional industry (one that is today considered to be relatively 'mature', not high growth) is the US automobile industry from 1900 to 1930, while the relatively new industry is the personal computer industry from 1975 to 2000. The similarities will lead us to ask whether we are really in a 'new economy' or simply in an economy driven, as in some past eras, by the development of new industries.

2.2 Technological change and economic growth

In this section I shall look at the way that technological innovations in previous eras, such as the invention of electricity in the early 1900s, radically affected the way society organized production and at how these changes spurred general economic growth. In many instances, the changes were so large that they defined an entire period, just as the rise of information technologies has led some to call the current era the 'information age'.

▨ ▩ ■ 2.2.1 Industrial revolutions and technological change

Industrial revolution

An industrial revolution occurs when technological change fundamentally transforms the way in which a society carries out the production and distribution of goods.

The way that technological change can fundamentally alter society is best viewed through the lens of previous industrial revolutions. The term **Industrial Revolution** usually refers specifically to the series of technological changes that occurred in England between 1760 and 1850 (such as steam power). More generally, the term refers to eras when rapid and significant technological changes fundamentally alter the way that production is carried out in society, affecting not only how people work but also how they live their lives. Consider the impact that electricity in the Second Industrial Revolution had not only on factories but also on the lives of families in their homes. Thus an industrial revolution occurs when new technological inventions and innovations fundamentally transform the production processes of goods and services to such an extent that all society is affected.

For our purposes the words 'invention' and 'innovation' can be used interchangeably. More specifically, however, the term 'invention' refers to the discovery of new products or processes, while 'innovation' refers to the commercialization (bringing to the market) of new products or processes. Furthermore, we can distinguish between *product* innovations and *process* innovations. Product innovations result in the production of a new product, such as the change from a three-wheel car to a four-wheel car, or the change from LP records to CDs. Process innovations increase the efficiency of the methods of production of existing products, for example the invention of the assembly-line technique.

The inventions and innovations that form industrial revolutions are those that open new doors and create new ways of doing things, not simply those that fill gaps in existing ways of doing things (Mokyr, 1997). The core of the First Industrial Revolution in the eighteenth century was a succession of technological changes that brought about material advances in three basic areas: (1) the substitution of mechanical devices (such as machines) for human labour; (2) the substitution of inanimate sources of power (such as steam) for animate sources of power (such as horse power); and (3) the substitution of mineral raw materials for vegetable or animal substances, and in general the use of new and more abundant raw materials (Landes, 1972).

These changes in technology and equipment occurred simultaneously with changes in *organizational* arrangements. For example, at the end of the nineteenth century the rise of electricity and the internal-combustion engine allowed the factory system to emerge, which radically changed the organization of work. The factory system, used first for the production of cotton but then extended to other industries, created a new, unified system of production which replaced the craft labour carried out in individual workshops. The main innovation of this new system was that it allowed workers to be brought together for the first time under common supervision with strict discipline, and it also introduced the use of a central, usually inanimate, source of power. The factory system enabled production to become more efficient as it allowed the company to spread its costs over a much larger output, a dynamic called 'economies of scale' which you will study in Chapter 3.

General purpose technology

A general purpose technology is a technology of sufficiently wide application to be used in various parts of the economy and whose impact is pervasive.

Economists interested in the pervasive effects of technological change in different industrial revolutions have devised the concept of a **general purpose technology** (GPT). A GPT is a technology that is general enough to be used in various industries and has a strong impact on their functioning. There are four main characteristics of a GPT (Lipsey *et al.*, 1998). As you read the list, consider how a new technology such as electricity or information technology fulfils each criterion.

1 It must have a wide scope for improvement and elaboration. This means that the technology does not appear as a complete and final solution, but as a technology that can be improved through the different opportunities for technological change that surround it.

2 It must be applicable across a broad range of uses. This means that its use is not restricted, for example, to only one industry but open to many different types of industries and consumers.

3 It must have a potential use in a wide variety of products and processes. This means that the new technology should not result in the creation of only one set of products (such as a computer), but a wide set of products (such as complex new air-traffic control systems or new inventory controls).

4 It must have strong complementarities with existing or potential new technologies. This means that the technology does not only replace existing methods but also works with them, ensuring an even broader impact on the systems of production and distribution.

Examples of GPTs include different power delivery systems (water-wheel, steam, electricity, internal-combustion engine), transport innovations (railways and motor vehicles), lasers and the Internet. The invention of the internal-combustion engine not only made possible personal automobiles, motor transport and air transport, but also created 'derivative' inventions such as the suburb, the motorway and the supermarket. Electricity allowed the work day to be extended (allowing for different shifts in a 24-hour period), gave a huge impetus to the entertainment industry, and greatly enhanced manufacturing process technologies. (We shall also see how it created the conditions for 'mass production' via the moving assembly line.)

GPTs are important because they spur technological change in different areas (and this effect is behind the first three characteristics of GPTs listed above). In fact, radical technological changes are often **cumulative changes**: change in one area leads to change in another area. David Landes is an economic historian and his account of the way in which the invention of the steam engine caused changes in many different industries has become well known. He calls this process 'technological interrelatedness'.

Cumulative change

Technological change is cumulative if change in one area of the economy leads to change in other areas.

In all this diversity of technological improvement, the unity of movement is apparent: change begat change. For one thing, many technical improvements were feasible only after advances in associated fields. The steam engine is a classic example of this technological interrelatedness: it was impossible to produce an effective condensing engine until better methods of metal working could turn out accurate cylinders. For another, the gains in productivity and output of a given innovation inevitably exerted pressure on related industrial operations. The demand for coal pushed mines deeper until water seepage became a serious hazard; the answer was the creation of a more efficient pump, the atmospheric steam engine. A cheap supply of coal proved a godsend for the iron industry, which was stifling for lack of fuel. In the meantime, the invention and diffusion of machinery in the textile manufacture and other industries created a new demand for energy, hence for coal and steam engines; and these engines, and the machines themselves, had a voracious appetite for iron, which called for further coal and power. Steam also made possible the factory city, which used unheard-of quantities of iron (hence coal) in its many-storied mills and its water and sewage systems. At the same time, the processing of the flow of manufactured commodities required great amounts of chemical substances: alkalis, acids, and dyes, many of them consuming mountains of fuel in the making. And all of these products – iron, textiles, chemicals – depended on large-scale movements of goods on land and on sea, from the sources of the raw materials into the factories and out again to near and distant markets. The opportunity thus created and the possibilities of the new technology combined to produce the railroad and steamship, which of course added to the demand for iron and fuel while expanding the market for factory products. And so on, in ever-widening circles.

(Landes, 1972, pp.2–3)

| Question | Can you think of new industries that have grown out of the PC and the Internet? |

You may have thought of online shopping, Internet banking, digital cameras, information services (such as online recipes) and computer desks. Having reflected on the nature of technological change and its role in defining industrial revolutions, we shall now examine how technological change affects the efficiency of firms and hence general economic growth.

■ ■ ■ 2.2.2 The effect of technology on productivity

In each industrial revolution, new inventions radically changed the way that production and distribution were organized, and often led to large and rapid increases in the efficiency of production. The rise of electricity, for example, allowed US productivity to increase in the manufacturing sector (as opposed to the agricultural or service sector) by more than 5 per cent per annum throughout the 1920s.

Productivity

Productivity is an indicator of the efficiency of production or distribution. Labour productivity can be measured as output produced per hour of labour.

Let us pause a moment and consider what this means. The term **productivity** refers to the amount of output that a given amount of inputs (such as hours of labour) can produce. For example, consider an automobile factory that is able to produce 10 cars per day using 100 hours of labour. If a new invention permits those same workers to produce 20 cars in the same amount of time, their productivity has been doubled.

The productivity of a whole economy, such as the UK economy – as opposed to a particular factory – is measured by first calculating the total output produced by the economy in one year. This is called the GDP or gross domestic product, and the calculation will be explained in Chapter 8. Total output divided by total labour hours in the year gives us a measure of labour productivity. A 5 per cent growth in UK productivity over a year means that the UK economy has become 5 per cent more productive than it was in the previous year. This should mean that the economy can produce 5 per cent more output (GDP) with the same amount of inputs.

Stop here and check your understanding of percentages and growth rates. They are quite simple, but it is important to get them clear. If a group of workers produces 10 000 units of output in one year, and 12 000 units the next year, how would you calculate the percentage increase in productivity?

You want to know the percentage increase represented by the second year's output, 12 000, over the first year's output, 10 000. Subtracting 10 000 from 12 000 gives us the increase. Divide the answer by 10 000 to calculate the increase relative to the first year. Then multiply by 100 to turn the answer into a percentage (the dot '·' means 'multiplied by').

$$12\,000 - 10\,000 = 2000$$

$$\frac{2000}{10\,000} \cdot 100 = 20$$

So, output increased by 20 per cent. As the number of workers stayed the same, this is also the increase in productivity.

Exercise 2.1

If you want to check your understanding of percentages, calculate the percentage increase in productivity if the output expands from 12 000 in year 2 to 15 000 in year 3.

In plumbing, for example, productivity would increase if the use of new materials enabled plumbers to fix broken pipes more quickly. This would free up more time for plumbers to work on other operations and hence increase their output per hour, that is, their productivity. Productivity can increase either when work methods are made more efficient without (necessarily) the introduction of new technology, perhaps from a better organization of the factory floor, or when new methods are introduced to the production process through the introduction of new technology – for example, when new machinery allows work to be done more quickly and with fewer mistakes. Adam Smith (1723–90), one of the founders of modern economics, claimed that increases in productivity lie at the heart of economic growth and prosperity. In his influential book *The Wealth of Nations* (first published in 1776), Smith uses the example of pin making to describe the process by which productivity can increase through a rise in the division of labour, that is, the degree to which workers divide tasks between themselves. The rest of his classic text is dedicated to describing the effect of increasing productivity on the development of markets and economic growth:

> The greatest improvement in the productive powers of labour, and the greater part of the skill, dexterity, and judgement with which it is anywhere directed, or applied, seem to have been the effects of the division of labour . . . To take an example, therefore, from a very trifling manufacture; but one in which the division of labour has been very often taken notice of, the trade of the pin-maker; a workman not educated to this business . . . nor acquainted with the use of the machinery employed in it . . . could scarce, perhaps, with his utmost industry, make one pin a day, and certainly could not make twenty. But in the way in which this business is now carried on not only the whole work is a peculiar trade, but it is divided

into a number of branches, of which the greater part are likewise peculiar trades. One man draws out the wire, another straightens it, a third cuts it, a fourth points it, a fifth grinds it at the top for receiving the head; to make the head requires two or three distinct operations; to put it on, is a peculiar business, to whiten the pins is another, it is even a trade by itself to put them into the paper; and the important business of making a pin is, in this manner, divided into about eighteen distinct operations, which, in some manufactories, are all performed by distinct hands, though in others the same man will sometimes perform two or three of them. I have seen a small manufactory of this kind where ten men only were employed, and where some of them consequently performed two or three distinct operations. But though they were very poor, and therefore but indifferently accommodated with the necessary machinery, they could, when they exerted themselves . . . make among them upwards of forty-eight thousand pins in a day.

(Smith, 1937, pp.65–6)

Question	What are the different tasks, outlined by Smith, involved in pin making? Why does productivity increase when these tasks are divided between workers instead of all being done by one worker, that is, when the division of labour increases?

Division of labour

The division of labour refers to the degree to which the various tasks involved in the production of a good or service are divided among different workers.

The **division of labour**, as described here by Smith, increases the productivity of workers by allowing them to concentrate on a fixed and simple task, and hence to become more efficient at that task over time. (Smith also warned of the negative effect that this repetition could have on the workers' intelligence and morale.)

The division of labour, and hence productivity, increased with the emergence of the factory system, in which many workers were brought together under one roof for the first time and each worker was responsible for a small part of the final product. This was very different from the craft manufacture system, in which each worker was responsible for producing the entire product.

Increases in productivity, even if just in one industry, can be transmitted throughout the economy for several reasons. First, increases in productivity can lead to higher incomes for an economy's citizens. All output must be transformed, through the process of production and sale, into someone's income (e.g. the boss's profits and the workers' wages). Hence, increases in productivity, which allow more output to be produced by a given amount of inputs, also lead to more income per head, that is, greater wealth for society. For example, if more cars can be produced due to increases in the productivity of car production, more cars are sold, which means that the car manufacturers' revenues increase. Furthermore, if, as is sometimes the case, increases in wages are linked to increases in productivity, then workers' wages may also rise (or, at least, their employment prospects may be more secure).

Second, increases in productivity diffused throughout the economy have an effect on prices. Increases in productivity tend to lower the cost of production, precisely because more output can be produced with the same amount of inputs. Since cost reductions tend to be translated into price reductions, increases in productivity eventually tend to reduce prices. Indeed, the introduction of assembly lines made a substantial contribution to the affordability of consumer durables such as the car. The increase in income per head and the reduction in prices allow consumers to be better off. This potential increase in the wealth of manufacturers, workers and consumers is the reason Adam Smith's book, which focused on the links between productivity and economic growth, was titled *The Wealth of Nations*.

Productivity may also increase for reasons not related to technological change, for example if workers are simply 'exploited' more (with or without new technology). Output per worker may increase if workers are forced to work more quickly or for longer hours, prevented from taking lunch breaks, or given no holidays. These are all conditions that still persist today in some low-income countries, as well as in some industries in those Western countries in which workers are not unionized and/or work in 'sweatshops', that is, factories that operate illegally in terms of international standards for wages and working conditions.

For a new technology to affect economy-wide productivity it must be widely adopted across industries instead of being restricted to a narrow domain. For example, full electrification of factories did not occur until the 1920s. Prior to that, from the 1890s to the beginning of the 1920s, most factories simply added electric motors to existing (older) equipment. Until the 1920s power transmission in factories was still operated through the 'group drive' system, in which only parts of the factory were electrified and electric motors turned separate shafts. The 'unit drive' system did not appear until the boom period of the 1920s, which opened up the potential for new, fully electrified plants (David and Wright, 1999). The switch from group to unit drive transmission allowed individual electric motors to run machines and tools of all sizes. The new unit drive not only allowed huge savings in fuel and energy efficiency, but also allowed the factory layout to be more amenable to the assembly-line system, which spread throughout the economy in the 1920s (although it had first been used by Ford Motors in 1910). The new technology facilitated the circulation of materials, made workers more productive and reduced downtime, as the entire plant no longer had to be shut down to make changes in just one department.

Exercise 2.2

Write a short paragraph (of not more than 100 words) describing the impact of technological change on economic growth. You should use the key concepts introduced in Section 2.2, although you do not have to define them.

2.3 Information technology, productivity and growth

Having discussed the radical and pervasive effect that inventions in previous eras have had on economy-wide productivity, and how they have even defined entire periods, we shall now ask how the rise of information technology compares to these previous revolutions. During the early growth phase of PC use, a leader article in *Fortune* magazine did not hesitate to compare the rise of the PC to previous technological revolutions.

> The chip has transformed us at least as pervasively as the internal-combustion engine or electric motor.
>
> *(Fortune, 8 June 1988, pp.86–7)*

In fact, the debate about the 'new economy' is a debate about whether the computer and the Internet have had an impact on the economy as great as that of other GPTs in previous eras.

Question Would you say that the personal computer is a GPT? (Hint: in what ways is it applicable across a broad range of uses?)

The personal computer (PC) qualifies as a GPT due to the wide-ranging and pervasive effect it has had on the economy. Given the four characteristics of GPTs, consider how it: (1) has continued to experience radical improvements, such as the doubling of processor speed every 18 months (known as 'Moore's Law'), (2) is applicable across a wide variety of industries, from online trading to inventory control in factories, (3) has created the need for new products and processes, such as the production of portable printers, and (4) is often used alongside older technologies, such as the use of computer-aided design/ manufacturing (CADCAM) to reduce inventory alongside traditional assembly lines. Furthermore, as happened with electrification, for many years the PC did not break free from its predecessor, the mainframe, but served mainly to support it (as display terminals). Only in 1990, with the emergence of the Wintel platform, that is, the interaction between the Windows operating system and the Intel processor, did the PC break free from IBM's grip on the mainframe computer market.

The emergence of IT has created new products, processes and distribution systems. New products include the computer, the Internet and digital TV; new processes include Internet banking, automated inventory control and automated teller machines; and new distribution systems include cable and satellite TV. But the evidence does not fully support the claim that IT has affected economy-wide productivity in the same way as technological change in previous eras. In the late 1980s Robert Solow, a Nobel prize-winning economist from the Massachusetts Institute of Technology, summarized the problem as follows: 'Computers appear everywhere but in the productivity statistics' (Solow, 1987). The 'Solow Paradox', as this is often called, addresses the fact that the wave of inventions based on the microprocessor and the memory chip failed to generate the economy-wide increases in productivity that previous technological revolutions had produced. Only in the mid 1990s did productivity growth seem to be on a rebound: between 1975 and 1995 the annual average productivity growth for the business sector in the USA (i.e. non-agricultural production) was only 1.4 per cent per annum; after 1996 the annual average rose to 2.9 per cent. In the first two quarters of 2000 the figure reached 5.2 per cent, putting it on a par with the productivity increase that occurred after the electrical revolution. In the past, new technologies such as electricity began to affect economy-wide productivity only once they had reached the 50 per cent penetration rate (i.e. when 50 per cent of households and/or businesses used the technology). For electricity, this occurred in the 1920s. Since PCs reached the 50 per cent mark in the USA only in 1999, it might still be too early to ask whether the computer is showing up in the productivity statistics.

Are the recent increases in productivity *sustainable*? The answer to this question, and the crux of the debate concerning the effect of IT, centres on distinguishing whether recent increases in productivity are just *cyclical*, and hence temporary, or whether they are the beginning of a new and long-lasting *trend*. If the increase in productivity in the USA in the late 1990s was cyclical, this means that it occurred simply because the US economy as a whole was undergoing a boom in the latter half of the 1990s, and the increases will disappear now that (as I write) the boom is over. All economies fluctuate in a **business cycle**. For a few years, growth is quite rapid, output and incomes rise, and unemployment falls. This is the 'boom'. Then the cycle turns. Growth slows, and in a true recession the total output of the economy falls. This is the down-turn of the cycle. The cycle is driven by changes in consumer spending and business investment and, historically, a boom or recession tends to last three to eight years.

Business cycle

The business cycle refers to the periods of boom and recession that succeed each other in market economies.

However, if the productivity increases of the late 1990s, especially in the USA, were a *trend* increase, this means that the rise in productivity was independent of the business cycle and resulted from the characteristics of new technologies or specific government policies. For example, if a new technology allowed the productivity of many industries to increase permanently, it would create a trend increase in productivity. If the rise in productivity persisted during a recession, it would be further evidence of a trend. Indeed, the word 'new' in the 'new economy' implies that the increase was a trend related to the characteristics of the new technologies (otherwise it would not be new).

IT can affect productivity by increasing the efficiency of the IT-producing sectors, such as computer manufacturers, and/or by increasing the productivity of the IT-using sectors, such as the service industries that process data using computers. There is really no debate at all on the former point: all agree that industries such as the computer and software industries have experienced great productivity increases due to the radical and rapid nature of technological change in these industries. In the 1990s the average productivity growth in the IT-producing sectors was 24 per cent per year, well above that of the other manufacturing sectors. The disagreement, therefore, is about the effect of IT on the rest of the economy.

The optimists in this debate, including Alan Greenspan, Chairman of the US Federal Reserve Bank, argue that the rise of IT has allowed most advanced capitalist economies to achieve a *permanent* (trend) higher level of productivity, because of the ways in which the new technologies have improved efficiency, for example through better control of inventories and cheaper access to information. They argue that IT has caused firms to increase their investment in capital equipment per worker and that this has occurred simultaneously with large increases in the productivity of other inputs, both machinery and labour, two-fifths of which has come from efficiency gains in computer production alone. These optimists argue that productivity increases will persist into the future, due to the rise in research and development spending and the rise in investments in business capital, including computers. Such investments, argue the optimists, should allow productivity to keep growing.

Pessimists, such as the US economist R.J. Gordon, claim that recent productivity gains have been only cyclical, that is, a result of the fact that the US economy has been experiencing a boom. A boom can cause productivity to increase because there is more work to be done during prosperous periods and hence there is a greater incentive for employers to work employees harder, making them more productive – and leading to an increase in productivity. To support his point, Gordon (2000) provides data showing that most of the productivity gains have been limited to the IT-*producing* sectors (such as the personal computer industry) and have not spread out to other sectors, including the IT-*using* sectors. In fact, after excluding the manufacture of durable goods and computers (12 per cent of the economy), and after adjusting for the business cycle, the statistics do not show any productivity increases in the remaining portions of the economy! And to make things even worse, it is in those sectors where IT has been used the most, such as financial services, that productivity increases show up the least.

Gordon (2000) claims that it is not so surprising that the rise of the Internet has not affected productivity to the same degree as the development of electricity did. Unlike electricity, the Internet has not produced new products; it has simply substituted for existing products (e.g. the substitution of online purchasing for mail-order catalogues). Likewise, most of the changes are in terms of market shares not productivity: what one company wins the other loses, as is evidenced by the effect that Amazon.com is having on the profitability of the big bookshop chains Borders and Waterstones. Electricity, however, made possible the invention of many *new* products such as the vacuum cleaner and

Figure 2.1
The Internet
increases
productivity at work
(or does it?)

the refrigerator. The electric motor, the aeroplane, the telephone and even the indoor flush toilet, invented by the Englishman Thomas Crapper in 1886, have had more effect on productivity than the Internet. Surfing the Internet may be fun and is often useful, but can its impact on production be compared to the effect of electricity on the illumination of factories and the rise of the assembly line? Some go as far as to say that, if anything, the Internet has *reduced* productivity by distracting people from serious work, a claim that is behind the popular joke that IT stands for 'insignificant toys' (Figure 2.1). Gordon (2000) quotes the finding by Active Research Inc., a San Francisco Internet-based market research company, that online shopping does not peak in the evening when workers are at home, but in the middle of the day when they are in the office!

Other sceptics point to the possibility that the rise in US productivity has been due more to the increased flexibility of the US labour market than to any specific characteristics of information technology. OECD studies comparing the US experience with that of other developed countries have found that the high US productivity growth in the mid 1990s was followed only in Australia, Finland and Canada, and not at all in Germany, Italy, France and Japan, which have less 'flexible' labour markets (Colecchia and Schreyer, 2002). Flexible labour markets are defined as those in which there are fewer government (and trade union) regulations concerning working conditions and pay scales and in which industrial trade unions are weaker or non-existent. For example, it is well known that in the USA workers can be fired much more easily (often indiscriminately) than in European countries. Hence, a lesson that may be drawn from the OECD reports, although it is not stated directly, is that the higher productivity of the 'flexible' countries might be due, not to IT, but to the fact that workers in those countries can be worked harder, paid less and fired more easily.

However, Gordon's (2000) findings have been criticized in turn for not taking into account the difficulty of measuring productivity in an economy characterized by rapid technological change. The issue here is that the traditional measurements of output used to calculate productivity figures do not take into consideration changes in the quality of output, such as improved product quality, choice, time savings and convenience. This is a big problem for productivity calculations as it means that if more change occurs on the quality side than on the quantity side, that is, better products rather than more products, the total change in output will be severely underestimated.

This problem is even greater in the service sector as most service improvements come in terms of not more services but better services. For example, output in the health-care industry will be underestimated if all that is counted is patient throughput or treatment episodes, without accounting for the extent to which consumers enjoy better treatment. Quality improvements in health care include better diagnosis, new medical equipment and less invasive treatments. Another example is provided in a study cited by *The Economist* (2000). This study claimed that when changes in the quality of output are not recognized, output in the US banking industry appears to have grown by only 1.3 per cent between 1977 and 1994. If quality changes are included, for example by taking into account the rise of automated teller machines and online banking, the study argued that output appears to have grown by 7 per cent!

Another way in which consumer satisfaction is not recognized in traditional productivity accounts is by neglecting the wider *choice* that people have in the products they buy. In the extreme case, if the same amount of output is produced in one year as in the previous year, but the choice of products has doubled, the official measures would not pick that up as a change in output. These are not problems in a world of mass production, where the point is to produce a lot of standard goods for the general consumer, but they are problems in the world of mass customization, where the point is to produce the 'right' goods for the specific consumer. Nonetheless, economists have devised methods to tackle these problems, some of which will be discussed in Section 2.4.

A summary

I have shown that, while IT has no doubt had an impact on productivity, it is not clear whether this goes beyond the IT-producing sector, or whether the gains will outlast the boom period of the business cycle. With so much debate, whom should we believe? Perhaps, as is often the case, the truth lies somewhere in the middle. The optimistic view highlights the way that IT has transformed society, and how this transformation has in many instances led to growth through the productivity-enhancing aspects of IT. The pessimistic view reminds us to be cautious in attributing such growth solely to the rise of IT, given that the rise in productivity has occurred during the boom period of the business cycle. Others argue that perhaps the productivity increase has occurred as a result of influences unrelated to IT, such as the rise of flexible labour markets. If the increase continues, it would appear that the productivity increases have been trend increases. If they fall, it would appear that they are more cyclical in nature.

Exercise 2.3

List two or three things that could happen in the US economy in the future that would go some way towards settling the debate between optimists and pessimists on the impact of IT.

2.4 'Garage tinkerers': new economy or industry life cycle?

As you have now seen, the concept of the 'new economy' has inspired a number of studies that compare the effect that new technologies have had on economy-wide productivity in previous eras with the effect that IT has – or has not yet – had in the current era. I shall now ask another question, still along the lines of 'what's new in the new economy?', but this time from a more microeconomic perspective, which focuses on the individual firm and industry rather than on the whole economy. (Look back at the distinction made in Section 2.1 between microeconomics and macroeconomics.) I shall ask whether the information revolution, that is, the emergence of IT as a new GPT, has changed the way that firms and industries evolve.

Why should we ask this question? Well, just as there is a debate about whether the 'new economy' has changed the dynamics of productivity, there is also a debate about whether the 'new economy' has changed the way that firms and industries operate and evolve. For example, some claim that the 'new economy' has made technological change and entrepreneurial activity more important to company survival than it was before, and hence has heightened the role of small, flexible and innovative firms. Others claim that technological change, new ideas and entrepreneurial activity were just as important in the early phase of industries that emerged before the 'new economy' era. Rather than investigating this debate through the views of optimists and pessimists, as we did above, we can dive right in by comparing an old-economy industry, the US automobile industry, which has been around for 100 years, and a new-economy industry, the US personal computer industry. The goal is to see whether patterns that are claimed to be characteristic of new high-tech industries were just as common in the early development of a traditional industry. These patterns include the role of small entrepreneurial firms ('garage tinkerers'), the rapidity with which firms rise and fall, and the importance of technological change for company survival.

▪▪▪ 2.4.1 The industry life cycle

The comparison between the automobile industry and the PC industry makes sense only if we concentrate on similar periods in their evolution. We will concentrate here on the 'early' development of both industries, in what will be called the 'introductory' and 'early growth' phases in their life cycles. This is the period running from 1900 to 1930 in the automobile industry and from 1975 to 2000 in the PC industry. The automobile industry refers here to all firms producing cars and trucks, and the PC industry refers to all firms producing personal computers (i.e. laptops and desktops rather than mainframes or workstations). To make the comparison as tight as possible, only the *US* market of each industry is studied, that is, US and foreign firms selling in the US market. Looking at the international market would inevitably cause us to consider other factors independent of industrial dynamics, such as different countries' business cycles and politics. We will not keep referring to US industries in what follows, but to help you to remember what we are discussing we will use the American term 'automobile' throughout this section rather than the British 'car'.

We will use the 'industry life cycle' framework to study the two industries side by side, highlighting similarities and differences in their development over time. The industry life-cycle framework, which you will study in more detail in Chapter 3, focuses on those economic mechanisms that cause firms to be born (to 'enter' an industry), to grow, and possibly to die (to 'exit' an industry). It also examines how these mechanisms affect changes in the industry structure. Industry structure refers to the characteristics of an industry, such as the number of firms operating in it, the distribution of power between them (whether some are very large and others very small, or whether they are all very large), and the degree to which new firms find it easy to enter the industry. Mechanisms affecting industry structure include the dynamics of entry and exit, technological change and falling prices. It is, therefore, on mechanisms such as these that we will focus.

The industry life cycle is characterized by different phases.

■ A *pre-market* or *hobbyist phase*, in which the product is produced more as a hobby or luxury than for commercial purposes. This phase is characterized by much variety in the characteristics of both firms and the product versions they produce.

■ An *introductory phase*, in which the product begins to be produced more for commercial purposes than for hobby reasons. This phase is characterized by the rapid entry of many new firms which seek to take advantage of the new profit opportunities. Entry occurs principally through technological change, that is, each firm enters with a different version of the product, so this phase is the one characterized by the most product innovation.

■ A *growth phase*, in which the industry grows rapidly due to the emergence of a standardized product. A standardized product refers to the convergence of industry production around a product with a given set of characteristics (e.g. a four-wheeled car with a roof). Efficiency in the industry increases, as the standardized product can be mass produced (not possible if the product is undergoing too much change), and demand for the product rises as consumers learn more about it. Those firms not able to produce the standardized product efficiently are forced to 'exit' the industry (more on this below).

■ A *mature phase*, in which demand slackens and fewer technological opportunities are available. If a new product innovation is introduced in the mature phase of the industry (e.g. the replacement of LP records with CDs in the music industry) the industry life cycle may start anew as new firms enter to profit from the new technological opportunities provided by the new product. However, whether the existing leaders remain the leaders will depend on whether the new innovations build on the leaders' existing capabilities and hence strengthen their position, or make those capabilities obsolete and hence threaten their position.

I shall now review these different phases in more detail through an analysis of the evolution of the US automobile and PC industries. We will see that there are some remarkable similarities in the early development of these two industries.

■■■ 2.4.2 Live fast, die young

Both the automobile and PC industries were characterized by a great deal of turbulence in the first 20 to 30 years of their existence. In both cases, many new firms entered the industry, introduced new varieties of the product, and soon left the industry, leaving only a few dozen firms to compete during the growth phase. By 1926 only 33 per cent of the firms that had started producing automobiles during the previous 22 years had survived. In the case of PCs, by 1999 only 20 per cent of the firms that had started producing PCs had survived. In both cases, the majority of firms did not last more than five years! This turbulent 'live fast, die young' period of great entry and exit is characterized by a lot of technological change. Let us look at this in more depth.

Figure 2.2
Some early
automobiles
Source: Epstein,
1928, pp.29, 48

The *hobbyist* period in the automobile industry lasted approximately from 1885 to 1900. The first internal-combustion engine was invented in 1877 by Nikolaus Otto in Germany, and the first car (three-wheeled!) was invented in 1885 by Karl Benz, also in Germany. The first four photographs in Figure 2.2 show that between 1893 and 1899 automobiles were simply 'horseless carriages'. They were the products of experiments carried out by 'tinkerers' in their homes or workshops. Carroll and Hannan (2000) document 3845 'pre-production' organizing attempts in the US automobile industry, of which only 11 per cent reached the market place.

The *introductory* period, in which cars began to be manufactured commercially, started in 1900. Before this date the automobile industry was not even listed in the census of manufacturers under a separate heading, yet by 1926 it had already attained an equal importance to shipbuilding and railroads (Epstein, 1928, p.30). In 1901 Oldsmobile produced the world's first mass-produced automobile, and in 1910 the Ford Motor Company used the industry's first branch-assembly plant, that is, an assembly-line system for mass-producing cars, to produce the Model T, which soon became close to an industry standard. The period between 1900 and the end of the 1920s witnessed the most variety in product versions ever experienced in the industry. The second set of four photographs in Figure 2.2 shows some of the automobiles that emerged from this period of experimentation and tinkering.

Before 1973, the computer industry was formed around the production of the *mainframe* computer, dominated by IBM since the 1960s, and the *minicomputer*, the embryonic form of today's PC, dominated by Digital Equipment Corporation (whose computer was called the PDP-8). The first mass-produced computer was introduced by Micro Instrumentation and Telemetry Systems in 1974 (the MITS Altair 8800). As in the automobile industry, in the early years (up to 1980) demand was concentrated among hobbyists. The new start-ups were very similar to the early 'tinkerers' in the automobile industry: production was often organized out of a structure that looked like a garage, and the producers were driven by creativity and a passion for the product. As in the automobile industry, entry occurred mainly through product innovation. Figure 2.3 illustrates the wide range of product designs in these early years.

The *introductory period* in the PC industry, in which real commercial growth began, occurred only after IBM introduced the IBM 'PC' in 1981, initiating the phase of IBM 'compatibility' (both hardware and software) which later allowed economies of scale to operate in the industry. Three further developments markedly increased the growth of the PC industry: (1) Intel's introduction of the 32-bit 386 processors in 1985, which

Apple Lisa

Amstrad PPC640D

Addressgraph-Farrington 1680

AT&T 3B2/300

Bondwell B2

Atari 800

Amstrad CPC464

MITS Altair 8800

Imsai 8080

AT&T PC 6300

Figure 2.3
Some early PCs

allowed graphical interfaces and hence a more user-friendly environment; (2) the introduction of Windows 3.0 in 1990, which standardized the PC on the Windows operating systems, allowing 'cloning' of the IBM PC; and (3) the rise of the World Wide Web in the 1990s. All three developments contributed to a rapid increase in sales and, later, to a rapid fall in prices.

Hence, in both industries the early years were characterized by a great deal of turbulence: new firms entering the industry with new product innovations, and industry growth taking off. Figure 2.4 depicts this turbulence graphically as the rise and fall of firm numbers (i.e. how many firms exist in the industry in a given year) for the first 30 years or so of each industry. The vertical axis shows the number of firms; the horizontal axis shows the age of the industry for its first 27 years.

| Question | Look at Figure 2.4. What was similar about the early years of the US automobile and PC industries? |

The two industries experienced a remarkably similar pattern of growth: both industries went from infancy to just below 300 firms in only 10 to 15 years. The peaks of the curves in Figure 2.4 illustrate that there was a maximum of 271 automobile firms in 1909 and a maximum of 286 PC firms in 1987. After this point, the industries experienced a 'shake-out', that is, the elimination of a large number of firms, which in the case of the US automobile industry culminated in the survival of only three domestic firms.

What caused the great number of exits, or 'shake-outs', from the two industries? As predicted by life-cycle theory, most of the firms left the two industries at around the time the product became standardized, that is, when the great experimentation with different

Figure 2.4
Number of
firms in the US
automobile industry
(1899–1925) and
the US PC industry
(1973–99)

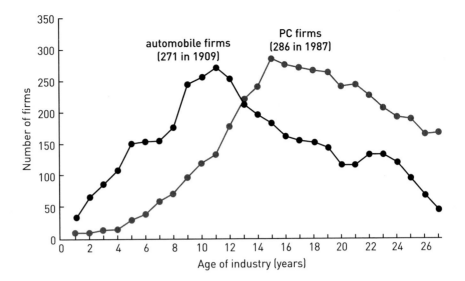

product types had ended and the industry had consolidated around a particular standard. In the automobile industry this occurred around 1910, soon after the Model T was introduced. In the PC industry it occurred around 1990, soon after the new Wintel platform emerged (the combination of the Windows operating system and the Intel processor), which set a new standard for the industry.

Once the product had become standardized, companies focused on increasing the efficiency of production through process innovations. For example, greater efficiency was achieved by introducing mass-production techniques, which allowed economies of scale. The term 'economies of scale', which you will learn more about in Chapter 3, refers to the dynamic by which an increase in the quantity produced allows the firm to spread its costs over a larger output, which lowers the cost of producing each unit of output. Mass production also allows improvements in efficiency from 'learning by doing': the more that is produced, the more that is learned, from experience, about how to make production more efficient. As large firms, by definition, achieve a higher scale of production ('scale' is measured by level of output), small firms are forced out of the market in the phase in which scale matters the most.

2.4.3 Prices and industrial change

Many of the new entrants entered by introducing a new variation of the product. In fact, the early period in both industries was characterized by much technological change in the form of product innovation. Once a product standard emerged, product and process innovations around that standard led to a drastic fall in the product price in both industries. We will now look at some of the indicators of this turbulence in technology and prices.

How can we look at price changes over time in industries in which the product undergoes so many changes, especially in the early stages? Economists have devised a way to do just that, called 'hedonic prices'. These are quality-adjusted prices, that is, prices that keep certain quality characteristics constant. In the case of automobiles over the last decade or so, the price might try to exclude changes such as the emergence of anti-lock brakes, the availability of engines with improved fuel consumption and reduced CO_2 emissions, airbags, stronger safety shells, traction control and central locking. In the PC industry, the

Figure 2.5
Hedonic prices in
the US automobile
industry
(1906–1926) and
the US PC industry
(1980–2000)

Source: Raff and
Trajtenberg, 1997;
Bureau of Economic
Analysis, 2000

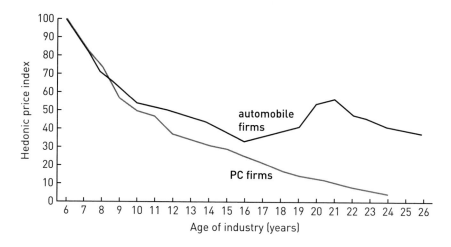

characteristics to be held constant might include available RAM, processor speed, screen size and weight.

Figure 2.5 illustrates the evolution of quality-adjusted hedonic prices in both industries. You can see that in both industries prices fell drastically over the first three decades. Between 1906 and 1940, quality-adjusted prices in the automobile industry fell by 51 per cent (i.e. they halved), with most of the change occurring between 1906 and 1918 (Raff and Trajtenberg, 1997). (The quality-adjusted price calculation also removes the effect of inflation, something that will be explained in Chapter 8.) This fall in price reflects the radical changes in technology, the spread of mass production and the general expansion in the market for cars.

The prices of personal computers were also greatly affected by technological advances. Berndt and Rappaport (2000) found that PC quality-adjusted hedonic prices fell by an average of 18 per cent between 1983 and 1989, 32 per cent between 1989 and 1994, and 40 per cent between 1994 and 1999. Prices began to drop significantly after Intel's introduction of the 32-bit 386 processors in 1985 and the introduction of Windows 3.0 in 1990. The latter allowed the production of PCs to be standardized (via cloning of the IBM PC). The rise of the Internet also increased sales and decreased prices. In recent years, quality-adjusted prices have fallen at an average annual rate of 24 per cent (Bureau of Economic Analysis, 2000).

Before we interpret what Figure 2.5 tells us about prices in the two industries, let me explain the meaning of the numbers on the vertical axis, which shows an *index* of (hedonic) prices. The concept of an index (plural indices) may be familiar to you. In case it is not, here is an explanation. It is worth getting this clear, as indices are used a lot in economics. They are basically a simple way of measuring change. The most widely used method of constructing an index is based on the notion of the percentage, as discussed earlier in this chapter (Section 2.2.2).

Suppose that the price of a product is €5 in 2000, €7.50 in 2001 and €10 in 2002 (just to keep the arithmetic simple). We want to start our index in 2000. So the price in that year is set equal to 100 per cent.

So €5 is the index base = 100

Then we compare all the other prices with the index base, using percentages. So to find the index for 2001, we divide the price in 2001 by the price in 2000, and multiply the result by 100 to give us a percentage.

Table 2.1

Year	Actual price of product €	Price index (base 2000)
2000	5.00	100
2001	7.50	150
2002	10.00	200

€7.50 as an index (base 2000) is €7.50/€5 · 100 = 150

For 2002, we do the same calculation, always comparing it with the *base year* (2000 in this example).

€10 as an index (base 2000) is €10/€5 · 100 = 200

So Table 2.1 shows the price index for the three years.

Question	Look carefully at Figure 2.5. What does it tell you about prices in the first three decades of both industries?

Focus on the slope of the curves, which indicates how prices are changing: a steep downward slope shows rapid price reductions. Figure 2.5 clearly indicates that in both industries prices fell drastically during the first three decades. One difference, however, between the two industries is that prices fell for a longer time in the case of PCs. We will examine the reasons for this difference after we have looked at the patterns of innovation.

Exercise 2.4

Complete Table 2.2.

Table 2.2

Year	Actual price of product €	Price index (base 2003)
2003	12.00	100
2004	16.00	
2005	19.00	
2006	21.00	

▧ ▨ ■ 2.4.4 Technological change

In both industries the fall in prices was driven by radical changes in the production of the products. How might we investigate the technological changes and the changes in quality that occurred in both industries simultaneously with the drastic fall in prices? There are various methods used by economists to measure technological change. Some methods focus on the 'inputs' into the innovation process, such as the spending on research and development by firms. But this is not ideal as it does not indicate whether the spending

Figure 2.6
Product and
process innovations
in the US
automobile industry
Source: Abernathy
et al., 1983

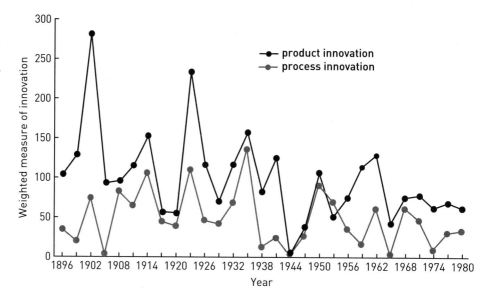

was successful, that is, it does not look at the output of the process, just at the intention. Some methods look at innovative output in terms of the numbers of patents issued by the firms. But this is not ideal either as it does not discriminate between patents which barely affect production and patents which cause major change to the industry. We will use two alternative methods here. One takes into account a list of innovations produced in the automobile industry, where each innovation is given a score according to its effect on the production process of automobiles. The other measures quality change and is derived from the quality-adjusted measure of prices explained above.

For the automobile industry, Abernathy *et al.* (1983) compiled a list of all the product and process innovations from 1893 to 1987 and gave each innovation a score on a scale from 1 to 7. This scale is similar to that used by market researchers who enquire how much you like a product on a scale from 1 to 5. The score is called a 'weight'. A weight of 1 means that the innovation affected the automobile very little (e.g. a new type of colour spray), while a weight of 7 means that it affected it a lot (e.g. the introduction of the assembly line or a new type of engine). The number of innovations per year and their weight produced a score for the year, which indicated the degree to which technological change had occurred. Product and process innovations were listed separately. Figure 2.6 illustrates this data by plotting the weighted measure of innovation in three-year intervals. The fact that both lines fall over time on average indicates that most product and process innovations occurred in the early years, when the industry experienced a high rate of new firm entry.

Although we do not have the same data for the PC industry, our second measure of innovation can be applied to both industries. This second measure looks at the degree to which the *quality* of the product has changed over time, a good proxy for innovation as innovation changes the quality of products and processes. To derive this measure of quality change, you start from the index of actual prices of a car or a PC. This is, in essence, the average price of each product sold in stores, turned into a price index as explained above. That is divided by the quality-adjusted hedonic price you have already studied. The first index shows the prices for goods of changing quality; the second, prices for goods of unchanged quality. Dividing the first by the second gives you a quality index: it will be high if there is a lot of quality improvement and low if there is little quality improvement.

Figure 2.7
Quality improvements in the US automobile industry

Source: Raff and Trajtenberg, 1997

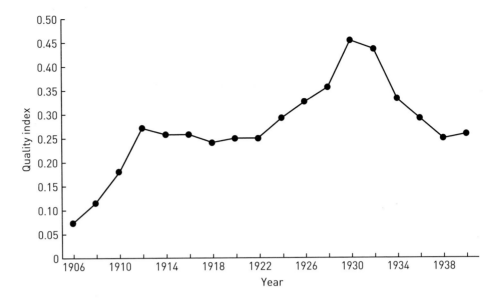

Figure 2.8
Quality improvements in the US PC industry

Source: Filson, 2001

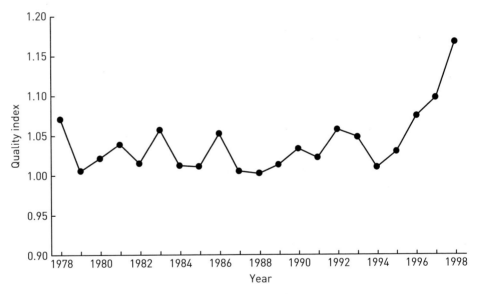

Question	Look carefully at Figures 2.7 and 2.8. How do quality changes compare at similar stages in the two industries' life cycles?

As in Figure 2.5, it is the slope of the lines that is important: how the quality index changes over time. A steep upward slope indicates a period of great increase in quality.

One difference between the two industries that you can see if you compare Figures 2.7 and 2.8 is that, whereas in the automobile industry the degree of quality change was greatest in the very early years (1906–12), in the PC industry it was greater during the third decade of its existence. This difference is due to the fact that the PC industry emerged from the existing mainframe and minicomputer industry, in which firms such as IBM and DEC controlled the industry and hence had little competitive stimulus to innovate. The reason is that a firm's goal when innovating is to out-perform its competitors; so if it is not being challenged by those competitors, it has less incentive to innovate. Radical innovation was not unleashed in the industry until those firms that had a technical lead lost their control of the innovation process. Innovation up until 1990 was to a large extent controlled by IBM, as everything had to be IBM compatible. Only once the Wintel standard (the combination of the Windows operating system and the Intel processor) replaced the IBM standard, did the industry experience the kind of turbulence experienced in the very early years of the automobile industry. Therefore, although there was a lot of entry into the PC industry during its first fifteen years (as seen in Figure 2.4), it took longer than that for the new firms to eliminate the lead of the giants that preceded them. Below we shall see the implications of this for the industry structure.

Furthermore, Bresnahan (1998) holds that the reason that technological change in the PC industry lasted into the third decade of its existence, instead of dying off as often happens during the growth stage of the industry life cycle (as in automobiles), is that technological leadership in this industry is not dominated by one firm or a set of firms but divided among firms in different parts of the computer industry. These firms are the makers of PCs themselves (e.g. IBM, Dell, Compaq); the makers of the microprocessors (e.g. Intel); the makers of the operating systems (e.g. Microsoft); and the makers of application software (e.g. Lotus, WordPerfect, Ashton-Tate). This divided technical leadership has ensured rapid advances from specialists and a very competitive market, as PC firms are forced to compete not only with other firms that produce PCs but also with firms that produce parts or complementary products that work with another firms' products.

■ ■ ■ 2.4.5 Changes in industry structure

How did the turbulence caused by new firms entering and leaving the industry, radical technological change and falling prices affect the overall industry structure? The term 'industry structure' refers mainly to the way in which power is distributed among firms. This can be described by factors such as the number of firms in the industry and the distribution of **market shares**.

Market share

The market share of a firm is its share of total industry production expressed as a percentage.

An industry that has one firm with 50 per cent of the market and 50 other firms with only 1 per cent of the market (market shares must total 100 per cent) has a very different industry structure from an industry in which 10 firms each have 10 per cent of the market. An industry is described as 'concentrated' when a few firms have large market shares. Economists are interested in industry structure because it has implications for consumers. One of the issues is the extent to which the existence of very large firms in the industry will prevent a competitive environment, for example whether they inhibit other firms from entering the industry and discourage innovation. This issue was at the heart of the Microsoft trial, which you will read more about in Chapter 4, in which a very large software firm, with almost complete domination of the market, was accused of hindering competition in the industry.

In both industries, the periods of greatest technological advance were also the periods in which market shares were the most unstable and industry concentration at its lowest. Market share dynamics are important because unstable market shares mean that the status quo in the industry is being disrupted: the leaders' lead is being challenged. When market shares are stable the existing leaders are not challenged by outsiders. Incremental technological change tends to be less disruptive to the leaders' position than radical technological change, which is often carried out by outsiders. In fact, some have argued that competition should be measured, not by the level of 'concentration' (i.e. whether market share gives some firms too much power), but by the level of market share instability. As long as there is some instability the existing leaders cannot relax and are thus forced to compete.

Case study: Cars – from technological change to marketing and back?

In the automobile industry, market share instability was especially strong during the period from 1910 to 1925, which witnessed not only high entry/exit rates but also some of the most radical innovations in the industry. Market share instability then decreased as entry fell and innovation became less important. The strong economies of scale that developed in the 1920s, when most of the industry (not only Ford) began to use mass-production techniques, alongside the fall in prices, caused the industry to become increasingly concentrated. The 'Big Three' US automobile producers (Ford, GM and Chrysler) have dominated the US industry for most of the post-Second World War period. Concentration stopped increasing in the 1970s when the entry of foreign firms into the US market created a more competitive market. Foreign firms especially profited from the opportunity to satisfy the high demand for small cars during the oil crisis of the 1970s, an area in which they had more experience. Since the 1970s, competition has been carried out principally via advertising wars and price wars. As the twenty-first century opens, however, the automobile industry stands on the brink of a new round of technological innovation, as hydrogen looks set to replace petroleum as the standard fuel (Chapter 3, Section 3.4.2).

Question

Do you think there are any economic factors underlying the varying importance of technological change over time? Is this pattern of structural change over time likely to be replicated in other industries (e.g. the PC industry)?

In the PC industry, market shares were the most stable and industry concentration the highest in the early years when IBM dominated the industry. During the late 1980s and early 1990s, the end of the IBM-compatibility era (with the rise of Wintel) and the emergence of the World Wide Web caused some disruption to the status quo, which resulted in unstable market shares and a fall in concentration. Concentration later rose again in the 2–3 year period up to the time of writing in 2001, because companies such as Dell were focusing less on innovation and more on simple measures to cut costs and hence prices so as to increase market share.

> Dell computers is vowing to remain on the offensive in an ongoing PC price war, sacrificing profits in a bid to gain market shares – a strategy that the company's founder admitted could ultimately kill off a competitor.
>
> *(Popovich, 2001)*

> A price war is hitting PC makers hard. Many well-known names could disappear from the high street . . . But not all the problems are due to the downturn in the economy or the bursting of the internet bubble. Much of the suffering has been caused by Dell computer which started a price war to gain market share.
>
> *(Schofield, 2001, p.1)*

You will study the concept of a price war in Chapter 6. For the present let us simply note that this recent trend has, in fact, been seen by many industry analysts as a threat to the industry. Unless the PC industry goes back to the era of competing via innovation (as in the early 1990s) it is bound to end up as a traditional, stagnant industry run by a few firms that are more interested in protecting their market shares (through price reductions and advertising wars) than in the future technological growth of the industry.

■ ■ ■ 2.4.6   The future?

In the USA, the automobile reached the 50 per cent household penetration rate in 1923, about 23 years into the industry's development. The PC reached that threshold rate in 1999, also about 23 years into its development. Given the discussion in Section 2.3, this suggests that the economy-wide effects of the PC have yet to be fully seen. And given the arguments in this section, it also suggests that the PC is now starting to reach the end of its growth phase. In fact, in 2001 PC sales fell for the first time. As a report in the *Financial Times* noted: 'Shipments of personal computers have suffered their first quarterly fall in at least 15 years' (Kehoe, 2001).

Given the similarities in the early development of the two industries, it is likely that some of the patterns that have characterized the mature phase of the automobile industry will also characterize the future of the PC industry, which is only now entering its mature phase. Using this logic we might expect the PC industry to be characterized by higher levels of concentration (already happening with the recently proposed merger between HP and Compaq, and with the price war led by Dell), more market share *stability* between the incumbents, and more focus on process innovation and advertising than on product innovation.

However, if future competition is carried out more through product innovation than through price wars and economies of scale (as it is currently), then this drift into stagnation may not occur. Instead, if innovations allow new firms to come forward and displace the old leaders, the characteristics of the early phase may reappear and the life cycle will start up again. We may witness new entries and exits and renewed market share instability. The future market structure of the PC industry will also be influenced by the nature of innovation in another sense: whether new innovations will continue to allow the technical leadership to be divided among firms, a situation which in the past has allowed new entry to occur and smaller firms to survive.

2.5   Conclusion

This chapter has enabled you to think about the essential role of technological change in determining economy-wide growth and the growth of firms and industries. We have seen that many issues surrounding the new economy are really issues around the dynamics of technological change: rapid increases in productivity, the emergence of many small firms, new products and new processes, and so on. The main lesson of the chapter has been to provide a historical perspective to the introduction of new technologies. Without such a historical perspective, patterns may falsely appear to be new: we have just forgotten!

Questions for review and discussion

Question 1   Suppose a firm uses 200 hours of labour per day and produces 4000 mobile phones. It then reduces its labour inputs to 100 hours per day and finds it can produce 3000 phones. Which one of the following is a correct statement about the change in the firm's productivity? Tick the letter corresponding to the correct statement from the list below.

A ❑ The firm now produces 25% fewer phones, so its productivity has fallen by 25%.

B ❑ The firm has cut its labour hours by 100 but its output has fallen by 1000, so its productivity has fallen.

C ❑ The firm employs 50% of the labour hours it employed before and produces 75% of its previous output, so its productivity has risen by 25%.

D ❑ The firm has increased its output per labour hour from 20 units to 30 units, so its productivity has risen by 50%.

Question 2   Some of the following features of industrial revolutions belong to a microeconomic perspective (as opposed to a macroeconomic perspective). Select the ones you think belong (there is more than one correct statement).

A ❑ There will be a rise in the level of productivity across the economy.

B ❑ There is rapid entry into and exit from a new industry in its growth phase.

C ❑ You will see cumulative technological change resulting from the birth of new general purpose technologies.

D ❑ There is an increase in the level of income per head.

E ❑ There will be a sustained fall in the price of a new product once a product standard has emerged.

Question 3   Which one of the following characteristics is most typical of an industry in its growth phase?

A ❑ There will be rapid entry of new firms, each producing a different version of the product.

B ❑ There will be firms of many kinds producing in a pre-commercial way.

C ❑ The emergence of a standardized product will be followed by the exit of firms unable to produce it efficiently.

Question 4   The table below is designed to give information about the price of a product in two years, 2000 and 2005. Write the correct values into the spaces in the table.

Year	Actual price of product (£ per unit)	Price index (base year 2000)
2000		
2005	£30	75

Question 5   Explain briefly using examples:

(a) how productivity may increase with the introduction of new technology;

(b) how the characteristics of a general purpose technology help us to understand industrial revolutions;

(c) how technological progress may increase economic growth.

3

Innovation, markets and industrial change

Graham Dawson and Judith Mehta

Concepts

- the market demand curve
- increasing and diminishing returns to a factor of production
- the short-run average cost curve
- the long-run average cost curve
- increasing and decreasing returns to scale; economies and diseconomies of scale
- the industry life cycle
- the learning curve
- network externalities

Objectives

After studying this chapter you should be able to:

- appreciate the importance of technological change, costs of production and consumer preferences to the changing organization of production
- understand the relation between the quantity demanded of a good and its price as represented by the demand curve
- understand economic models of the relation between firms' costs and output
- analyse the role of technology and costs in influencing industry structure over the life cycle.

3.1 Technological change, demand and costs

The new economy

Over the past 40 years global computing power has increased a billionfold. Number-crunching tasks that once took a week can now be done in seconds. Today a Ford Taurus car contains more computing power than the multimillion-dollar mainframe computers used in the Apollo space programme. Cheaper processing allows computers to be used for more and more purposes. In 1985, it cost Ford $60,000 each time it crashed a car into a wall to find out what would happen in an accident. Now a collision can be simulated by computer for around $100. BP Amoco uses 3D seismic-exploration technology to prospect for oil, cutting the cost of finding oil from nearly $10 a barrel in 1991 to only $1 today . . .

Thanks to rapidly falling prices, computers and the Internet are being adopted more quickly than previous general-purpose technologies, such as steam and electricity. It took more than a century after its invention before steam became the dominant source of power in Britain. Electricity achieved a 50% share of the power used by America's manufacturing industry 90 years after the discovery of electromagnetic induction, and 40 years after the first power station was built. By contrast, half of all Americans already use a personal computer, 50 years after the invention of computers and only 30 years after the microprocessor was invented. The Internet is approaching 50% penetration in America 30 years after it was invented and only seven years since it was launched commercially in 1993.

(The Economist, *23 September 2000, pp.5, 10*)

That is how *The Economist* discussed the issue you studied in Chapter 2: the role of information technology as a general purpose technology.

Question	How would you summarize the argument about prices, costs and information technology put forward in *The Economist*?

It seems to us that the argument is that improvements in information technology caused a decline in the costs that firms face in producing goods. Falling prices have in turn encouraged a rapid take-up by consumers of products embodying information technology. Economists place costs on the supply side of markets, where firms produce and sell goods such as cars, oil, personal computers and Internet access. Take-up by consumers is on the demand side of the market. The quotation suggests that new information technology *causes* a decline in costs and hence in prices that enables large numbers of consumers to buy safer cars, personal computers and so on. Technological change, a supply-side phenomenon, is seen as a prime cause of economic change.

In the previous chapter, Mariana Mazzucato looked at the impact of newly introduced technologies in the early phase of the US auto industry and the PC industry, highlighting the similarities between what we are observing today in the IT-based industries and what we observed 100 years ago in an industry we now consider mature. As we write, technological change continues to be very rapid, and two particular technological developments will be used in this chapter to illustrate our discussion of the forces shaping the organization of industrial production. The dilemma faced by car manufacturers in adjusting to the 'hydrogen economy' of the future will be discussed in Section 3.4. We also discuss digital technology, which has revolutionized sound reproduction as well as the capture and transmission of visual images in DVD, digital television and digital cameras. Car manufacturers are also exploiting its potential. For example, the Citroën C5 'bristles with the latest digital technology to improve your motoring experience' (see Figure 3.1). An advertisement for the C5 alludes to the origins of digital technology, showing instructions as sequences of 'switches' in a computer as being 'on' or 'off', or set to '1' or '0'.

In this chapter we will introduce the use of economic models of markets, firms and industries to examine the relationships among consumer demand, technological change and costs. Section 3.2 develops the idea expressed in *The Economist* extract that falling prices were responsible for the rapid take-up of new products by consumers. This is an example of a widely observed relation between the quantity demanded of a good by consumers and the price of the good: the lower the price, the greater the quantity demanded. However, there are other influences on market demand. For example, consumers are likely to buy more goods if their incomes increase. So Section 3.2 explains how economists analyse the interaction between price and other influences. This analysis is the first part of the theory of consumer demand, which will be further developed in Chapter 8.

Figure 3.1
An advertisement
for the Citroën C5

Technology as it should be. 100% useful.

The rest of the chapter focuses mainly on the supply side of the market, exploring the role of costs and technological change in the organization of production. The objective is to understand the process by which a firm – initially one among many similar firms jostling for position – emerges ahead of the pack to achieve an advantage over its competitors, as Ford did in the US automobile industry (Chapter 2). What was so special about Ford? More generally, how can we account for the change in structure that so many industries seem to undergo? Why do most of the many small firms so common in the early years of new industries disappear to leave an established industry dominated by a few large firms? Why does the heterogeneity or extreme variety of those small firms in new industries give way to a much greater degree of similarity, indeed standardization, among the few survivors?

In exploring these questions, economists use models of the relation between the output, technology and costs of firms. In Section 3.3, we define technology in an economic model of a firm, and use it to explore the link between technology and costs. We begin from a model in which firms take technology as given and their ability to change their costs is severely constrained, and then build in progressively more decision-making flexibility over the adoption and use of technology.

Section 3.4 links this analysis of technology and costs to the model of the industry 'life cycle' introduced in Chapter 2, Section 2.4.1. The life-cycle model represents an industry as if it were a biological organism going through the stages of birth, growth, maturity and decline, and is used to consider the interaction of demand and technology in shaping industrial structure. This section further extends the analysis of firms, technology and costs to include models where firms' freedom to learn and create is one driver of technological change itself. This helps us to understand how a particular firm can become the 'leader of the pack' through innovation and how it can then gain an advantage over competitors by reducing its costs through large-scale production.

3.2 Market demand

Case study: Digital outsells film

Sales of digital cameras have overtaken traditional 35 mm cameras for the first time. According to monthly figures collated by national electric and photo retailer Dixons, digital camera sales outstripped 35 mm cameras during the month of April. 'This is a sea change in consumer photography,' said Dixons marketing director Ian Ditcham. 'As a leading photographic retailer, Dixons is a clear barometer of consumer trends,' he said. The main reasons for the popularity of digital cameras are falling prices, the growth of home PC and internet usage and the instant delivery of images without the need for processing.

(Adapted from Outdoor Photography, *August 2001, no.15, p.4)*

Questions

1 What do you think are the main similarities between the arguments in this case study and the second paragraph of 'The new economy' quotation discussed in Section 3.1?

2 Figure 3.2 illustrates a number of different makes of digital camera. What other products do you normally associate with the manufacturers of these cameras?

The quotation and the case study describe the take-up by consumers of new products embodying innovations in information technology. Both link the popularity of new technology among consumers with falling prices and draw attention to the rapidity of consumer take-up. There is something new for Dixons and other retailers to sell and for consumers to buy. A new product, the digital camera, has created a new market. Figure 3.2 shows that this market is supplied by a number of manufacturers normally associated with the production of a range of other consumer goods. Nikon and Olympus make traditional cameras. Epson is a well-known brand of personal computers and printers. Sony is probably best known for the Walkman, the first personal audio-cassette player. Casio puts its name on watches and calculators. Fuji is particularly interesting as a manufacturer not only of cameras but also of film, the medium under challenge from digital.

It seems natural to us to say that these firms from different **industries**, including computers, electronics and optical equipment, have together created a new **market**, that is, a market for a new product, the digital camera. This suggests that industries can be thought of as being about the production of a range of broadly related goods, and markets are about the sale and purchase of a more narrowly defined set of goods. For example, the optical equipment industry produces cameras, photocopiers, microscopes, telescopes and so on in order to supply different markets. There are consumer markets for disposable cameras, entry-level compact cameras or cameras for the serious amateur and so on. There are industrial markets for cameras for professionals or microscopes for specialist use in medical and scientific research. So markets can be identified in terms of their consumers and the purposes for which those consumers are buying goods, as well as in the more familiar terms of the goods themselves. Phrases such as 'the market for medium format

Industry

An industry is a group of firms producing a broadly related range of goods using similar technologies.

Market

A market is constituted by the buying and selling of goods or services.

Figure 3.2
A selection of digital cameras from the buyer's guide of *What Camera?* magazine
Source: *What Camera?*, winter 2001, pp.16–20

cameras' are common. But a medium format camera might appeal to the serious, and affluent, amateur as well as the professional. It is not easy to say where one market ends and another begins.

Precisely where we draw the line between 'industry' and 'market' depends on which aspect of economic activity we want to analyse. Producing and selling are both stages in a single complex process of making profits from the *supply* of goods by turning inputs into outputs that consumers are willing and able to buy. It is helpful to use the term 'industry' if we want to direct attention towards suppliers (as producers) and the technologies they are using. Most countries use a system known as the Standard Industrial Classification to assign organizations to industries. Under this system, each organization is assigned to an industrial category according to the principal goods or services it produces. The system is essential to the collection of statistics that enable us to estimate the relative contributions of the different industries to national income, and to detect which parts of the economy are growing or contracting over time.

To speak of a market directs attention towards the relations between suppliers (as sellers) and buyers of a particular good. It is usually taken for granted that buyers and sellers are engaged in *voluntary* exchange, of money for goods, and that buyers are able to exercise *choice* (to buy or not to buy, to buy this good rather than that one). 'Market' is therefore a politically charged term, unlike 'industry', shown, for example, by the prevalence in political debate of the expression 'free market'. (The nature of markets, including this political dimension, is also discussed in Chapter 5, Section 5.1.)

The focus in Section 3.2 will be on consumer demand for products and in particular the price at which they are offered for sale. It is therefore appropriate to use the term 'market' in this section, reserving 'industry' for later sections where our attention is directed towards the costs incurred by firms in producing goods.

Figure 3.3
A market demand
curve for electronic
personal organizers

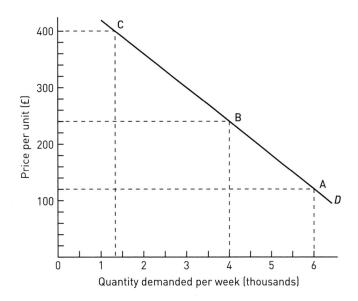

3.2.1 Market demand and price

This subsection will explore the widely observed relationship between the quantity demanded of a good by consumers and the price of the good: the lower the price, the greater the quantity demanded. This relationship underlies the way in which falling prices are responsible for the rapid take-up of new products by consumers, as reported in the quotations above. We focus on the market demand curve, which represents the demand of all the consumers in a given market. However, as well as the price of the good, there are other influences on market demand, discussion of which will be postponed until Section 3.2.2. This makes it possible to take a step-by-step approach and to begin by considering the influence of price alone.

The relationship between demand and price can be represented in different ways: in words, in a diagram or by using algebra. We expressed it in words in the preceding paragraph: the lower the price, the greater the quantity demanded. This relationship can also be shown in a diagram, known as a demand curve (always by convention a 'curve' though it may be drawn as a straight line). Figure 3.3 shows a demand curve, and we look at it in detail in a moment. Note first that as part of the step-by-step approach, the demand curve is drawn on the assumption that the price of the product is the only relevant variable influencing demand for the product. A 'variable' is a precisely defined aspect of the economy, such as the price of a good, that can take a range of values (such as £1, £2, £3, . . .).

All the other influences on market demand are held constant while we look at the relationship between demand and price. This procedure is usually known by the Latin phrase *ceteris paribus*, which means 'other things being equal'. It is the foundation for constructing economic models, which abstract from the complexities of real economic life to concentrate on one or two variables that seem to be important. Once we have understood how two variables are related – how a change in one affects the other, *ceteris paribus* – it is possible to move on, dropping the assumption that other things have remained equal. We can introduce other variables, gradually making the model more complex by considering the effects of changes in them.

An economic model therefore provides a systematic way of thinking about causal relationships. We can use them to formulate hypotheses about cause and effect, such as 'lower prices caused the increase in sales'. That puts us in a position to look for evidence that might lead us to accept or reject the hypothesis.

The market demand curve is a very simple economic model in that it abstracts from the many things going on in a market to focus on only two: the quantity demanded of the good and its price. Look at Figure 3.3, and notice that the vertical and horizontal axes are 'anchored' at the zero point, called the origin. As with all such diagrams, movements up the vertical axis, and along the horizontal axis to the right, represent higher values. Each point on the curve D shows the quantity demanded (measured on the horizontal axis) at a particular price (measured on the vertical axis). The market demand curve therefore shows the quantity demanded at each and every price by all the consumers in a particular market. We say 'each and every price' to draw attention to the fact that in drawing the market demand curve as a continuous line, economists are making estimates. The good may not have been offered for sale at 'each and every' price but only a small number of selected prices. Drawing the market demand curve as a continuous curve on a diagram such as Figure 3.3 shows estimates of what demand would be at other prices.

Figure 3.3 shows a hypothetical market demand curve for electronic personal organizers (hypothetical because it is not based on actual sales figures but is being used purely as an illustration of market demand curves in general). Electronic devices are particularly good at storing files, allowing them to be used in different ways, and have come to dominate the market for portable information storage. The market demand curve depicts the quantity consumers demand, depending on price. This 'quantity demanded' is not necessarily the number of electronic personal organizers that people need, but what they are willing and able to purchase at different prices.

The demand curve in Figure 3.3 shows that with a price of £120, the quantity demanded of electronic personal organizers is 6000 units per week (point A). For a higher price at, say, £240, *ceteris paribus*, we can find out how many units will be purchased by moving along the demand curve to point B, where the quantity demanded is only 4000. If the price was as high as £400 smaller quantities would be purchased; we move along the demand curve to point C, and see that the quantity demanded is only 1300 units. This inverse relationship between the price of a good (or service) and the quantity demanded (shown by the market demand curve sloping downwards and to the right) is known as 'the law of demand'.

So economic models can be stated in words and represented in diagrams. They can also be represented by using algebra. The claim that demand depends on – or changes in response to – price can be written as:

$D = f(P)$, *ceteris paribus*

which is read as demand (D) *is a function of* price (P), all other influences held constant. Both demand and price vary in this model; quantity demanded is the *dependent* variable, since it changes in response to price, the *independent* variable. So this algebraic statement makes clear the causal relation proposed by the model, while the diagram, Figure 3.3, showed the *negative* relationship it proposes between demand and price: a higher price results in a lower quantity demanded (*ceteris paribus*).

However, there may be some exceptions to this 'law' of demand. Early in the twentieth century, Thorstein Veblen, an American institutional economist, analysed cultural influences on consumption. In *The Theory of the Leisure Class* (Veblen, 1912) he suggested that it can be important to show off your wealth by means of conspicuous consumption. The rich can demonstrate their wealth by buying goods that are widely known to be very expensive and beyond the reach of most consumers. The term *Veblen goods* is used to denote luxury items, such as exclusive jewellery, cars or designer clothes which may therefore be in greater demand at higher prices.

At the lower end of the income scale, consumers in very poor countries may actually buy less of a very basic good, such as rice, when its price falls. This is because they can use the spending power released by the fall in the price of the basic foodstuff to replace some rice with a greater variety of foods. Such goods are called *Giffen* goods because the influential economist Alfred Marshall, apparently in error, gave Sir Robert Giffen credit for discovering this exception to the general law of demand.

▨ ▩ ■ 3.2.2 Other influences on market demand

What about other variables which may affect demand? Let us consider four such variables. As is often the case in economics, the first two points involve understanding some rather formal relationships between variables, in this case price and income.

1 *The price of other goods.* Two goods x and y are known as *substitutes* if the quantity demanded of good x increases after a *rise* in the price of good y. The rise in the price of good y causes consumers to switch to good x. For example, if the quantity demanded of electronic personal organizers increases after a rise in the price of (print) diaries, these goods are substitutes. On the other hand, two goods x and y are *complements* if the quantity demanded of good x increases after a *fall* in the price of good y. The fall in the price of good y causes consumers to buy more and also to buy more goods that are used with it, such as good x. For example, if the quantity demanded of electronic personal organizers increases after a fall in the price of desktop computers (to which data can be downloaded), these goods are complements.

2 *The incomes of consumers.* The amounts of income consumers have at their disposal determines the absolute level of consumption: people with high incomes tend to purchase more of most goods and services than people with low incomes. But the level of income also influences the kind of things that people buy. If a country's national income goes up, households have more total purchasing power, and more goods and services of most types will be bought. A *normal good* is one for which the quantity demanded increases when incomes rise. In countries where the average level of income is relatively high, most goods are normal goods (e.g. refrigerators, cars, haircuts, houseplants and electronic personal organizers). Studies of households in poverty show their very limited purchases. There are some products, such as basic foodstuffs, or black and white television sets, of which fewer items will be purchased as income rises. For example, if poor households in low-income countries get richer, they are able to substitute beans, meat or fish for part of their basic grain diet of rice, maize or millet. Less rice will therefore be purchased. When demand for a commodity falls as incomes go up, the commodity is called an *inferior good*.

3 *Socio-economic influences.* J.S. Duesenberry, an American economist, suggested that demand for particular commodities, as well as consumption expenditure in general, is affected by a 'demonstration effect', where people feel social pressures to purchase what others have. J.K. Galbraith, another American economist, talks of a dependence effect, where wants are dependent on the very process by which they are satisfied, since producers use advertisements and sales people to persuade us to purchase what they are making. Many commentators suggest that for a wide range of goods 'consumption to be' has replaced 'consumption for use'. That is, the consumption of many goods and services has become an expression of identity and self-definition, with less emphasis

placed on the use value of the product. As more people turn to shopping for entertainment and leisure, and as the phrase 'retail therapy' increasingly enters into everyday language in high-income countries, it becomes more difficult to understand the demand side of the economy without taking account of society's norms and values.

4   *The expected future price of the good.* Expectations about future prices may affect demand. People may buy non-perishable goods now because they think that prices will be higher in the future or delay purchases in the belief that price cuts are imminent.

We can use algebra to express very concisely what it will take us a paragraph to say in words. A demand function is an algebraic expression of the idea that the demand for a good depends on its price and on the other variables discussed above. We can now write the demand function for a commodity, x, in the following expanded form:

$$D_x = f(P_x, P_r, Y, Z, P_e)$$

This demand function states that the market demand for commodity x D_x is a function of, or depends on, five variables. P_x is the price of commodity x itself, while P_r stands for the price of related goods, that is, substitutes and complements. Y is the standard symbol in economics for the income of all consumers or households together. Then there are socio-economic variables, labelled Z. Finally, P_e stands for expected future prices. The number of variables on the right-hand side of the equation shows that the complete market demand function for a good is quite complex.

So far we have looked at a hypothetical market demand curve for electronic personal organizers on the assumption that while the price of the good changes other things remain equal. What happens if we relax the *ceteris paribus* assumption? In other words, supposing that commodity x is electronic personal organizers, what happens if any of the items on the right-hand side of the demand function change? A change in any of the variables other than the price of electronic personal organizers can be shown by a *shift* in the whole demand curve, because the *ceteris paribus* assumption, on which the original curve was drawn, has been dropped. The shift may be to the left or right, depending on the cause of the change.

Figure 3.4 shows such a shift in demand. This figure does not have a numerical scale on the axes, as in Figure 3.3. Instead, the axes are just labelled 'Price' (P) and 'Quantity'

Figure 3.4
A shift in a market demand curve

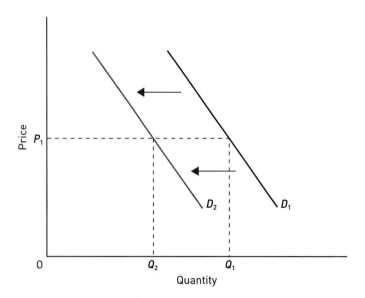

(Q). 'Quantity' should be understood as 'quantity per period of time', such as a day, a week or a year. Diagrams such as this allow us to focus on the direction of change of variables and their implications, rather than exact magnitudes. Let us suppose that consumer incomes fall, so that everyone has less to spend on normal goods. The quantity demanded will therefore decrease at all prices. For example, at price P_1 quantity demanded falls from Q_1 to Q_2. This means that we now have a new relationship between quantity demanded and price, and this is shown by the new market demand curve D_2 in Figure 3.4 lying to the left of the original one, D_1.

The key points about movements along and shifts of the market demand curve are:

- If the price of the good changes while all other variables remain the same, this is reflected in a movement *along* the market demand curve.
- If a variable other than the price of the good itself changes, the whole curve shifts, showing that after the change in the variable more (or less) is now demanded at each price.

Here is an exercise to help you think about shifts in the market demand curve.

Exercise 3.1

Think for a few minutes about how other things besides price may *not* remain equal in the market for electronic personal organizers. Work out what effect each will have on the demand curve. Then see if you can complete Table 3.1 below.

Table 3.1 Shifts in the market demand curve for electronic personal organizers

Change in variable	Effect on demand curve
Decrease in income	Decrease in quantity demanded at all prices Demand curve shifts to the left
Increase in income	
Rise in price of a substitute	
Fall in price of a substitute	
Rise in price of a complementary good	
Fall in price of a complementary good	
Change in socio-economic influences in favour of electronic personal organizers	
Change in socio-economic influences away from electronic personal organizers	

3.3 Firms, costs and technology

In this section the focus turns towards the supply side of the market, towards firms and industries, exploring the importance of costs and technological change in the organization of production. The objective is to understand the kinds of change in industrial structure discussed in Chapter 2, that is, changes in the number and size of firms in an industry. One such change saw the emergence of Ford, initially one among many similar firms jostling for position in the US automobile industry, as the industry 'leader'. What was so special about Ford? Henry Ford was the first car maker to introduce an innovative assembly-line production technology. This gave him a competitive advantage over firms using more traditional and, for that reason, more expensive processes. Since consumers were unwilling to pay higher prices for broadly similar products, Ford's rivals were forced to take up the same new methods of production if they wanted to compete.

This story raises some important questions about competition, technology and costs. How do firms respond to changing conditions in their industry? What can a 'typical' firm do to cut its costs? What are the main constraints on its behaviour? Economists use models of the relationships between technology, costs and output of firms to explore these questions. This section examines these relationships in a basic economic model of a firm. It explores the scope the firm has for cutting its costs in the short and long run, and the impact of changing technology on the firm's costs. The distinction between the short run and the long run is important because it is based on assumptions about how much room to manoeuvre the firm has in responding to changing market conditions and draws attention to the role of investment in the firm's response. It is in the short run that the firm's actions are subject to the greatest constraint. In the analysis in this section, firms take technology as given. In Section 3.4 we remove this constraint, restoring to firms some influence in shaping technology and hence their costs to their own advantage.

■ ■ ■ 3.3.1 Technology and costs in the short run

Advertising leaflets are dropping through letter boxes around the UK, as we are writing this chapter, from cable suppliers trying to attract new customers for their services. They promise to provide a telephone line, a bundle of television channels, an Internet connection, home shopping and movies-on-demand, all at a 'bargain price'. These leaflets raise some interesting questions. How does expanding output of cable services by selling to new customers make it possible to offer them for sale at a lower price? What happens to the costs of producing cable services as the firm increases its output of them?

In analysing the costs, technology and output of firms, economists create a model of the typical or representative **firm**. A firm is an organization that buys inputs, such as land, labour and capital, and transforms them into output for sale. We call these inputs to the firm's production process *factors of production*.

A firm that wants to expand output is likely to need more inputs. For example, in order to increase output the cable supplier would probably recruit more workers, such as the technicians who install cable boxes in customers' homes and the telephonists who respond to customer enquiries. It might also need to buy in more of the equipment used by these workers, such as telephones, computers and engineering tools, and it might need to rent more office space. In other words, the firm increases its input of factors of production, namely labour (the technicians and telephonists), capital (telephones, computers and engineering tools) and land (office space). The firm is assumed to have done this by purchasing the additional inputs it needs from the relevant factor markets, for example by recruiting new workers in the labour market.

The firm can combine factors of production in various ways to create output, but is limited by the technology available to it. The best production methods available to the firm are summarized in its **production function**, which identifies the maximum output a firm can produce from each available combination of inputs. We can write it out using algebra in exactly the same way as we wrote out the demand function in Section 3.2:

$$Q = f(F_1, F_2, \ldots, F_n)$$

The firm

The firm is an organization that transforms inputs of land, labour and capital into an output of goods and services for sale.

Production function

The production function specifies the maximum output a firm can obtain from each available combination of inputs.

This says that the firm's output (Q) (the dependent variable) is a function of the various factors of production (the different Fs, up to any number 'n' of them) such as land, different types of labour and machinery (the independent variables). This production function is the firm's *technology*. The firm is assumed to do the best it can with its inputs, without waste. If there is technological change, the firm can get more output from its inputs, that is, increase their productivity (Chapter 2, Section 2.2.2). In the models we discuss in this section all firms have access to the same technology.

The firm's objective is not to produce maximum output, but rather to make as much profit as possible. However, reducing costs is an important competitive tool in the search for profits, as the cable supplier's offer of a 'bargain price' to new customers illustrates. So how do firms' costs change as output changes? What makes it possible to supply more customers at a lower price? Are there any limitations to this process? The distinction between the short run and the long run helps to answer these questions.

Question We referred above to the cable supplier recruiting new workers. Can you think of any employers or industries that have found this difficult?

In 2001 in the UK the health and education industries were beset with staff shortages and in some areas recruited from overseas. It is likely to take most employers longer to increase the quantity of skilled than unskilled labour. Skills may not be available in the locality and workers may have to be enticed to move from other jobs, involving periods of notice. New workers may have to be trained and the training period may well be lengthy. BBC television reported on 4 September 2001 that Arriva, a UK train and bus operator, had announced the cancellation of up to a hundred services a day because of a shortage of train drivers. Arriva had the capital equipment, the trains, to run the services but could not do so until it had increased the amount of skilled labour at its disposal by training new drivers. In this example the firm is constrained in its response to the demand for rail services because the quantity of one factor of production, labour, is fixed.

The short run

A firm is operating in the short run when it is unable to change the quantity it uses of at least one of its factors of production.

Economists describe the situation in which Arriva finds itself as **the short run**. In the short run the firm can vary the quantity it uses of some of its factors of production but there is at least one which is fixed. The term denotes this constraint on the firm's behaviour rather than a particular period of historical time. The firm's actions take place in actual or historical time and so the short run will eventually come to an end, in Arriva's case when the drivers have been trained in a matter of months. Therefore, the short run, understood as the condition of being unable to change the quantity used of at least one factor, refers to different periods of historical time, depending on the circumstances of each particular firm. Another example from transport illustrates this variety. London's Heathrow, Stansted and Gatwick airports are constrained in responding to rising demand for air travel from London and south-east England by the planning process required before new runways or terminals can be constructed. In this case the fixed factor is capital and the short run is measured in years, perhaps even decades.

Heathrow Terminal 5 to get go-ahead

After an inquiry that began in 1995, the government is poised to give the go-ahead for Heathrow's Terminal 5. It is due to open in 2007, subject to final approval.

(*Adapted from* The Sunday Times, *4 November 2001, p.2*)

In the short run, therefore, the firm has one or more variable factors of production but at least one fixed factor. How does the firm's output change in the short run as it increases the amount of a variable factor? For example, let us suppose that the cable supplier recruited more labour, such as technicians and telephonists, while using unchanged quantities of both capital and land. Hiring more labour allows it to increase output. Initially, output may rise faster than the inputs of labour. Each additional worker may not need a computer all to themselves and, up to a point, extra workers can share the same office space. So initially increases in the amount of labour may generate larger 'returns' in the form of increases in output. At this stage in its expansion of output in the short run, therefore, the firm is experiencing increasing returns to a factor of production, in this case labour.

However, this fortunate situation has its limits. If the firm continues to expand output by increasing the input of labour with unchanged inputs of capital and land, a point will be reached after which the employment of even more workers brings successively smaller increases in output. For example, there may be so many workers that each one spends some time idle in the queue waiting to use a computer. The input of labour is rising faster than output, and the firm is now experiencing diminishing returns to a factor of production. Diminishing returns pose a serious constraint on the expansion of a firm in the short run.

These relationships between inputs and outputs in the short run influence the firm's costs. Returning to the cable supplier, it is now possible to frame a more precise question: what happens to the costs of producing these services as the firm increases its output of them in the short run? To analyse this, we need to distinguish **total costs** (*TC*) and the **average cost** (*AC*) of production. A firm's total costs are the expenses incurred in buying the inputs necessary to produce the firm's output. Average cost is the cost per unit of output. Average cost (*AC*) is therefore the total cost of production (*TC*) divided by the number of units produced (*Q*):

Total costs

The total costs of the firm are the expenses incurred in buying the inputs necessary for production.

Average cost

The average cost of production is the total cost of production divided by the number of units produced.

$$AC = \frac{TC}{Q}$$

We can draw a short-run average cost (*SRAC*) curve that models the relationship between different levels of output and average cost (*AC*) in the short run (Figure 3.5). Each point on the *SRAC* curve represents the average cost in the short run (measured on the vertical axis) of producing a quantity of output (measured on the horizontal axis). Output (*Q*) is measured per time period, such as a year. The *SRAC* curve is expected to be 'U'-shaped, as shown in Figure 3.5. The downward-sloping section of the *SRAC* curve indicates that as output expands from a low level, average costs in the short run fall. Eventually, however, the *SRAC* curve begins to slope upwards, showing that at output levels above Q_1 average costs rise as output increases.

The shape of the *SRAC* curve arises from the technical constraints on short-run output expansion just described. We assume that the price of inputs is constant. As output expands the fixed cost of the fixed factors of production, such as the cable system itself, is being spread over an expanded number of customers. Increasing returns to a factor of production means that output rises faster than the variable input, so the cost of the variable factor per unit of output falls too. So initially the average cost of production (*AC*) falls as output rises.

Eventually, however, diminishing returns to the variable factor of production sets in. Output starts to rise more slowly than the variable input so the additional cost required to produce additional units of output starts to rise. Eventually total cost (fixed plus variable costs) will start to rise faster than output: that is, average costs will start to rise. On Figure 3.5 this happens as output rises above Q_1.

Figure 3.5
A short-run average
cost (*SRAC*) curve

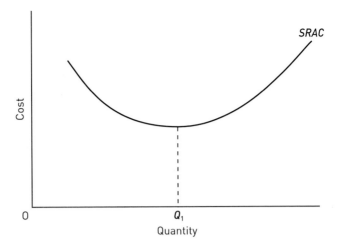

To sum up, in the short run the firm's ability to reduce costs as output rises is constrained by diminishing returns. In the long run, opportunities to invest in factors such as plant and machinery mean that the quantity of all factors of production can be varied. How does that affect the firm's costs?

▪▪▪ 3.3.2 Long-run costs and economies of scale

What makes it possible to offer more output for sale at a lower price? That was one of the questions with which Section 3.3.1 opened. Part of the answer is that the firm's cost curves, which reflect the technology it is using, may display falling average cost as output increases over a range of output levels. The other part of the answer is that market demand must be sufficient to justify successive expansions of output. A firm such as the cable supplier seeking to increase sales by offering 'bargain prices' to its new customers is making an assumption about the size of the market. This section examines the relation between output and average cost on the assumption that the size of the firm's market is sufficiently large to justify increases in its input of all factors of production.

The long run

In the long run
the firm is able
to change the
quantity of all of
its factors of
production.

There is greater scope for cutting costs in **the long run**. In the long run the firm can increase inputs of all factors of production: labour, capital and land. This corresponds in reality to firms making investments. Firms invest in labour by training key personnel such as train drivers, technicians and telephonists. They may invest in items of capital equipment from telephones and computers to new factories or warehouses. They may invest in land by buying more office space or, literally, perhaps by buying a 'greenfield' site for a new runway. In modelling firms in the long run, it is still assumed that they are operating with given technology available to all firms.

How exactly do economists analyse the effects of investment of this kind on the firm's costs? The long-run average cost (*LRAC*) curve models the relationship between changes in output and average cost (*AC*) in the long run (Figure 3.6). Each point on the *LRAC* curve represents the average cost, in the long run, of producing a given quantity of output. The shape of the *LRAC* curve varies with the technology in use by firms in a particular industry. An increase in output in the long run is described as an increase in the *scale* of production, the phrase reflecting the implications of investment in plant and equipment. In the long run, a firm can adjust the quantities of all its factors of production to produce its desired level of output at the lowest possible cost. To achieve higher levels of output, a firm will need to buy more factors of production. How will costs change?

Figure 3.6
Long-run average cost (*LRAC*) curves.
(a) *LRAC* curve displaying increasing, constant and decreasing returns to scale;
(b) 'L'-shaped *LRAC* curve; and
(c) downward-sloping *LRAC* curve

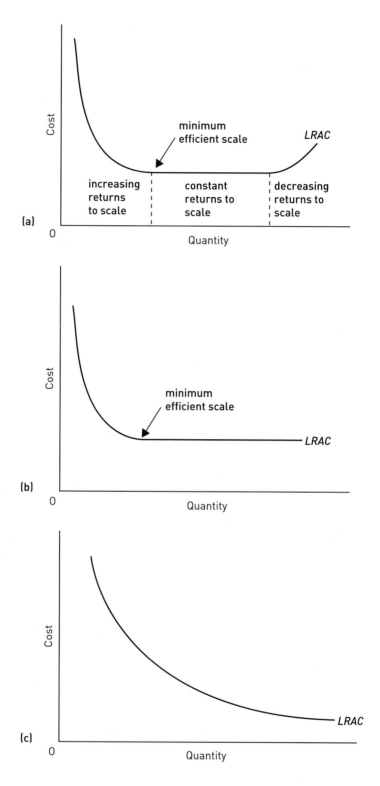

Increasing returns to scale/ economies of scale

Increasing returns to scale/economies of scale exist when long-run average cost falls as output increases.

Figure 3.6 shows three possible shapes for the firm's long-run average cost (*LRAC*) curve. All three have a downward-sloping section: in (a) and (b) this occurs at low output levels; in (c) *LRAC* slopes down continuously over the whole output range. If the *LRAC* slopes downwards, the firm is benefiting from **increasing returns to scale or economies of scale** over the relevant range of output. We will use these two terms interchangeably. They imply that as output increases, long-run average costs fall.

Increasing returns to scale arise within the firm from the firm's production function. Increased output may allow a firm to use inputs more productively. If doubling all the firm's inputs more than doubles output, there are increasing returns to scale. This may be because there are economies of increased dimensions. For example, enormous oil tankers and very large lorries can transport goods at lower cost per unit than smaller ships and vehicles because their capacity rises faster than the materials needed to make and run them. Industrial plant displays the same effect: building a factory extension that doubles the output capacity of the firm may be possible without doubling the costs of using and maintaining it. Furthermore, larger scale may also allow the more efficient use of inputs through specialization of tasks that was described in Chapter 2, Section 2.2.2.

The firm may also benefit from economies of scale that arise from sources outside the firm. These are reductions in a firm's average costs arising from the expansion of the industry to which it belongs. For example, the first IT firms which located in what has become known as Silicon Valley in the USA – or in Silicon Fen as the area around Cambridge, UK, is sometimes called – gained economies of scale when the industry began to expand. The concentration of numerous, closely related high-tech companies in a single geographical area meant that highly specialized factors of production (e.g. computer technicians and silicon chips) were available to them more cheaply and easily than they were to firms located elsewhere.

Minimum efficient scale (MES)

Minimum efficient scale refers to the output at which long-run average costs first reach their minimum level as output rises.

Firms may find that there is a limit to the economies of scale that they can achieve, a situation shown in Figure 3.6(a). They will reach a level of output after which no further reductions in average cost can be obtained. This level of output is known as the **minimum efficient scale (MES)**. The MES marks the size of the firm beyond which there are no cost advantages to be reaped from operating at a larger scale; it is the point at which all economies of scale have been taken up. As Henry Ford's smaller rivals discovered, once large-scale assembly-line production had been developed serious cost disadvantages were incurred by a firm operating below the MES, where average cost is higher than it would be if all scale economies were to be exploited. The MES is located at the beginning of the flat section of the *LRAC* curve, over which average cost is constant in Figure 3.6(a). The firm is experiencing **constant returns to scale** over this range of output.

Constant returns to scale

Constant returns to scale exist when long-run average cost remains unchanged as output increases.

The *LRAC* curve depicted in Figure 3.6(a) rises at high levels of output. Average costs increase as output increases. The firm is now experiencing **decreasing returns to scale or diseconomies of scale**. Decreasing returns to scale or diseconomies of scale arise from the disadvantages that large-scale production may entail. The major source of diseconomies of scale is the co-ordination problems that beset management in large bureaucratic organizations. The rapid expansion of an industry may also cause external diseconomies of scale, if labour costs increase as more and more firms chase scarce supplies of specific skills. For example, firms in some 'new economy' industries find wages are being bid up because of a shortage of workers with the appropriate IT skills.

Decreasing returns to scale/ diseconomies of scale

Decreasing returns to scale/ diseconomies of scale exist when long-run average cost rises as output increases.

The 'U'-shaped *LRAC* curve shown in Figure 3.6(a) is only one of three possible shapes that are usually distinguished. If the technology of the industry in which the firm is active is different from that of another industry, this will be expressed in a different *LRAC* curve. In Figure 3.6(b) the *LRAC* curve is 'L'-shaped, indicating that the firm continues to experience constant returns to scale across its output range once output is above the MES. This might correspond to a firm that can continue to replicate its production processes, for example by adding additional assembly lines, each one exactly like the others.

A third possibility is depicted in Figure 3.6(c), where the firm enjoys economies of scale right across its output range. There is, therefore, every incentive, in the form of ever lower average costs, for firms to continue to expand output. A single firm can supply the whole market at a lower cost than could be achieved by a number of firms in competition with each other. Network industries such as gas, water and electricity distribution, fuel retailing, railway track and cable networks in telecommunications are examples of industries where firms are appropriately modelled by the *LRAC* curve shown in Figure 3.6(c) (see Chapter 4, Section 4.4.2).

The three *LRAC* curves in Figure 3.6, considered together, imply that the technology of an industry is expressed in the shape of the particular *LRAC* curve used in modelling that industry. There is a further implication, which is that technology, reflected in costs, shapes the structure of the industry. If, for the moment, the 'structure' of an industry is understood to mean the number and size of firms that are active in it, this point can be illustrated in a number of ways. You have already seen that the US automobile and PC industries experienced a 'shake-out' of small firms as product standardization enabled the exploitation of economies of scale.

In industries in which firms experience constant returns to scale there will be a minimum level of output, the MES, at which constant returns set in, that firms must be able to sustain if they are to remain competitive. The MES varies with the particular technologies characteristic of different industries. For many parts of the clothing, footwear and furniture industries, all economies of scale may be exploited at relatively low levels of output and so the MES is low relative to market size. By contrast, in industries such as automobiles and chemicals where economies of scale are available over much greater ranges of output, the MES is much higher in relation to the size of the market.

Question	What does this suggest to you about the number and size of firms in the clothing, footwear and furniture industries compared with those in automobiles and chemicals?

There are likely to be fewer but larger firms in the automobile and chemical industries compared with the clothing, footwear and furniture industries. In the former, the exploitation of economies of scale up to high output levels relative to market size leaves room for only a few large firms in the market. In the latter, increasing returns to scale are exhausted at lower output levels relative to market size so there is room for more firms. In automobiles and chemicals the model predicts greater pressure for mergers and acquisitions as firms seek to expand output by taking over rival firms.

The existence in some industries of a level of output beyond which decreasing returns are experienced sets a limit to the size of firms and hence to the pressure for mergers and acquisitions. In fact, decreasing returns to scale can lead to the break-up of very large firms so that management can focus on making the 'core' business more competitive. The break-up of the chemicals firm ICI into ICI and Zeneca in 1993 can be interpreted as an example of this kind of behaviour.

If increasing returns are available across the whole output range required to supply the market, this has dramatic implications for industry structure. A single producer can supply the entire market at a lower cost than two or more competing firms. This is because a single firm avoids the cost of duplicating distribution networks such as gas, water and electricity pipes, railway track and telecommunications cables; its consequences for consumers are discussed in Chapter 4.

Figure 3.7
A downward shift in
the *LRAC* curve

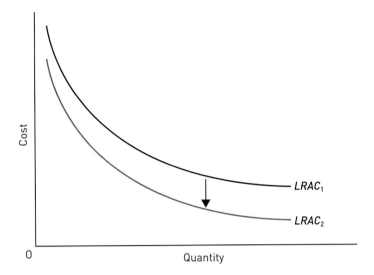

The technology of an industry, expressed in the shape of the *LRAC* curve of its firms, is therefore a major influence on the structure of that industry. However, in modelling firms' costs in the short run and the long run, it has been assumed that firms are operating with given technology. It is now appropriate to relax this assumption and investigate the role of technological change in shaping industrial structure.

As Section 3.3.1 explained, a firm's production function embodies its technology. The model assumes that technology is given and is available to all firms in an industry. We can therefore think of technological change as a change in each firm's production function. Particular input combinations now become more productive, producing more output. What effect does this have on the long-run average cost curve?

The *LRAC* curves in Figure 3.6 were drawn on the assumption of given technology. Technological change can therefore be understood as a *shift* in the average cost curve. Figure 3.7 shows a downward shift in an *LRAC* curve like that shown in Figure 3.6(c). The shift of $LRAC_1$ downward to $LRAC_2$ in Figure 3.7 shows that long-run average costs have fallen at each and every level of output, or scale of production.

Technological change may not affect average costs at all levels of output. Henry Ford's introduction of moving assembly-line production methods is an example of a technological change that changed the shape of the *LRAC* curve for firms in the industry, shifting it downwards at high levels of output. The new methods hugely extended the range of output over which firms could benefit from increasing returns to scale. In this way, technological change, and its associated cost changes, exert a major influence on industrial structure. We explore this further in Section 3.4.

Exercise 3.2

A revision exercise before you move on.

1 Explain the meanings of the concepts listed below and how the items in each pair of concepts are related:
   (a) increasing and diminishing returns to a factor of production
   (b) economies of scale and increasing returns to scale
   (c) decreasing returns to scale and diseconomies of scale.
2 Why do short-run average costs differ from long-run average costs?

3.4 Technological change and industrial structure

This section will explore the interaction of technology and costs with market demand in shaping industrial structure throughout the industry life cycle. Many industries begin as a numerous and turbulent group of firms jostling for position, experimenting with new and idiosyncratic products, and turn into a much smaller, more stable number of firms, making standardized products by routine methods. In this section we add a rather different view of firms to that developed in Section 3.3, modelling firms as dynamic agents engaged in a learning process and an active search for technological innovation. The term 'dynamic' signifies that the model constructs firms and industries as acting and undergoing change in historical time. The technology available to firms is no longer being assumed to be given from outside the firm. The industry life cycle, outlined in Section 3.4.1, provides a theoretical framework for identifying general patterns of structural change across different industries. Section 3.4.2 discusses some additional concepts used in modelling the dynamics of industrial structure.

▩ ▨ ■ 3.4.1 The industry life cycle

The model of the industry life cycle outlined in Chapter 2 represents an industry as if it were a biological organism going through the stages of birth, growth, maturity and decline. This helps us to understand how a particular firm can become the 'leader of the pack' through innovation. In Section 3.2 it was explained that an economic model is a deliberate simplification of the world, which helps to provide a systematic way of thinking about causal relationships. The industry life cycle is a rather different type of model. The aim is still to provide a systematic way of thinking about economic activity but not by analysing particular interactions between variables. The industry life cycle is instead a systematic way of thinking about general patterns of structural change across different industries. In this sense, the industry life cycle is an 'ideal type', enabling us to bring order to the complexity of historical events by classifying them as belonging to this or that phase of an identified pattern of industrial change.

The industry life cycle models industries as following a similar pattern of development as industry output changes, moving from many small and different firms to a few large and similar firms. This change in industrial structure is driven by the interplay between consumer demand and technology throughout the industry life cycle. Section 3.2 examined some of the influences on market demand and the particular importance of price. In fact, price and non-price factors are of varying importance at different phases of the life cycle. Section 3.3 analysed the firm's *SRAC* and *LRAC* curves, which reflect the technology available to the firm. Costs are of crucial importance to the firm at each phase of the industry life cycle but firms are driven to focus on costs in different ways at different phases.

The model of the industry life cycle is depicted in Figure 3.8. The curved line traces how the total output of a typical industry changes over time. In this diagram, the total output of the industry is measured along the vertical axis. The horizontal axis shows the passage of time.

The introductory phase is characterized by *product innovation*, that is, the introduction of novel products for which there are no close substitutes. At this stage the scale of production is low, costs are high and demand for the new industry's products is limited to relatively few consumers. There will be considerable variety among firms in the industry, ranging from small firms that are as new as the industry to large firms with established products in other industries that are diversifying into the new one. Some firms will have entered the industry

Figure 3.8
The industry life
cycle

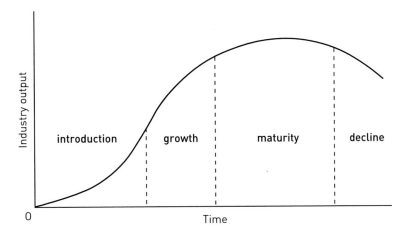

right at the start, while others enter more gradually as the profit opportunities created by the original 'pioneers' become clear. This 'heterogeneity' among firms, that is, their variety, will be reflected in differences in the technology they use and hence in the costs that they face. Hence technology is no longer understood as 'given' and common to all. The experimental nature of production at this stage favours firms that can learn quickly and are therefore able to be more flexible and better able to adjust output rapidly in response to changing conditions. In the introductory phase of the industry life cycle, production is a risky business and firms cannot be sure that their product is exactly what consumers want.

You can see, in Figure 3.8, that, as the industry moves from the introductory phase into the growth phase, the size of the industry, measured in terms of its output, increases. Firms will be able to exploit economies of scale. There is, however, a condition. The selection of 35 mm SLR film cameras and digital cameras shown in Figure 3.9 holds a clue about the condition for achieving economies of scale.

Question What do you think is the main difference between the appearance of the 35 mm SLR film cameras and that of the digital cameras in Figure 3.9?

There is considerable variety among the digital cameras. At first glance the Fuji Finepix 6800 resembles a hand-held computer; the Fuji Finepix 40i looks to us like a portable CD player and is in fact an MP3 player as well as a digital camera; and the Nikon Coolpix 950 is perhaps too radical a design to be mistaken for anything else. On the other hand, the Fuji Finepix 4900 looks much more like a 35 mm SLR film camera. This variety and sense of experiment is consistent with the digital camera industry being in its introductory phase. Manufacturers seem undecided whether a digital camera should look like a computer with a lens or a camera with some data-processing software. By contrast, it seems to us that the 35 mm SLR cameras are remarkably similar in appearance and they are also similar in technical specification. Standardization is evidently lacking among digital cameras. Product standardization is symptomatic of a move to the growth phase of the industry life cycle. Once firms have standardized the product, they can also standardize the manufacturing process and move to production on a large scale.

Question What advantages will this move to production on a large scale confer on firms in the growth phase of the industry life cycle?

Figure 3.9
A selection of 35 mm SLR film cameras and digital cameras
Source: *What Camera?*, winter 2001, pp.17–24, 47, 48

Film cameras

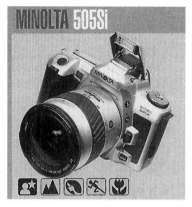

Digital cameras

The advantages of large-scale production, summed up in the concept of economies of scale, or increasing returns to scale (Section 3.3.2), generate a revolution in industrial structure once the expansion of demand gets under way. On the supply side, increasing returns to scale at the growth stage of the cycle can be exploited by the largest and most efficient firms as they compete and survive. Those firms that have failed to keep pace with changing opportunities exit from the industry; that is, a 'shake-out' takes place. This contraction in the number of firms means that the industry exhibits a greater degree of concentration as a few large firms dominate the industry. If you look back at Chapter 2, Figure 2.4 you can see that from 1909 to the mid 1920s the number of firms in the US automobile industry fell from 271 to approximately 50 and the number of firms in the US PC industry showed an equally dramatic decline during the years from 1973 to 1999.

How might this be explained? On the demand side, the fall in average costs resulting from increasing returns makes it possible for the firm to reduce the price it charges for the new product. This sequence of events was encountered in the extract from *The Economist*'s survey of the new economy at the beginning of Section 3.1. The suggestion was that new technologies are a major cause of the decline in costs and hence in prices that enables large numbers of consumers to buy safer cars, personal computers and so on. In terms of the model of market demand explained in Section 3.2, the fall in price leads to a movement along the market demand curve, bringing the product into the range of many more consumers. This is reinforced by a shift in the market demand curve caused by a change in socio-economic influences, in particular the demonstration effect that describes the tendency of people to imitate the consumption decisions of those who have already bought the product (Section 3.2.2).

The phase of maturity is reached as the market approaches saturation and replacement demand becomes important. By now there are many similar products for consumers to choose from, as they replace their first car or washing machine – or 35 mm SLR camera – and price exerts a major influence on demand. By the mature phase, the product has become well established and most of the consumers who would like one have already acquired it. The quantity demanded is therefore relatively stable and this is reflected in a flattening of the curve in Figure 3.8. Firms now have to work hard to reach those consumers who still have not bought the product and to create a demand for replacement purchases. The UK domestic appliance industry provides a good example of this phase. Most of the consumers wanting to own a refrigerator now have one and so the main source of market demand lies with consumers setting up home for the first time, and those needing to replace old equipment. Since there are plenty of very similar products available, price is a key determinant in deciding which one to buy.

On the supply side the focus of the firm's attention therefore shifts to *process innovation* aimed at securing reductions in the average cost of production. For example, Henry Ford found that the way to drive down costs is through the introduction of innovative new manufacturing processes. The firm that fails to innovate and to adopt industry best-practice technologies of production soon finds that it cannot compete with the lower prices offered by its rivals and is forced to exit the industry. In these circumstances the aim of investment may be to enable a firm to 'catch up' with its competitors by introducing the best available technology already in use elsewhere. A good example of this is provided by the German car manufacturer BMW when it took over the Longbridge car plant in the UK. BMW brought the factory up to date with the technologically advanced methods of car production introduced into the UK when the Japanese firms Nissan and Toyota set up new factories near Sunderland and Derby respectively.

Finally, the industry enters into decline when new industries with new products embodying superior technology render the old industry's products obsolete. This phase may be brought on by further product innovation giving rise to a new industry with its own introductory phase so that radically new products replace the obsolete ones. For example, the development of synthetic materials in the 1960s meant that a wide range of industries using 'natural' materials went into decline. Some of the firms in these industries, such as carpet manufacturers, were able to draw on the new materials to reinvent their products, but others disappeared altogether as demand for their products dissolved.

Each stage of the model of the industry life cycle presented above is fixed and distinct. In reality, the boundaries between stages in the development of an industry are blurred and can be difficult to observe in a short time horizon. The length of the life cycle also varies with the extent to which the products it makes can be reinvented. The personal stereo industry offers an example. By the 1980s, many consumers already owned a personal stereo that played audio-cassettes. With the arrival of new technologies for recording music on CDs, consumers shifted from cassettes to CDs in order to benefit from better recording quality. This stimulated a replacement demand for personal stereos that could play CDs, extending the life cycle of the personal stereo industry.

▪▪▪ 3.4.2 Industrial dynamics: knowledge and network industries

This final subsection introduces two more concepts that develop further our analysis of the dynamics of industrial structure, with particular reference to the 'new economy' industries. A dynamic approach to industrial change places considerable emphasis on innovation and learning, seeing firms as actively searching out innovative products and processes and learning how to produce and sell them. Some of the novelty of the new economy is reflected in the concepts used in trying to understand it, which are applied here to a brief analysis of network industries.

Knowledge and learning in the industry life cycle

In Section 3.3 we described technology as 'given' to firms. Now let us reflect on that idea. We can think of technology as consisting in bodies of knowledge necessary to produce artefacts. An appreciation of the importance of knowledge to economic activity is not new, for it was recognized by the eminent economist Alfred Marshall, who wrote that 'Capital consists in a great part of knowledge and organisation' (Marshall, 1925, p.138). What Marshall meant can perhaps best be understood by considering two 'thought experiments' broadly similar to those conducted by the philosopher Sir Karl Popper. In the first, all human artefacts, and hence all capital equipment, are wiped out in an extraordinary natural disaster. Human beings survive unharmed and set about constructing their capital stock, and other artefacts, all over again. This is an immense task but in a decade or so the job is done. In the second thought experiment we imagine once again that all capital equipment is destroyed. The difference is that this time human knowledge is also lost. All memories of how to build lathes, computers, robots, cars, combine harvesters and all the other machines the human race has ever invented are annihilated and so too are all the skills acquired in learning how to use them. The human race effectively returns to a much earlier period in its evolution when the capital stock consisted perhaps of stone tools. Even supposing that history repeats itself and people eventually reinvent the technologies leading up to the capital stock of twenty-first century humanity, it would take thousands of years to get back to where we were. The hardware is important but it is human knowledge that really matters. Learning how to use the hardware most effectively is therefore a crucial capacity for firms.

The 'learning curve' captures the idea that turning technological change to competitive advantage is a skill that has to be learned like any other. Figure 3.10 depicts this idea. It shows a fall in average cost that occurs as learning takes place over time after the firm starts up in production. This figure looks rather like the *LRAC* curve in Figure 3.6(c) but depicts a different relationship between output and costs. The horizontal axis, labelled

Figure 3.10
A learning curve

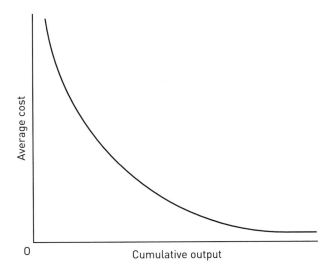

'cumulative output', shows the output a firm produces each year *added together* over time. This contrasts with the *SRAC* and *LRAC* diagrams in Section 3.3, where output was measured per time period, such as a year, and the diagrams picture the firm's costs at any given output per year. In Figure 3.6, a firm might move left or right, depending on its output decisions for the year. However, in Figure 3.10 you should think of the firm as moving rightwards over time, since each year it continues in business cumulative output will necessarily increase.

Learning-by-doing

Learning-by-doing refers to a fall in unit costs and cumulative output increases.

When a firm benefits from **learning-by-doing**, it is said to be 'moving along the learning curve' or gaining from 'experience effects'. Imagine that the production process involves the use of a new machine. When a worker first starts to operate the machine, lack of familiarity means that mistakes are made and progress is slow. However, the worker learns from these mistakes and as the hours spent operating the machine increase, productivity improves, that is, more units of output are produced per unit of input. The more cumulative output is produced, the more efficiently it is produced. The cost of producing a unit of output therefore declines as cumulative output increases, as Figure 3.10 shows.

Learning effects are not confined to assembly-line tasks but can occur throughout the firm wherever repetition gives rise to experience. Their significance in the industry life cycle is greatest when firms are learning how to use new technology. This occurs both in the introductory phase, as firms experiment with new products, and in the mature phase, as firms learn how to use new processes to improve the manufacture of a standard product. As the point is reached when all the cost savings derived from experience have been extracted, there is a flattening of the learning curve (Figure 3.10). From then on the firm diverts its attention to other ways of reducing its costs as a means of gaining an advantage over rivals.

A firm's capacity for learning how to use new technology depends in part on whether innovations build on its existing strengths or render them obsolete. Many historical studies have documented how technological change (process or product innovation) does not evolve in a continuous and smooth manner but discontinuously. A long period of incremental change may be punctuated by episodes of radical change. These discontinuities that are introduced by technological innovation can be classified as either 'competence enhancing' or 'competence destroying' (Tushman and Anderson, 1986).

To understand this, we need to recognize that once we allow firms to learn and innovate individually, we have moved away from the model of the firm presented in Section 3.3.

That section modelled a 'representative' firm among very similar firms. Once firms can learn, we move away from this approach, towards modelling firms as diverse organizations that develop distinct capabilities or competencies over time (Chapter 4 develops this idea further). Competence-enhancing innovations are innovations that develop new products, or improvements to existing products, which build on a firm's existing competence and strengthen its market position. This cumulative 'success begets success' dynamic causes the market structure to become more concentrated, stable and less friendly for new firms:

> Existing firms within an industry are in the best position to initiate and exploit new possibilities opened up by a discontinuity if it builds on competencies they already possess . . . the rich are likely to get richer.
>
> *(Tushman and Anderson, 1986, p.444)*

Competence-destroying innovations have the opposite effect. They develop new products or changes in existing products which require completely new skills and knowledge to be developed. These innovations disrupt industry structure, rendering current capabilities obsolete. Existing firms, set in the old way of doing things, are often not quick or ready enough to adapt to this radical change, allowing new flexible firms (not always small) to enter, remaking industry structure – and perhaps starting a whole new life cycle. Innovation can therefore either stabilize or destabilize industrial structure.

Network externalities and increasing returns to scale

> The reader should ask herself the following question: Would I subscribe to a telephone service knowing that nobody else subscribes to a telephone service?
>
> The answer should be: Of course not! What use will anyone have from having a telephone when there is no one to talk to?
>
> *(Shy, 2001, p.3)*

Network externalities

Network externalities arise when the value to one consumer of joining a network depends on the number of other consumers joining the network.

The uncertainty surrounding production in the introductory phase, which places such importance on the ability of the firm to secure quick benefits from learning effects, is particularly acute in 'network industries', such as telecommunications, computers, video players, banking services, fuel retailing and many others. On the demand side, the example of a telephone service shows that the benefit (or 'utility', see Chapter 8) that people get from consuming such goods depends on the extent to which other people also use these goods. These goods are said to display **network externalities**, because the value one consumer gets from, say, a telephone depends on factors external to their own consumption of it. The idea of externalities is widely used in economics (see Chapter 9). Network externalities (which can also be referred to as 'network effects') thus 'arise when the attractiveness of a product to customers increases with the use of that product by others' (Fisher and Rubinfeld, 2000, p.13). The more people who subscribe to the same standardized system, the more services and people the user can access, and so the greater the value of that system to each individual user. The implication is that firms that are in the introductory phase of a network industry life cycle face huge rewards from establishing an early lead for their product. Even if competing products have more useful features, the product with the largest network will be difficult to dislodge simply because the number of its subscribers make it the most attractive option for new subscribers.

On the supply side there is considerable scope for the firm with the largest network to achieve increasing returns to scale. The firm faces the cost of developing and maintaining a single network, and that cost can be spread over a large and rising quantity of output, reducing average cost (*AC*). The industry life cycle models the transition to the growth phase as depending in part on product standardization (Section 3.4.1). A stronger version of standardization is present in network industries. The cost advantages are particularly dramatic for a firm that can establish its own network, or a technical component essential to the functioning of a network, as the industry standard.

Network industries have in common a number of characteristics including *complementarity*, *compatibility* and *standards* (Shy, 2001, pp.1–3). A network industry produces complements, such as trains and railway tracks, cameras and film, computers and software, CD players and CDs, and cars and fuel. These complementary products must be compatible with one another in the sense that trains are no use unless they fit the tracks, film is needed if you want to use a film camera and so on. In other words, complementary products must operate on the same standard. For example, in the nineteenth century it was impossible for regional railway companies in the UK to run rolling stock on each other's tracks until a national gauge or width was established. This gauge is an example of an industry standard. Without a standard gauge or film size or computer operating system, product standardization cannot take place and economies of scale are unobtainable. Establishing an industry standard may involve a struggle between competing would-be standards. When video players were first introduced in the 1980s, two different recording formats appeared on the market, VHS and Betamax. It was some years before VHS was established as the industry standard.

Case study: BMW wants to make internal-combustion engines that run on hydrogen

One way that global warming might be reduced is by powering cars with something that does not release carbon dioxide when it is burned. That is part of the idea behind a 'hydrogen economy' – a future in which hydrogen, which can be produced from renewable sources, takes over from hydrocarbons as the world's principal fuel.

Several of the world's car makers – notably Ford, DaimlerChrysler and Honda – are studying fuel cells. These react hydrogen and oxygen together to produce electricity. Fuel cells certainly work but they are still some years from commercial viability in cars. There is, however, an alternative: burn the hydrogen in a conventional internal-combustion engine. And that is what BMW proposes to do.

Converting an engine to run on hydrogen is relatively simple. There are, however, two catches. The first is that fuel cells are a far more efficient way to use hydrogen than burning it

in a conventional engine. The second is that, gram for gram, hydrogen contains significantly less energy than petrol. Performance will reflect that, unless those clever engineers at BMW can somehow overcome the difference. If they cannot, then BMW, whose prestige and independence rely largely on its engine-making ability, may be in trouble. Were fuel cells to become the standard, the firm's future could be bleak.

(Adapted from The Economist, *21 July 2001, p.86)*

Question

This case study describes the situation facing car manufacturers as they develop new technology for the 'hydrogen economy' of the future. How does BMW's decision to use hydrogen in an internal-combustion engine illustrate the uncertainties confronting firms in network industries in the introductory phase of the industry life cycle?

The new network industry in this case is hydrogen fuel production and retailing. A means of propulsion, such as an internal-combustion engine or a fuel cell, and a fuel, such as petrol or hydrogen, are complementary goods. The means of propulsion and the fuel must be compatible, in the sense that a conventional internal-combustion engine is compatible with petrol and a fuel cell with hydrogen. The industry can progress to the next phase of the life cycle only if an industry standard can be agreed upon. There seems to be a consensus that hydrogen will become the standard fuel. Beyond that, however, there is uncertainty. Ford, DaimlerChrysler and Honda are investing in fuel cell technology in the belief that it will become the industry standard in the 'hydrogen economy', while BMW take the view that the internal-combustion engine will retain that position in the new circumstances. The industry dilemma highlights the role of technological change in shaping industrial structure. If BMW have 'backed a loser' and invested in a technology that fails to become the industry standard, they may, as the case study suggests, lose their independence. The number of firms in the industry will decrease if BMW's destiny is to fail, as part of the process by which technological change shapes a new industrial structure.

Network externalities on the demand side and increasing returns on the supply side may interact in what is colloquially termed a 'double whammy' to produce a dramatically different industrial structure as an industry moves into the growth phase. A firm that benefits from such a double whammy will secure monopoly power in its industry. The economic analysis of monopoly power is the subject of Chapter 4.

3.5 Conclusion

The idea of the double whammy brings together the two driving forces behind changes in industrial structure, with which the chapter opened and now closes. The use of a new technology causes a decline in the costs of production, which in turn encourages a rapid take-up by consumers of products embodying the new technology. The chapter has explored the factors affecting consumer demand. While the price of the product was found to be of crucial importance, socio-economic influences such as culture and identity were seen to have an important role to play, especially in the introductory phase of the industry life cycle. Chapter 8 will explain the foundations of consumer demand with an account of utility theory and its role in understanding individual choice and equilibrium.

On the supply side the firm's cost curves reflect the technology it uses to produce goods and services. An analysis of cost curves showed the constraints imposed by technology on the firm's development and how technological change creates new opportunities. Technology is ultimately a matter of knowledge and technological change can best be modelled in dynamic terms, as firms search creatively for new products and processes and learn how to make and employ them.

In the network industries, prominent in the new economy, the demand- and supply-side factors interact in particularly striking ways. Network externalities and industry standards combine to push the industry from a turbulent crowd of heterogeneous firms to a small number of similar firms. In Chapter 4 we put together the analysis of demand, costs and technology into a study of firms' decision-making and of the behaviour of firms in industries where one firm is big enough to wield monopoly power.

Questions for review and discussion

Question 1   Complete the following sentences by selecting the correct word or phrase from the list below to fill in the spaces:

Independent   dependent   positive   negative   Giffen   Veblen
slope downwards from left to right   slope upwards from left to right
are horizontal   are vertical   are indeterminate

A market demand curve shows the relationship between quantity demanded (the . . . variable) and price (the . . . variable). According to the 'law of demand', this relationship will be a . . . one. Some luxury goods called . . . goods, and some very basic goods, called . . . goods, are exceptions to the 'law of demand', and their market demand curves . . .

Question 2   Figure 3.11 shows a hypothetical demand curve for cartridge pens. Draw a shift in the curve leftwards or rightwards as appropriate to illustrate the likely effect of each of the following:

(a) An increase in the price of fibre-tipped pens
(b) An increase in the price of ink cartridges

Figure 3.11
Hypothetical
demand curve for
cartridge pens

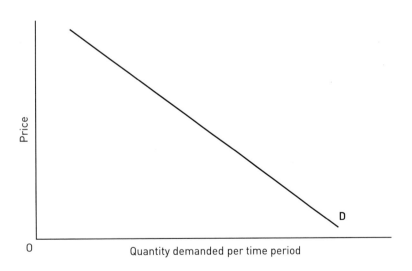

Question 3   Say which is the most appropriate phrase to complete the sentence below:

A firm is operating in the short run when

A ❑ It cannot change the quantity it uses of any of the factors of production, so some inputs are being wasted.
B ❑ It is suffering diminishing returns to its fixed and variable factors.
C ❑ There is not sufficient time for it to raise its output.
D ❑ It cannot change the quantity it uses of at least one of its factor inputs.

Question 4 Figure 3.12 shows a short-run average cost curve for a firm. Select *two* statements from the list below. The statement you mark '1' should state what happens as output rises from Q_1 to Q_2. The statement you mark '2' should state what happens as output rises from Q_2 to Q_3.

Note: 'average' means 'per unit of output'.

A ❑ Average fixed cost falls, average variable cost falls then rises.
B ❑ Falling average variable cost outweighs rising average fixed cost.
C ❑ There are diminishing returns to the variable factors throughout.
D ❑ Average fixed cost and average variable cost both rise.
E ❑ There are increasing returns to the variable factors throughout.

Figure 3.12
Short-run average
cost curve

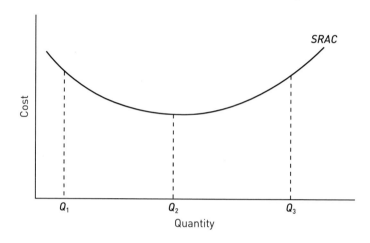

Questions 5 Figure 3.13 shows long-run average cost curves for two firms, A and B, each in a different industry. Select from the list of statements below the one that is consistent with what is shown in the diagram.

A ❑ Firm A attains minimum efficient scale (MES) at a lower level of output than Firm B.
B ❑ Both firms experience diseconomies of scale at the highest levels of output shown.
C ❑ Firm A operates in an industry where there is great pressure to expand output, for example by merger.
D ❑ Firm B has higher fixed costs than Firm A.

Figure 3.13
Long-run average
cost curve

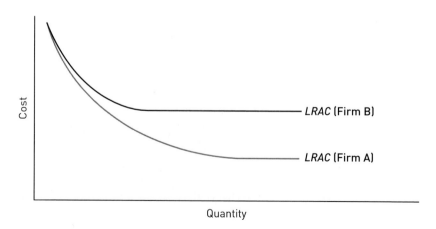

Question 6   Figure 3.14 shows a learning curve for a firm. The curve is similar in shape to a long-run average cost (*LRAC*) curve, but the relationship it depicts is different. Select from the list below the *three* statements that correctly identify differences between curves of these two kinds:

A ❑ The horizontal axis of the learning curve shows cumulative output; that of the *LRAC* curve shows output per time period.

B ❑ The costs shown by the learning curve exclude capital costs; those shown by the *LRAC* curve include capital costs.

C ❑ The firm moves rightwards along its learning curve over time; the firm may move leftwards or rightwards along its *LRAC* curve.

D ❑ At some points on the learning curve, factor inputs are being wasted owing to mistakes and inexperience; at all points on the *LRAC* curve, the firm uses all inputs to their full potential and there is no waste.

Figure 3.14
Learning curve

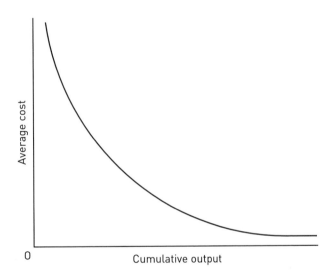

Question 7   Complete the following sentences by selecting words or phrases from the list below.

Representative competence-enhancing mature distinct competencies
competence-destroying manufacturing network reproduce competencies

In analysing the costs, technology and output of firms, we can use a model of a . . . firm. But when thinking about innovation, we need to model firms as diverse organizations that develop . . .

. . . innovations tend to cause market structure to become more concentrated. The need to secure quick benefits from learning effects is particularly acute in . . . industries.

Question 8   The table below gives information about a firm's costs in the short and long run.

	Output (000s)					
	1	2	3	4	5	6
Short-run average cost (£)	18	9	9	11	14	14
Long-run average cost (£)	18	6	5	5	5	6

(a) Draw a diagram showing each of the above curves and explain briefly what distinguishes the short run from the long run.

(b) With reference to the diagram, explain how (i) diminishing returns and (ii) diseconomies of scale affect the production costs of a firm.

(c) With reference to the diagram, give an example of a change which can cause (i) a movement along the long-run curve and (ii) a shift of the long-run curve.

Question 9   Essay: Using examples, explain how network externalities and economies of scale interact to determine industrial structure.

4

Monopoly power and innovation

Neil Costello and Maureen Mackintosh

Concepts

- the firm's demand curve
- average and marginal revenue
- marginal cost, average cost and total cost
- profit maximization
- price elasticity of demand
- a firm's capabilities or competencies
- barriers to entry and contestability of a market

Objectives

After studying this chapter you should be able to:

- understand, and apply to cases, economic models of pure monopoly and monopolistic competition
- explain how monopoly power may be sustained over time and how it may be undermined by competition
- examine the relationships between monopoly power and innovation
- discuss some implications for competition policy of high rates of innovation.

4.1 Monopoly, innovation and competition

Case study: Breaking up Microsoft?

It was an interesting week for the 'New Economy'. On Monday, federal Judge Thomas Penfield Jackson declared that Microsoft had violated the antitrust laws by engaging in predatory tactics that discouraged technological competition. On Wednesday, the White House staged a conference that credited the New Economy's technological advances for raising living standards . . . Connections and contradictions here beg to be explored.

Among the panelists at the White House conference was Microsoft Chairman Bill Gates. Presumably, he was not invited because he is a corporate thug, which is – by inference – how Jackson depicted him. What are we to think of Gates? A larger contradiction looms. If Microsoft is such an anticompetitive monster, how has the New Economy become (at least by reputation) so competitive that it raises efficiency and lowers inflation? . . .

Case study continued

Because Microsoft's operating systems (Windows and its offspring) control roughly 90 percent of personal computers, it's hard to separate the company from this larger transformation [of the economy]. Microsoft's central contribution was (and is) standardization. This meant that applications programs – from spreadsheets to photo processing – didn't have to be written for multitudes of operating systems. Software markets expanded, so writing programs became more profitable. Computer networks could be more easily constructed. People who learned computer skills at one company wouldn't lose them by moving elsewhere . . .

The question posed by the Microsoft case is whether antitrust laws can cope with technological competition. When Congress passed the Sherman Antitrust Act – under which Microsoft was convicted – in 1890, the evils of monopoly power seemed obvious. A monopolist might restrict supply and prop up prices. Competitors might conspire to do the same thing. Competition meant price competition; the antitrust laws aimed to preserve it.

But today's most significant competition doesn't involve identical products sparring over price. It involves rival technologies struggling for superiority. Cable TV competes against satellite TV. Wireless communication competes with land lines. The Linux operating system is beginning to challenge Windows. For most technologies, standards are vital. Without them, mass markets are impossible. Sometimes standards arise by voluntary agreements among firms; sometimes they result from the triumph of one or a few firms. The check on this dominance – if there is a check – is the threat of a new technology.

Source: Robert J. Samuelson, Washington Post, *11 April 2000*

Question

Why was the United States government trying to break up one of the most successful companies in the world?

Microsoft was at the time one of the world's largest firms. In its financial year to June 2000 it had net income of US$9.42 billion and in July 2001 employed nearly 44 000 people worldwide. It claimed to be 'Building on the popularity of the Windows operating system and the Office productivity suite, [and] on developing technology for the next-generation Internet' (www.microsoft.com, 6 July 2001).

The US 'antitrust' authorities – what in Europe are called the competition authorities – took the opposite view, arguing in court that Microsoft was misusing its dominance in computer operating systems to try to become dominant in the market for Internet browsers. Judge Thomas Penfield Jackson recommended that Microsoft should be broken up into two companies. Microsoft immediately launched an appeal.

A number of the themes of this chapter and this part are raised in the *Washington Post*'s commentary on these events. Microsoft, a big winner in the consolidation of the computing industry, is a firm with great monopoly power; that is, it can greatly influence a whole market by its behaviour. The Microsoft court case turned on the effects of its monopoly power: was it developing its products to the benefit of users, the industry and the economy, or was it merely defending its own huge profits by blocking beneficial competition and innovation?

Journalists, government agencies, firms and judges draw on economic theory in trying to answer questions like that; in this chapter you will study some of those theories. The central theme of the chapter is the interaction of monopoly power with competition, especially competition through innovation.

Figure 4.1
The *New Yorker*
pictures the
proposed break-up
of Microsoft

Look back at the *Washington Post* commentary. It contrasts two kinds of competition. What are they?

Robert Samuelson contrasts 'technological competition' – what we call competition through innovation – with 'price competition'. Price competition occurs when firms gain customers by selling goods more cheaply than their competitors. Competition through innovation occurs when firms introduce new products and improve old ones. The distinction between them is not quite as sharp as the article seems to suggest: as Chapter 3 showed, innovation can also reduce costs and allow firms to lower prices and increase their market share.

In this chapter we look more closely at how firms compete for monopoly power, how they behave when they have it, and how market dominance is undermined. Section 4.2 defines monopoly power in terms of the demand for a firm's products. Section 4.3 builds up, based on the analysis of costs in Chapter 3, the economic model of 'pure monopoly' that is frequently employed by governments attacking monopoly power. Section 4.4 turns to competition between firms with monopoly power, and the ways in which dominant firms fight to sustain market dominance. Section 4.5 analyses innovation as a competitive weapon of market dominance, and introduces an alternative economic model of the firm that pays attention to firms' internal organization and capabilities. Section 4.6 pulls together some implications of these theories for the Microsoft case and for the general issue of appropriate government policy towards big powerful companies in innovative market contexts.

4.2 Monopoly power and the firm's revenues

■ ■ ■ 4.2.1 Pure monopoly and monopoly power

The extent to which a firm can exercise influence over its market – as Microsoft clearly did at the time of the court case discussed in the *Washington Post* – depends both on the nature of the demand for its products and on the kind of competition it faces in that market. This section and the next introduce some economic theory that gives a rather precise meaning to those statements, and hence helps us to begin to define and assess the extent of a firm's monopoly power.

In Sections 4.2 and 4.3 we analyse the decisions a firm will make in an economic model of a firm and a market. Some basic elements of this model were introduced in Chapter 3: market demand for a product, a firm's costs and market price. Economic models that simplify markets and firms right down to interactions of demand, costs and price can, as we hope to show, produce strong results that are influential in policy making.

However, these models do contain a rather 'transparent' notion of a firm, reducing it, as Graham Dawson and Judith Mehta explained in Chapter 3, Section 3.3.1, to a set of specified relationships between inputs and outputs. In the simplest versions of these models, with which we begin, firms compete solely on the basis of price. The models can also be used, as in Sections 4.4 and 4.5, to analyse competition through innovation and what the *Washington Post* called, above, 'predatory' behaviour. However, the models seem to miss something: they offer little understanding of why particular firms, propelled by large personalities such as Bill Gates, are so successful in pursuing monopoly power. Chapter 3, Section 3.4 introduced models that help us to understand how a particular firm can gain an advantage over its competitors through innovation. Section 4.5 builds on these models to analyse the role of individual entrepreneurs and the organizational basis for particular firms' competitive success.

Monopoly power or market power

A firm has monopoly power (market power) if it has some choice in setting the price of its product and its decision about how much to supply influences the price it can charge.

Economic models of the interaction of demand, costs and price give us a clear initial definition of **monopoly power or market power**. These two terms are often used interchangeably, and will be throughout this text. A firm with monopoly power (market power) has some influence over its market; in particular it has some discretion about the price it charges for its product. Firms are particularly likely to exercise such monopoly power if they are large relative to the size of the market as a whole. That is, firms in relatively concentrated industries can be expected to have more monopoly power than firms in industries that contain many small firms.

Question	You met the concept of industry structure in Chapter 2, Section 2.4.5. Look back at that now. What are the two ways of measuring industry structure?

Industry structure can be measured in terms of the number of firms in an industry or in terms of the market share of the largest firms expressed as a percentage of total industry production. The smaller the number of firms or the greater the market share of a few large firms in an industry, the greater the degree of industrial concentration. The most extreme concentration – hence on this measure the greatest market power – occurs when a single firm supplies the whole market. This is called a **pure monopoly**.

Pure monopoly

A pure monopoly exists when a single firm is the sole supplier in a market.

Chapter 3, Section 3.2 discussed some of the difficulties of defining 'industry' and 'market'. For the purposes of this chapter, we are going to assume that each industry, composed of one or more firms, supplies a single market. This means that a 'pure monopoly' is therefore both the sole firm in an industry and the sole supplier to its market.

Question	Look back at the *Washington Post*'s commentary on Microsoft in 2000. Did the firm fit the definition of a pure monopoly?

Microsoft held in 2000 something close to a pure monopoly in the market for Intel-compatible operating systems for personal computers: around 90 per cent of sales worldwide. Personal computer (PC) manufacturers, the most important direct customers for operating systems, testified at Microsoft's trial that they believed there were no reasonable substitutes: they had to buy and install Windows (Fisher and Rubinfeld, 2000).

▨ ▨ ■ 4.2.2 The demand curve of a firm with monopoly power

We now look in more detail at the way demand conditions influence market power. Graham Dawson and Judith Mehta introduced the market demand curve for a good or service in Chapter 3, Section 3.2.1. They explained that this is a model of the relationship between quantity demanded by consumers of a particular good and the market price of that good. If all other influences on demand are held constant, then normally quantity demanded will rise as price falls.

Question	Can you draw a market demand curve and distinguish the causes of movements along the curve from the causes of shifts in the curve? If not, revise Chapter 3, Section 3.2 before reading on.

The demand curve for the output of a pure monopolist is the market demand curve, since the firm has the market to itself. However, most firms do not have a market to themselves, not even Microsoft: only some of the market demand is typically demand for a particular firm's product. If a market is supplied by several firms with market power, then each firm faces a downward-sloping demand curve for its product.

In markets for many familiar products, each firm develops a specific profile or 'brand' for its product, to differentiate it from competing products and attract customers. Kellogg's, for example, promotes its breakfast cereals as distinctively different to those of other companies, and is at pains to point out that it does not provide breakfast cereals under 'own label' brands for supermarket chains. One of the company's advertising slogans has been 'if it doesn't say Kellogg's on the box, it isn't Kellogg's in the box'; the implication is that its products are superior in some way. This is known as *product differentiation*.

Question	Try to think of some more examples of product differentiation before reading on.

Product differentiation is characteristic of markets where the products are broadly similar and a firm wants to make sure that its own product is easily recognized by consumers. Examples include detergents, cigarettes, soft drinks, instant coffee and petrol. In all of these markets the products are seen by consumers as quite close substitutes, but not identical. For example, if Kellogg's put its prices up by 20 per cent some consumers would still buy Kellogg's.

We can therefore model each firm as facing a downward-sloping demand curve for its products. Figure 4.2 shows the demand curve facing a supplier of a product in a market where firms have some monopoly power: it might be, as shown, a supplier of PCs.

Figure 4.2
A demand curve for
PCs supplied by a
single firm with
market power

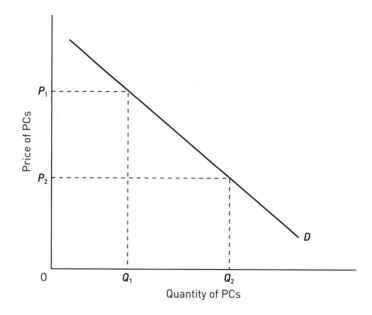

| | **Question** | Explain carefully what Figure 4.2 shows. |

The demand for the firm's PCs is assumed to be a function of the price of the PCs. The model abstracts from, or 'holds constant', every other influence on the demand, such as people's incomes and the price of other companies' PCs. If price rises, quantity demanded (in a given time period) will fall. Conversely, if the firm reduces its price from P_1 to P_2, the quantity of its PCs demanded will increase from Q_1 to Q_2. Both the quantity demanded and price vary in this model; the quantity demanded is the dependent variable, since it changes in response to price, the independent variable.

▨ ▨ ■ 4.2.3 Average revenue and marginal revenue

We defined a firm with monopoly power in Section 4.2.1 as a firm with some choice in setting the price of its product. This is reflected in the downward-sloping demand curve faced by such a firm, showing that if the firm sets a lower price it can increase the quantity demanded. The demand curve for a firm's goods determines the *total revenue* the firm would earn at each price it might set. With price P_1 in Figure 4.2, the firm's total revenue (*TR*) is P_1 multiplied by the quantity demanded Q_1. More generally, a firm's total revenue is the quantity of its goods demanded times price:

$$TR = P \cdot Q$$

It follows that the demand curve (*D*) of the firm is also its *average revenue* (*AR*) curve. The average revenue is the revenue per unit sold: in Figure 4.2 it is the firm's revenue per PC. Average revenue is therefore total revenue divided by quantity demanded, and is equal to the price per PC. That is:

$$AR = \frac{TR}{Q} = P$$

Marginal revenue

Marginal revenue is the change in total revenue resulting from the sale of an additional unit of output.

which reads, average revenue is total revenue divided by quantity demanded, which is equal to price. Each point on the demand curve therefore shows the average revenue (equals price) of the firm for each quantity demanded.

This analysis of a firm's revenue is a building block for analysing a firm's decision about the price it should charge for its goods. To complete it we need one more concept, **marginal revenue** (*MR*). Marginal revenue is the change in total revenue resulting from the sale of an additional unit of output.

Question	Look again at Figure 4.2. Suppose that demand is currently Q_1 at price P_1. Now the firm wants to sell an extra PC. How will price and total revenue change?

If the firm wants to increase demand by one PC it will have to reduce its price. And that means it will receive a lower price for all the PCs it sells, not just the additional one. That is the snag about a downward-sloping demand curve. So the marginal revenue – the change in total revenue – the firm receives from selling an extra PC is positive if the extra revenue from selling one more PC outweighs the drop in revenue from reducing the price of all the others.

'Marginal' concepts such as marginal revenue identify the effects of small changes in one variable (such as quantity demanded) on another variable (such as total revenue). Marginal concepts are used quite a lot in economics because they offer a useful way of analysing decision-making, as this chapter will illustrate. Section 4.3 introduces another marginal concept: marginal cost. Section 4.4 brings marginal cost and marginal revenue together to analyse a firm's decision on what price to set for its goods. Make sure you have got to grips with the revenue concepts by doing Exercise 4.1 before moving on.

Exercise 4.1

Suppose that our computer firm has a demand for only one PC at €1000, and has to reduce the price steadily to increase demand for PCs. Complete columns 3 and 4 on Table 4.1, using the data in the first two columns. Look back at the explanations of average, total and marginal revenue to help with your calculations.

Table 4.1
Price, quantity demanded and revenue of a computer firm

(1) Price (P) = average revenue (AR) €	(2) Quantity (Q) of computers demanded	(3) Total revenue (TR) €	(4) Marginal revenue (MR) €
1000	1	1000	–
950	2	1900	900
900	3	2700	
850	4		
800	5		

Question	Look at your completed Table 4.1, and state carefully the relationship that it shows between marginal revenue, average revenue and total revenue as price falls.

Figure 4.3
Average revenue
and marginal
revenue curves of a
firm with monopoly
power

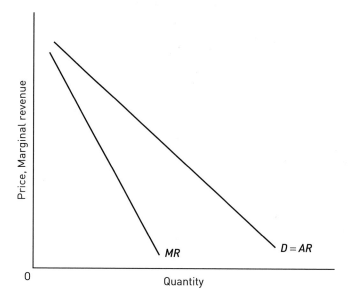

As price (average revenue) falls (column 1), quantity demanded rises (column 2). Total revenue increases as demand rises (column 3). The addition to total revenue from each additional unit of demand is the marginal revenue (column 4). Marginal revenue falls as quantity demanded rises. Furthermore, if you compare marginal with average revenue, you will see that marginal revenue is less than average revenue at each quantity demanded.

This relationship between marginal and average revenue is implied by the downward slope of the demand curve. Average revenue (price) declines as quantity rises. Marginal revenue must therefore (arithmetically) be less than average revenue for the reason explained above: the marginal revenue is the price (average revenue) of the extra PC *less* the revenue lost by reducing the prices of all the others in order to raise demand.

A marginal revenue (*MR*) curve traces the marginal revenue received by the firm at each price set and each quantity demanded. A downward-sloping demand curve is therefore always associated with a marginal revenue curve that lies below it, as in Figure 4.3.

▪ ▪ ▪ 4.2.4 The price elasticity of demand

Suppose that our computer firm decides to reduce its price in order to increase the quantity of its PCs demanded. The number of extra PCs sold will depend on how steeply the demand curve for its PCs slopes downwards. A shallower (flatter) slope means that a given price reduction (e.g. from €1000 to €950) will sell more extra PCs than would be sold if the demand curve sloped more steeply at that point.

The firm's most important concern, however, is likely to be with the effect of the price decrease on its total revenue. This will depend, as we saw in Section 4.2.3, on the balance between the loss of revenue from lower prices and the gain in revenue from extra sales. This section shows that the effect of a given price change on a firm's total revenue varies as the firm moves along a straight line demand curve.

If the firm finds that a small percentage drop in price produces a large percentage increase in sales, then it will see its total revenue increase. However, if a large percentage price reduction is needed to sell just one more PC, the marginal revenue might be negative, and total revenue would fall.

Figure 4.4
Average revenue
(demand) curve for
a computer firm
with monopoly
power

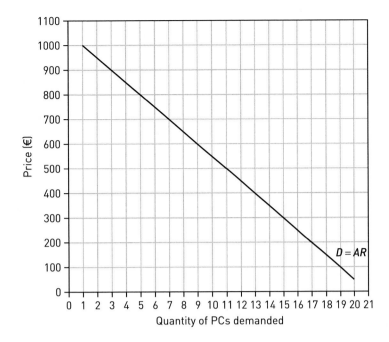

Question	Explain that last statement to yourself, looking back at Section 4.2.3 if necessary.	

Marginal revenue will be negative if the revenue raised by selling the extra PC is less than the revenue lost by reducing the price for all other units that could previously be sold at a higher price.

Hence, the firm's revenue prospects as its price changes depend on the responsiveness of demand to price changes. Economists call this responsiveness the **price elasticity of demand**. It is measured by dividing the proportionate change in quantity demanded by the proportionate change in price that brought it about:

Price elasticity of demand

The price elasticity of demand measures the responsiveness of the quantity demanded of a product to changes in its price.

$$\text{price elasticity of demand} = \frac{\text{proportionate change in quantity demanded}}{\text{proportionate change in price}}$$

You can express the proportions as percentages. Exercise 4.2 asks you to review your understanding of percentages (see Chapter 2, Section 2.2.2) and also gives you practice in calculating elasticities.

Exercise 4.2

Figure 4.4 shows our computer firm's average revenue curve, plotted from the data on Table 4.1 and extended to price = €50.

The firm reduces price from €800 to €600.

1 What is the percentage decline in price?
2 What is the resultant percentage increase in quantity demanded?
3 What is the price elasticity of demand when price falls from €800 to €600?

Price elasticities of demand are generally negative, as Exercise 4.2 showed, because price and quantity demanded move in opposite directions. In practice we calculate and compare elasticities by ignoring the minus sign and just looking at the number. So we say that an elasticity of −4 is greater than an elasticity of −0.5. If quantity demanded is very responsive to price, so that the percentage change in quantity is greater than the percentage change in price, then demand is price **elastic**. If highly unresponsive, so that the percentage change in quantity is smaller than the percentage change in price, it is **inelastic**.

Elastic and inelastic demand

Demand is price elastic if the price elasticity is greater than 1.
Demand is unit elastic if the price elasticity = 1.
Demand is price inelastic if the price elasticity is less than 1.

So you found in Exercise 4.2, that between €800 and €600 per computer, demand was price elastic since the elasticity is (minus) 3.2. However, on Figure 4.4, if price falls from €250 to €200 (−20 per cent) quantity demanded rises from 16 to 17 (only 6.25 per cent). So the price elasticity of demand is

$$\frac{6.25}{-20} = -0.3125$$

which is inelastic. We can conclude from this example that price elasticity is not constant along a straight line demand (average revenue) curve but declines as we move from left to right.

Question	Did you understand the last paragraph fully? Calculate the price elasticity of demand between different points on the $D = AR$ curve in Figure 4.4, in order to check your understanding.

A firm's output decision will be influenced by its elasticity of demand. To see why, consider what happens if a firm lowers its price in the face of inelastic demand. The proportionate increase in demand will be less than the proportionate change in price (the elasticity is less than 1). If price falls by 10 per cent, quantity demanded rises by less than 10 per cent. Result, total revenue falls, and marginal revenue is therefore negative. A wise firm with monopoly power will not expand output to the point where each additional unit of output sold reduces its total revenue in this way. That is, the firm will not operate on the inelastic part of its demand curve.

Finally, what influences a firm's elasticity of demand? Look back at the earlier discussion of product differentiation. The price elasticity of demand is strongly influenced by the ease with which consumers can substitute a firm's good with another. For example, to Neil Costello's unsophisticated culinary eye, one bag of salt seems to be exactly the same as any other bag of salt. Thus he would always buy a cheaper bag of salt rather than a more expensive one. Conversely, to his gullible(?) eye, one medium-sized car is not exactly the same as any other, so he is prepared to pay more for particular cars which he sees as superior in some way. What this means is that in a world of consumers with Neil's characteristics the price elasticity of each brand of salt is high. A price increase for one brand results in a big shift to other brands. But the price elasticity of each brand of medium-sized car in a world of Neil lookalikes is not so high. A price increase in one brand does not produce such a big shift to alternatives. The extent to which goods are substitutes for each other is a major determinant of price elasticity of demand.

However, this does not mean that the price elasticity of demand cannot be influenced by the firm. Firms try to differentiate their brands through advertising in markets where there is monopoly power; that is, they try to reduce the extent to which their products are perceived as similar to other products. There are other ways too for a firm to reduce the price elasticity of demand for its product, such as tying its use to complementary products the firm also supplies. Microsoft, for example, sought to tie users of Windows software into using the Internet Explorer browser rather than alternative methods of browsing the Internet such as Netscape's Navigator. PC manufacturers that installed Windows could neither remove Internet Explorer nor feature a rival browser more prominently. Microsoft also offered Internet service providers, including America Online, a feature in its operating system to make it easy for users to establish an account, but only if the service provider denied most of its subscribers an alternative browser. One effect would be to make it more likely that consumers would continue to use the Microsoft browser if its price went up, since switching to another browser became more difficult.

4.3 Pure monopoly

The Microsoft court case pitched two economics professors against each other: Franklin Fisher from the Massachusetts Institute of Technology, expert witness for the government, and Richard Schmalensee on behalf of Microsoft. Both employed in their arguments the economic model of pure monopoly presented in this section. The model is useful because it examines an extreme case of monopoly power. Studying it can allow us to draw some conclusions, not only about how monopolies are likely to behave if unconstrained, but also about the conditions that sustain monopolies and the implications for policy.

To construct the model, we bring together the analysis of a firm's costs developed in Chapter 3 with the analysis of revenues in the last section, in order to study the pricing and output decisions of a pure monopolist.

▩ ▨ ■ 4.3.1 Marginal and average costs

In Chapter 3 Graham Dawson and Judith Mehta argued that the shape of firms' cost functions is of considerable relevance to understanding how industries change over time. The average cost curve traces average or unit costs of production at different levels of output, in the short and long run (Chapter 3, Section 3.3). From the shape of the average cost curve, whether downward sloping, 'U'-shaped or horizontal, we can deduce the pattern of the firm's total costs and marginal costs (just as a pattern of marginal and total revenues were implied by the downward-sloping average revenue curve).

The firm's total cost (TC) at each level of output is, by definition, the quantity produced (Q) multiplied by average cost (AC):

$$TC = AC \cdot Q$$

Marginal cost

Marginal cost is the change in total cost incurred as a result of producing an additional unit of output.

Marginal cost (MC) is then the change in total cost incurred when the firm produces an extra unit of output. The shape of the marginal cost curve is closely related to the shape of the average cost curve. Figure 4.5 shows the shape of the marginal cost curve associated with a 'U'-shaped average cost curve.

At levels of output below Q_1 on Figure 4.5, average cost falls as output increases. Marginal cost is therefore less than average cost. This is the same arithmetical relationship as we explained above between marginal revenue and average revenue. If average cost is declining, the addition to total cost as a result of producing the last unit must be less than average cost, because as output rises the cost of producing each unit declines. At

Figure 4.5
Marginal cost curve
with a 'U'-shaped
average cost curve

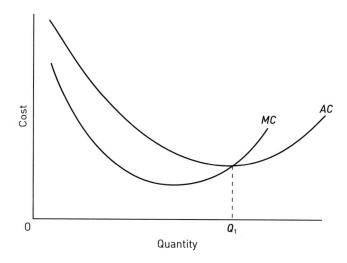

Q_1, average cost has reached its minimum. As output rises above Q_1, average cost starts to rise. Marginal cost is therefore now above average cost. This is because an increase in output raises the average cost of producing each unit, so the addition to total cost required to produce an extra unit must be larger than average cost. It follows that the marginal cost curve crosses the average cost curve at its lowest point.

Exercise 4.3

A numerical exercise may help to understand this. Table 4.2 shows output and average cost for a hypothetical firm. Complete the last two columns and graph the average and marginal cost curves on a single diagram.

Figure 4.5 showed a 'U'-shaped average cost curve. This might be a short-run or a long-run curve. Short-run average cost curves will be 'U'-shaped, since the firm cannot alter its fixed costs such as investment in plant and machinery. In the long run the firm can invest in additional plant, and, unless prevented from doing so, new firms can also invest and enter an

Table 4.2
A firm's average
and marginal costs

Units of output (Q)	Average cost (AC)	Total cost (TC)	Marginal cost (MC)
1	100	100	–
2	90	180	80
3	80	240	60
4	75	300	
5	72	360	
6	72	432	
7	75	525	
8	80		
9	92		
10	115		

Figure 4.6
Horizontal long-run average and marginal cost curves of a firm

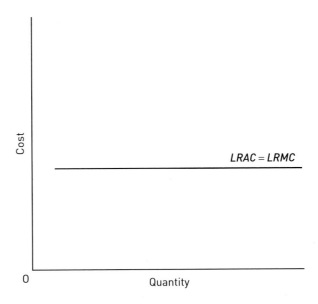

industry. Chapter 3, Section 3.3 noted that long-run average cost curves may be 'U'-shaped, or may decline continuously over the output range relevant to a particular market.

Question	What is the shape of the marginal cost curve associated with a continuously declining long-run average cost curve?

The marginal cost curve will lie below the average cost curve at all levels of output. This answer follows directly from the discussion of the relationship between average and marginal revenue curves. Look back at Section 4.2.3 if you were not sure of the answer.

A firm may also have long-run average costs that are constant over a large output range. This would mean that the long-run average cost (*LRAC*) curve was horizontal at these output levels (Figure 4.6). In this case, long-run marginal costs (*LRMC*) will be equal to average costs: each additional unit of output adds the same amount to total cost.

4.3.2 The profit-maximizing monopolist

We can now analyse the pricing and output decisions of a pure monopolist. We will assume that the firm has a sole objective, to maximize its profits. This is not an unrealistic assumption, though it is unlikely to be the only aim firms pursue. Firms whose shares are quoted on the stock market have constantly to chase higher profits in order to satisfy shareholders' desire for maximum returns. Even firms with no competitors in their product markets need to try to keep their share prices buoyant in this way, in order to be able to continue to attract investors and raise funds.

The profits our firm is seeking to maximize are the difference between its total costs and its total revenues. It can alter profits by altering output and hence the price at which it must sell. A pure monopolist faces no competition, so it does not have to worry about other firms' responses to its pricing and output decisions. Its constraint is the demand function for its product. The monopolist can choose the price at which it sells its output, and that will determine the quantity sold. Alternatively, it can choose its desired output

Figure 4.7
Profit maximization
by a pure
monopolist

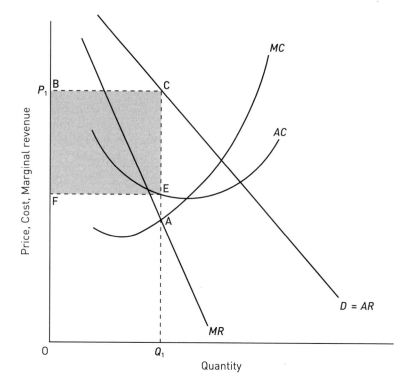

(sales) level, and that will determine the price that can be charged. Its aim is to choose the price/quantity combination that maximizes profits.

A firm that is seeking to maximize profit will choose the level of output (sales) that maximizes the difference between total cost and total revenue. To get an intuitive grasp of how it might do this, think of a firm gradually increasing output. Each additional unit produced and sold increases total revenue, so long as marginal revenue is positive. Producing the additional unit also adds to total cost so long as marginal cost is greater than zero.

If the marginal revenue is higher than the marginal cost, the addition to total revenue is larger than the addition to total cost and profit rises. Total revenue has increased by more than total cost. Conversely, if marginal cost is larger than marginal revenue, then producing and selling the additional unit has reduced profits. Where marginal revenue and marginal cost are equal, profit is maximized. This **condition for profit maximization** applies to firms in all market structures, not just to pure monopolists.

Now let us apply this condition to the monopolist. Figure 4.7 puts the firm's cost and revenue curves (Figures 4.3 and 4.5) together on a single diagram. What output will the monopolist choose in order to maximize profits? On Figure 4.7, the marginal revenue curve MR crosses the marginal cost curve MC at point A with output Q_1. Suppose the monopolist chooses to produce Q_1. What price will have to be charged to sell the whole of that output?

The monopolist's demand curve (average revenue curve) is $D = AR$. If the firm wishes to sell Q_1 it will charge P_1. A higher price will leave it with unsold goods, while a profit-maximizing firm will not charge a lower price, since that would reduce revenue.

The firm will make total profits equal to the shaded area BCEF on Figure 4.7. The vertical distance BF (= CE) measures the profit per unit, that is, the difference between the price P_1 and average cost. The horizontal distance BC (= FE) is equal to Q_1, the

The condition for profit maximization

Profit is maximized at the level of output at which marginal revenue = marginal cost: $MR = MC$

Equilibrium

In an economic model, an equilibrium is a situation from which there is no incentive for change.

output produced. Total profits are therefore BF times BC, the area of the rectangle BCEF.

At output levels below Q_1 the marginal revenue curve MR is above the marginal cost curve MC. So increasing output towards Q_1 will add to profits. At output levels above Q_1 marginal revenue is below marginal cost, so reducing output will reduce costs more than it reduces revenue, hence profits will rise. It follows that Q_1 is the firm's profit-maximizing output. Once it is producing Q_1 it has no incentive to change its output. Q_1 is therefore the firm's **equilibrium** output in Figure 4.7, and P_1 the equilibrium price.

▧ ▦ ▰ 4.3.3   Market dominance and supernormal profits

The rewards of market dominance can be large. The model of pure monopoly shows that a monopolist may be able to make high profits. Furthermore, these are not just short-run profits. The model rules out by assumption the possibility that other firms can enter the market, attracted by those profits, and compete away the monopolist's customers by charging a price for the product lower than P_1 in Figure 4.7. Hence a pure monopolist may be able to earn supernormal profits in the long run.

To see what this means, consider the firm's decision to invest, for example, in more machinery. This investment will only be worthwhile if the return on the investment is as good as, or better, than returns available if the funds had been invested elsewhere. So the cost of making the investment is the return from the alternative activity forgone, which might, for example, be the profit from investing in another industry. This alternative return forgone is the **opportunity cost** of the investment. You will meet this concept of opportunity cost often in economics.

Opportunity cost

The opportunity cost of using a resource is the amount it would have earned in its best alternative use.

The opportunity cost of investment determines the profit that would be just sufficient to keep the firm in the industry. This level of profit, called *normal profit*, is included in the economic definition of a firm's costs, odd though it may seem to call a profit a cost. The average cost curve of the monopolist thus includes normal profit because it is considered an (opportunity) cost. If average cost equals average revenue, only normal profits are being made; if average revenue exceeds average cost, as in Figure 4.7, the firm enjoys *supernormal profits*.

We now have another possible indicator of monopoly power, in addition to concentration ratios: the extent to which a firm can set price above average cost. Section 4.4 will show how competition even in markets with some monopoly power can drive out supernormal profits. Furthermore, a pure monopolist will always set a price above marginal cost. You can see this in Figure 4.7, where P_1 is greater than marginal cost (MC) at point A. Chapter 5 explores a model of competition without monopoly power, where price is forced down to marginal cost. So a further indicator of the extent of monopoly power in a market is the mark-up of price over marginal cost. This can be measured as:

$$\frac{P - MC}{P}$$

a measure sometimes called the 'degree of monopoly'.

Lest all this seems too detached from the real world, note that these indicators of monopoly power were at issue in the Microsoft court case. Expert witnesses for the government argued that Microsoft was exploiting its market power to earn supernormal profits by charging consumers more than they would pay if there were more competition in the market for computer operating systems. They pointed to the high observed levels of company profitability as evidence that Microsoft was using market power to raise prices significantly above long-run average costs (Gilbert and Katz, 2001, p.29).

Furthermore, the economists for both sides tried to calculate whether the observed gap between Microsoft's marginal cost and price was at the level to be expected if Microsoft was behaving like a profit-maximizing monopolist. To do this, they started from precisely the model of monopoly behaviour outlined in Section 4.2.2. They made estimates of marginal costs and of the elasticity of demand for Windows software; and from these they estimated the price a pure monopolist would be expected to charge.

From these calculations they drew opposing conclusions. Schmalensee, for Microsoft, argued that the short-run monopoly price for Windows should have been at least 16 times the price actually charged. Fisher, for the government, argued that Microsoft was charging a long-run monopoly price for the software. The argument turned in part on the distinction between short and long run, and in part on the objectives of the firm. The government argued that Microsoft's price for Windows reflected monopoly pricing tempered by the broader objectives of the firm, including expanding the installed base of Windows, encouraging the use of complementary products such as applications software and discouraging software pirating (Gilbert and Katz, 2001, p.29).

The model of pure monopoly described in this section is a *static* model, in a number of senses. First, it holds many things constant: technology, for example, and the way the firm organizes production. Most crucially, it rules out competition by assumption, thus removing the main force for change in industrial markets. Second, the model is designed to explore the firm's *equilibrium* price and quantity; it is a model of a firm at rest, not one that is changing. Models of this kind can be used to analyse change – we will do so in the next section – but there is no doubt that they miss the sense of turbulence and continuous change conveyed by Mariana Mazzucato in Chapter 2 when discussing the automobile and computer industries over time. Sections 4.4 and 4.5 reintroduce competition and technological change to our analysis.

4.4 Contestability and barriers to entry

Economists have long recognized that almost all monopolists face potential competition, and that this will influence their behaviour. Joseph Schumpeter was an influential economist working in the first half of the twentieth century. He was deeply interested in social relations and social philosophy and is particularly well known for his theory of economic development. He was an early critic of the model of monopoly just outlined, arguing that its emphasis on profit maximizing with given technology (Section 4.3.2) focused too much on 'data of the momentary situation', rather than being concerned, as firms were, with the past and the future and 'the competition from the new commodity, the new technology' (Schumpeter, 1942, p.84).

Schumpeter's arguments seem highly contemporary. He emphasized innovation and the destruction of sections of the economy and whole ways of life by new techniques of production and new products. Firms that hold strong monopoly power in one era can find that their markets disappear through industrial transformation. Schumpeter's examples included transport: canal companies driven out of business by the railways; the railways threatened by the motor car. In the current era, a comparable transformation has come in information technology. The large producers of mainframe and midi computers who once exercised enormous market power, seemingly invulnerable, disappeared or were completely transformed at the end of the twentieth century with the advent of the personal computer. For example, during the late 1970s IBM dominated the market for large mainframe computers. In 1981 it launched the IBM personal computer – a relatively late entrant into the market for small portable machines. Its relationship with Microsoft, then a small 32-person company supplying the DOS operating system, and the successful marketing of its new range saved it from extinction, though it has never regained the dominance it held in earlier decades and the changes of the 1980s 'fundamentally rocked' the business (www.ibm.com, 3 October 2001).

In this section and the next, we respond to Schumpeter's critique in two stages. We first drop the assumption that a monopolist faces no competition, and instead assume that in the long run – that is, once firms are able to invest in new capacity – firms can enter new markets. Indeed, they can create whole new markets for innovative products. We explore in this section the barriers that can be established, by technology and by the conduct of established or 'incumbent' firms, to the entry of new firms into an industry, and some consequences of lowering barriers to entry, drawing on the model of the profit-maximizing firm developed in Sections 4.2 and 4.3. In Section 4.5 we then look specifically at competition through innovation, drawing on an alternative model of firms as evolving institutions with specific skills or 'capabilities'.

▨ ▧ ■ 4.4.1 Economies of scale and barriers to entry

Graham Dawson and Judith Mehta analysed in Chapter 3 one of the most important sources of monopoly power: economies of scale. If there are economies of scale in an industry, firms' long-run average cost ($LRAC$) curves are downward sloping: average cost falls as output rises. If a firm expands ahead of its rivals it can take advantage of these economies of scale in such a way that it can dominate the industry. The firm's combination of low average costs and high output become a *barrier to entry* to other firms. This means that other firms, attracted to the industry by the profits they see the existing firm making, find that they cannot profitably enter and supply part of the market.

Let us look a little more closely at why not. Figure 4.8 shows the long-run average cost curve and the demand curve for a single firm that currently monopolizes its market. Average costs fall as the scale of the firm's operation is increased, up to the point of minimum efficient scale A at output level Q_1. Beyond A, costs per unit of output are constant. The market demand curve is D, the firm supplies the whole market. For simplicity

Figure 4.8
Barriers to entry under economies of scale

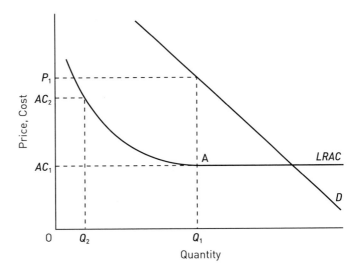

we have omitted the marginal cost and marginal revenue curves. Let us just assume that Q_1 and P_1 are the profit-maximizing price and quantity for the monopolist.

Now consider the position of another firm trying to muscle in on the market. All firms in the industry have (by assumption) the same cost curves. Suppose that a new firm sets up production sufficient to supply a small part of current demand (Q_2). You can see that at that level of output its average costs are considerably higher (AC_2) than those of the established firm (AC_1).

| Question | However, the new firm's average cost AC_2 is less than the market price P_1. So surely it can come in and make a profit. What is the problem? |

Natural monopoly

A natural monopoly exists if, as a result of economies of scale, a single firm can supply the market at a lower average cost than a number of smaller firms.

There are two problems. First, there is additional output in the industry from the new firm. To sell the new output, the new firm will have to drive down the price, undermining its own profitability. Second, the incumbent firm is making supernormal profits per unit equal to $(P_1 - AC_1)$. It is likely to be willing to sacrifice some of those profits for a while, reducing price to make entry unprofitable, in order to sustain its monopoly power. (You will study 'strategic' behaviour by firms, of which this is an example, more systematically in Chapter 6.)

There is room for only one firm in this market, since a single firm can supply the market at lower average cost than any combination of smaller firms. Industries of this kind are called **natural monopolies**. The barrier to entry to the market characterized by natural monopoly is therefore the downward-sloping part of the average cost curve.

| Question | To reinforce this conclusion, study Figure 4.9. This is identical to Figure 4.8 except that each firm now has constant average costs. Assume again that the incumbent firm produces output Q_1. Could a second firm now come in and compete for part of the market by producing Q_2? |

Yes. The new firm's average costs are identical to those of the incumbent firm, at AC_1. Because there are no economies of scale, the larger firm has no cost advantage over the

Figure 4.9
Barriers to entry under constant average costs?

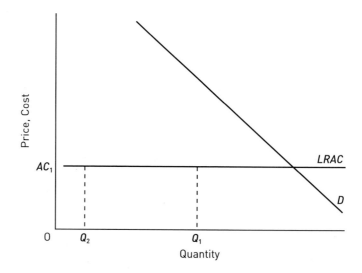

new entrant, and the market will be divided between a number of competing firms. There is no cost barrier to entry.

There are many areas of the economy where the cost conditions generate strong barriers to entry. Software, Microsoft's product, is a good example. The initial cost of producing software is very high. IBM, for example, is reported to have spent US$1 billion to develop, test and market its OS/2 operating system as a (failed) alternative to Windows (Gilbert and Katz, 2001, p.28). Once software is produced, the marginal duplication costs to produce additional copies are close to zero, as Microsoft's chief economic witness assumed in his calculations. Major pieces of software, such as PC operating systems, therefore exhibit very large economies of scale, and this is a major source of Microsoft's monopoly power. One economic commentator (Klein, 2001) described Microsoft as operating in a 'natural monopoly market'.

However, the phrase 'natural monopoly' suggests a permanency that economic history belies. The industries that most closely fit the natural monopoly model are the 'network industries' (Chapter 3, Section 3.4.2). There are a number of 'old economy' industries where economies of scale are generated by physical infrastructural supply networks that are inefficient to duplicate, such as gas pipes, water pipes and cabling. Even in these industries, however, technology can undermine the economies of scale. Perhaps the best example is telecommunications, where mobile telephony has destroyed the natural monopoly characteristics of the supply of telephone services.

▪▪▪ 4.4.2 Network externalities and market contestability

There are also barriers to entry on the demand side of some markets. A key characteristic of a number of 'new economy' industries, explained in Chapter 3, Section 3.4, is network externalities. These imply that the value of an item – such as a particular computer operating system – to consumers rises as the use of the product by others increases.

From the point of view of firms supplying computer operating systems, for example, these network externalities operate as a barrier to entry in a way that is comparable to economies of scale. The first firm into the market can rapidly build up a customer base, since the more people buy in, the greater the incentive for others to do so too. Once there is an established incumbent firm, the barrier to other firms' entry is formidable: it will be hard to persuade existing customers to switch supplier, since they will lose key network benefits. This effect of network externalities is called 'lock-in': once consumers are integrated into a network it is expensive to shift them.

Microsoft dominated the operating systems market in this way. The more users adopted the Microsoft operating system (MS-DOS and Windows), the more it became advantageous for other users to do the same, so that they could communicate easily with existing users, share files and learn from each other. Microsoft was able to benefit from these network externalities to establish its operating system as the standard system, even though a number of other operating systems, notably Apple, were seen as superior by many commentators and users. Because Windows was widely used, there were strong incentives for new computer users to purchase machines operating with that system. Software developers wrote additional programs for the operating system – such as specialist software used by economists – and users became 'locked-in' to Microsoft's systems and products. In these circumstances, even if better software had existed, the costs of training staff in the new systems and changing hardware could have been prohibitive, and the inconvenience of using a different system from others reinforced the incentive to stick with Microsoft products. The government labelled this, in the Microsoft case, the 'applications barrier to entry'.

Network externalities and 'lock-in' on the demand side thus pose a barrier to entry even in industries where there are not large economies of scale. They become formidable barriers when they are associated with economies of scale, as in the Microsoft case.

Firms wishing to compete with Microsoft in the operating systems market thus faced a dual barrier to entry: economies of scale on the supply side and network externalities on the demand side. As a result, the PC operating systems market displayed a particularly severe lack of **contestability**.

Complete or 'perfect' contestability is very rare since virtually all industries and markets display some entry barriers, although they vary greatly in severity.

Contestable market

A market is perfectly contestable if entry and exit are costless.

Question

If you were setting up your own business, which of the following ideas would you consider to be the most viable? Note down, for each, one barrier you would face in setting up such an undertaking.

■ **a sandwich shop**
■ **selling antiques via the Internet**
■ **brain surgery.**

It may be very difficult to set up a sandwich shop without approvals from the relevant health and safety authorities. *Regulations* thus affect the ease with which firms can enter markets or operate once they have established themselves. In addition, it may be the case that you do not have the necessary *skills* to operate in some sectors of the economy. Brain surgery is an obvious example. Thus barriers to entry can be related to ownership of particular skills or *resources*. If you wanted to use the Internet to sell antiques you would need the skills to establish and run a website. You would also need to be able to source and deliver antiques, perhaps requiring the creation of a network of antique dealers. So you would already need to have resources such as a good knowledge and set of contacts in the trade. If a firm was already undertaking this kind of e-commerce in antiques, dealers might be tied into it by exclusive deals that prevented you working with them.

■■■ 4.4.3 Artificial barriers to entry

The last example illustrates a general point: barriers to entry may be 'natural' in the sense that they are inherent in the product or service, or they may be deliberately created by firms in a deliberate attempt to prevent competition. The more a firm can prevent other firms from entering a market, the more freedom it will have to exercise monopoly power to the detriment of consumers, by charging high prices and making supernormal profits. If a market is contestable, incumbent firms realize that any monopoly profits will be short lived, because new firms will come in and compete them away. Section 4.4.4 analyses that process. Competition authorities are particularly concerned to ensure that firms do not create artificial barriers to contestability.

However, effective competition does not necessarily require firms actually to enter a market. Firms already in a market will be aware that if they make high profits they will create strong incentives for competitors to move in. Hence, they may be prevented from exercising monopoly power by fear of generating entry by competitors where barriers to entry are low. Hence, an industry with few firms may display competitive behaviour, so long as barriers to *potential* competitors are low.

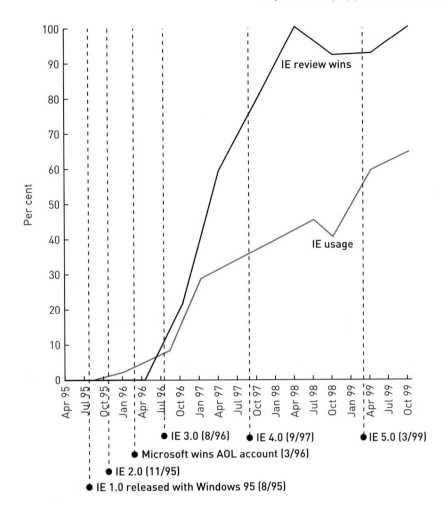

Figure 4.10
Trends in Internet Explorer's share of review 'wins' and usage, from April 1995 to October 1999

Source: Klein, 2001, p.48

The debate in the Microsoft case turned in part on the extent of contestability of its market. The government argued that the reason Microsoft was putting so much effort into gaining market share for their Internet Explorer browser was that Netscape represented a source of potential competition for Windows. The reason for this was that Netscape had the potential, along with the Java language, to grow into a layer of 'middleware' – software that lies between the operating system and the applications software – that would separate the software applications of interest to users from the underlying operating system. This would break the link, described above, between the network externalities on the demand side and the economies of scale in operating system software, and hence largely remove the 'applications barrier to entry'.

Microsoft put more than US$100 million per year during 1995–97 into improving its browser Internet Explorer. It also gave away Internet Explorer for free, and paid Apple to use the browser (Klein, 2001). Figure 4.10 illustrates the effects of these efforts on market share. Internet Explorer started to win approval from reviewers by comparison with other browsers ('IE review wins') and market share ('IE usage') increased.

Economists differ on the implications of these effects for users. Nicholas Economides argues that the direct benefits to the consumer of cheaper and higher quality net access were very large; he emphasizes the benefits to users of the shared software standards created by Microsoft operating systems software. Fisher and Daniel Rubinfeld, for the government, argued that Microsoft's actions were 'predatory'. That is, they were making investments and charging prices that were only profitable in the long run taking into account the supernormal profits that could be earned once the competition was eliminated (Fisher and Rubinfeld, 2000). The government emphasized the long-term potential damage to users from eliminating future competitive pressure on prices and quality (Gilbert and Katz, 2001).

▨ ■ ■ 4.4.4 Monopolistic competition

Given the central role of competitive pressure in the case against monopoly, let us look more closely at the effects of competition in contexts where firms have monopoly power but markets remain contestable. This section examines competition on the basis of price. Section 4.5 turns to competition through innovation.

The model of monopolistic competition builds on the pure monopoly model, but drops the assumption that new firms cannot enter the market. It shows that entry of new firms can result in the disappearance of supernormal profits, but there are some less satisfactory effects on costs.

Look back at Figure 4.7, and think of this now as the short-run profit-maximizing position of a firm holding a temporary monopoly in a market open to entry. In the long run, new firms can freely enter the industry by investing in their own plant, and the incumbent firm can also invest in new plant and equipment.

Question	What happens to the demand curve of the original or 'incumbent' firm when others come in?

There is now a distinction between the demand curve facing the firm and the market demand curve. The firm's demand curve lies to the left of the market demand curve, since only part of the market demand is now demand for its product. This is a market where (by assumption) firms have market power. There will be product differentiation (Section 4.2), and we can picture the new firms coming in with a similar but slightly different product. Consumers can choose between them. The slightly different product may also attract some new consumers, but as new firms enter the market, the original firm's demand curve is likely to shift to the left.

How far left will the demand curve shift? This is a question about the *equilibrium* of the firm in an industry where firms have monopoly power. Section 4.3 analysed the equilibrium for a pure monopoly. Once firms can enter the industry, they will continue to move into it so long as there are supernormal profits being made, since supernormal profits mean, by definition, profits higher than the return available elsewhere. Figure 4.11 shows the point of long-run profit-maximizing equilibrium of a firm in a monopolistically competitive industry after entry has ceased.

We have drawn the firm's long-run average cost curve as 'U'-shaped but flatter than the short-run cost curve in Figure 4.7. The demand curve $D = AR$ is the *firm's* demand curve. As other firms have come in, the demand curve has shifted left. At the same time, the firm has moved leftwards along its long-run average cost curve: it may have disinvested as demand has decreased at each price for its product. The firm's equilibrium is at the point where there are no longer any supernormal profits to be made. This happens at point A on Figure 4.11, where the demand curve is tangent to the average cost curve, that is, it just touches it. At this point with output Q_E the firm maximizes profits by setting $LRMC = MR$ (point B). Supernormal profits have fallen to zero because price equals average cost. There is therefore no longer any incentive for new firms to move into the industry.

Figure 4.11
The equilibrium of a
firm in monopolistic
competition in the
long run

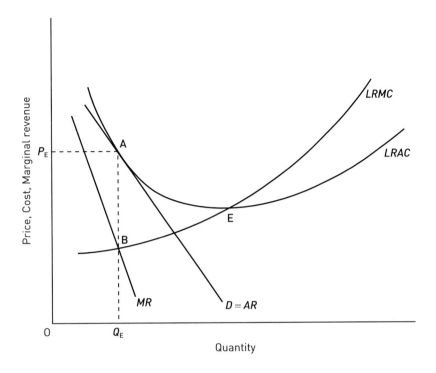

This model is only relevant to cases where the minimum efficient scale of firms is such that there is room for a number of firms in the market. Notice, however, that at output Q_E and price P_E the firm is not operating at the point of minimum efficient scale E. Average costs are higher than they would be if the firm was supplying a larger part of the market. So monopolistic competition can drive up costs above their minimum level, and although there are no supernormal profits, consumers may not be getting the best possible deal. On the other hand, competition has brought product diversity to the market.

4.5 Competition through innovation

In the model of monopolistic competition firms compete on price, and by product differentiation. However, as Schumpeter pointed out, firms also compete by creating radically new products, changing consumers' lives in the process. This process of product innovation may be particularly marked at the early stage of an industry life cycle. Later, as an industry consolidates, process innovation may sustain a firm's grip on the market. Being first into a market can have benefits, as discussed in Chapter 3, Section 3.4; they are further explored in Chapter 6. This section analyses competition through innovation, drawing on a rather different theory of the firm from the one we have used so far in this chapter.

▩▦■ 4.5.1 Capabilities, resources and the entrepreneurial firm

A company producing a new product has to create a market for it, and the more innovative the product is, the more the firm has to work to persuade customers to understand it and to buy it. For example, TranscenData was at the time of writing in 2001 a small high-tech company based near Cambridge, England. It was built up by an academic engineer, Geoff Butlin, on the basis of his research interests. Geoff's attempts to commercialize his ideas had mixed success but he learned from his experiences and in the middle of the 1990s began to develop a new product which he realized had potentially a global market. The product was about data exchange. In building other products earlier, Geoff had used his complex technical ideas to produce computer-aided design tools. To do that he had to learn how to move data from one computer design system to another and he recognized that his small company had a world lead in that area.

TranscenData decided to develop this new product and finally gave it a name, CADfix, which the market loved. The name was very expressive of what the product was doing – fixing computer-aided design (CAD) models. Geoff was taking a new product to market. He also knew, from hard-earned previous experience, that excellent technical solutions were not a guarantee of commercial success and that other companies, with perhaps greater commercial acumen, were only too ready to run with new ideas. He was very much aware of the potential competition from new entrants, though initially there were no close substitutes so he enjoyed considerable monopoly power.

What kind of economic model would help us to analyse the chances of a particular firm building on and holding on to monopoly power? The question creates particular problems for the model of the firm studied so far, because this is a question about how particular firms *differ* from each other in ways that gain some potential advantage. The model used so far in this chapter has, however, assumed that competing firms are the *same*: they have the same technology, and react in standard ways to market conditions. Chapter 3 described the model, for this reason, as analysing a 'representative firm' (Section 3.3.1). The moment we look at innovation we clearly have to drop that assumption, and consider individual firms as innovators. Technological change in the model becomes uneven, and particular firms can build up a dominant market position – or disappear.

There is an alternative tradition in economics of modelling the behaviour of firms, one that has recently taken on a new lease of life as innovation has again become a central concern. This approach sees individual firms as evolving organizations – as TranscenData evolved – that develop particular resources and capabilities over time. You can think of 'capabilities', or 'competencies' as they are also known (Chapter 3, Section 3.4), as the things a firm is good at. Two influential theorists in the evolutionary tradition, Nelson and Winter (1982), model these organizational capabilities as embedded in the 'routines' of a company. Routines are practices in which firms engage in a taken-for-granted way. A firm's routines are acquired in the same way as skills are acquired by individuals, by learning or sometimes by accident. When organizations become 'skilful', they respond to situations effectively through taken-for-granted patterns of behaviour, without thinking each situation through from scratch, rather as a skilful sports star performs.

Particular firms can thus become good at certain activities, such as spotting the next technological breakthrough early, or providing good customer service, and reproduction of those skills and capabilities becomes part of the firm's way of operating. Alongside organizational skills, firms also develop particular organizational resources: for example, networks of suppliers they can rely on; particular highly skilled groups of staff; or large investments in specialized plant. This model of firms is 'evolutionary' in the sense that firms develop distinct capabilities over time, and those most effective in current market contexts win the competitive battle – for a time. This approach assumes firms may pursue a range of objectives, one of which is chasing enlarged market share.

So in an evolutionary model history matters. Joseph Schumpeter, cited at the beginning of the last section, argued that models based on price and quantity, where all firms have the same technology, lack a sense of past and future. An evolutionary model overcomes that: it analyses how particular firms build on their past to create scope for future success – or to drive the firm to bankruptcy by being unable to change. TranscenData is an example of a firm that built on past skill and experience to create a market niche for a new product.

■ ■ ■ 4.5.2 Innovation and monopoly power

Successful product innovation is particularly characteristic of 'entrepreneurial' firms, led by individuals and reflecting their character. The evolutionary model allows space for considering the impact of the personality of a firm's founder on its fortunes. Microsoft was a firm still run and part-owned by a dominant entrepreneurial founding figure, Bill Gates. These issues too find their way into policy debate: part of the debate around Microsoft was about what *kind* of firm Microsoft had become. Was it one that, through its own organizational culture and routines, was constantly searching for improvement, responding to competitive threat with better products? Or had it, as it gained monopoly power, stopped innovating and gone over to defensiveness, trying to prevent competition through innovation rather than winning through innovating?

For Microsoft, Schmalensee argued that, whatever the arguments about the extent of the threat from competitors, Microsoft 'behaves as if it faces ... intense dynamic competition', and presented evidence of 'relentless innovation to improve its operating system'. He concluded that

> despite what would appear to be an ironclad monopoly, the evidence based on real world observations is that Microsoft does not *behave* like a firm with monopoly power.
>
> *(www.microsoft.com, September 2001, Microsoft's emphasis)*

Here Schmalensee is contrasting the evidence relevant to the standard pure ('ironclad') monopoly model with evidence of the behavioural characteristics of the firm, relevant to the evolutionary model. Fisher and Rubinfeld (2000) for the government agreed that behavioural evidence was also relevant. They used company emails to support their argument that Microsoft displayed the opposite behavioural tendency: an organizational focus on suppressing competition to the detriment of product improvement and consumer choice.

So there is no single answer to the question, do firms with monopoly power continue to innovate? A firm's behaviour will depend on its history and its current competitive challenges. Firms with monopoly power may continue to face competition through product innovation. In that case, a highly concentrated industry – one containing very few firms – may continue to behave competitively in a dynamic sense: the incumbent firms innovate constantly, since they perceive barriers to entry through product innovation as low, and entry always a potential threat. Schmalensee argued that Microsoft faced constant competitive threats of this kind.

As industries consolidate, some large firms may shift from product to process innovation (Chapters 2 and 3). Process innovation involves producing existing products more efficiently, using new production technology, or merely organizing production more efficiently using existing technology. Process innovation can therefore shift a firm's long-run average cost curve downwards (Chapter 3, Section 3.3.2).

Figure 4.12 analyses such an innovation by a profit-maximizing monopolist. For simplicity, we have this time drawn the firm's *LRAC* curve to display only the range where constant returns to scale exist (*LRAC* = *LRMC*). The monopolist's profits are maximized

Figure 4.12
The effect of a
monopolist's
innovation on price
and costs

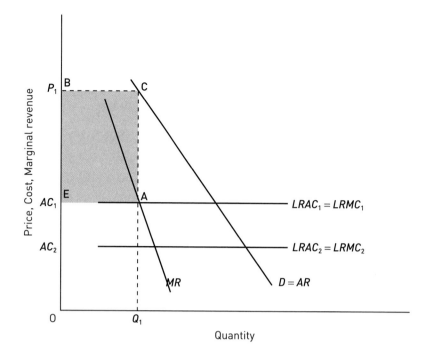

initially where $LRMC_1 = MR$ at point A. Output is Q_1 with an average cost per unit of AC_1 and price P_1. Supernormal profits are initially shown by the rectangle BCAE. The process innovation shifts the long-run cost curve downwards to $LRAC_2$.

Exercise 4.4

Indicate on Figure 4.12 the monopolist's new profit-maximizing price and quantity after the innovation. What has been the effect on price?

Your answer should show that even a pure monopolist, as defined in Section 4.3, will charge a lower price after the innovation than before; the innovation benefits consumers.

Schumpeter argued in the 1940s that large firms with monopoly power may be particularly likely to pursue this and other kinds of innovation. They are more likely than firms with little market power to be able to obtain financial backing from banks for risky innovation, and they may have a flow of supernormal profits to be reinvested. Furthermore, large firms with monopoly power have incentives to innovate since they can hope to benefit from their innovations by reaping further monopoly profits, hence monopoly power can drive industrial growth and create cheaper products for consumers.

These benefits of innovation can be threatened by contestability. In highly contestable markets, there is little incentive for a firm to innovate, if imitators will quickly compete away the market advantage gained by the innovator. Thus for policy purposes contestability has to be tempered with the opportunity for firms to make adequate returns. This is the key argument for allowing firms to take out patents on inventions that are the basis for innovation, allowing them to protect and exploit for profit the intellectual property rights in their ideas for a limited period. Competition authorities are increasingly concerned to get the policy framework right to promote and sustain competition through innovation.

4.6 Monopoly power and competition policy dilemmas

We can now draw together some implications of our study of monopoly power for competition policy. The antitrust prosecutors in the United States, like the competition authorities in Europe, including the UK's Competition Commission, have as their objective the prevention of the abuse of monopoly power to the detriment of consumers. The theory in this chapter helps to identify some central dilemmas policy makers face, especially when dealing with firms in highly innovative and rapidly changing industries. We start with another look at the Microsoft case, concentrating this time not on the economic analysis presented but on the remedies proposed by the government.

▪ ▪ ▪ 4.6.1 Structure and conduct

Appeals court rules against Microsoft break-up

Microsoft on Thursday won its battle against being broken up when a US appeals court threw out a lower court ruling that split the company in half, and closed almost all doors for another try at a break-up.

But the seven-judge panel, in a unanimous decision, also upheld many of the key charges in the government's landmark lawsuit, finding that Microsoft was a monopoly that acted illegally in an attempt to maintain its dominance in personal computer operating systems.

Bill Gates, Microsoft chairman, said he was 'pleased' with the court's decision, which had removed the threat of break-up. 'We feel very good about what the court has written here. The decision is consistent with our ability to go forward with our new products.' . . .

In a 125-page ruling, the appeals court found that Microsoft had not illegally tried to monopolise the internet browser market, as the government had charged. It also asked a lower court to reconsider a ruling that Microsoft's practice of including its web browser, Internet Explorer, in its Windows operating system was illegal 'tying' . . .

The court did find many of Microsoft's business practices to be unlawful, particularly contracts it signed with a wide array of companies in the industry – including computer manufacturers, internet service providers, and independent software vendors – that shut rival browsers out of the market.

Source: Peter Spiegel and Paul Abrahams, http://www.financialtimes.com,
28 June 2001

Government authorities who are considering acting against a firm for abuse of monopoly power will investigate both market *structure* – the extent of monopoly power enjoyed by the firm – and market *conduct* – the behaviour of a firm with monopoly power. In the Microsoft case, as in others on both sides of the Atlantic, the assessment of the extent of market power is the 'initial step' in tackling the problem, since a firm without monopoly power cannot abuse it. Gilbert and Katz list the methods used by the US courts to assess the extent of market power: they first define

the relevant market(s) affected by the firm's conduct. A market is a set of products that consumers consider to be reasonably close substitutes for each other [then] the assessment of market power moves on to the calculation of market share, examination of competitive interactions, determination of the conditions of entry and analysis of other pertinent structural features of the market.

(Gilbert and Katz, 2001, pp.29–30)

The 'structural' features of the market that determine the assessment of monopoly power cover a broad range, including barriers to entry and the pattern of interaction with actual and potential competitors. In many cases, a pertinent issue is the size of the relevant market: an industry dominated by a single firm in one country may operate in and face competition in integrated international markets.

The analysis then moves on to the *market conduct* of the firm. Here, the behaviour of the firm is scrutinized for abuse of monopoly power, such as monopoly pricing and deliberate blocking of competition by 'predatory' behaviour against the interests of consumers. European Union legislation bans the abuse of a 'dominant position' in a market by a monopolist, and that wording was brought into UK law by the Competition Act of 1998. In the USA, similarly, for the courts to act against Microsoft, they needed to be convinced *both* that the firm held monopoly power and that it had abused it to the long-term detriment of computer users. The possession of monopoly power alone is not an offence; as Gilbert and Katz (2001, p.30) put it: 'Indeed it would not make economic sense to punish a firm that possesses market power solely as a consequence of its having developed a superior product, because doing so would erode the incentives for innovation.'

The structure/conduct distinction is a fuzzy one: evidence of conduct can be and is used to assess the competitiveness of a market structure. But the distinction between the extent of monopoly power and its abuse is central to policy options. Competition authorities, whether in the USA or Europe, once convinced that a firm is abusing monopoly power, can seek to remedy the situation by *structural remedies*, that is, reducing the extent of market power by, for example, breaking up a dominant firm into two or more smaller ones. Alternatively, they can seek to impose *conduct* (or *behavioural*) *remedies* that seek to change market conduct by directly prohibiting or penalizing particular forms of conduct. Policies in both Europe and the USA typically mix structural and behavioural remedies, but there are nevertheless different policy traditions on the two sides of the Atlantic.

The US policy stance has displayed, since the Sherman Act cited at the beginning of this chapter, a greater emphasis on 'structural' remedies. This was the type of remedy that Judge Thomas Penfield Jackson sought to impose on Microsoft, breaking it up into two companies. One company would have held the Windows operating system, and the other all the applications and Microsoft's other lines of business. The Appeals Court, in June 2001, overturned that order (see above), arguing (among other points) that it was not clear that splitting the company would prevent the behaviour by Microsoft that the court found anti-competitive. In September 2001 the US Justice Department announced it was abandoning the effort to break up the company. Instead, it sought to address conduct through imposing penalties to prevent certain types of behaviour it regarded as designed to exclude competitors from its market.

The European Union approach, and the UK policy tradition, both permit structural remedies. However, there is greater emphasis on conduct remedies for the abuse of market power. The UK Competition Commission investigates cases referred to it by the Office of Fair Trading (OFT) and focuses on the *effects* of firms' behaviour on a case by case basis. Conduct remedies, when firms have been found to be abusing market power (e.g. through monopoly pricing) or acting to create artificial barriers to entry by competitors, have included price reductions and changes in pricing structure. For example, in October 1999, following an OFT investigation, football clubs in the UK agreed that licensing contracts with shirt manufacturers would include a requirement that retailers would not be prevented from discounting replica kits. A number of Premiership clubs had used their dominant position to encourage manufacturers to withhold supplies to retailers who were selling at a discount. The OFT ruled that where contracts were already in place, manufacturers had to tell dealers that they could sell kits at whatever price they chose. The OFT's intention was that supporters and parents of young fans would benefit from lower prices for replica kits.

■ ■ ■ 4.6.2 Monopoly power and competition policy in dynamic markets

Highly innovative industries with fast changing market structures pose very particular dilemmas for competition policy, and the analysis in this chapter helps to identify some of these dilemmas and their implications.

Perhaps the sharpest dilemma relates to the incentive to innovate. It is hard for competition authorities to distinguish between high profits from innovations that benefit consumers, on the one hand, and high profits that result from short-run profit extraction against consumers' interests, on the other. Policy needs to protect the incentive to make profits through innovation, while attacking monopoly profits of the type identified in the static model.

This is not an easy balance to achieve. In a famous phrase, John Hicks, a British economist writing in the 1930s, said 'The best of all monopoly profits is a quiet life' (Hicks, 1935, p.8). Schmalensee, for Microsoft, picked that up:

> Far from living the quiet life of a monopolist immune from entry, Microsoft
> perceived itself as being in a constant struggle to maintain its leadership in
> computer operating systems.
>
> *(www.microsoft.com, 5 September 2001)*

The key word is 'leadership'. As we have argued above, Microsoft was operating in a market where a high level of concentration was 'natural'. The market for operating systems was likely to have one 'leader' at a time. A difficult question for policy was, how serious was the competitive threat that it faced? There was room for a huge amount of debate on this question, not least because it turned in part on what might happen if Netscape software developed in particular directions.

This in turn makes it hard in highly innovative markets to distinguish vigorous competition from deliberate creation of barriers to entry. In markets with economies of scale and network externalities, the common standards created by a dominant supplier such as Microsoft, and the low costs associated with high volume, benefit consumers. Entry by competitors is very difficult, and when it happens it is 'catastrophic entry' – catastrophic, that is, for the incumbent firm. A new firm grabs the leadership. It is hard for policy makers to spot the moment when the old market leader tips over from innovator to blockage on progress. If government tries to force entry too soon, it may just slow innovation; if it lets an incumbent block entry through tactical behaviour, it may have the same effect. Hence the importance of the issues raised by the evolutionary models of the firm: the extent to which innovation is built into the incumbent firm's culture and organizational style.

We can draw a few tentative conclusions. In innovative markets, barriers to entry remain important policy issues: competition through innovation can be shut out by artificial entry barriers, and there needs to be a very strong argument why such barriers should persist. One such argument, however, is the effect on incentives for innovation. Firms need to know that if they spend on developing new products they can gain a return: but not one that prevents the next wave of innovation. Furthermore, there are industries where monopoly power is highly transitory. New firms pick up the new technologies in months, and the initial firm's market power disappears: in these markets, there may be no role for competition policy, however monopolized the markets (briefly) appear. Geoff Butlin's experience showed that TranscenData was operating in a market constantly threatened by new entry. And, finally, innovation is expensive: large firms have a continuing role to play in generating investment in innovation, but there also need to be sources of funds for the next set of innovative firms.

4.7 Conclusion

Competition policy is an area of government policy strongly built on economic analysis. The focus of this chapter has been competition in innovative markets in which firms have monopoly power. We have argued that the static models of monopoly and monopoly power have a lot to teach us – and policy makers – still. But they miss crucial issues relevant to dynamic market environments. The evolutionary models of the firm address different questions, notably about the role of innovativeness and entrepreneurial behaviour in competition, that are particularly relevant in dynamic markets. The next chapter turns from markets where firms have market power to markets where they do not.

Questions for review and discussion

Question 1   The table below shows data for a firm selling watches. The firm's marginal revenue from the sale of the thirteenth watch is (tick the letter corresponding to the correct amount):

A ❑ £155
B ❑ £–25
C ❑ £2015
D ❑ £–15

Quantity of watches sold	Price of a watch (£)
10	200
11	185
12	170
13	155

Question 2   Figure 4.13 shows cost and revenue for a firm. Complete the following explanatory statement by placing in the spaces the most appropriate words from the list below:

Total revenue   marginal revenue   average revenue   average cost   total cost marginal cost   output

At output level Q_1, the . . . . . . earned by the firm is P_1. Since . . . . . . is greater than . . . . . . at output Q_1, the firm could increase profits by increasing . . . . . .

Figure 4.13
Cost and revenue
curves

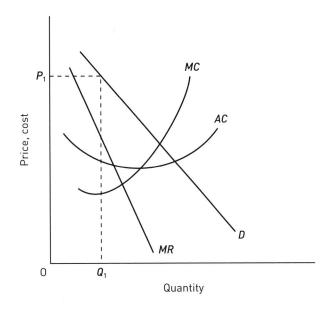

Question 3 The graph (Figure 4.14) shows the demand curve and the marginal revenue curve for a firm. At which point on the demand curve (Q_a, Q_b or Q_c) is demand price inelastic?

Figure 4.14
Demand and
marginal revenue
curves

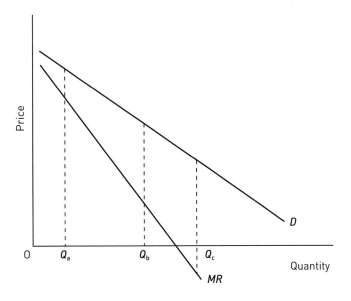

Question 4 Figure 4.15 represents the initial cost and revenue curves of a monopolist producer of low-fat ready meals.

(a) Assuming profit maximization, redraw the diagram and indicate and explain the output level 'Q_1', the price at which this output is sold 'P_1', and the area of profit.

(b) Given the level of demand, use the concept of price elasticity of demand to explain why the monopolist will not necessarily maximize output.

(c) If the monopolist was required to charge a price equal to marginal costs, mark on your diagram the new output level.

(d) Explain why the above decision would be advantageous to consumers.

Figure 4.15
Initial cost and
revenue curves
of a monopolist
producer of low-fat
ready meals

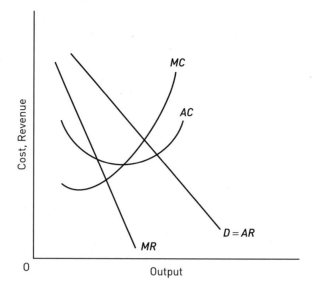

Question 5 Essay: Explain the distinction between 'structure' and 'conduct' in the study of industry. How do these features of the industry landscape influence competition policy?

5

Competitive markets

Judith Mehta

Concepts

- perfect competition
- perfect information, homogeneous products and freedom of entry and exit
- equilibrium of the perfectly competitive firm
- supply curves of the firm and industry in the short and long run
- market equilibrium

Objectives

After studying this chapter you should be able to:

- analyse the behaviour of firms and industries in the model of perfect competition
- understand how demand and supply interact to establish market equilibrium in perfect competition
- appreciate the significance of the model of perfect competition as a policy benchmark.

5.1 Introduction

Article 81

1. The following shall be prohibited as incompatible with the common market: all agreements . . . which have as their object or effect the prevention, restriction or distortion of competition within the common market, and in particular those which:

   (a) directly or indirectly fix the purchase or selling prices . . . ;
   (b) limit or control production, markets, technical development or investment;
   (c) share markets or sources of supply;
   (d) apply dissimilar conditions to equivalent transactions with other trading parties, thereby placing them at a competitive disadvantage;

   . . .

3. [Paragraph 1 may be inapplicable if an agreement] contributes to improving the production or distribution of goods or to promoting technical or economic progress, while allowing consumers a fair share of the resulting benefit . . .

(Treaty of Amsterdam, 1997)

Question	In Chapter 4 it was suggested that highly innovative industries pose an acute dilemma for policy makers (Section 4.6.2). What is this dilemma and how is it reflected in the extract from the Treaty of Amsterdam (1997), which sets out the framework for European Union competition policy?

The policy dilemma is how to protect the incentive to make profits through innovation, while seeking to curb monopoly profits of the kind identified in the static model of monopoly. The influence of the static model is evident in Article 81, paragraph 1's prohibition of agreements (among firms that wield market power) which 'directly or indirectly fix the purchase or selling prices' and 'limit or control production'. You will recall that the model predicts that a monopolist will restrict output to sustain a higher price. However, paragraph 3 acknowledged the importance of dynamic considerations concerning innovation, stipulating that paragraph 1 may be inapplicable if an agreement 'contributes to . . . promoting technical or economic progress'.

At the root of this policy dilemma is an ambiguity in the concept of competition: does competition consist in selling as much output as possible at the lowest possible price or in bringing new products to market? If the former, it seems logical that policy should be guided by the objective of securing the market structure that is as far removed from pure monopoly as possible. In economic theory this is perfect competition and it is the subject of this chapter.

The model of perfect competition is also a source of ideas that inform political as well as economic discussion. You may be familiar with debates in the media in which the advantages and disadvantages of 'the market system', or 'free markets', are discussed. These terms describe a particular way of organizing economic activity. Under the market system, firms are free to decide what to produce and how to produce it, while households are free to decide which to buy of the consumption goods available to them. The plans of all the millions of individual firms and households in the economy are co-ordinated through the adjustment of prices which takes place when buyers and sellers come together in competitive markets.

There are, of course, other ways of organizing an economy. One example is the system of 'central planning', sometimes described as the 'command economy' because it is the government that decides on the level and kind of production and consumption, and the government that determines prices. That is, production and consumption take place 'by command' rather than through voluntary transactions in markets.

In practice, most Western economies (e.g. the US and the UK) are 'mixed economies'. A mixed economy is one in which for the most part firms and households are free to pursue their plans through free market transactions. However, the government exerts some control over production and consumption through taxation and the transfer of payments to those with low incomes, and through the provision of certain goods and services, such as defence, health care and education. It is conventional to refer to this kind of economy as a market economy, while recognizing that it is not a pure case of the market system.

Since the 1980s there have been three contexts in which the market system has featured heavily in public debate. First, many of the erstwhile socialist countries of eastern Europe have moved away from central planning and towards the market system. Second, a programme of privatization has been taking place in the UK and elsewhere under which many organizations previously owned by the government are being transferred into private ownership. In both these cases the idea has been to reduce the role of government in decision-making in favour of a greater role for free markets; you may have seen this idea expressed rather grandly as 'rolling back the frontiers of the state'. Third, as the market system has reached out to almost every corner of the globe, pressure groups have formed to express concern at the impact of free markets on the natural environment and on the world's poorer countries. At the time of writing, these concerns were being expressed under the banner of 'the anti-capitalist and anti-globalization movement'.

Given the intense debate which the market system engenders, why is this particular way of organizing economic activity seen as desirable by so many politicians and economists?

Policy is informed by the belief that markets – or, more specifically, *perfectly competitive markets* – are good for us. It is argued that when consumers are free to 'shop around' for the best bargains, and when firms must compete with rivals selling similar goods and services, then there is pressure for resources to be used efficiently, for goods and services to be produced of the kind and quality that consumers want, and for prices to reach the lowest possible level. These virtues are reflected in the assumptions of the model of perfect competition. When compared with other types of market structure (say, monopoly) and other forms of economic organization (say, central planning), perfect competition leads to better outcomes for consumers. The fact that in reality few, if any, markets in a modern market economy can be characterized as perfectly competitive all of the time does not reduce the relevance of perfect competition as something to aim for.

Because the idea of perfect competition has come to provide such an important, if sometimes contentious, policy benchmark, we need to look carefully – and critically – at how perfectly competitive markets are depicted in the economic models which inform policy decisions. That is the task of this chapter. We will be developing models of the perfectly competitive firm and the perfectly competitive industry, and showing how, according to economic theory, the activities of the supply side of the economy (i.e. producers or sellers) and the demand side (consumers or buyers) are co-ordinated. We will then compare the outcomes of firm behaviour under perfect competition with monopoly and question the realism of this approach to the competitive process: is the model of perfect competition a 'well-designed machine', or does it merely describe a 'special case' where 'its sleek design is too smooth to grasp more than a smaller and smaller fraction of what economists regard as market behavior' (Makowski and Ostroy, 2001, p.531)? By the conclusion of the chapter, you will have acquired deeper insights into competitive market structure; you will also be sensitive to some of the limitations of this approach and, hopefully, feel eager to join the debate.

5.2 The perfectly competitive firm

Do you remember what a model is and what its purpose is in economics? A model is a deliberate simplification of some part of the real world. It is always underpinned by some simplifying assumptions so that we may focus our attention on a clearly defined set of circumstances. The value of models is that they help to develop insights into relations of cause and effect. In order to do this, models emphasize some facets of the real world while playing down or omitting others.

Decisions about what to leave in and what to leave out of a model can be highly contentious, because the insights we get out of a model are sensitive to the assumptions we put into it: change these assumptions and the model will generate different results. This may be an unsettling thought if we would like economics to deliver 'hard and fast' truths. However, it is also an exciting thought because there is the potential to use models to engage in debates about the way the economy works. Perhaps, like me, you are one of those who are attracted to economics for exactly this reason.

There are four simplifying assumptions that underpin the perfectly competitive model. These are that all firms and consumers are price-takers, that buyers and sellers are fully informed, that products are homogeneous, and that there is free entry into and exit from the market. These assumptions are explained in the next section.

▪▪▪ 5.2.1 The assumptions of the model of perfect competition

The reliance of the model of perfect competition on simplifying assumptions is sometimes understood to imply that it need not be taken very seriously. As I suggest in Section 5.5, there is some force in the claim that the model is unrealistic. However, new communications technologies, such as the Internet, have enhanced the potential realism of the perfectly competitive model.

> Visionaries of the 'new economy' tend to present it as getting closer than ever to the universal free market, letting perfectly informed buyers confront perfectly competitive sellers. On the demand side, the new 'friction-free capitalism' promises consumers access to perfect information about all comparable products and their prices. On the supply side, production becomes sufficiently competitive to meet new demand because: (a) there are no economies of scale, so that every product has many competing suppliers; (b) there is costless entry and exit, so that even suppliers with no obvious rivals must set competitive prices to avoid having sales snatched by new arrivals; and (c) there are generic processes and products, giving consumers a wide choice among products that are essentially identical.
>
> *(Adapted from Shipman, 2001, pp.334–5)*

Let us keep these points in mind as we examine the assumptions of the perfectly competitive model.

All firms and consumers are price-takers

You saw in Chapter 4 that under pure monopoly the industry consists of a single firm supplying the whole market for a product. This firm can exercise monopoly or market power because there are no substitutes for the goods or services it supplies. In contrast, a competitive industry is one in which all firms and consumers are small *relative* to the size of the market, so that none of them wields any market power.

The relation of the firm's size to the market is crucial: a 'small' firm in this context may have a very large turnover but still counts as 'small' if it is unable to influence the market price. For example, a city may support many large general music stores but only one small seller of classical music appealing to specialist tastes. The latter is large relative to the local market for such specialized tastes (and hence has monopoly power in the local market) while the general music stores compete with each other despite their greater size. By the same token, a large steel firm may be small compared with the world market for the product.

In determining whether a firm counts as 'small' we therefore have to pinpoint the relevant market. There are general music stores all over the world, but the relevant market is highly localized geographically because consumers will not want to travel far for relatively low-value purchases. In contrast, the relevant market for steel is global; because of the high value of transactions, and the importance to buyers of getting the right kind and quality of steel, the proximity of the firm to the buyer is of less importance.

In a perfectly competitive market, no firm has any monopoly power. What precisely does this mean? One way to model this idea is to suppose that each firm's impact on their market is too small to influence the market price. While a monopolist has to reduce price to sell more, a perfectly competitive firm knows it can sell as much as it likes at the market price. It is so small relative to the market that price reductions are unnecessary even to sell additional quantities that seem large by the firm's standards. And if the firm were to try to raise its price above the market level, it would simply lose sales to rivals who continued to sell at the lower price. Such a firm is described as a **price-taker**. Under these conditions, firms can only choose how much output to sell, rather than being able to choose from among the range of combinations of quantity and price. As a consumer you are probably aware of what it means to be a price-taker in this way; most of us demand quantities which individually are so small relative to the entire market (say, for clothes, CDs or stereo systems) that we are used to taking the market price as given and do not expect to be able to negotiate a lower price. Similarly, many firms are also so small in their market that they must sell what they produce at the 'going rate'.

Price-taker

A price-taker is a firm or consumer whose output or demand is so small relative to the market that it has no effect on the market price.

> **Question** What examples can you identify of goods or services that can only be sold at a price determined by the market?

Many markets contain large numbers of price-taking firms. In the area where I do my shopping, for example, there are many small independent retailers selling eggs whose revenues are determined by market conditions; I can go to any one of them and the price of a box of six medium-sized white eggs will be the same. Similarly, individual operators on the foreign exchanges sell euros for dollars and other currencies at a price dictated by overall market conditions. The clothing industry also contains many small producers who can exercise little individual influence on market prices. The perfectly competitive model supposes a market composed entirely of such small 'actors' with no dominant operators.

Buyers and sellers have perfect information

The significance of this second condition is best illustrated by considering what might happen if it were *not* true. If buyers are poorly informed about the range of prices available and are unable to 'shop around', they have no way of judging whether the particular price being offered by one particular seller is reasonable. Consider a traveller visiting a town for the first time and needing a local guide book. They will be poorly informed about the price of local guide books and the location of shops selling them. A seller who is aware of the customer's lack of knowledge (say, a vendor located immediately outside the railway station) can exploit the situation by raising the price of guide books above the market level; under these conditions, we would say that the seller has a degree of monopoly power.

Local fruit and vegetable markets (see Figure 5.1) are often regarded as highly competitive. They fit the information requirement very well because of the ease of price comparisons: by wandering around the stalls, buyers can easily discover the different prices and qualities on offer. This example shows how important it is for information to be easily available. If it is very difficult to find the price which different suppliers might charge (e.g. for a non-standard car repair), then gathering information becomes costly and consumers may not be prepared to pay these 'search costs'.

Figure 5.1
Price comparisons
are easily made in
fruit and vegetable
markets

Question Can you think of examples of markets in which information about the range and price of products is easily available to buyers and sellers? What mechanisms exist to improve the amount of information available?

In recent years the amount of information available to buyers and sellers has increased because of easier and cheaper access to the Internet. Anyone with access to a computer can log on to any of the many websites provided by suppliers which describe their product range and menu of prices, while suppliers can make themselves known through 'email marketing'.

> We're in a very competitive environment where we're up against huge companies like Mr Kipling and McVities . . . Email has brought us new customers but more importantly it has done the awareness thing for us. If people do not think you exist, they are not going to buy your product.
>
> (The Guardian, *4 October 2001*)

There is evidence that the impact of the Internet on competitive conditions is strongest either where the good or service has very precise characteristics, as in the transactions in stocks and shares, or where it is extremely simple, such as plastic cups or paper napkins, and that it is especially in business-to-business markets that these effects are being felt. Other areas of potential competitive gain are where information between buyers and sellers was previously poorly matched, such as consumer durables, and in the online job market where job posting has grown spectacularly. While it is too soon to be certain about what is happening, it is possible that the information flows generated by new technologies may be leading to more competitive trading conditions, making 'real world' markets more closely resemble the perfectly competitive model (Graham, 2001, pp.145–58).

Products are homogeneous

This is the third assumption. Shopping around by customers is a more effective discipline on the pricing behaviour of firms when the products of the various firms are more similar, or 'homogeneous', in the perceptions of buyers. Moreover, if prospective buyers can see nothing to differentiate one firm's product – say, detergent – from another's, individual suppliers of the product have little room to manoeuvre with respect to price because buyers will simply opt for the cheapest product available. Conversely, if it is believed that the detergent produced by firm A gets clothes cleaner than the detergents produced by all the other firms, firm A will be able to charge more, even if its product is manufactured to the same formula as all the others. Firm A is not then a price-taker. This example tells us that if firms are to be price-takers, products must be regarded as homogeneous in the markets in which they sell.

The discussion of the industry life cycle in Chapter 3 showed that trading conditions can change over time. Consider the market for eggs again. At one time this market could be characterized as perfectly competitive. After all, eggs are easy to standardize (by size and colour), leading buyers to regard one egg of a given grade as the same as another. Moreover, there were many retailers selling this homogeneous product at the prevailing market price. But then some consumers developed a preference for free-range eggs. Eggs are no longer regarded as homogeneous and so we may say that the market has split into two market segments. For a short while, these market segments had different market structures. The original market remains competitive but, because there were only a few suppliers of free-range eggs, each one had an element of market power and was able to command a large premium for its products. As more retailers entered this new market, market power was dissipated. Free-range eggs still cost a little more than those produced using the cheaper intensive-farming methods but, since all of the many retailers of free-range eggs have no choice but to charge the prevailing market price, the market in free-range eggs resembles the model of perfect competition.

There is freedom of market entry and exit

In Chapter 4, you saw that barriers to entry are crucial to the establishment and retention of monopoly or market power. Conversely, for there to be no market power, it must be the case that potential entrants are free to enter the market. This is most likely to be the case when minimum efficient scale is small; set-up costs are then likely to be relatively low, and economies of scale will not pose an entry barrier.

This condition does not require that new entry actually does take place; what matters is that the threat of new entry is real, that is, that the market is *contestable*. There is then no opportunity for existing firms to restrict supply so as to raise prices and profits above the competitive level. Firms already in the market will know that prices and profits would simply be bid downwards by the entry of new firms until each firm is once again earning normal profits; at this point there is no longer any incentive for new entry.

It must also be the case that firms can exit the market at zero cost in the event that production is no longer profitable. The firm which is making a loss (e.g. because it is using outmoded and hence more costly production techniques) then has an incentive to leave the market rather than continuing to produce. As the number of firms falls, and total industry output is reduced, price is bid up until the point is reached at which all remaining firms are making normal profits and there is no longer any incentive to exit. In the model of perfect competition, the firm faces the greatest pressure to use efficient production processes and to produce the kind and quality of products that consumers want to buy.

These four assumptions that underlie the perfectly competitive model are quite tough conditions and few actual markets will satisfy all of them. However, there *are* real-world markets in which monopoly power is very limited. A model of perfect competition, based on price-taking firms exercising no monopoly power, can provide some useful insights into market competition.

▨ ▨ ■ 5.2.2 The competitive firm's demand curve

The demand curve facing the individual perfectly competitive firm reflects its position as a price-taker. Let me remind you of what is being represented when we graph a demand curve. The vertical axis measures price, while the horizontal axis measures the quantity demanded per time period. Each point on the demand curve therefore indicates the quantity demanded per time period at a particular price. In Chapter 3, you saw that the *market* demand curve slopes downwards, indicating that a lower price is required to sell a greater quantity of goods (Chapter 3, Figure 3.3).

The demand curve for the market as a whole slopes downwards whatever the market structure (e.g. monopoly or perfect competition). But for the individual firm in the market, the shape of the demand curve for its own product depends crucially on the structure of the market in question. The shape of the demand curve facing a *price-taking* firm is different from the market demand curve.

Question	What do you think the demand curve facing a price-taking firm will look like? Think about a market you are familiar with in which there are numerous rival suppliers. What do you think would happen if just one supplier were to raise its price while all the others maintained the same lower price?

Let us return to the market for eggs in my locality. Because there are many different suppliers of eggs, if one shop raises the price of eggs while all the others maintain a lower price, I will simply make my purchase at one of the many rival outlets selling identical eggs for less. Since we may expect my neighbours to behave in the same way, the expensive shop will soon find its customer base has dissolved. It will either have to restore the price of eggs to the original lower level or close down.

The greater the choice the consumer has between competing suppliers, the more responsive a firm's demand will be to changes in the price of its own product. This implies that a firm with many competitors will face a fairly flat demand curve; the flatness of the curve indicates that a small price rise will choke off demand. So we can conclude that the price responsiveness of the firm's demand curve tends to increase with the degree of competition, because consumers have plenty of alternative sources of supply if the price is raised. In the extreme case the firm is left with no discretion about price at all. If it raises its own price above the market price, all sales are lost to competitors. At the same time, there is no point in lowering its own price because it can sell as much as it wants at the market price and need not reduce price to sell more. In such a case the firm observes the prevailing market price, and then decides how much to produce. This quantity decision will depend on the firm's costs, as we will discuss below.

Figure 5.2
The horizontal
demand curve
facing a perfectly
competitive firm

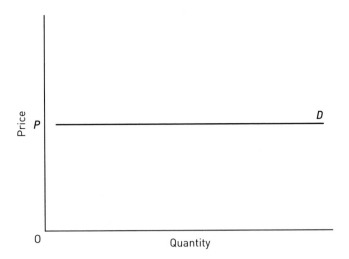

The firm's demand curve gets flatter and flatter as more and more competition is introduced. The perfectly competitive model represents the limiting case, in which there is such a large number of firms selling identical products that the individual firm has no influence on price at all. The perfectly competitive firm's demand curve is therefore horizontal, indicating that it has no discretion at all about what price to charge and is a price-taker (Figure 5.2).

What is the price elasticity of demand of a horizontal demand curve? Recall that its definition is: the price elasticity of demand (ε_D) = proportionate change in quantity demanded divided by the proportionate change in price. As the demand curve gets flatter and flatter, the top part of the equation increases enormously. The proportionate change in quantity demanded becomes very large, for a small proportionate change in price. In the limiting case of a horizontal demand curve, ε_D becomes infinitely large, and the firm's horizontal demand curve is said to be infinitely elastic.

The firm producing in such a market realizes that its actions are insignificant in their effect on price. The market itself determines at what price the product or service should be traded, and the firm determines only how much to sell. Because the individual firm is so small relative to the market, it can sell as little or as much as it likes without affecting market price. But remember: the horizontal demand curve is the demand curve facing the price-taking *firm*. The market demand curve will still be downward sloping.

■ ■ ■ 5.2.3   The competitive firm's output decision

Not all industries are the same. Some industries see the rapid entry and exit of firms as conditions change and market prices fluctuate. This is particularly likely in the early stages of the industry life cycle when the market has yet to be established. Other industries, particularly those that have reached maturity, are relatively stable. The behaviour of the firm will be modelled under both circumstances. We will therefore begin with the output decision of the firm at a single moment holding market conditions constant, and then move on to discuss events taking place as market conditions change and entry and exit occur. Throughout this chapter 'industry' means all the firms supplying a particular homogeneous product to a competitive market.

In modelling perfect competition, firms are assumed to choose their actions so as to maximize profits. We have seen that the perfectly competitive firm has no room to manoeuvre with respect to price. What factors determine the quantity of output produced, given that the firm can sell as much as it wants at the market price? Like the firm with a degree of monopoly power, the perfectly competitive firm will expand output as long as the extra benefits of doing so exceed the extra costs, that is, until marginal revenue is exactly equal to marginal cost. Let us revisit the horizontal demand curve to see what this means and how we can represent it.

Question	Look back at Figure 5.2. Can you draw onto it the marginal revenue curve for the firm facing a horizontal demand curve?

Chapter 4, Section 4.2.3 explained the relationship between the total, average and marginal revenue of a firm. The marginal revenue is the change in total revenue as a result of the sale of an additional unit of output. A firm with monopoly power faces a downward-sloping demand curve. It will therefore find that its marginal revenue curve will be *below* the demand curve because, to sell one more unit, the firm not only has to lower the price of that unit but of all the other units which could otherwise have been sold at a higher price.

However, the relation between demand and marginal revenue looks different for the perfectly competitive firm. With a horizontal demand curve, the price is dictated by the market. The perfectly competitive firm can sell as many units as it likes at the market price and therefore the addition to total revenue from selling one more unit is simply the price for that unit. That is, marginal revenue equals price. For the perfectly competitive firm, marginal revenue does *not* change as output expands. We can now add the marginal revenue curve to the first diagram of the chapter. As Figure 5.3 shows, in perfect competition a single horizontal line represents both the demand (D) and marginal revenue (MR) curves.

What is implied when the demand and marginal revenue curves can be represented by a single curve? You will remember from Chapters 3 and 4 that the demand curve traces the firm's average revenue (AR) at each level of output. As we have just seen, for the perfectly competitive firm, marginal revenue equals price ($MR = P$). Since the firm faces a given market price (P), and since marginal revenue equals price, we have our first conclusion from the model. In perfect competition:

$$AR = MR = P$$

Figure 5.3
Demand and marginal revenue for the firm in perfect competition

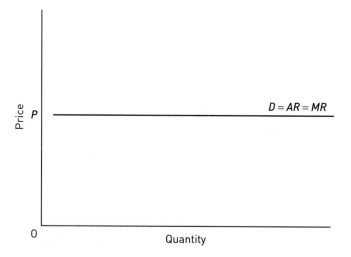

The profit-maximizing output

We can now identify the level of output that will maximize profits for the firm. Intuitively, the argument is as follows. For a given market price, the firm should produce the quantity of output at which the marginal cost of production is equal to marginal revenue; that is, where:

$$MC = MR$$

The argument here is the same as for firms with market power. That is, if marginal revenue is above marginal cost, the firm will increase profits by producing and selling more output. Conversely, if marginal revenue is below marginal cost, the firm can increase its profits by reducing output.

As just noted, for a competitive price-taking firm, marginal revenue is equal to the market price at all levels of output. So for the competitive firm, the condition for profit maximizing reduces to:

$$MC = P$$

This condition is illustrated in Figure 5.4. The only difference between this diagram and the previous one is the introduction of the marginal cost curve, which you will recognize from Chapter 4. Q is the profit-maximizing output. This is the equilibrium output because the firm has no incentive to change its output. To see this, compare Q with Q_1 and Q_2. At Q_1, marginal revenue is above marginal cost, so increasing output will increase profits. Conversely, at Q_2, marginal revenue is below marginal cost, so output should be reduced. There is only one profit-maximizing level of output, Q, which is where $MC = MR = P$, represented by the intersection of the two curves.

Figure 5.4
Profit-maximizing output of a firm in perfect competition

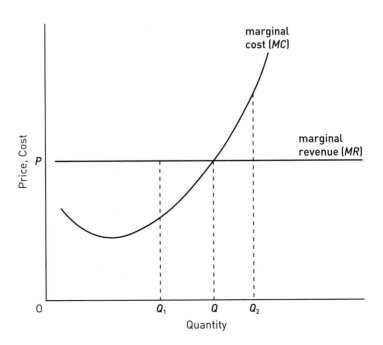

Table 5.1
Output and total
cost of a shirt
manufacturer

Output (shirts/day)	Total cost £
0	12
1	17
2	20
3	21
4	24
5	29
6	36
7	45
8	56

In order to reinforce these ideas, it will help to work through a numerical example, which will be developed further below. Suppose that the firm is a small owner-managed shirt manufacturer operating in a perfectly competitive market. Table 5.1 shows the firm's total cost for different levels of production.

From these figures you can derive the firm's marginal cost for the different levels of output shown. Marginal cost enables the profit-maximizing output to be identified.

Exercise 5.1

1 Derive the marginal cost for each level of output from the data in Table 5.1.
2 If the market price is £7, what output of shirts maximizes the firm's profits?

Exercises like this are not meant to suggest that firms think in terms of marginal revenue and marginal cost curves when deciding on the amount of output to produce. Terms like 'marginal revenue' and 'marginal cost' are parts of the economist's apparatus for modelling decisions, but they may not be part of the vocabulary of the firm. Perhaps it is helpful to imagine a discussion at a board meeting between the marketing director and the production controller along the following lines. If the marketing director believes that the revenue from increased sales will be more than the extra costs which the production manager says would be incurred, the firm will decide to produce more output; conversely, if the revenues from increased sales would be less than the extra costs, the firm will decide not to increase output. The discussion taking place between these individuals is the same as the decision process described by economists but the argument is framed in different terms.

■ ■ ■ 5.2.4 The supply curves of the perfectly competitive firm

Supply curve

The supply curve of a firm indicates how much it will supply at each market price.

Section 5.2.3 concluded that under perfect competition, the firm produces where price is equal to marginal cost:

$$MC = P$$

With a little more analysis of a firm's decision-making we can use this information to derive a supply curve for the firm. The **supply curve** is analogous to the demand

Figure 5.5
The supply
decisions of
the perfectly
competitive firm as
price changes

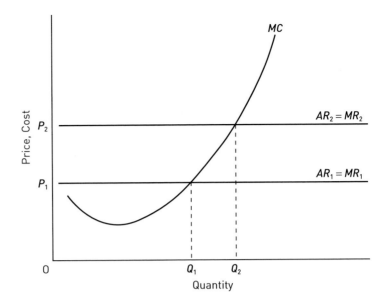

curve in that it provides information about how much the firm will supply at each price, just as the demand curve shows how much consumers will buy at each price. To trace out the firm's supply decisions as prices change, we need to look at the firm's marginal cost curve.

Figure 5.5 shows the profit-maximizing output quantities, Q_1 and Q_2, for a perfectly competitive firm facing two different market price levels, P_1 and P_2. When the price rises from P_1 to P_2, the firm will supply more since the profit-maximizing output has risen. Given the shift of the marginal revenue curve, from MR_1 to MR_2, the extent of the increase in output is determined by the shape of the marginal cost curve. As you know from Chapter 3, the firm's costs depend on the time period specified, whether it is the short run or the long run, so I will look at each of these in turn.

Short-run supply

In order to examine the firm's costs more closely, it is helpful to review the distinction between fixed (or overhead) costs and variable costs (Chapter 3, Section 3.3.1). Fixed costs are those costs which are unavoidable and which do not vary with the level of output in the short run; they include things such as the rent on factory buildings. Variable costs are the costs of those factors of production that vary with the level of output, such as the price of raw materials and the wages paid to labour. The firm's total costs comprise both of these elements.

Figure 5.6 shows the cost curves of the perfectly competitive firm in the short run. We have distinguished between variable and total costs, since this distinction is important to the firm's short-run supply decision. The firm's short-run average cost (*SRAC*) is calculated by dividing the firm's *total* cost in the short run by the number of units produced, for each level of output. The short-run average variable cost (*SRAVC*) is the *variable* cost per unit at each level of output. The two curves converge because a fixed overhead cost is averaged over a larger number of units as output rises. At a market price of P_1 the output level at which marginal cost equals price is Q_1.

Figure 5.6
The short-run cost curves and supply curve of the perfectly competitive firm

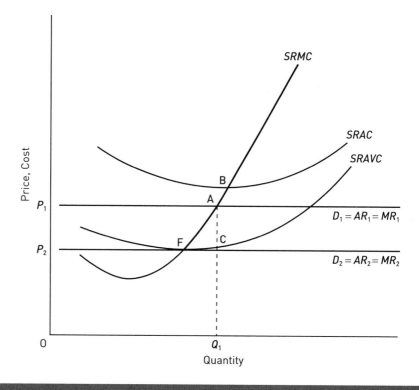

Exercise 5.2

This exercise consolidates your understanding of short-run cost curves. Table 5.2 builds on Table 5.1. We now assume that the shirt manufacturer is operating in the short run. Total cost (and therefore your calculations of marginal cost) remain as before. We assume that the owner-manager of the shirt factory incurs £12 per day in fixed costs for renting premises and equipment. By subtracting £12 from total cost at each output level, Table 5.2 adds a column for short-run variable cost of labour, materials and equipment maintenance to produce each level of output.

Calculate short-run *average* total cost (*SRAC*) and short-run *average* variable cost (*SRAVC*) from Table 5.2. Then draw, using graph paper, the marginal cost, average variable cost and average total cost curves of the firm. Check that the marginal cost curve cuts the average total and average variable cost curves at around their minimum point.

Table 5.2
Output, variable and total costs of a shirt manufacturer in the short run

Output (shirts/day)	Short-run total cost £	Short-run variable cost £
0	12	0
1	17	5
2	20	8
3	21	9
4	24	12
5	29	17
6	36	24
7	45	33
8	56	44

Question Now look again at Figure 5.6. At price P_1, MC = MR at point A, with output Q_1. Will the firm in fact choose to produce Q_1 or will it prefer not to produce at all?

The firm's decision to produce or not to produce depends on the relation between costs and revenues. At Q_1 on Figure 5.6, the price the firm receives for its goods, P_1, is high enough to cover its average variable costs at that output (point C). But P_1 is not high enough to cover its average total costs (*SRAC*) at any output. However, each unit sold is making a contribution to its fixed costs of a size represented by the distance AC on Figure 5.6. The firm is therefore making a loss at Q_1: it is not covering total costs. But its fixed costs are unavoidable in the short run. So in the short run, as long as price is above average variable costs, the firm is better off continuing to produce rather than ceasing production altogether. Q_1 is the loss-minimizing output and the best the firm can do in the short run. The excess of price over variable costs at least makes some contribution to fixed costs.

In the financial pages of the press, you will often come across reports of firms that are operating at a loss. At the time of writing, examples include several airlines, a number of 'dot.com' companies and a football club. Now why would a firm want to continue production in these circumstances rather than simply close down?

Short-run supply curve

The short-run supply curve of the perfectly competitive firm is that part of the short-run marginal cost curve above the short-run average variable cost curve.

We can now identify the **short-run supply curve** of the perfectly competitive firm. The short-run marginal cost curve in Figure 5.6 cuts the short-run average variable cost curve at its minimum point, which is F. If market price falls below price P_2, then the firm is not covering even its average variable costs. This creates a loss which can be avoided if the firm stops producing altogether. At any point on the marginal cost curve between F and B (where B is the point of minimum average total costs) the firm will continue to produce in the short run despite an overall loss. At any point above B, price is above average total costs and the firm will be making supernormal profits. It follows that the emphasized bold part of the firm's short-run marginal cost curve, above point F in Figure 5.6, is also its supply curve.

In order to illustrate these ideas, let us return to the example of the shirt manufacturer appearing in Exercises 5.1 and 5.2. Look again at the marginal cost data that you calculated from Table 5.1. At each price, the firm will supply the quantity at which price equals marginal cost. If the market price is £7, six shirts will be produced per day; if £9, seven shirts.

You can also use your answer to Exercise 5.2 to check the minimum point of average variable costs below which the shirt manufacturer will cease production. When the price is £5 per shirt the manufacturer will make five shirts per day; average variable cost at this output is £3.4 per shirt, leaving a contribution of £1.6 per shirt to fixed costs. So the firm will continue to produce in the short run. As prices fall, the firm will cease production once the revenue from output does not cover the variable costs. For example, at a price of £1, the best the firm can do is to produce three shirts, but to do so it incurs variable costs of £3 per shirt. The firm will do better by producing nothing, forgoing £1 per shirt in revenue but saving £3 per shirt in variable costs. In the short run the minimum price which covers average variable costs is £3. At prices lower than this the firm stops production.

Long-run supply

So far, the analysis has identified the outcome of the supply decision in the short run when the firm's fixed costs are unavoidable. In the long run, the firm has more options available to it.

In the long run, the firm is able to vary all its inputs. There are no fixed costs. Chapter 3 showed that the long-run average cost curve varies in shape depending on the technology the firm is using (Section 3.2, Figure 3.6). The persistence of many small competitive firms in an industry suggests that the minimum efficient scale (MES) is small relative to the size of the market and that economies of scale are limited. Otherwise a dominant firm would emerge. In these circumstances the firm will face a 'U'-shaped long-run average cost curve, the upward-turning portion showing that diseconomies of scale (or decreasing returns to scale) set in at a scale that is small relative to the size of the market.

Let us now derive the long-run supply curve of the perfectly competitive firm just as we did for the short run. Once again, the firm's supply decisions as prices change are traced out by its marginal cost curve. However, the long-run marginal cost (*LRMC*) curve, and hence the *LRAC* curve, is flatter than the short-run curves. The reason is that costs can be reduced in the long run by adjusting capacity as output rises or falls towards the lowest point on the average cost curve (point A in Figure 5.7). This is the MES and marks the level of output at which long-run costs are minimized. The firm will produce where price equals long-run marginal cost provided that price is not below long-run average costs. This means the firm's *long-run supply curve* is traced by that part of the *LRMC* curve which is above minimum average costs, that is, the emphasized bold part of the *LRMC* curve above point A in Figure 5.7.

Before leaving this model of the firm, it is worth noting a further assumption on which it is based, that the firm is endowed with complete information about its own costs, and about trading conditions in the market. A look at the financial pages of any national daily newspaper shows that the real world is characterized by change and uncertainty, which in some cases includes uncertainty about the prevailing market price of a product, or the cost of the inputs required to make that product. For example, a recent press report pointed to the finding that firms can seriously underestimate total costs when venturing into the use of computers by failing to understand what is involved in maintenance and repairs. As a consultant observed, 'Small and medium-sized enterprises generally don't have anyone in-house who can offer them a detailed explanation of all the issues' (*The Guardian*, 4 October 2001).

Figure 5.7
The long-run
supply curve of
the perfectly
competitive firm

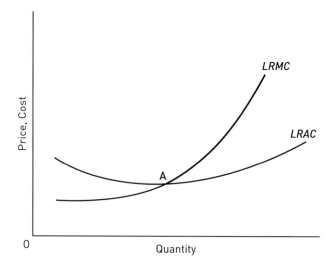

In ignoring the uncertainty that characterizes much of the real world, we are following a practice that is common in economic modelling. We omit certain factors from our analyses, not because they are unimportant, but because they allow the simplest set of circumstances to be examined. Within these limitations, the model has provided answers to three questions faced by the perfectly competitive firm: how much to produce, whether to produce in the short run, and whether in the long run to remain in the industry.

5.3 The perfectly competitive industry

It is nearly 10 years since Body Shop was at its peak [. . .] Since then, the only way for the chain that revolutionised the beauty business with raspberry bath bubbles sold in refillable urine sample bottles has been down [. . .] the real damage has been done by the big corporations, such as Boots in Britain and Bath & Bodyworks in the US, which saw a good idea and decided to do the same. When Body Shop was flavour of the month on the stock exchange, there were no similar products or green-tinged outlets [. . .] Now there are 'natural' products on every supermarket shelf [. . .] Boots was first to copy the formula and now there are new competitors like Lush, that make Body Shop look like a member of the establishment [. . .] Shoppers, meanwhile, are going to supermarkets.

(*Julia Finch,* The Guardian, *3 October 2001*)

The entry of new firms into a market is a common feature of economic activity, as the newspaper article illustrates. When we turn our attention from the competitive *firm* to the perfectly competitive *industry* as a whole, we therefore have to add to the model the entry and exit of firms. Recall that an industry consists of the firms supplying the market for a particular product. The perfectly competitive industry therefore consists of a large number of price-taking firms. Each supplies only a small part of total industry supply and is hence unable individually to influence the market price. In the perfectly competitive model, as in monopolistic competition (Chapter 4, Section 4.4.4), the entry of firms is explained as a response to the existence of supernormal profits, building on the assumption that firms have a single goal, to maximize profits. This is an abstraction from motivations such as 'seeing a good idea and deciding to do the same', which is justified on the grounds that it enables us to construct a systematic model, not trying to explain everything at once but isolating one factor at a time.

Supply by a perfectly competitive industry is determined by two variables: the supply decisions of each firm within the industry, and whether there are new entries or exits. In the short run there is a fixed number of firms in the industry, each deciding on a short-term basis how much to produce according to their marginal costs and the market price. At each market price we can deduce how much each firm will produce and sell, and we can add up these outputs to find the total supplied. The firms' marginal cost curves, and therefore the industry short-run supply curve, will be relatively steep, since some of the factors of production are fixed (e.g. firms can increase output only by more intensive use of existing capital equipment).

In the long run, existing firms can change the scale of their operation, moving along their long-run average cost curve, and firms may enter or leave the industry. The role of supernormal profits in this process can be understood by considering a perfectly competitive industry in which the market price has recently risen sharply. Perhaps the product has suddenly become fashionable. As a result, in the short run, firms in the industry are making supernormal profits, as depicted in Figure 5.8.

Figure 5.8
Short-run
supernormal profits
of a perfectly
competitive firm

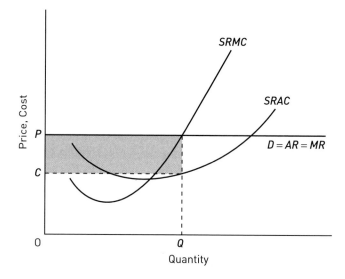

Recall that one of the assumptions of the perfectly competitive model is that firms and consumers are perfectly informed, so the profitability of firms, and their costs and market conditions, are common knowledge. The objective of the firm is to maximize profits – and supernormal profits are, of course, higher than normal profits. The firm depicted in Figure 5.8 will produce output Q at the ruling market price P. It is making supernormal profits equivalent to the shaded area, that is, the difference between price P and average total cost C, multiplied by the number of units of output produced Q.

Question	What effect will supernormal profits have on firms within the industry and those outside it?

Supernormal profits entice existing firms to expand in the long run when all factors can be adjusted, including those which are fixed in the short run. And they attract new firms into the industry. Perfect competition assumes there are no barriers to new entry (Section 5.2.1). If the industry's products call for readily available standardized inputs (e.g. unskilled labour and non-specialized components) then new firms will be able to reproduce the conditions of the existing firms at the same cost levels without any difficulty.

Question	Assuming there are no barriers to entry, what will happen to market price as new firms enter the industry?

As new firms come in, prices are likely to be bid downwards by the increased competition for sales. The supernormal profits depicted in Figure 5.8 will be squeezed. If we assume that firms continue to enter the industry until there are no more supernormal profits to be made, then prices will fall until firms are in the situation depicted in Figure 5.9. It is possible for falling prices to have dramatic effects on the industry. If eager entrants find they have together driven prices below long-run average costs, many firms will fail. This may allow prices to rise again until the remaining firms can cover costs. One example of expansion and new entry occurred in the late 1990s when it became fashionable in the

Figure 5.9
The perfectly
competitive firm
in long-run
equilibrium

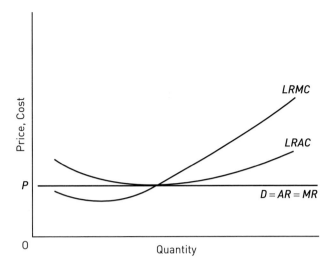

**Price elasticity
of supply**

Price elasticity
of supply is a
measure of the
responsiveness of
supply to changes
in price.

UK to take a break from work or shopping in one of the new-style coffee shops. Existing chains of coffee shops expanded and new firms moved into the market to take advantage of the profits to be made. It is now the case that most large towns and cities have so many alternative coffee shops that it is difficult to see how profitability can be maintained.

Figure 5.9 supposes that the firm shown is representative of the whole industry. However, if all the firms in the industry were exactly identical, using the same technology of production and, hence, with the same cost curves, we would have an 'all or nothing' situation in which all firms would leave the industry when price was below the minimum average cost, or all would enter for prices above this cost level. This does not seem realistic. It is perhaps more reasonable to think of this firm as the *marginal* firm in the industry, where its normal profits represent the best new entrants can expect. Some older firms may be doing rather better, say, as a result of being the first to enter the industry.

What shape is the industry supply curve in the long run? Industry supply is likely to be more price-elastic (**price elasticity of supply**) in the long run than in the short run, as illustrated in Figure 5.10. (Price elasticity of demand was explained in Chapter 4, Section 4.2.4.) If prices rise from P_1 to P_2, supply will increase in the short run to Q_2. In

Figure 5.10
Short-run and long-run supply curves of a perfectly competitive industry

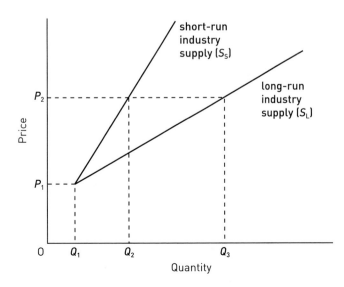

the long run it will rise further from Q_2 to Q_3 as new firms come in. The long-run supply curve (S_L), however, is still likely to be upward-sloping. New firms may be less efficient than older firms and the industry as a whole may experience cost constraints on expansion. For example, the labour needed by firms entering an expanding industry may not be attracted away from other industries except at increased wages. The industry supply curve then slopes upward, showing the higher price needed to coax in additional factor inputs and, hence, the rise in costs as total industry output increases.

The model of perfect competition thus allows us to construct short- and long-run supply curves for the perfectly competitive industry. These industry supply curves are the supply curves for a product in a perfectly competitive market. We can draw these supply curves independently of the particular demand conditions obtaining at any moment in the market as a whole.

This completes the analysis of supply under perfect competition. In the next section we will draw together the supply side and the demand side of the market.

5.4 Market demand, supply and equilibrium

In a competitive market, prices of goods and services can change with some rapidity, and people react to price changes. The model of the perfectly competitive market assumes that buyers as well as sellers are price-takers. Individual consumers make their buying decisions in response to the prevailing market price, and market demand is the sum of their decisions. As you know, for the market as a whole the demand curve is downward sloping, implying larger total demand at lower prices. This section brings together market demand and supply curves to show the results of the interactions between a great many price-taking individuals.

■ ■ ■ 5.4.1 Reinterpreting demand

The downward-sloping market demand curve can be thought of as the sum of many individual consumers' demand curves for an industry's product. As Chapter 3 noted, *ceteris paribus* (all other things being equal) people can be expected to buy less of a product as its price rises. If we take the *ceteris paribus* qualification seriously, and set aside the socio-economic influences on consumption discussed in Chapter 3, we can interpret the demand curve in a way that will be useful for evaluating perfect competition in Section 5.5.

We can consider each consumer as an independent decision maker, and make similar assumptions about self-interest as we made for firms. Just as the firm is assumed to pursue the maximum possible profits, so the consumer is assumed to pursue the maximum possible satisfaction, or 'utility'. (The concept of utility will be explained in Chapter 8.) Consumers are assumed to know what is in their own best interests and to make choices consistent with these interests, given the income at their disposal. Within such a framework we can analyse how a consumer will choose between the different products available. It quickly becomes clear that it is purchases at the *margin*, that is, the last music CD or the last can of cola purchased, that are particularly important in influencing market prices. This is similar to the earlier analysis of the firm where it is the cost of the *marginal* unit, that is, of the last unit produced, which is relevant to the decision about how much to produce.

Like the firm, the consumer in a perfectly competitive market is a price-taker, facing market prices over which she or he has no control. To allocate income so that utility is maximized, she or he must spend it in such a way that the last euro's worth of each product provides her or him with equal utility. If this was not the case, the consumer could still transfer a euro from a product which provides less utility, to one which provides more, thereby increasing total utility. Without such adjustment the consumer would not be acting in the rational way which this model of decision-making requires (as Chapter 8, Section 8.3.2 explains in more detail).

The implication of this line of thought is that, in allocating income among competing possible purchases, the consumer will adjust consumption until the ratio of the utility derived from the last or marginal euro spent on a good to the price paid for that good is the same for all the goods the consumer purchases. So, for example, if a new stereo system costs twice as much as the cost of the last improvement made to your home, then it must have been worth twice as much to you. If that stereo system was worth any less, you could have maximized your satisfaction by buying a cheaper system and spending more on home improvements.

There are two assumptions that are important to this analysis of demand. The first is that more consumption increases satisfaction. The second is that the more we buy of something, the less the last or marginal unit is worth. So as we buy more of something, the price we are willing to pay for it falls. For example, when I am ravenously hungry I am willing to pay a great deal for a bar of chocolate which provides some satisfaction. A second bar provides extra satisfaction but by an amount which is less than the first bar because the edge has been taken off my appetite; as a consequence, I'm willing to pay less for it. The amount of extra satisfaction I gain from a third bar is even less, and so on.

This approach enables us to interpret the demand curve in a new way. The demand curve is not only a description of how much is bought at each price, but for each individual it represents the *willingness-to-pay* for the last unit of each good bought. Under this interpretation we can see that price-taking consumers both contribute to total market demand and at the same time determine their own demand depending on the given market price.

How, then, is market price determined in an environment in which no single actor has any influence? We need to bring the information about supply and demand curves together.

■■■ 5.4.2 Market equilibrium

The individual firm, the individual consumer and the industry can be brought together in a three-part diagram, Figure 5.11. Figure 5.11(a) shows a typical price-taking consumer, with a downward-sloping demand curve. This curve shows how much this individual will buy of the good in question at each price. Total market demand is the horizontal addition of individual demand. That is, if there are a million consumers just like this one, the total demand for the good will be one million times that quantity at each price. This aggregate demand is described by the market demand curve in (b). Notice that the units of measurement of output on the horizontal axis of (b) must be much larger than those on (a) (or (c)).

Similarly, Figure 5.11(c) shows the marginal cost curve of a typical price-taking firm. The firm maximizes profit at the point where (horizontal) marginal revenue is equal to marginal cost, so at levels of marginal cost above minimum average costs, this becomes the firm's supply curve. The industry supply curve *is* the market supply curve. Therefore if there are 500 such firms in the industry, the supply to the market will be 500 times the supply from each individual producer. Total market supply is the horizontal addition of the individual supply curves and is shown in (b).

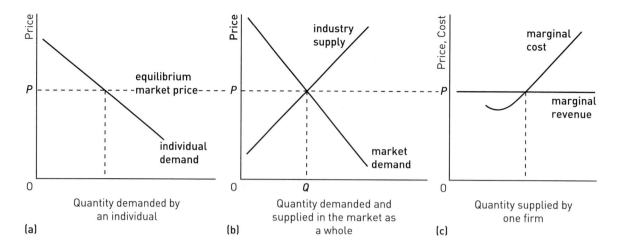

Figure 5.11
Consumer's demand (a), market equilibrium (b), and firm's supply (c)

Figure 5.11 (a) and (c) therefore represent the equilibrium for each price-taking consumer and producer, that is, the best position they can achieve given the market price. Figure 5.11(b) shows how the individual decisions of consumers and producers interact in the market to determine the equilibrium price, *P*. The point of intersection of the market demand and supply curves identifies the point at which the market is in equilibrium, that is, the price at which quantity supplied equals quantity demanded. By following the dashed line across to the vertical axis, you can read off the equilibrium price, *P*; and by following the line down to the horizontal axis, you can read off the equilibrium quantity, *Q*. At this point there is no pressure for change from within the market: given the market price, *P*, no consumer wishes to purchase any more or less, and no producer wishes to supply any more or less. So this is the *market equilibrium*.

The market price that each consumer observes determines the amount they choose to buy (represented by their individual demand curves); by the same token, the market price also determines both the quantities supplied by individual producers and how many producers choose to be in the market. There is thus a constant interaction between buyers and suppliers in the market: the market sends price signals which are in turn translated into quantity decisions by individual actors, which feed back into the market to determine the equilibrium price.

▨ ▧ ▪ 5.4.3 Changes in market conditions

We know from earlier analysis that the slope of the supply curve depends on whether we are considering the short or long run. Similarly, consumers will be able to make a fuller response to price changes (say, changing the type of heating system if there is a change in the price of a fuel) over a longer period. Once the time period is established, supply can be analysed in the same way as demand. The same distinction between shifts in the curves and movement along them is valid.

Question	Which types of change would cause a shift in a supply curve, and which a movement along it?

The important distinction, again, is between responses to price changes (movements along the supply curve) and to changes in other factors (shifts of the curve). Variables that affect the amount a firm is prepared to supply at a particular price are reflected in the marginal cost curves from which the supply curve is derived. Changes in these variables therefore cause the supply curve to shift. The effect on the industry supply curve depends on whether the cost changes are particular to the firm or experienced across the industry as a whole. For example, fluctuations in the world price of oil are a common occurrence and have an industry-wide effect where oil and oil-based products are a significant factor input. When the oil price rises, all airlines find their operating costs rising, and may 'ground' a proportion of their aircraft. Conversely, a single airline may find itself in trouble for firm-specific reasons, such as poor management.

Question	A virulent disease destroys a high proportion of the year's crop of coffee beans. What effect will this have on the market supply curve for coffee beans and on the equilibrium price? What will be the wider effects of this event? What would you expect to happen in the long run? Assume that the market for coffee is perfectly competitive.

The drop in output of coffee beans as a result of the disease reduces market supply at each price, shifting the short-run supply curve to the left. Figure 5.12 shows this leftward shift of the supply curve from S_1 to S_2. At the old equilibrium price, P_1, there is now *excess demand*. At P_1, people still wish to buy Q_1, but only Q_3 is now on offer. The price will have to rise to P_2 before the supply of and demand for coffee beans are back in equilibrium at output Q_2. The effect of the shift of the supply curve is to raise the market price.

Events taking place in this market will have a knock-on effect in other markets. For example, at higher coffee prices, we would expect consumers to buy more of cheaper substitutes such as tea, increasing the demand for tea and hence its price. We cannot say precisely what will happen in the long run. Firms which are badly hit by higher coffee prices may decide to exit from the industry, particularly if the disease proves difficult to eradicate and expectations of future profits are diminished.

Figure 5.12
A shift in the market supply curve for coffee beans

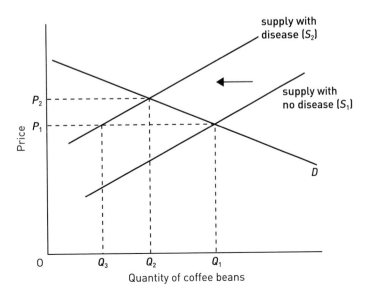

Question	A new technology for the transmission of electric power is developed. Only 7 per cent of the energy originally generated is lost in transmission, and one super-conductive cable can transmit the same quantity of electricity as three of the old-style copper cables. What effect will this have on the supply curve and the equilibrium price?

This is a rather trickier case to analyse. This innovation has already taken place and at the time of writing new super-conductive cables are beginning to be laid in Detroit in the USA. The new technology will reduce costs once electricity suppliers have had time to invest in the new distribution process. Assuming for the sake of argument that the market is perfectly competitive, we can speculate on what will happen to the price of electricity on the assumption that the technology is widely adopted by the industry.

Assume that the new technology reduces the average cost of production of power at all levels of output. The effect is to shift each firm's cost curves downwards. As a result, each firm will be willing to supply more output at the current market price and also at all other market prices that allow profitable operation; that is, the firm's supply curve shifts to the right.

Exercise 5.3

This exercise will ensure that the last point is clear. Look back at Figure 5.4, which is the same as Figure 5.11(c). Copy the *MC* and *MR* curves and then sketch on your diagram the effect of the new technology on the marginal cost curve. Show the new profit-maximizing output, assuming market price remains constant.

Adding up the firms' new supply curves implies that the market supply curve shifts to the right. Firms already in the industry will together supply more at each market price. Figure 5.13 shows the shift in supply from S_1 to S_2. At the old equilibrium price, P_1, there is *excess supply*: people still want to buy Q_1 but Q_2 is available. Price will have to fall to P_2 before the supply and demand for electricity are back in equilibrium at Q_3.

Figure 5.13
A shift in the supply
of electricity

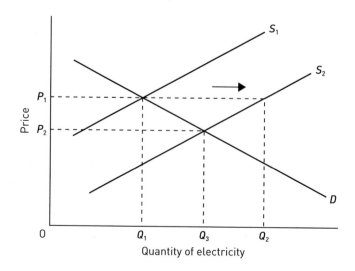

This analysis has identified the characteristics of market equilibrium; it does not tell us anything about the process by which the market moves from one equilibrium to another but compares two equilibrium positions. This kind of analysis is called a *comparative static* analysis of changing market conditions. The results of the analysis can be very useful when applied to real market situations. For example, they can be fed into the calculations of electricity suppliers to help them decide if it would be worthwhile to invest in the new transmission technology.

Exercise 5.4

Suppose that unexpectedly warm weather has a beneficial effect on Florida's orange groves leading to an increase in the supply of orange juice. Assuming that the market is perfectly competitive, what will happen to the equilibrium price? Illustrate your answer with a diagram, and comment on the way in which the market might shift from the old equilibrium to the new one.

In each example of a change in market equilibrium, shown in Figures 5.12 and 5.13, the initial disturbance was caused by a shift in the supply curve. The new equilibrium was found at another point along the demand curve, which did not shift. In the real world, there are continuous shifts in both demand and supply, as tastes and preferences change, new technologies are introduced and unexpected events take place. As the coffee bean case demonstrates, the effect of a change is unlikely to be restricted to a single market. Under these conditions, long-run equilibrium really does seem like a distant horizon – always in sight but never quite reached!

Case study: An economic history of chocolate

The story of chocolate can be traced backed at least as far as the Mayan Indians who described cocoa as 'the food of the gods'. Thought to contain chemicals that, when consumed, stimulate the production of natural opioids in the brain, the cocoa bean was revered also by the later Aztecs who used it as a form of currency. Around 1500, Spanish explorers were the first to bring cocoa beans to Europe where they were used to make drinks until the mid nineteenth century when an English company introduced the first solid bar, a product subsequently refined by Swiss candle-maker, Daniel Peter, who gave the world its first taste of 'milk' chocolate.

For most of the twentieth century (1910–79), Ghana was the world's largest supplier of cocoa beans, though trade with the outside world was heavily influenced by companies who used their market power to buy beans from producers at the lowest prices possible. During the late 1920s and 1930s a number of Ghanaian farmers boycotted these trading companies who had tried to avoid increasing prices to producers. Much later, towards the end of the 1970s, as cocoa prices plunged, many Ghanaian farmers cut down trees for timber and planted other food crops in their place.

Like many other commodities, cocoa prices have oscillated dramatically during the past 30 years. High market prices during the 1970s encouraged an expansion of production to the point where, by the end of the 1980s, world production had reached 2.4 million tonnes. Prices fell in response to this increase in supply and consumption rose too, but only slowly. As a result, stocks of cocoa accumulated, and prices began to fall again.

This behaviour illustrates two important aspects of market behaviour. First, both supply and demand are subject to long-term changes. Second, there is a lag between crop planting and production which means that, when prices are high, producers invest in more plants but the effect on supply has

Case study continued

to wait for the plants to mature. At that time, the market becomes flooded and prices plummet.

By 2004, the USA was still the largest consumer of cocoa in the world, taking up 22 per cent of the world's production each year. In recent years, Brazil's demand has grown dramatically and new markets in Asia, where there has been little tradition of cocoa consumption in the past, are expected to develop rapidly.

On the production side, supplies have benefited from a range of government policies in a number of countries. In Brazil and the Côte d'Ivoire, development and rehabilitation programmes encouraged farmers to use modern hybrid plants. Indonesia also promoted cocoa production as a means of generating economic growth in rural areas.

In 2005, the Head of Economics and Statistics in the International Cocoa Organization concluded

that the future for cocoa was 'bright' as demand was expected to exceed supply in the medium term while promotional campaigns and scientific advances in production were thought likely to have effects on the market over the longer term.

Questions

1 What factors have encouraged the growth in demand for chocolate?

2 How would you represent a shift in demand on a price–quantity diagram?

3 Do you think the demand for chocolate will continue to grow in future?

4 What impact will changes in demand have on the equilibrium price of chocolate?

Figure 5.14
Scene from the film *Chocolat*

5.5 Monopoly and perfect competition compared

Just one task remains to complete our analysis of competition within a comparative static framework and this is to compare the outcome of perfect competition with the outcome of pure monopoly for a particular industry. The only difference under consideration is a difference in the number of firms from just one to 'very many'. This means we can compare

Figure 5.15
Monopoly and
perfect competition
compared

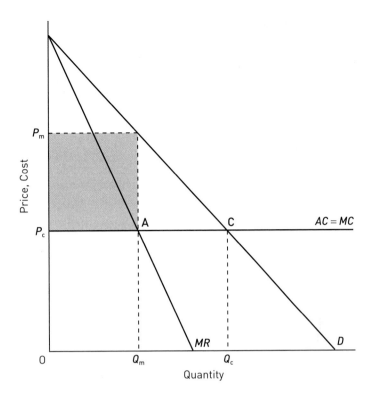

the behaviour of the *same* industry under monopoly and perfect competition. All the components of the analysis will be familiar to you; it is simply a case of bringing them together.

Figure 5.15 shows a firm, a monopolist, producing for a market that is *potentially* perfectly competitive. Let us imagine that government regulations have protected the industry from new entry. *D* is the market demand curve; because the firm is a monopolist, *D* is also the demand curve facing the firm. *MR* is the monopolist's marginal revenue curve. Notice that *MR* is downward sloping and lies below the demand curve at every point. This indicates that, in contrast to the perfectly competitive firm, the monopolist must reduce price in order to sell more output (and must reduce output in order to set a higher price). As a consequence, marginal revenue falls as output increases. *AC = MC* is the firm's average cost and marginal cost curve, showing that the firm faces constant returns to scale across the output range.

Question	Think back to Chapter 4. How does the monopolist decide on the quantity to produce and the price to charge? What is the size of the monopolist's profits?

The profit-maximizing level of output for any firm, whether in monopoly or perfect competition, is found where marginal cost is equal to marginal revenue. For the monopolist, this is Q_m in Figure 5.15 (follow the dashed line down from point A). The market demand curve shows that at output Q_m the price is P_m (follow the dashed line up from Q_m, through point A, to where it just meets the demand curve). The size of the monopolist's profits is represented by the shaded rectangle in the diagram. The supernormal element is measured by the excess of price over average cost, multiplied by the quantity sold:

$$(P_m - AC) \cdot Q_m$$

What happens under perfect competition? Let us suppose that the government has deregulated the industry, allowing in new entrants. The market is now supplied by a large number of broadly similar price-taking firms. The cost conditions in the industry are being held constant, and so the constant returns to scale experienced under monopoly are carried over into perfect competition. The line $AC = MC$ is therefore the industry supply curve in the long run as industry output expands. You can think of the industry as composed of many small firms, all operating at minimum long-run average cost as in Figure 5.9. Industry output expands at price P through the entry of new firms operating at the same cost. The effect is a horizontal industry supply curve.

The intersection of that supply curve and the market demand curve D at point C gives the equilibrium level of output in the market under perfect competition. This is Q_c at the equilibrium price P_c. Since price equals average cost, the firms in the industry are making normal profits.

Question   What does Figure 5.15 tell you about consumer satisfaction under monopoly and perfect competition?

The monopolist charges a higher price and produces a lower quantity than the market price and quantity under perfect competition. Consumers are therefore worse off under monopoly than under perfect competition. Not only do they face higher prices under monopoly, they are not able to buy the quantity of output given by $Q_c - Q_m$. The introduction of competition therefore benefits consumers in these two important respects.

The result of the comparison of the models of monopoly and perfect competition is an important one. It is often called upon to justify the use of perfect competition as a benchmark for industrial policy.

Question   To see what this might mean, look back at the quotation from the European Union's Treaty of Amsterdam in Section 5.1. Can you see an influence of the model of perfect competition in these clauses?

The prohibition on activities that prevent, restrict or distort competition reflects a belief that competition is the most important safeguard of consumers' interests. The particular prohibition on limiting production and on creating competitive disadvantage for particular firms reflects the comparison you have just studied between monopoly and perfect competition: free entry of firms and competition on equal terms defines competition in these documents. Article 81, paragraph 3 picks up the model in another way. Competition is desirable – as the comparison between models suggests – because it produces benefits for consumers. Hence paragraph 3 permits exceptions to competition regulations only where, as a result of agreements to promote innovation, it is clear that consumers still reap 'a fair share of the resulting benefit'. Chapter 6 will further analyse competition policy and agreements between firms.

As a result of these considerations, European competition policy has frequently promoted market conditions that bring markets closer to meeting the assumptions of the model of perfect competition. This is what we mean by the model being used as a 'benchmark' for industrial policy. For example, the European Commission – like the UK competition authorities – has blocked mergers between firms that would reduce the total number of firms in the market. More generally, the effort to integrate the European economies to create the single European market is aimed, in part, at creating competition among firms that previously held protected positions in national markets. A larger integrated market implies more competing firms. The presumption underlying these policies is that a larger number of firms in a market implies more competition and benefits for consumers. This presumption is rooted in the economic comparison outlined in this section between monopoly and perfect competition.

While the perfect competition model has in this way influenced industrial policy, the model is nevertheless the subject of considerable criticism from economists. A particularly severe critic of the realism of the perfect competition model was offered by Friedrich Hayek, an economist who thought of competition not in terms of models of market equilibrium but as a dynamic process:

> The theory of perfect competition has little claim to be called 'competition' at all. If the state of affairs assumed by the theory ever existed, it would not only deprive of their scope all the activities which the very verb 'compete' describes but would make them virtually impossible.
>
> Advertising, undercutting, and improving ('differentiating') the goods and services are excluded by definition – 'perfect competition' means the absence of all competitive activities.
>
> *(Hayek, 1976)*

The model of perfect competition provides one interpretation of competition. The perfectly competitive firm is a price-taker and cannot survive unless it can maintain its costs at a level that allows it to earn normal profit by selling its output at the prevailing market price. This is certainly a form of competition many of us encounter when we go shopping at the fruit and vegetable stalls illustrated in Section 5.2. However, as the quotation from Hayek (1976) reminds us, this form of competition is only one way in which firms may compete. In concentrating exclusively on it, the perfect competition model fails to accommodate competition through differentiating goods and services in the manner discussed in Chapter 4, Section 4.2.

Furthermore, although the effects of widely available technological change can be analysed in the model, as in Section 5.4.3, the concept of perfect competition cannot easily accommodate competition through innovation. The industry life cycle, explained in Chapter 3, suggested that individual firms often compete through innovation, by introducing new products or new technologies of production. This form of competition lies beyond the perfect competition model and calls for a different kind of analysis of industrial dynamics, moving away from the models of representative firms to models that allow firms to be very different. This theme from Chapters 2 and 3 is taken up again in Chapter 6.

The policy implication is that an industry consisting of many small firms cannot necessarily be relied upon to remain in that condition. If it is an industry in the introductory phase of its life cycle, the likeliest prospect is of increasing concentration and the emergence of a dominant firm. Competition policy must therefore be sensitive to the particular characteristics of each market.

> There are rather few examples of market structures or conduct which we can condemn unambiguously as not being in the public interest. Similarly, there are few market practices to which we can give a definitive assent. In most examples, 'it all depends' on the particular circumstances under consideration.
>
> *(Hay and Morris, 1991, p.609)*

5.6 Conclusion

The general result of the model of perfect competition is that in a market where firms and consumers are price-takers, we are more likely than in a monopolized market to observe low prices, higher output and profits at no more than the normal level. There are markets in the real world which satisfy, or very nearly satisfy, the conditions for perfect competition. Under these conditions, the model generates some real insights into the outcomes of a competitive market structure. Many markets are, however, as we have discussed in earlier chapters, far removed from the ideal described by 'perfect competition'. These markets are supplied by industries that supply differentiated rather than homogeneous products; they are characterized by poor information, a high level of instability and change, competition over non-price aspects of products, barriers to entry and exit, and a tendency towards a small number of large firms rather than a large number of small firms. This does not mean that competition is absent from such markets. However, under these very different conditions a different approach to the modelling of competition is required. In the next chapter, Vivienne Brown will develop an approach to competition that can shed more light on the behaviour of firms in these markets.

Questions for review and discussion

Question 1 Complete the following sentence:

For a market to be highly contestable, there must be

A ❏ a large number of firms already in the market.
B ❏ extensive network externalities.
C ❏ virtually costless entry to and exit from the market.
D ❏ significant economies of scale in production.

Question 2 Complete the following sentence:

A firm in perfect competition

A ❏ unlike a monopolist, can increase its marginal revenue by increasing output.
B ❏ that is maximizing profits in the short run must be producing at a level of output where $MR = SRAC$.
C ❏ may be able to lower its average costs to a limited extent in the long run by adjusting its capacity.
D ❏ that is maximizing profits in the short run should increase its output in response to a fall in the price of its product in order to continue to make maximum profits.

Question 3 Figure 5.16 shows cost curves and revenue curves for a firm in perfect competition and currently making normal profit.

Label the diagram correctly by inserting appropriate labels, from the selection provided below, on the graph.

LRMC   AFC   SRAVC   SRAC   SRMC   AR   LRAC   MR

Figure 5.16
Cost and revenue
curves for a firm in
perfect competition
and making a
normal profit

Question 4 Figure 5.17 shows cost and revenue curves for a firm in perfect competition. Which of the following is true?

A ❑ The firm would do better not to produce at all rather than produce output Q_1, as revenue at output Q_1 is not sufficient to cover total costs.

B ❑ The firm is making supernormal profit in the short run, as price is greater than average variable costs.

C ❑ The firm could raise its profit/reduce its losses in the short run by increasing output to bring in higher revenue.

D ❑ The firm cannot raise its profit/reduce its losses in the short run by increasing output to bring in higher revenue.

E ❑ The firm cannot raise its profit/reduce its losses in the short run by adjusting output.

Figure 5.17
Cost and revenue
curves for a firm in
perfect competition

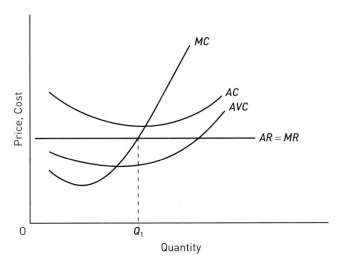

Question 5 Figure 5.18 shows cost and revenue curves for a Firm A, a firm newly attracted into a perfectly competitive market by the availability of supernormal profits. Draw a shift in the AR curve as necessary to illustrate each of the following:

Figure 5.18
Cost and revenue
curves for Firm A

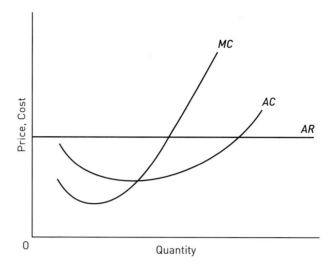

(a) More new firms enter the industry, reducing but not eliminating Firm A's supernormal profit.
(b) The entry of new firms continues, leading to a situation in which Firm A will decide to leave the industry.

Question 6   Figure 5.19 shows the cost curves of a firm operating in a perfectly competitive market.

Use the letters on the diagram in answering the questions below:

(a) Indicate the short-run supply curve of the firm.
(b) Assuming a marginal firm in long-run equilibrium, redraw the diagram and mark in the average and marginal revenue curves.
(c) Indicate on your diagram as 'Q' the level of output and as 'P' the price charged. What is the level of profit? Explain your answer.
(d) Assume the demand for the product of this industry declines. Using a diagram, illustrate the effect of this on the industry price and output, and briefly discuss the wider effects of this change.

Figure 5.19
Cost curves of a
firm operating
in a perfectly
competitive market

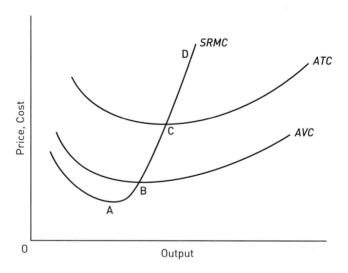

Strategic competition: conflict and co-operation

Vivienne Brown

Concepts

- strategic competition
- oligopoly
- duopoly
- game theory
- dominant strategy
- commitment
- cartel; explicit collusion
- implicit collusion

Objectives

After studying this chapter you should be able to:

- understand what is meant by strategic competition and how this may include elements of conflict and co-operation
- understand what is meant by game theory and be able to apply the prisoners' dilemma game and first-mover advantage game
- analyse issues in strategic competition such as advertising, output cartels, price fixing, price wars and strategic alliances
- understand some issues concerning competition policy as applied to strategic competition.

6.1 Introduction: strategy matters

Competitive behaviour between firms is sometimes described in the language of 'war'. We read in the newspapers of a 'price war' among firms when prices are reduced aggressively to try to boost market share by taking sales away from rival firms. This happens from time to time in many sectors of the economy, including the major retailing sectors and the markets for specific consumer goods or services. Rival supermarket chains keep a close watch on their market shares and periodically battle for customers by slashing prices. In 2001, at a moment when four supermarket chains – Tesco, Sainsbury's, Asda and Safeway – controlled half of the grocery sector in the UK, another price war seemed to be under way. Claims and counterclaims were made about price reductions, and some of these were even taken to the Advertising Standards Authority. In price wars of this sort, firms seem to have opposing interests.

At other times, relations between firms competing in the same market seem to go to the opposite extreme; instead of the language of 'war', it is now the language of 'alliance' and 'partnership' that provides the keywords. For example, in 1999 an alliance was formed between France's Renault and Japan's Nissan when Renault took a 36.8 per cent stake in Nissan. At that point Nissan was ailing, but within two years Nissan's loss had been turned into a profit, and the success of the Renault–Nissan alliance had become the subject of numerous books and business-school case studies, including one by the Harvard Business School (*The Economist*, 2001a). Here, corporate profits had been given a boost by the formation of an alliance with a rival firm rather than by attempting to wage war against it. In cases of this sort, firms seem to have mutual interests.

Although these two types of firms' behaviour – waging war and forming alliances – are so different, there is one thing that they have in common: firms are *interdependent*, in that each firm's actions will affect rival firms, whose reactions will in turn affect their rivals. A firm in this situation will have to take into account the expected reactions from rivals in making its own plans, and if a firm is really smart it will prompt rivals into reacting in ways that are beneficial to it. In such cases the simple contrast between opposing interests and mutual interests seems to break down, and what we see are various mixes of conflict and co-operation. Competition between firms that is characterized by interdependence is known as **strategic competition**. This type of competition is different from both perfect competition and monopolistic competition, and we are going to be analysing it in detail in this chapter.

In the perfect competition model, which you studied in Chapter 5, firms take the market price and technology as given and so do not go in for price cutting or innovation. In the monopolistic competition model, that is, competition between firms with monopoly power (Chapter 4), firms typically compete through product differentiation or innovation. But in neither of these types of models do firms take into account the expected reactions of rivals when deciding what to do. So these models miss a key feature of many important markets, including the grocery sector, the motor industry, the airline industry, commercial banks and the markets for many basic household items, including foods, soft drinks, cigarettes . . . the list goes on and on.

Firms in these markets certainly find it profitable to cut prices, or to innovate, or to advertise. In so doing, however, they may well take into account their interdependence with rivals, and the smartest of them will choose their actions to ensure a favourable reaction from other firms. Sometimes, firms compete globally, as in the case of automobile producers, but they could be competing for a national market, as in the case of supermarket chains, or even a local market, as in the case of two restaurants facing each other across a town square.

The practical examples of strategic competition are thus extremely wide-ranging, encompassing both markets supplied by a very few firms and those supplied by a sizeable number of firms. The term for a market comprising a few firms is **oligopoly** and a firm operating in an oligopoly market is known as an *oligopolist*. If there are only two firms, the market is known as a **duopoly** and the two firms are *duopolists*. Oligopolistic markets typically display strategic competition, but the crucial point about strategic competition is the interdependence of the firms not the number of them. Strategic competition is less likely if the number of firms is large, but the number of firms that may compete strategically depends on the characteristics of specific markets.

Strategic competition is the subject of this chapter, and we shall study it using a new modelling technique: *game theory*. The policy implications of strategic competition will be considered briefly in the final section of the chapter.

Strategic competition

Strategic competition means that firms need to take account of expected reactions by rivals when making their plans.

Oligopoly

An oligopoly is a market supplied by only a few firms.

Duopoly

A duopoly is a market supplied by two firms.

6.2 Introducing game theory

▪▪▪ 6.2.1 Game theory

The analysis of strategic competition uses *game theory* because it provides some of the conceptual tools required for modelling interdependence. Game theory has applications beyond economics, including the modelling of war, politics, business and personal and family relations. In an introductory book on game theory entitled *Thinking Strategically: The Competitive Edge in Business, Politics, and Everyday Life*, the authors Avinash Dixit and Barry Nalebuff compare game theory with planning a war.

> [T]hink of the difference between the decisions of a lumberjack and those of a general. When the lumberjack decides how to chop wood, he does not expect the wood to fight back; his environment is neutral. But when the general tries to cut down the enemy's army, he must anticipate and overcome resistance to his plans. Like the general, you must recognize that your business rivals, prospective spouse, and even your child are intelligent and purposive people. Their aims often conflict with yours, but they include some potential allies. Your own choice must allow for the conflict, and utilize the co-operation.
>
> *(Dixit and Nalebuff, 1991, pp.1–2)*

Dixit and Nalebuff explain that the general must think strategically in planning ahead and anticipating the enemy's reactions. So, if the general's objective is to win the war, not just the next battle, he has to have a forward-looking strategy. The general needs to look ahead to where he wants to be at some point in the future, and then think backwards to the present from that desired point. The same follows for a firm: if a firm wants to increase its market share or eliminate a rival, it has to look ahead to that future, and then think back to the present and plan accordingly. This implies that the environment facing the firm is not neutral, as firms' actions produce feedback effects that influence their environment. Thus theories of strategic competition emphasize that the business environment – the market or industrial structure – within which firms operate is not simply given to them as a natural part of the landscape, but may be constructed by their own actions. This is something we shall examine later in this chapter.

Dixit and Nalebuff argue that life is itself a 'game', and that strategic thinking is required in just about all aspects of life; just as a general calculates his best strategy vis-à-vis the enemy, so business rivals, spouses and parents calculate the best course of action. You may think this claim is inappropriate (or offensive) but the thinking behind it has been extensively applied in economics. Notice, too, how Dixit and Nalebuff incorporate both conflict and co-operation in the passage. They recognize that players will not always have aims that conflict, and they advise them to utilize the potential for mutually bene-ficial co-operation as well as allow for conflict. Just as a general needs to cultivate allies as well as to isolate the enemy, so a firm sometimes needs to establish co-operative relations with others as part of its overall competitive strategy to advance its own aims. Here again we see the combination of conflict and co-operation that is so typical of strategic competition.

It is worth pausing a moment here to note some of the basic terms you will need in this chapter.

- A *game* is a situation involving interdependence.
- The *players* in a game are decision makers.
- A *strategy* is a plan of action available to a player.
- *Strategic decisions* recognize the mutual interdependence.
- A *pay-off* is a player's gain (or loss) from particular strategies. A pay-off can be anything that is valued (or disvalued) by the players. In economic games, the pay-off will be an economic variable such as profit, revenue or sales.

Game theory

Game theory is a technique for modelling strategic choice as a game between players.

These terms help to define what is meant by **game theory**, which analyses the range of 'best moves' available in a situation of mutual interdependence such as strategic competition. Thus game theory is the study of *strategic decision-making*.

Game theory assumes that players are self-interested in that they try to maximize their own *pay-off* from the game. In economic games, the pay-off is usually taken to be profits, output or sales, but there is no restriction on the form the pay-off can take. A game may be a one-off game or it may be a repeated game played again and again.

The behavioural assumptions of game theory are:

1 *individualistic* – the pay-off is calculated individually for each player without recourse to wider notions of collective well-being; and

2 *rationalistic* – players are deemed able to calculate pay-offs correctly and then select the one that will maximize individual pay-off.

In presenting a game, the range of potential pay-offs are presented in a *pay-off matrix*, which is a tabular array showing all the various possible outcomes on the basis of which the players individually select their own preferred strategy. The actual values of the pay-offs are normally selected arbitrarily to illustrate particular outcomes of a game and are not intended to represent realistic values for actual games played out in real situations. This means that it is the structure of pay-offs that is important rather than their absolute levels.

■ ■ ■ 6.2.2 Introducing the prisoners' dilemma

Have you ever wondered why there is so much advertising, and whether it would be better for firms if they spent less on it? If all firms were to reduce their advertising, then perhaps each would increase its profits; if sales are unaffected and costs are lower, the profits should be greater. Why don't firms try this? One answer to this question is derived from game theory using one of the most famous of all games: *the prisoners' dilemma*.

The prisoners' dilemma game has been applied to many different situations. The interest of the game lies in the paradox that it highlights, namely that individual decision-making can lead to an inferior outcome for the players in comparison with joint decision-making. The name of the game comes from a story that illustrates the nature of the paradox. This story involves two prisoners who are held for questioning concerning a crime which they are alleged to have committed together. The prisoners would each do better if they were both to deny the crime, but when they are interrogated separately each one confesses. How can such an apparently paradoxical result happen?

In this game the prisoners (the players) are faced with just two options (the strategies): to deny having committed the crime, or to confess and thereby implicate the other player. Each prisoner must decide individually which strategy to choose. The terms of the game are such that the prisoners have no experiences beyond the game, so that only the pay-offs matter; there are no shared norms of behaviour, for example, or enforcement agencies.

In addition, assume for the moment that the game is played just once; this kind of game is called a 'one-shot' game. The pay-offs for the prisoners take the form of years of imprisonment, so the objective of each prisoner is to minimize their individual pay-off. The question is: which strategy – confess or deny – will each prisoner choose? Any moral considerations (e.g. the virtues of telling the truth) are set to one side.

As each of the two players faces two options, there are four possible strategy combinations or strategy pairs: each prisoner confesses; each prisoner denies; the first prisoner confesses and the second denies; and the first prisoner denies and the second confesses. The structure of the pay-offs is such that individual decision-making leads each prisoner to confess, as this yields a lower pay-off whether the other prisoner confesses or denies. But if each of the prisoners confesses, they both end up worse off than if each had denied.

The significance of this result is that it shows how individual decision-making can, in certain circumstances, lead to an inferior outcome for each player in comparison with joint decision-making. If the prisoners are indeed guilty, you might think that it is good that they are not able to achieve a better outcome for themselves by falsely denying the crime – but the result of the analysis also applies if the prisoners are innocent! There are many situations in the real world in which the details of the 'story' are different but the structure of the problem is the same.

■ ■ ■ 6.2.3 The prisoners' dilemma game

I said above that it is the particular structure of the pay-offs in the prisoners' dilemma game that results in the paradox. Let us now see how this works. The prisoners' pay-offs are set out in Figure 6.1, in a form called a pay-off matrix. Take some time to look at Figure 6.1 carefully. There are two prisoners, A and B. Each of the prisoners has a choice of two strategies: 'confess' or 'deny'. There are $2 \times 2 = 4$ possible strategy pairs: A and B deny, A and B confess, A denies and B confesses, and A confesses and B denies. These four possible strategy pairs are represented by the four cells in the pay-off matrix; inside each cell is written the prisoners' pay-offs to each strategy pair. The pay-offs are given in terms of years of imprisonment. A's pay-offs are the first entry in each of the four cells, followed by B's.

The aim of the game for each of the players is to minimize the period of imprisonment. The actual values in this matrix have been chosen to illustrate the structure of the pay-offs (i.e. the relationship among the pay-offs) that is characteristic of the prisoners' dilemma. To keep the arithmetic simple, each of the players here faces the same pay-offs as the other player; this means that the matrix is symmetrical. The game does not depend on this, however, and you will meet a matrix that is not symmetrical in Exercise 6.1.

Figure 6.1
Pay-off matrix showing the prisoners' dilemma

		Prisoner B	
		confess	deny
Prisoner A	confess	3, 3	1, 4
	deny	4, 1	2, 2

Dominant strategy

A dominant strategy is a strategy that has the better pay-off for a player irrespective of the other player's strategy.

Which strategy will each prisoner choose? Let us start from A's point of view. If B confesses (reading down the first column of Figure 6.1), A would get 3 years for 'confess' and 4 years for 'deny'. So it is better for A to confess. If B denies (reading down the second column), A would get 1 year for 'confess' and 2 years for 'deny'. So again it is better for A to confess. Thus, whether B confesses or denies, it is better for A to confess. In the terms of game theory, 'confess' is the **dominant strategy** for A, as this is better for A no matter what B's strategy is.

| Question | Now try it for yourself. What is B's dominant strategy? |

The analysis here is symmetrical with that for A. If A confesses (reading across the first row), B's pay-off is 3 years for 'confess' and 4 years for 'deny', so B would be better off confessing. If A denies (reading across the second row), B's pay-off is 1 year for 'confess' and 2 years for 'deny'. Again, 'confess' is the dominant strategy for B.

It follows that, in the prisoners' dilemma game, each player has a dominant strategy: 'confess'. This is the outcome of the game. According to the matrix in Figure 6.1, if each prisoner confesses then each receives 3 years' imprisonment (top left-hand cell). But if each denies, each one receives only 2 years' imprisonment (bottom right-hand cell)! Individually choosing the best strategy leads to an outcome that is inferior for both of the players. It follows that a better outcome requires the prisoners individually to choose a strategy that appears to be worse for them. That is the paradox of the prisoners' dilemma.

Exercise 6.1

Another example of a prisoners' dilemma game is shown in Figure 6.2. The strategies are expressed quite generally as 'co-operate' and 'not co-operate'. The pay-offs here can be anything that is valued by the players; this implies that the players are trying to *maximize* their pay-offs. Note too that in this example the two players are not facing the same pay-offs, so the matrix is not symmetrical.

What is the outcome of the prisoners' dilemma game shown in Figure 6.2?

Figure 6.2
A prisoners' dilemma game

		Player B	
		co-operate	not co-operate
Player A	co-operate	3, 5	1, 6
	not co-operate	4, 3	2, 4

▨ ▪ ■ 6.2.4 Advertising as a one-shot prisoners' dilemma game

Now we are ready to go back to the issue of advertising. How can the one-shot prisoners' dilemma game help us to understand why firms spend so much on advertising? Figure 6.3 presents an advertising game. In this, we assume that there are two duopolists, A and B,

Figure 6.3
An advertising game

		Firm B	
		high advertising	low advertising
Firm A	high advertising	4, 4	12, 2
	low advertising	2, 12	10, 10

each producing mobile phones, and that each has a choice of two strategies: 'high advertising' or 'low advertising'. The economics behind the matrix is as follows. If A goes for high advertising expenditure and B goes for low advertising expenditure, then A has greater profits than B because B loses business to A. But if each firm chooses high advertising each one receives lower profits than if each firm chooses low advertising, since in the latter case each is spared the expense of advertising and the sales are largely unaffected. In the pay-off matrix in Figure 6.3, the pay-offs are the individual firms' profits. Note that in this case each firm is trying to *maximize* its pay-off.

Question   **What is the dominant strategy for each firm in the advertising game in Figure 6.3?**

In this game the dominant strategy for each firm is high advertising, as whatever the other firm's strategy, there is a greater pay-off individually to high advertising than to low advertising. Consider A. If B's strategy is high advertising, then high advertising is better for A than low advertising (4 > 2). If B's strategy is low advertising, then high advertising is better for A than low advertising (12 > 10). So A goes for high advertising. The same holds for B. Thus each firm goes for high advertising and the pay-off is 4 for each firm (top left-hand cell).

Of course, the firms would have been better off with the strategy of low advertising, with a pay-off of 10 each (bottom right-hand cell). Modelling the choice of advertising strategy as a prisoners' dilemma game may thus explain why each firm individually chooses a high-advertising strategy, even though a low-advertising one would have been more profitable for both.

▪▪▪ 6.2.5   The paradox resolved?

Surely, you might say, intelligent players can find a way to resolve the paradox illustrated by the prisoners' dilemma? If individual decisions do not lead to the co-operative outcome, why don't the players abandon individual decision-making in favour of joint decision-making, and thereby jointly choose the 'co-operative' outcome: the prisoners could agree jointly to deny and the firms could agree jointly to choose low advertising? In the prisoners' dilemma game, however, decisions are made *individually*, not jointly; and what the one-shot prisoners' dilemma game shows is that an agreement will not be kept in the presence of individual decision-making unless that agreement coincides with individual choices. In other words, individual decision-making will not support an agreement unless there is some **commitment** that binds players to a joint agreement by making individual decisions coincide with the joint decision.

Commitment

Commitment binds players to a joint agreement by making individual decisions coincide with the joint decision.

A fundamental point about the one-shot prisoners' dilemma game is that commitment is absent: there are no mechanisms for committing individuals to a joint decision by making individual decisions coincide with the joint one. This is why agreements collapse and the co-operative outcome eludes the players. As an illustration of this, consider a slight variation to the one-shot prisoners' dilemma story. Suppose the authorities allow the prisoners to meet beforehand to discuss their strategy. The prisoners promise to deny when the time comes. The trouble, however, is that there is nothing to bind the players to this promise. When the prisoners return to their cells, the decision to be taken is still an individual decision, not a joint decision. Individually, the pay-offs are still such that A and B each works out that, whether or not the other player keeps to the promise, confessing is the better strategy. This follows from the terms of the one-shot game: decisions are made individually by the players; only the pay-offs matter to the players; and the game is played once. In these circumstances, when they are back in their cells, each player still confesses. It turns out that having a meeting and agreeing beforehand makes no difference to the outcome of the game: the co-operative outcome is as far off as it was before.

This analysis shows that players cannot resolve the paradox of the one-shot prisoners' dilemma game within the terms of the game as stated above. As the paradox follows strictly from the terms of the game, however, we can work out how the paradox could be resolved if those terms were different. If the pay-offs are not all that matters to the players, or if the game is repeated, then it may be possible for the players to achieve the co-operative outcome even when the strategies are chosen individually. We will consider each of these situations separately.

If the pay-offs are not the only thing that matters, then there might be shared norms or practices that could provide commitment and so ensure that individual promises are kept. For example, returning to the prisoners, if shared norms strongly proscribe implicating others (honour among thieves), or if the prisoners are members of a gang and know that other gang members will harm them for confessing after their imprisonment is over, these norms and practices could provide commitment by ensuring that the prisoners individually choose to deny.

However, if the norms and practices *themselves* ensure commitment, making a promise beforehand may be redundant! The reason for this is that if the norms and practices that provide commitment do not depend on the existence of a promise, then the promise is not necessary. For the prisoners, this implies that if the norm of honour among thieves is an unspoken norm, or if gang members know about the likelihood of reprisals, then either of these could be sufficient to ensure commitment without the need for a promise beforehand. What emerges from this analysis is that an agreement without commitment is ineffective, but commitment may not require an agreement. We shall return to this result when we consider implicit collusion.

The story of the prisoners was presented above as a one-shot game, but the prisoners' dilemma game may be played repeatedly. When the prisoners' dilemma game is repeated, players need to look ahead and take the pay-offs in further rounds into account. In this case, each prisoner wants to minimize imprisonment over the repeated rounds of the game, not just the current round. Looking ahead in this way over many rounds of the game may result in individual decisions that lead to the co-operative outcome. Thus, in repeated prisoners' dilemma games, commitment may be provided by the individual incentive to minimize imprisonment over repeated plays of the game.

These two basic approaches to resolving the paradox of the prisoners' dilemma can be applied to cases of strategic competition. The next two sections consider different types of strategic competition: Section 6.3 examines output restrictions and Section 6.4 examines pricing and strategic competition.

Exercise 6.2

It was emphasized above that it is the structure of the pay-offs, not their absolute levels, that is significant. To see more clearly what this means, try to construct your own version of the one-shot prisoners' dilemma game using your own numbers. Try this for yourself before looking at the answer to this exercise. The answer presents a general form of the pay-off matrix for a one-shot prisoners' dilemma game, showing the relationships among the pay-offs, which you can use to check your own matrix.

6.3 Collusion to restrict output

■ ■ ■ 6.3.1 Cartels and the prisoners' dilemma

During the late 1990s and early 2000s the price of unprocessed coffee fell sharply because increased world production was outstripping sales. This sharp fall in price hit coffee producers, including the many small family producers of unprocessed coffee in countries such as Tanzania, Columbia and Brazil. Individual producers of unprocessed coffee are too numerous and too small relative to the world market to have any impact on the world price, and in this respect the world market for unprocessed coffee can be modelled in terms of a perfectly competitive market (Chapter 5). But if the producing *countries* could get together perhaps they could jointly decide on market supply; this would help to smooth out fluctuations in market price and possibly maintain a more remunerative price over the longer period. This would involve suppressing competition between them and jointly exercising some monopoly power (Chapter 4). The countries might thus be able to achieve a better outcome by forming a **cartel**, which could take joint decisions on behalf of its members.

Cartel

A cartel is a group (of firms, countries) which makes joint decisions with a view to increasing the combined profits of its members by suppressing competition between them. This behaviour is also known as *(explicit) collusion.*

Ideally for the members (although not necessarily for consumers), a cartel could function as a monopolist in trying to maximize combined profits for the cartel, although it might also try to use its regulatory power to improve the functioning of the industry. It would be up to the individual members to negotiate their output quotas and their shares of the profits. In practice, cartels are unlikely to control all the output in an industry and so cannot aspire to a pure monopoly; the question is whether they can control sufficient output to meet their objectives.

This is what the Association of Coffee Producing Countries (ACPC) tried to do. In 2000 a Retention Plan was agreed in which members would reduce their exports of coffee by 20 per cent in order to increase (and stabilize) the world price. An earlier scheme to buttress the price of coffee by reducing the quantity coming onto the market had broken down in 1989, but in 2000 the ACPC had high hopes that its plan would work.

We can use the analysis in Section 6.2 to model the problems that cartels face in sustaining agreements of this sort. Member countries have a joint incentive to keep to the agreement, but each individual country has an incentive to break it. If all member countries break the agreement, however, the agreement collapses. This is a classic example of the tensions between conflict and co-operation that can be modelled using the prisoners' dilemma game.

Assume that there are two countries which produce good *x*, country A and country B. The two strategies are 'restrict output' and 'default' (by not restricting output). These options are shown for A and B in the pay-off matrix in Figure 6.4, which represents a one-shot prisoners' dilemma game. The pay-offs are the individual countries' profits. The economics behind this matrix is that if each country restricts exports, the price rises and

Figure 6.4
Cartel to restrict output

		Country B	
		restrict output	default (not restrict output)
Country A	restrict output	200, 200	100, 250
	default (not restrict output)	250, 100	150, 150

so the pay-offs increase for each country. If neither country restricts, the price falls and so the pay-offs fall for each country. If one restricts and the other defaults, the restricting country has a lower pay-off and the defaulting country has a higher pay-off, because the restricting country suffers from the price fall caused by the other country without the benefit of the defaulting country's extra sales. Will the cartel be successful?

Question	Will the cartel be successful according to the pay-off matrix in Figure 6.4?

Consider A's strategy. If B restricts output it is better for A to default, as this gives a pay-off of 250 rather than 200. If B defaults it is better for A to default, as this gives a pay-off of 150 rather than 100. So A goes for the 'default' option. As this game is symmetrical, the same holds for B. The outcome of the game is that each player defaults with pay-off of 150 (bottom right-hand cell).

The outcome of the game is inferior to one in which each country restricts output with a pay-off of 200 (top left-hand cell). Although the best outcome for the players (not the consumers!) is that each should keep to the agreement, deciding on output levels individually means that both countries default. Again, deciding on strategy individually results in an inferior outcome for the players.

Thus, although it might seem that a cartel could achieve a better outcome for the players, this is not possible if there is no commitment to the joint decision; and cartel members cannot be committed to the joint decision if each has an individual incentive to break it. If default remains on a small scale, the cartel may survive but, as soon as default becomes sizeable, the cartel will collapse as the increased output drives down the price. This is what happened to the ACPC in 2001 when the Retention Plan was formally abandoned in the face of a failure to reduce exports. The ACPC is an example of a country cartel but the same analysis holds for a cartel of firms.

Exercise 6.3

There are two firms. If each one increases output, the pay-off for each firm is 300. If each one reduces output, the pay-off for each firm is 500. If one increases output and one reduces output, the pay-off for the increasing firm is 600 and the pay-off for the reducing firm is 200.

1 Draw the pay-off matrix and fill in the pay-offs for the two firms to the strategies 'increase output' and 'reduce output'.
2 If the pay-offs are all that matter to the firms, explain whether they could successfully collude to reduce output.

▨ ▪ ■ 6.3.2   Successful cartels

Not all cartels collapse. OPEC (Organization of Petroleum Exporting Countries) is one of the best-known of all output cartels. OPEC monitors a reference basket of crude oils and seeks to maintain price (and an orderly market) by means of output quotas for member countries. There are three main problems for OPEC in doing this. The first problem is controlling the members' output of oil. The second problem is forecasting demand, as the demand for oil is sensitive to world economic growth (which in turn responds, with a time lag, to the price of petrol). The third problem is that OPEC members do not account for all oil production and OPEC has little influence over non-OPEC oil production; at the time of writing in 2001, OPEC members accounted for about 40 per cent of world oil output.

In spite of the ups and downs it has experienced, OPEC has not broken up as ACPC has. This implies that in spite of the difficulties involved, especially the second and third problems just mentioned, OPEC is managing to control its members' output of oil to some degree. How can this be explained? Remember that, in the prisoners' dilemma game, only the pay-offs matter, and in the one-shot version the game is played only once. Both of these features of the game may be unrealistic in real-world applications.

In a real-world application of the game, whether repeated or not, the pay-offs may not be all that matter. This means that norms of behaviour, institutional practices and non-economic factors extending beyond the pay-offs may also influence behaviour. Furthermore, for many real-world situations it is more appropriate to think of the game as being played repeatedly. Output is always measured over a period of time, but this time element is missing from the matrix in Figure 6.4. The matrix needs to be reinterpreted in terms of output produced over a specified period of time, say a day, a week or a month, so that the game would be played repeatedly, every day, week or month. This implies that players would need to look ahead and take into account not only the current pay-offs but also those in further rounds. This in turn requires that players consider the reaction of the cartel or of other members if they default in the current play of the game. It is the presence of both these factors that helps to account for the fact that some cartels achieve a measure of success.

A cartel is successful only if members are individually committed to a course of action that supports it, so the question is: what provides commitment to the agreement? As we know from the analysis in Section 6.2 of the one-shot prisoners' dilemma game, players may be bound to the agreement if there is something beyond the pay-offs that matters to the players. This 'something' may be rooted in the experiences, relationships, practices or cultures beyond the game that provide norms, social sanctions or incentives for the players in deciding on their strategy. For example, a cartel composed of countries may punish cheating by political means, or there may be ways in which the cartel can exert other forms of economic pressure on members to conform. A cartel composed of firms is unlikely to be able to exert non-economic forms of pressure against defaulting members, but it may have different ways of exerting economic pressure against firms that default on the agreement.

Furthermore, we know that commitment may also be secured by players individually maximizing their pay-offs in a repeated prisoners' dilemma game as they look ahead and think back. In this case, the strategies chosen individually by players over many repetitions of the game may lead to a co-operative outcome for the players. For example, a cartel could create incentives for individual members to keep to the agreement if it imposed penalties for default in the form of lower pay-offs in future rounds of the game, such that overall pay-offs were lower for default than for keeping to the agreement. If the cartel members look ahead and realize this fact, the threat of punishment by the cartel might provide commitment. Changing the pay-offs by punishing default would thus provide commitment by ensuring that the strategies chosen individually by players coincide with those that are needed to maintain the agreement.

For commitment of any sort to be effective, defaults have to be detected. This may be easier if the number of players (countries or sellers) is small and the game (setting output or price) is repeated frequently, or if information about the members is readily available. Furthermore, influences beyond the pay-offs or further repetitions of the game have to matter for present choices. If players do not care about anything beyond the pay-offs or about what happens in further rounds of the game, then the pay-off in the present game is all that matters. For the threat of punishment in repeated games to have an effect, it is also necessary for the game to be played indefinitely without a known end-point. The reason is that there must always be a further round of the game in which the punishment can be carried out, but a known end-point undermines this. Finally, the punishment has to be certain; this implies that the threat of punishment has to be 'credible', that is, players must believe that they will indeed be punished if they default. If the threat is not credible, players will ignore it.

Thus cartels may sometimes be able to achieve greater combined profits (or greater stability of market shares) by means of explicit collusion in the form of agreements over, say, output levels or prices. As we found out in Section 6.2, an agreement without commitment is likely to be ineffective. This implies that a successful cartel needs to provide some means of binding players to the agreement by making players' individual decisions coincide with the joint decision (e.g. by punishing defaulting firms). But we also saw in Section 6.2 that commitment may not require an agreement as such; and this implies that commitment may not depend on the cartel's activities at all. This brings us to the paradoxical secret of successful collusion: if the commitment necessary for successful collusion does not depend on the *explicit* collusion provided by a cartel, successful collusion may not require a cartel at all! In this case, the players are said to be engaged in *implicit* collusion. This is an important point, because it implies that explicit collusion may not be necessary for collusive behaviour. Implicit collusion is the subject of the next section.

▪ ▪ ▪ 6.3.3 Implicit collusion

Implicit collusion

Implicit collusion occurs when firms behave as if they are colluding but there is no agreement to do so.

Implicit collusion occurs when players individually choose strategies that lead to those outcomes that would have been agreed jointly by the players, although agreement has not in fact taken place.

Implicit collusion also requires commitment. Mechanisms that might provide commitment for implicit collusion may be provided by the practices of the market; even though each player decides on strategy individually and there is no collusive agreement, the market context may provide commitment to collusive behaviour. We shall examine an example of this in connection with pricing in the next section.

Implicit collusion may also be sustained in repeated prisoners' dilemma games by players individually learning which strategies promote the collusive outcome. For example, strategies that punish defaulting firms in a repeated game may emerge without joint agreement. A big player may come to assume the role of 'enforcer' in punishing defaulting firms by flooding the market and letting prices fall. Small defaults may be tolerated, but if they become widespread the big player punishes the others by itself defaulting. The big player may thus periodically have to reinforce the point that pay-offs in further rounds of the game will be severely reduced if players default in the current round. Such a punishment strategy works by making default less profitable to players individually over repeated games.

Another strategy is known as 'tit-for-tat': a player follows another player's default with default but follows co-operative play with co-operation. Cheating is punished and good play is rewarded. As the game is repeated indefinitely, players come to learn that it is not in their interests as individuals to cheat on others, even though there is no joint agreement. Players need to implement some 'forgiveness', so that co-operative play is reinstated and another's default is not punished for too long, otherwise the players would get stuck in default mode with no one backing down. The strategy of a 'forgiving' version of tit-for-tat has been found to be very effective in securing the co-operative outcome in simulated prisoners' dilemma games (Axelrod, 1990).

Returning to OPEC, it is possible that different kinds of co-operative behaviour may help to explain its continued existence, if the cartel is modelled as a repeated-play prisoners' dilemma game. There may be a sense of common cause that helps to bind members to the joint decision, but individual incentives to co-operate are based on each member's realization that cheating (or, at least, too much cheating) reduces individual pay-offs over repeated plays. Furthermore, Saudi Arabia with its high output and large reserves has functioned as the big player that is prepared to flood the market and punish default by smaller countries.

Similarly, in a cartel of firms, shared activities such as trade associations or social inter-connections may help to promote implicit collusion. Firms may also learn over repeated plays that it is not in their individual interests to cheat, and, again, large firms may function as the enforcer of last resort in maintaining discipline even in the absence of any explicit agreement to do so.

This section has shown that explicit agreement is not necessary for collusive behaviour. Section 6.4 examines the possibilities for implicit collusion over pricing.

6.4 Pricing and strategic competition

We saw in Section 6.1 that price wars sometimes take place. But one puzzle is why price wars do not occur more frequently. This section presents a game theory approach to price wars and non-price competition.

6.4.1 Price wars

In 2001 a price war hit PC makers. This was partly a defensive reaction to poor sales growth, as the PC market was reaching saturation just as the global economy was thought to be sliding into recession. The headlines of such price wars make dramatic reading, and consumers benefit from the low prices, but out-and-out price wars are relatively rare. We will build on the argument of the previous section to show how implicit collusion can enable firms to escape from the prisoners' dilemma that can lead to a price war.

The extent to which price cutting increases a firm's profits depends partly on the elasticity of the firm's demand curve and partly on how rival firms react. For any given demand conditions, we can model price cuts for two firms by supposing that there are two strategies: 'leave price unchanged' and 'cut price'. The pay-offs are the firms' profits and these are shown in Figure 6.5. The economics behind this matrix is that if one firm cuts price and the other does not, then the price-cutting firm gains. If each firm cuts price they both lose out; there may be some increase in the total quantity demanded at the lower price, but it is not enough to compensate for the reduction in price.

Figure 6.5
A price war:
Round 1

Firm B

		leave price unchanged	cut price
Firm A	leave price unchanged	100, 100	80, 110
	cut price	110, 80	90, 90

Question   Start with B this time, and identify the firm's dominant strategy.

As in the earlier one-shot prisoners' dilemma games, each player has a dominant strategy. B will note that whether A leaves price unchanged (top row) or cuts price (bottom row), B's best strategy is to cut price. A's dominant strategy is the same. The outcome is that each firm has a pay-off of 90. But each firm would have been better off leaving its price unchanged, with a pay-off of 100! Each firm calculated individually that it was better to cut price, but when they both did so they simply spoilt the market for themselves. Again, individual decision-making yields an inferior outcome for the players.

What can each firm do now? Should each fight to the finish? To answer this we need to consider what would happen if a similar game were played again, that is, we need to model what would now be Round 2 of a price war. This is shown in Figure 6.6. Starting from the end of the first round of the price war with pay-offs of 90, the economics behind the matrix is the same as in Figure 6.5 but the price at which firms start the game is lower. So 'leave price' in Figure 6.6 refers to the 'cut price' in Figure 6.5, which is where the firms finished in Round 1.

Question   Is there a dominant strategy in the game shown in Figure 6.6?

The game in Figure 6.6 is similar to the one in Figure 6.5. Each firm has a dominant strategy which is to cut price and so each firm ends up with a pay-off of 80, although both firms would have been better off if each had left price unchanged. What we now have is a price war that is harming both firms.

The two rounds of the price-cutting shown in Figures 6.5 and 6.6 illustrate the cumulative nature of change as firms interact with each other over time. But could there

Figure 6.6
A price war:
Round 2

Firm B

		leave price unchanged	cut price
Firm A	leave price unchanged	90, 90	70, 100
	cut price	100, 70	80, 80

Figure 6.7
An alternative
round 2: Reversing
the price war?

		Firm B	
		leave price unchanged	increase price
Firm A	leave price unchanged	90, 90	110, 60
	increase price	60, 110	100, 100

have been a different Round 2 in which firms reversed the price cuts of Round 1 and put the pay-off back to 100 from 90, instead of further reducing it from 90 to 80 as we saw in Figure 6.6? Let us consider an alternative scenario for Round 2 by considering two strategies 'leave price unchanged' and '*increase* price'. This is shown in Figure 6.7. If each firm leaves price unchanged then each has a pay-off of 90; this was the outcome at the end of Round 1. The strategy 'increase price' for one firm with 'leave price' for the other firm would result in profits of 60 for the former and 110 for the latter, as customers switch to the firm with lower prices. If each firm raises price then each would have a pay-off of 100. The question is: can the firms reverse the price war on the basis of individually choosing their strategies?

Question	To see whether the firms can reverse their price war, consider the outcome of the game in Figure 6.7.

Each firm has a dominant strategy of 'leave price unchanged' with a pay-off of 90. Neither firm individually has an incentive to raise price as doing this will cause sales to be lost to the rival firm, even though each would be better off if they were both to do so. The lesson is that once a price war has started it is not easy for firms individually to return to the pre-war situation.

If firms are forward-looking, however, they can look ahead and see this too! Firms can thus recognize that destructive price wars may be the outcome of current price cutting. Once we move from a one-shot game to the idea that similar games may be played indefinitely, players need to look ahead and anticipate the consequences of their actions. As we saw earlier, just as an army general needs to look ahead and then think back to the present and plan accordingly, so too does a firm. This suggests that firms individually may well learn how *not* to engage in price wars, that is, they learn to co-operate.

Exercise 6.4

Two rival airlines, FlyingHigh and HighFlights, with similar levels of quality and service, are each considering whether to introduce a discounted fare below the current standard fare. With present standard fares, each airline has a profit of £60 million. If each of the airlines introduces the discounted fare, each would have a profit of £40 million. If one airline introduces the discounted fare and the other does not, then the profit of the former is £80 million and the profit of the latter is £30 million.

Using a pay-off matrix, explain the firms' dominant strategies.

▨ ▨ ■ 6.4.2 Price fixing

Implicit collusion may also result from the practices of the market. The ready availability of information on rivals' prices facilitates implicit collusion by enabling firms to monitor each others' prices without explicit agreements, and this makes it easier for firms to keep prices in line – or to fix prices – without formally agreeing to do so. This openness may be brought about by such apparently innocuous activities as the publication of trade price lists, consumer magazines or online information. The practice of making 'meet competition' promises to customers may also facilitate collusion by providing commitment. This is the subject of this section.

Some shops offer a 'meet competition' promise to their customers: if a buyer finds another seller who can offer the same goods at a lower price, then the first seller is obliged to sell at that price too. Buyers generally see this promise as a sign of intense competition, but it can also be seen as a form of commitment in a strategic game that makes credible the threat of punishment against a player who cuts prices. Price cutting by a 'rogue' store now has to be matched by the other stores; this functions as a commitment to punish default by matching the price cut, and so commitment is secured by removing the individual incentive to reduce price. Furthermore, detection of default is now easier for the firms as price-conscious customers provide it free of charge by informing a seller whose product can be bought more cheaply elsewhere.

Note, though, that the punishment hurts the non-defaulting stores that have to match the price cuts as well as the rogue stores that are cutting prices. This is where the credibility of the threat of punishment comes into play. Rogue stores know that punishment will hurt the non-defaulting firms, and so the threat of punishment is credible only if the non-defaulting firms are bound to administer the punishment and reduce their prices too. The 'meet competition' promise thus binds the non-defaulters to administer the punishment. As all firms know this, however, there is no individual incentive for any firm to reduce price. As we saw earlier, the essence of commitment is that it binds players individually to adhere to what would be the joint decision.

In terms of a prisoners' dilemma game, the effect of the 'meet competition' promise is that it eliminates the strategy combinations in which just one player cuts price. So, returning to the pay-off matrix in Figure 6.5, the bottom-left and top-right cells are effectively eliminated. What remains of the pay-off matrix is shown in Figure 6.8.

The strategy of undercutting a rival is now eliminated. Given the choice of leaving the price unchanged with a pay-off of 100 and cutting the price with a pay-off of 90, each firm chooses to leave the price. The game is no longer a prisoners' dilemma game and price competition is eliminated! The 'meet competition' promise thus resolves the prisoners' dilemma for the firms, and so the game is no longer a prisoners' dilemma game.

Figure 6.8
'Meet competition'

		Firm B	
		leave price unchanged	cut price
Firm A	leave price unchanged	100, 100	
	cut price		90, 90

Exercise 6.5

Assume that there is a 'meet competition' promise by each firm in the airline industry. What difference would this make to your answer in Exercise 6.4? Use a pay-off matrix to explain your answer.

■ ■ ■ 6.4.3 Non-price competition

The absence of price competition does not imply that there is no competition between firms. Instead of cutting prices, firms may engage in *non-price competition*. This suggests that firms are limiting the area of conflict by co-operating to prevent a potentially ruinous type of competition while competing in other areas. Firms thus use non-price competition to enhance their competitiveness even if – perhaps especially if – the product is fairly standardized.

Firms may improve services as a form of non-price competition, but the dividing line between the product and the service is often fuzzy. Airline competition was once strongly characterized by non-price competition focusing on improved service for business travellers, such as better in-flight meals, more comfortable seats, on-board massages, free gifts, executive lounges with office machines and so on. Classic airline policy was to offer these improved services to the front-of-cabin passengers who provide most of the revenue, and reserve their price cutting for the largely leisure travellers at the back of the plane. This traditional airline policy has been dramatically challenged by budget airlines, however, as pioneered by easyJet and Ryanair, which slash prices by cutting out all unnecessary costs and offering a strictly no-frills service. At the time of writing it is too early to say whether this budget approach will transform air travel, although the increased security provisions and fall in consumer demand following the terrorist attacks in the USA in September 2001 look set to prompt some rethinking of airline policy and a restructuring of the industry in response to sharp falls in profitability.

Non-price competition also includes advertising to heighten the effects of product differentiation and promote brand loyalty for what might otherwise appear to be similar products, such as breakfast cereals, detergents, confectionery, cigarettes and soft drinks, which are the focus of extensive advertising (Chapter 4, Section 4.2). For example, the cola market has some features of a classic duopoly with heavy advertising expenditures by the two leading brands, Coca-Cola and Pepsi-Cola. In addition, there may be inducements such as free gifts, stamps or coupons to buy particular brands. Competition between petrol stations, where there is relatively little scope for product improvement, may take the form of free gifts or shopping and restaurant facilities. Non-price competition between rival supermarkets is often linked to the quality of the service, such as the width of the shopping aisles, the speed of the check-out and customer loyalty cards. It may also involve extensions in the product range, including delicatessen items, in-store bakery items and non-food products such as consumer durables, clothing and banking facilities. More recently, retailing has included online customer services.

Sometimes design factors and designer labelling are an important element in non-price competition, especially as higher prices can then be charged for products with a superior design or brand image, thus moving even further away from a potential price war in which firms try to maintain competitiveness by cutting prices. This may be seen in the fashion industry, for example, not only in exclusive fashion shops but also in high-street stores.

▥ ▨ ■ 6.4.4   Explaining price wars

The analysis in the previous sections helps to explain why price wars are not more frequent and why non-price competition is important. But price wars do sometimes occur and so it is worth pausing to consider why this happens.

There is some evidence to suggest that price cutting is linked to the cyclical state of the economy: if the economy is in recession and sales are depressed, there may be more of an incentive for firms to reduce prices aggressively. In terms of our game theory model, this may be explained by saying that the time period of the analysis is suddenly shortened, such that the model of repeated plays of the prisoners' dilemma game becomes less relevant: in a recession there is often a fear that there may be no tomorrow! As we have seen, in 2001 price wars were taking place in UK supermarkets and in the PC industry at a time when the global economy was sliding into recession. Similarly, if an economy is shortly expected to come out of a recession, firms may cut prices as an aggressive policy to try to improve market share and establish new customer loyalties in preparation for the coming up-turn.

Another factor is that different firms may be able to offer different levels of price cuts because they have different capabilities and different costs (Chapter 4, Section 4.5.1). If a firm has lower costs than its rivals then it can potentially make price reductions that the others cannot match. This would yield high pay-offs to the more efficient firm. An example of this situation is provided by discount stores. Another example is provided by budget airlines such as easyJet and Ryanair, which have slashed costs compared with conventional airlines by rethinking the economics of air travel. As we saw in Section 6.4.1, however, these budget airlines would be ill-advised to get into a price war with each other.

On the other hand, firms may be reluctant to change prices in response to small changes in costs for fear of setting off the unfavourable reactions of their rivals. When cost changes are significant, however, aggressive price cutting may be based on falling costs over time, and this is likely to be more important when there is dynamic competition (Chapter 3, Sections 3.3 and 3.4; Chapter 4, Section 4.5). The race to cut costs can therefore very easily turn into an aggressive price war as firms desperately try to sell their increasing output. In a dynamic industry where firms have increasing returns to scale, the competition between them can become a fight to the death, as the market may be too small for them all when they are producing at their lowest-cost output levels. This is illustrated by the microchip industry which has experienced enormous shake-outs. (See Chapter 2, Section 2.4 on the consolidation of the PC industry.) This situation can also be analysed using the first-mover advantage game, which we'll be considering in the next section.

As in the conduct of war, some moves in a price war may be aggressive or aggressively self-defensive; others may be exploratory, testing the other side, and testing the market, too, to see how responsive consumers are to price and quality changes. In these cases, the price cuts are part of the learning process for firms that are exploring the limits of their rivals' responses. Sometimes, too, a price war is initiated as a retaliatory move to punish other firms who have defaulted on a collusive agreement to fix prices (see Section 6.3). Furthermore, some firms may take a long-term view of these skirmishes in an attempt to drive out weaker rivals. For example, a firm may temporarily reduce price to the absolute minimum to try to drive out weaker firms that it thinks will be unable to bear the short-term losses. If the price is reduced below costs, this behaviour is known as 'predatory pricing'; the objective is to force weaker firms out of the industry, and then increase prices and take advantage of reduced competition in the future. In many countries, predatory pricing is illegal. (Chapter 4 discusses the court case against Microsoft, which was accused of predatory behaviour towards its competitors.)

In Sections 6.2 to 6.4 we have been examining forms of strategic competition in which there are different mixes of conflict and co-operation. In Sections 6.5 and 6.6 we will consider two different models which lie at opposite ends of the spectrum: the first-mover advantage game in Section 6.5 concerns conflict, and the discussion of strategic alliances in Section 6.6 concerns co-operation.

Exercise 6.6

In this section we have seen that firms may engage in non-price competition to avoid price wars, and that this may include advertising or improvements in product quality or service. In Section 6.2.4, however, we saw that advertising may itself be modelled using the prisoners' dilemma game. It follows from this that improvements in product quality or service may also be modelled in this way. Similarly, investment in innovation in processes or products may also be modelled as a strategic choice using the prisoners' dilemma game.

Two firms, LeadTheWay and FastForward, produce state-of-the-art electronic goods. Each knows that it needs to innovate ahead of its rival to increase its profit, but engaging in extensive R&D is very expensive and risky. If neither goes for a new R&D project, each has existing profits of £100 million. If one goes for the R&D project ahead of the other and the other does not, the more innovative firm has profits of £180 million and the less innovative firm has profits of £10 million. If each one goes for a new R&D project, each has profits of £80 million.

Using a pay-off matrix to model this as a one-shot prisoners' dilemma game, explain whether the firms will opt for the new R&D project.

6.5 First-mover advantage

If an industry has substantial increasing returns to scale this may limit the number of firms which can survive (Chapters 2 and 3). Strategic competition tends to be most applicable in cases where the number of firms is relatively small, so it follows that industries with substantial increasing returns, in which firms' optimal scale of production is large relative to market demand, may also be those for which models of strategic competition are particularly relevant.

Firms may gain market advantage by exploiting economies of scale with given technology (Chapter 3, Section 3.3.2), or dynamic cost reductions as technology progresses, especially when production methods are being transformed as the scale of production increases (Chapter 3, Section 3.4.1). Particular firms may gain market dominance through learning-by-doing where the technology is new and firms work out cheaper ways of implementing new technology as they become more experienced (Chapter 3, Section 3.4.2). Network externalities are another source of market dominance by particular firms (Chapter 3, Section 3.4.2). As noted earlier, examples of industries where increasing returns generate high degrees of market concentration include the motor industry, chemicals, personal computers and microchips.

In these industries it may matter a great deal which firms start out first because the early firms have a *first-mover advantage*. This advantage may arise from learning-by-doing or from any of the other cumulative advantages that can be exploited by getting into the market early (Chapter 3, Section 3.4). This situation can be modelled strategically using a quite different game from the prisoners' dilemma: the first-mover advantage game.

Figure 6.9
First-mover
advantage

		Firm B	
		produce	not produce
Firm A	produce	−100, −100	100, 0
	not produce	0, 100	0, 0

Like the prisoners' dilemma game, the first-mover advantage game assumes individual decision-making and that players seek to maximize individual pay-offs. The structure of the pay-offs is different, however, and so the first-mover advantage game is a different kind of game. Suppose that there are two firms, A and B, and that the market is large enough for only one of them working at full capacity. The game is shown in Figure 6.9. The firms' strategies are 'produce' and 'not produce'. If each of the firms produces they make losses of 100 each (i.e. profits of −100 each). If only one firm produces it has a pay-off of 100.

Question | Study Figure 6.9 carefully. What is the better strategy for A?

Figure 6.9 is not a prisoners' dilemma game. Here the better strategy for A depends on B's strategy. If B produces, it is better for A not to produce with a zero pay-off. If B does not produce, A's best strategy is to produce with a pay-off of 100. A symmetrical analysis applies to B. There is therefore *no* dominant strategy because the better strategy for each firm depends on the strategy of the other. There are therefore two possible outcomes to this game: either A produces or B produces.

What will be the outcome? The game implies that if one firm is sure the other will produce, then its best strategy is to stay out. A firm that successfully occupies the market first will therefore scoop the whole available return. Hence the name of the game. The example of Microsoft, which you studied in Chapter 4, illustrates the point. Producing software is characterized by extensive increasing returns to scale and by huge network externalities generated by the benefits to users of compatible systems. By establishing Windows as the market standard, Microsoft gained overwhelming dominance over the operating systems market. Others were then deterred from entering because of the scale of the investment required and the difficulty of establishing a new standard. The Microsoft court case turned in part on whether Microsoft was using Internet Explorer to fight off a prospective challenge from Netscape to this dominance.

In any real situation, what is likely to determine which of the rival firms survives in this fight to the death? It may not be the first firm into the market that survives, but it may well be the firm that manages to achieve the first sustained cost advantage and sustained market coverage. If a firm is early in the market, it can start travelling along its learning curve; it becomes familiar with the technology, it can build on its initial customer loyalty, it can benefit from network externalities, it can buy up relevant patents, it can establish its distribution network and so on. Cumulatively, a market leader emerges and then is hard to compete out – until the next major technological change.

Perhaps this explains why existing firms are eager to keep their options open in developing new market opportunities, even rashly so. For example, many firms in 1999 and 2000 were keen to move into dot.com industries for fear of being left behind on new economy developments. As it turned out, the dot.com expansion proved to be a speculative bubble ready to burst and many firms lost heavily, but their instinct not to be left behind is indicative of the acknowledged benefits of first-mover advantage. Once a firm loses contact with a new market, it is often harder to gain a presence there in the face of established competition.

6.6 Strategic alliances

The pervasive metaphor of game theory is that of 'war', but as we have seen firms facing strategic competition may develop co-operative forms of behaviour as well as engage in conflict with rival firms. As noted above, a strategy to limit the potential destructiveness of all-out war may require co-operative behaviour. This implies again that firms cannot always be thinking in terms of conflict with their rivals but must also think in co-operative terms.

In recent years, many firms have begun to experiment with a further type of co-operation in the form of strategic alliances, an idea that was pioneered by Japanese firms but widely adopted by others. Toshiba Corporation was one of the pioneers in developing strategic alliances as a way of securing global growth by sharing the costs and the risks with other firms.

> When you consider the severe economic environment today in Japan and the unsettled nature of most major overseas markets, you can understand our desire to try to turn yesterday's competitors into tomorrow's partners. We still compete with most of the companies with whom we have formed alliances. But we have found that co-operation is often more sensible in certain markets where it involves creating a new business opportunity.
> *(Fumio Sato, President of Toshiba, quoted in* Fortune International, *1993, p.S5)*

According to this view, strategic alliances allow the partners to develop into areas that would otherwise have been inaccessible, and so they help to promote competition in such areas. This context for strategic alliances is thus one of a dynamic and global competition in which only the most efficient and innovative firms can prosper (Chapter 4, Section 4.5). This view sees strategic competition as a journey into unknown territory, but a journey that is becoming increasingly specialized and expensive, and one on which travellers are ill-advised to venture alone. It is also a journey that is becoming increasingly risky, as Exercise 6.6 illustrates, although the returns to successful innovation may be considerable. In this context, a large, established firm may form a partnership with a small, specialist start-up; or traditional rivals find that they can co-operate in a specific area of their activities so that each may enhance its competitiveness on a global basis; or a global corporation needs a local partner in exploring foreign markets. As noted in *The Economist*: 'At a time of rapidly developing technologies, alliances provide a way to dip a toe in the water with minimum risk' (*The Economist*, 2001b). This raises two sorts of questions: the first concerns the kind of co-operative behaviour that is implied by alliances; the second concerns whether such alliances are beneficial.

We have so far met co-operative behaviour among firms that are colluding over output or price. The colluding firms have separate interests, although these interests are

Figure 6.10
Strategic alliances can be important in the growth phase of new knowledge-based industries . . . and in the mature phase of older manufacturing industries

Left: Nick Winton of UK eUniversities Worldwide and Greg Stroud of Sun Microsystems sign a strategic alliance in the British Library Reading Room

Right: Suzuki and Kawasaki co-produce motor bikes to cut costs

interdependent. The interests are separate in the sense that Firm A's interest is to increase Firm A's profits and Firm B's interest is to increase Firm B's profits. They are inter-dependent in that an increase in A's profits depends on what B does, and vice versa. In the case of strategic alliances, firms also have *mutual* interests, that is, Firm A's interest includes directly increasing B's profit as well as its own, and Firm B's interest includes directly increasing A's profit as well as its own. The degree of interdependence and of co-operation between the firms is thus of a higher order than in the case of collusion.

One example of a strategic alliance is provided from the new-economy side of retailing (or 'e-tailing'). In 2001 Tesco (UK)'s online deliveries system was adopted by Safeway (USA) in California to support its GroceryWorks online channel. Tesco was said to be contributing its technology and US$22 million of a US$35 million refinancing of GroceryWorks, taking a 35 per cent stake in the business in return. The partnership was seen as giving a boost to 'old-economy' Tesco's more economical system of in-store 'picking' for the online deliveries (i.e. the online orders are picked off the shelves in the supermarkets), whereas other online grocery businesses had invested in costly warehous-ing for storing the online goods (Voyle and Edgecliffe-Johnson, 2001; *Financial Times*, 2001). What is significant from the point of view of our discussion of co-operation is that both Tesco (UK) and Safeway (USA) had a mutual interest in the success of Safeway's adoption of Tesco's online delivery system in that Tesco (UK) had a financial stake in Safeway (USA).

Another example is provided by the motor industry alliance of France's Renault and Japan's Nissan referred to in Section 6.1. In 1999 Renault took a 36.8 per cent stake in Nissan and Carlos Ghosn moved from Renault to Nissan to overhaul its manage-ment practices. The fruit of this managerial rethink was not only to turn a loss into a profit for Nissan, but also to design a new fleet of cars for Nissan based on ten basic platforms which would be shared with Renault. The mutual advantage for the firms thus included a sharing of floorpans and basic body parts which was expected to provide enormous cost savings for both firms in producing their separate fleets of cars, which would look different although based on identical platforms. As Ghosn reportedly remarked, the alliance depended on 'managing the contradiction between synergy and identity' (*The Economist*, 2001a).

Strategic alliances are often looked upon more favourably by economists than cartels or collusion, and this is reflected in the use of terms such as 'alliance' or 'virtuous collusion'. The reason is that alliances are thought to improve the efficiency of the firms, either managerially or in terms of innovation, production, distribution or the develop-ment of shared networks, such that costs are reduced and consumers benefit. In the case of cartels and collusion, however, costs remain unchanged but prices are increased and the firms are thought to benefit at the expense of consumers.

Alliances are thought to be beneficial to consumers if they are directed at promoting innovation. Economists agree that there tends to be an under-investment in innovation and insufficient dissemination of information on innovation. Investment in innovation is very expensive, risky and long-term, and firms calculate the profitability of such investment only by taking into account the impact on their own profits individually, without regard to wider benefits. To the extent that sharing the costs and risks of such investment encourages firms to do more of it than they would otherwise, and to share or exchange the information that they have, strategic alliances are thought to be beneficial not only to the firms involved but also to consumers. Alliances are also thought to be beneficial if they bring together complementary activities and capabilities rather than competing ones. Even if the partners are competing directly in the same market, complementary capabilities – such as skills, knowledge, facilities or networks – may provide the basis for a beneficial alliance. Where the partners are not competing directly, mutually beneficial inter-firm co-operation may come from technology licensing, supply arrangements, joint ventures, research agreements, mutual training schemes or the exchange of people and ideas. Thus strategic alliances tend to be most successful between firms that have complementary strengths.

So, returning to our examples: the alliances between Tesco (UK) and Safeway (USA) and between Nissan and Renault were based on enhanced investment and complementary inputs from the two partners. The Tesco/Safeway alliance promoted e-tailing by allowing Tesco to share its expertise with Safeway, and the Nissan/Renault alliance promoted the sharing of better management and larger economies of scale in car production. Both alliances were expected to be financially beneficial to the individual firms, but appraisal by economists tries to look beyond the individual firms' profitability to assess the likely impact on costs and, hence, the benefits to consumers. Sharing investment and production in some areas is thought to provide one way of improving efficiency in production while maintaining competitition for the benefit of consumers.

It is recognized that strategic alliances may not last very long and sometimes raise difficult issues associated with different corporate cultures. Sustained co-operation may thus not be feasible over long periods because of different business cultures, different objectives of the partners or changing external circumstances, or because the initial objectives of the alliance have been more or less fulfilled. It may be that part of the synergy of such alliances arises precisely because of the interaction of two different corporate cultures, but that this arrangement will often be short-lived. As Ghosn remarked, there is a tension between creating synergies between firms and maintaining their sense of individual identity. Strategic alliances also raise the more delicate question of the cultural context in which such partnerships are viable, and this in turn sometimes requires a different conception of business ethics and inter-firm relations. This issue has been the subject of considerable interest recently among economists trying to learn about best practice in firms from different cultural contexts.

6.7 Strategic competition policy

This section briefly considers some of the implications of our analysis of strategic competition for competition policy. You have already met some of the difficulties involved in framing competition policy (Chapter 4, Section 4.6). In this section we shall see that reframing policy questions in strategic terms leads to some unusual – and sometimes counterintuitive – results.

▨ ▨ ■ 6.7.1 Collusion

Competition policy tries to put an end to anti-competitive behaviour. The analysis in Sections 6.3 and 6.4, however, underlines just how difficult this can be in practice. Collusion may be sustained not only by explicit agreements but also by implicit collusion resulting from practices which, on the face of it, might not appear to be anti-competitive. We have seen that apparently competitive practices such as 'meet competition' promises may provide the commitment that sustains collusive behaviour.

What has emerged from the analysis of strategic competition is that anti-competitive behaviour does not necessarily imply secret agreements in smoke-filled rooms – or even discreet gentlemen's agreements in exclusive clubs – but may be the result of ordinary practices of day-to-day trading or trade association activities. This makes it harder for governments and regulatory authorities to establish whether behaviour is collusive. In the case of explicit collusive agreements there is the possibility of finding clear evidence, but in the absence of this all that can be done is to examine whether the outcomes in terms of prices and output are more consistent with collusion than with competition. To establish whether price fixing has taken place, for example, it is necessary to look at the relation between firms' costs and prices, and to try to establish whether there is evidence of 'parallel' pricing across firms, that is, whether firms' prices tend to move together. But if the firms are facing similar costs, it is hard to know whether parallel prices follow from the similar costs faced by the firms or whether the firms are colluding over price.

In spite of these difficulties there have been some successful crackdowns on cartels over the years, and some of these suggest that large numbers of firms may be involved, showing that collusive behaviour is not the preserve of markets with few firms. For example, it was reported in *Fair Trading*, the magazine of the Office of Fair Trading, UK, that in 2000 the German competition authority undertook its largest ever cartel prosecution against 62 companies in the ready-mixed concrete industry, which were fined DM 320 million for operating an output cartel. In Denmark the discovery of an alleged cartel in electrical wiring was expected to lead to 200 to 300 firms being prosecuted (*Fair Trading*, Issue 29, February 2001, p.12).

In the UK, the Office of Fair Trading was given enhanced powers in the Competition Act 2000 and is planning new competitive measures under its new Director General, John Vickers, previously Chief Economist and Executive Director at the Bank of England and Professor of Economics at Oxford. These include a new 'leniency' policy, influenced by the US policy, which offers leniency, that is, total immunity from legal penalties, to the first cartel member to provide information on other cartel members (plus some discretionary limited leniency for other cartel members), together with the imposition of financial penalties of up to 10 per cent of a company's UK turnover for the period of infringement (up to a maximum of three years). It was reported that in the USA over the last five years such a leniency policy 'has been responsible for detecting and cracking more international cartels than all of our search warrants, secret audio and videotapes and FBI interrogations combined' (Scott Hammond, Director of Criminal Enforcement for the US Department of Justice's Antitrust Division, speaking at the International Cartels Workshop hosted by the Office of Fair Trading in November 2000, which was attended by over a hundred international cartel busters, as reported in *Fair Trading*, Issue 29, February 2001, pp.13–14).

In 2000 the UK government announced a proposal to make it a criminal offence for individuals to engage in cartels, thus also threatening to jail business executives who take part in price-fixing cartels rather than simply impose fines on their companies, and bringing UK legislation more in line with the USA rather than the EU. Explicit cartel

Case study: From collusion to art wars

A dramatic example was the explicit collusion between the auction houses Christie's and Sotheby's between 1993 and 1999 to fix prices by agreeing on the commission that clients were charged for selling their fine art, jewellery and furniture. The prosecution alleged that clients were cheated of as much as $400 million during the period. Sotheby's pleaded guilty to price fixing and was fined $45 million; and the former chairman, Alfred Taubman, was liable to up to three years' imprisonment as well as a large fine. Christie's, on the other hand, received immunity for being the first to provide evidence of the collusion, and its former chairman, Sir Anthony Tennant, could not be extradited from Great Britain to the USA and so remained free. The trial in New York during 2001 held the elite art world transfixed, and there were reportedly plans to make a Hollywood movie based on the price fixing and the ensuing humiliation of two of the most prestigious auction houses in the world (Eunjung Cha, 2001).

Question

What factors aided the identification of collusion in this case? Do you think implicit collusion would have been possible for the auction houses and, if so, how difficult would the practice have been to uncover?

agreements and implicit concerted practices which are anti-competitive in their objectives or effects are prohibited under Article 81(1) of the Treaty of Amsterdam (previously Article 85(1) of the Treaty of Rome) (see also Chapter 5, Section 5.1). It is widely thought, however, that the European Commission has been hampered in cracking down on cartels by lack of resources, legal restraints and bureaucratic delays. The Commission also lacks the threat of jail for convicted price-fixing executives; and observers have noted that the threat of claims for damages by consumer groups against convicted companies which are present in the USA is not available in the EU. During 2000 and 2001, however, partly helped by new rules to reward 'whistle-blowers', Mario Monti, the European Competition Commissioner, launched a new offensive against cartels. During 2001 the competition department reportedly raised €1.8 billion in fines on cartels, and these included illegal agreements on Nordic airline routes, graphite electrodes, sodium gluconate, vitamins, brewing, citric acid, zinc phosphate, carbonless paper and euro bank charges. The euro bank charges cartel involved five German banks which operated a price-fixing cartel on foreign exchange transaction charges in order to compensate for the anticipated loss of revenue caused by reduced opportunities for foreign currency speculation with the introduction of the euro. The banks were fined £63 million (Guerrera, 2001; Osborn, 2001).

■ ■ ■ 6.7.2 Strategic alliances

As was argued in Section 6.6, there are some sound economic arguments in favour of strategic alliances, so policy makers accept and even encourage those alliances while being wary of alliances that do not offer these benefits. In principle, this implies that alliances promoting the production and diffusion of innovation and/or involving complementary skills and resources are regarded as beneficial. It also implies that alliances involving co-operation other than at the R&D stage (e.g. marketing and distribution stages), and those co-operating over non-complementary activities, are more likely to be regarded as anti-competitive.

Although, in principle, the issues might seem straightforward, in practice it is often not clear how to keep these various aspects separate. First, in practice it is sometimes difficult to separate the different stages of research, product development, manufacturing and marketing. Second, given the risks and long-term nature of investment into new products and processes, the co-operating firms might want to argue that they also need to co-operate at the manufacturing and marketing stages to make the investment financially attractive. Third, applying these principles to the complexities of real circumstances can be extremely difficult. Thus finding the right balance between beneficial alliances and anti-competitive collusion is often difficult in practice.

As we saw above, agreements and practices are prohibited by Article 81(1) of the EC Treaty if they are held to be anti-competitive, but there are exemptions from this under Article 81(3) if the agreements and practices contribute to 'improving the production or distribution of goods or to promoting technical or economic progress, while allowing consumers a fair share of the resulting benefit'. The grounds for exemption thus reflect our economic analysis of strategic competition that, although such agreements and practices are harmful if their effects are solely anti-competitive, on balance they may be beneficial if there are improvements in efficiency that outweigh the negative effects arising from the reduction in competition.

■ ■ ■ 6.7.3 Picking winners?

The first-mover advantage game in Section 6.5 highlights the importance of being in at the start of new developments. Should government policy try to anticipate this by picking winners? This policy question is illustrated in Figure 6.11, which is the same as Figure 6.9 except that A, the preferred firm, is now subsidized by 150 to produce when it would otherwise make a loss (top left-hand cell).

A receives a subsidy of 150 if it would otherwise make a loss, that is, the negative pay-off of −100 is converted into a positive pay-off of 50 if both firms produce. It follows that A now has a dominant strategy 'produce' as this has the better pay-off whatever B's strategy. But in this case, B's best strategy is 'not produce' (0 as opposed to a negative pay-off).

Question	Does the government actually have to pay the subsidy for its policy to work?

This is an interesting question as it depends on how we are modelling the government. At one time, in the UK at least, the answer to this question would have been 'yes'. An issue might have been whether or when the government should or could put an end to the payment. This kind of case is similar to the 'infant industry' argument, which asserts that new industries should be supported while establishing themselves, particularly in the context of low-income countries. The problem is deciding when the moment has come for the industry to become independent of government support.

Figure 6.11
Picking the winner

		Firm B	
		produce	not produce
Firm A	produce	50, −100	100, 0
	not produce	0, 100	0, 0

In strict game theory terms, however, if the government's subsidy policy is a credible policy that is made known in advance, B's best strategy is not to produce. In which case the government does not actually have to pay any subsidy! This is the equivalent of the credible threat already discussed, and it raises the question of how the government's promise could be made credible.

But if we are considering how the government's policy is to be made credible, we are now treating the government as a player in the game.

■ ■ ■ 6.7.4   The government as player?

Once we conceive of the government as a player in a strategic game we need to specify its pay-offs too. What are its interests? Does the government have its own pay-offs, or does it identify with the pay-offs of particular players? And how well informed can the government be? If everyone is acting strategically, how can the government gain independent information about which firm is likely to be better in the long run? The firms concerned are not going to be truthful but will present information to their own advantage, and why should the government know better than firms in the market what will be the better bet in the long run?

Once the government and its authorities – and even its appointed regulators and commissioners – are seen as players in a game, their interests, their credibility and their pay-offs have to be taken into account. But this changes the nature of the policy analysis in ways that become highly complicated and not fully understood. As we saw above, the UK government has recently proposed that the Competition Commission should be free of political control and that stiffer penalties should be introduced for company executives found to be engaged in collusive behaviour. It remains to be seen whether these proposals find their way onto the statute book, but perhaps they will be seen as a credible commitment on the part of the government to change the structure of the pay-offs facing firms.

6.8   Conclusion: why strategy matters

This chapter has examined different kinds of strategic competition and has introduced game theory as a way of modelling this competition. One of the interesting results to emerge from this analysis of firms' interdependence is that conflict and co-operation are not necessarily opposites, as firms may be faced with situations that include a mixture of conflict and co-operation. As in many situations in social life, firms need to handle both the conflict and the co-operation, but an implication of this is that it may sometimes be harder to identify anti-competitive practices. Game theory can help us to understand firms' co-operative and conflictual behaviour, complementing the models you studied in Chapters 2 and 3.

Questions for review and discussion

Question 1   Complete the following by placing in the first space a phrase from the left-hand column and in the second space a phrase from the right-hand column.

superior to	the worst individually
inferior to	the best individually
the same as	between the best and the worst individually

In the prisoners' dilemma game, if each player chooses their dominant strategy, the outcome will be . . . that resulting from each player going against their dominant strategy. If player A chooses a dominant strategy and player B goes against his, this will result in an outcome that is . . . for player B.

Question 2 In Figure 6.12, A and B are firms; X and Y are the strategies available to them. The pay-offs represent profits, and we assume that each firm wishes to make as much profit as possible. Insert the numbers from the list to fill in the blank spaces in the matrix in such a way that the two firms, A and B, are faced with the prisoners' dilemma. The pay-offs should be symmetrical for the two firms. Also, if both firms choose the same strategy, each should receive the same amount of profit. Each number needs to appear twice on the matrix. One number is filled in for you.

3 5 5 8 8 10 10

Figure 6.12
Game strategy matrix

Question 3 Rearrange the numbers from the answers to question 2 in Figure 6.13 so that each player has the same dominant strategy as before but there is no prisoners' dilemma. Once again, pay-offs for the two firms should be symmetrical. One number is filled in for you (note there is more than one combination that is correct).

3 5 5 8 8 10 10

Figure 6.13
Game strategy matrix

Question 4 This question has five True/False statements associated with it.

The matrix in Figure 6.14 shows pay-offs to each of two firms, A and B. Each prefers higher profit to lower profit. The two firms choose their strategies simultaneously.

For each part of the question, indicate whether the statement is true or false.

Figure 6.14
Game matrix
showing possible
pay-off

		B	
		produce	not produce
A	produce	−50, −75	70, 0
	not produce	0, 80	0, 0

(a) Firm A has a dominant strategy.

(b) Firm B does not have a dominant strategy.

(c) (0, 80) is a possible equilibrium solution, since with this outcome neither firm has an incentive to change strategy.

(d) The offer of a subsidy of 65 to firm B if both firms produced would be sufficient to ensure that firm A would not produce.

(e) The offer of a subsidy of 60 firm A would be sufficient to ensure that firm B would not produce.

Question 5 Read the following extract:

> This week, two of Monopoly's biggest players landed on a square they were hoping to avoid. A throw of the enforcement dice by the Office of Fair Trading (OFT) left Argos and Littlewoods with a £22 million fine for fixing the price of toys. The £22 million fine is the OFT's biggest yet. Its investigation uncovered correspondence between the companies individually and 'Hasbro' the toy maker about an agreement not to sell below the recommended retail price. Hasbro managed to use the game's famous 'get out of jail' card, by telling the OFT about the secret arrangement. The admission meant that Hasbro escaped punishment for its part in the scheme.
>
> The fine is part of an OFT plan to concentrate on eliminating price-fixing above all other anti-competitive practices.
>
> (The Sunday Times, *Business Section, 23 February 2003*)

(a) With the aid of the prisoners' dilemma game, explain why the firms colluded to fix the price of toys.

(b) What are the problems faced by firms when they act as a cartel?

Part 3

What makes an
economy successful? Work,
well-being and the state

7

The labour market

Francis Green

Concepts

- the perfectly competitive model of the labour market
- marginal revenue product
- human capital
- imperfectly competitive models of the labour market
- marginal factor cost
- institutional interventions in labour markets
- minimum-wage legislation
- trade unions
- segmentation and segregation
- efficiency wages
- the worker discipline effect

Objectives

After studying this chapter you should be able to:

- understand the scope and limits of the perfectly competitive model of the labour market
- appreciate the greater explanatory power of imperfectly competitive models of the labour market incorporating institutional factors
- explain recent changes in the UK labour market by applying models of the labour market
- explain some general characteristics of labour markets by applying models of the labour market.

7.1 Introduction

Some salient changes have taken place in labour markets throughout the industrial economies in recent years. The UK, for example, has seen an increase in the relative wages of skilled workers, a rise in the proportion of skilled workers, an increase in the intensity of work effort and the introduction of minimum-wage regulation. In this chapter we will examine these recent changes in the UK labour market and some other, more lasting, features of labour markets in general.

7.1.1 Relative wages, skilled workers and work effort

Three recent changes in the UK labour market – an increase in the relative wages of skilled workers, a rise in the proportion of skilled workers and an increase in the intensity of work effort – are illustrated by the evidence given in Table 7.1. The first row of Panel A shows

Table 7.1
British jobs have
become more
intensive and more
skilled

Panel A	1979–81	1993–95
Ratio of the average wage for university-educated workers to the average wage for workers with no qualifications		
Males	1.63	1.93
Females	1.92	2.11
Ratio of university-educated workers to workers with no qualifications		
Males	0.19	0.71
Females	0.07	0.43
Panel B	**1992**	**1997**
Proportion of workers who strongly agree with the statement: 'My job requires that I work very hard'		
Males	30	38
Females	33	42

Source: Machin, 1999; Green, 2001

that the average wage of workers who have a degree rose, relative to the wages of workers with no qualifications, by about 30 percentage points for men and 19 percentage points for women from 1979–81 to 1993–95. In other words, the value of a degree increased during this period. Over the same period, those with degrees became more numerous in the workforce than those with no qualifications. For example, in 1979–81 there were roughly two men with a degree in the workforce for every ten with no qualifications at all. By 1993–95 the ratio had risen to more than seven degree-holders for every ten with no qualifications.

Panel B of Table 7.1 gives evidence about the increasing intensity of work effort, although effort is difficult to measure objectively. A representative sample of the British workforce was asked an identical question in 1992 and 1997. The interviewees were asked whether they agreed with the statement: 'My job requires that I work very hard.' The proportion of men and women strongly agreeing with the statement rose between 1992 and 1997.

Employers often describe jobs as 'more demanding' than they used to be. Although this term is rather vague, if we interpret it as a statement that jobs are becoming more skilled, and require workers to work more intensively than they used to do, then we can see from Table 7.1 why employers hold this view. The employers' view seems to be accurate in this case.

An important factor driving the changes shown in Table 7.1 is the nature of modern technology. The computer and a range of other new technologies, such as biotechnology, are thought to generate an increase in the demand for skilled workers. Actually, the effect in many industries may be a sharp decrease in the demand for less-skilled workers, because routine work is the most easy to automate. For example, in the 1990s large numbers of non-manual back-office staff in the financial industry lost their jobs in this way. But whether new technologies increase the number of highly educated workers in an industry or decrease the number of less-educated workers, the effect is to raise the *relative* demand for the more highly educated workers.

A similar argument suggests that the new technologies of the modern age demand the sort of worker who is prepared to put in high levels of effort. For example, the technologies to be found in call centres – which grew from nothing to become an industry employing more than 400 000 workers by the end of the 1990s – are widely thought to both enable and demand high levels of effort. Each call can be delivered instantaneously to workers, and their effort can be monitored with great precision. The system offers rewards to workers who are prepared to endure the high pace of the work.

■■■ 7.1.2   The labour market

A financially starved student goes into town one day, knocks on a factory door and asks if there is any work going: perhaps there is a half-day's labouring to be done, perhaps not. On the other side of the globe, a 40-year-old man goes to work in an office in one of the large Japanese corporations: he has been working there for 20 years already and confidently expects to do so for 20 more. These two people are doing the same thing in one general respect: they are both participating in a labour market.

They seem poles apart. The student works just a few hours in return for equivalent wages and may never again have any relationship with the company. The Japanese worker benefits from the 'nenko system', which guarantees lifetime employment in the firm for a proportion (largely male) of the Japanese workforce. The relationship between the worker and the firm is still an exchange of work for wages, but the implications of its long-term character are very different from those of the 'casual' labour market of the student.

Most workers participate in labour markets that lie between the poles of the casual labour market and the nenko system. Some jobs are more stable and secure, and are regarded as long-lasting or even as 'permanent', in contrast to others which are subject to a greater likelihood of closure and are typically more short term. But of course many 'permanent' jobs cease to exist in the event of dismissals for misconduct or, more commonly, redundancy. Even the seemingly 'safe' IBM, which for a century or so had never made any workers redundant anywhere in the world, found itself declaring massive redundancies in the 1990s' shake-out of the computer industry (Chapter 2).

So, while it is correct, if somewhat trite, to define a labour market as the place where wages are exchanged for labour, it is already clear that one striking feature of labour markets is that jobs vary so much in their length and degree of security. What else is special about labour markets that merits our exclusive attention in this chapter? You can probably think of a number of factors in answer to this question, but for the purposes of this chapter we need to emphasize three significant points.

First, in a labour market the money that is being exchanged is wages (or salaries), and these form a very large part of most people's income. On average about 60 per cent of income in the UK is derived from the reward for labour (*Economic Trends*, April 2001). Hence the factors that determine wages have a great effect on income distribution. Moreover, our welfare is directly linked to our employment prospects. When unemployment looms as the result of a failure of the labour market it is a matter of great concern.

A second reason why the analysis of labour markets is special is that the wages paid to an employee do not automatically guarantee that a satisfactory job is done from the firm's point of view. When we buy apples from a street seller it is relatively easy to see if any are rotten and insist on replacements if necessary. By contrast, to motivate workers to work in return for their wages requires that they be managed somehow. The economic analysis of labour markets cannot properly be considered completely separately from the issue of worker motivation. Later on in the chapter we will consider a model which highlights the consequences of this link between wages and worker motivation.

The third reason why labour markets are different from many others in the modern world is that their scope is geographically far less wide than other important markets. We have become accustomed to thinking in global terms in relation to the money market or to many product markets: UK-based banks, for example, by no means confine their operations to UK lending. Yet firms based in a particular country or area largely recruit their workforces from that area. For many types of work, and those below the highest grades, that area is usually taken to be the town and its surroundings; the UK Department of Employment delineates them as 'Travel-To-Work Areas' on maps. For other types of work, such as senior management, the market may be national in scope. International recruitment occurs in a relatively small number of cases, with the important exception of the large-scale migration of labour. Yet despite occasional mass migration, the fact that labour markets remain distinctly national is evident, if only from the different wages paid to the same type of labour in different countries. In developing countries, wages are typically a small fraction of even unskilled manual workers' wages in the industrialized world. And between countries of the advanced industrialized world there remain distinct differences in wages and conditions of work.

In this chapter we will primarily, although not exclusively, draw examples from the UK labour market. The relatively high economic, social and political barriers to mass migration mean that this remains a sensible region to examine.

In the light of these special characteristics of labour markets, the aim of this chapter is to address two broad questions about how they operate.

1 What are the determinants of wages and employment? Why do some workers get paid more than others?

2 How do institutional interventions in the free operation of labour markets affect their performance? By 'institutions' here we mean anything other than individual workers or firms (e.g. trade unions, employer organizations, or the various arms of government).

We will begin the analysis of these questions by elaborating on the 'perfect competition' or 'competitive' model of the labour market. The chief reason for beginning with this is that many official policy analyses and positions have traditionally emerged from this approach. For example, it used to be assumed that minimum-wage legislation tended to raise wages at the expense of employment. A related policy has been to reduce the power of trade unions, which are also thought to contribute to inefficiency and to high wages at the expense of potential jobs for the unemployed. All of these conclusions can be drawn from the perfect competition model. Minimum-wage legislation and trade unions are two distinct but related themes, which we will examine in detail later in this chapter.

As the chapter proceeds you will see that, although there are useful insights to be gained from the perfect competition model, most of the assumptions that underpin this model are unrealistic. Nevertheless, the model can serve as a benchmark against which to contrast the assumptions of other models based on imperfect competition, which are regarded as the normal or most widespread structure of the labour market. You may judge these assumptions for yourselves.

7.2 The perfectly competitive labour market

The perfect competition model is primarily an analysis of a 'spot market' in which an amount of labour (e.g. measured in hours) in the present is sold for wages. Both the price of labour – the wage rate – and the level of employment are determined by the intersection of demand and supply, just as in many commodity markets. A number of assumptions form the starting point of this model.

A1 Buyers and sellers of labour are price-takers: they cannot individually alter wages.

A2 All participants are perfectly informed: workers know the available job and wage opportunities, while firms know the potential workers in the labour market.

A3 Workers can move freely between jobs or in and out of work.

A4 Labour hours, once purchased from the workers, are used without problem as effective labour to produce output.

A5 Firms aim to maximize profits.

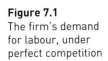 **7.2.1 The demand for labour**

The demand for labour is the demand for a factor of production. It is commonly referred to as a 'derived demand' since the labour is wanted not for itself but for the profits which it brings to the company. Let us consider how the demand for labour is determined in principle by a firm using just this one variable factor, labour, to produce an output, that is, to maximize its profits. The marginal physical product of labour (MPP_L) is the extra output produced by utilizing an extra unit of labour. The MPP_L declines as labour increases, in accordance with diminishing returns to a factor of production (Chapter 3, Section 3.3.1). In the analysis here we are particularly concerned with the **marginal revenue product** (*MRP*), which is related to the MPP_L.

Marginal revenue product

The marginal revenue product is the extra revenue obtained by the firm from employing an extra unit of labour.

If *P* is the price of the product we can write:

$$MRP = P \cdot MPP_L$$

Because we assume that in perfect competition the firm is a price-taker, the decline in MPP_L means that the *MRP* curve is also declining. The *MRP* curve is illustrated in Figure 7.1.

Suppose that the market wage rate is given by *W*. The theory of the firm's demand for labour may now be simply stated: the firm that maximizes profits will demand labour up to the point at which the wage equals the marginal revenue product, or:

$$W = MRP$$

Figure 7.1
The firm's demand for labour, under perfect competition

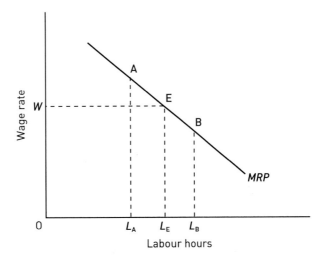

This is illustrated by the point E on Figure 7.1, where employment is L_E. How do we know this is the optimal amount to employ? We can reason by considering alternative points. At A, with only L_A employed, the *MRP* is above *W*. This means the firm could get extra profits by employing one more unit of labour, since the extra revenue, *MRP*, is greater than the cost, *W*. Conversely, at B, with *MRP* below *W*, the firm could get more profits by cutting a unit of labour, since the cost saving, *W*, is more than the lost revenue, *MRP*. Thus, neither A nor B is a point at which profits are maximized; but at E, no change in employment could raise profits further.

If the wage rate were raised or lowered, the profit-maximizing firm would simply alter its employment according to its *MRP* curve. The curve thus traces out the **demand for labour**.

Demand for labour

The demand curve for labour in a perfectly competitive model is given by the marginal revenue product curve.

Not all firms are the same, of course, and so their labour demand curves may have different slopes and shapes, but they are expected to be downward sloping. Hence, when we aggregate all firms to obtain the market demand for labour, we would also have a downward-sloping demand curve. This is a key conclusion emerging from the analysis and it will be used again, below. But before leaving this topic we must consider some loose terminology we have been using so far: in talking about labour we have not discussed different types of labour, such as carpenters, labourers, managers and so on. Implicitly, we have been assuming that all labour is the same. Nevertheless, the same arguments can apply to any specific type of labour, leading to the conclusion that there are downward-sloping demand curves for each type.

Exercise 7.1

The proposition that the demand for labour rises when the wage rate falls is widely believed. Can you trace the steps in the argument leading to that conclusion?

7.2.2 Labour supply

We turn next to look at the underlying determinants of labour supply. These can be divided into: (a) the factors determining overall labour supply, and (b) the factors determining the supply of a particular type of labour, relative to alternative types of labour. Let us look at each in turn.

Overall labour supply

In any country the ultimate boundary affecting labour supply is population. Table 7.2 contains some summary data for the UK. You will see that although there are nearly 60 million people, only just under half are in the workforce (meaning that they are either employed or officially unemployed). A number of factors play a part in determining this overall figure. There are social and demographic factors, such as the proportion of people of normal working age and society's attitudes towards women or younger or older people working, which have changed gradually over the years. There are technical factors, such as the availability of washing machines, which have made work in the home more productive than in earlier times, thereby in principle freeing up time for paid work. There are also political factors, such as the availability of state-financed child-care facilities or

Table 7.2
UK population and
labour statistics,
2001

	Thousands
Population	59 954[1]
Workforce	29 619
Workforce in employment	28 142

1 Mid-year projection.
Source: *Annual Abstract of Statistics*, 2001; *Labour Market Statistics*,
June 2001

the provision of full-time education or higher education. And there are private economic factors, such as the availability of private sources of income, that may alter the incentive to work. Someone with a large private income will be able to afford the cost (in terms of lost wages) of not going to work.

Labour supply to a particular line of work

Now we have considered the overall supply of people wishing to work, we need to consider the supply of potential workers to particular kinds of work. It is this supply, together with the demand for particular types of labour, that provides an explanation of relative wages – that is, wages in one job relative to those in another. This is crucial both for reasons of distribution and for reasons of economic incentives.

For the moment we shall set aside the question of different skill requirements for different jobs. Suppose we consider two jobs, A and B, with the same skill requirements but with different conditions of work: job A has poorer conditions than job B. This might mean more risky or less pleasant work surroundings in some way. Job B might, for example, be window cleaning, while job A is window cleaning on high-rise buildings. The supply of high-rise window cleaners is going to depend on the wages and riskiness of the high-rise jobs *relative to* those for the ordinary window cleaners. A typical supply curve might look like the one in Figure 7.2.

Figure 7.2
Labour supply for
high-rise window
cleaning

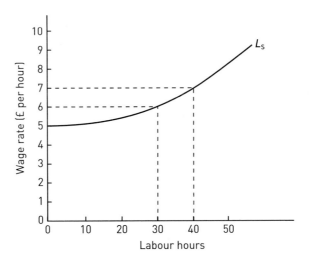

Figure 7.3
The determination of wages and employment in high-rise window cleaning under perfect competition

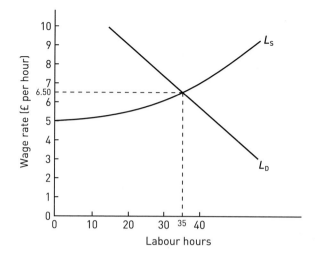

Suppose that workers could get £5 per hour for ordinary window cleaning. Assuming no one prefers the extra risks of high-rise work, the labour supply L_S will be zero for any wage at or below £5. At £6, however, a certain number (30) are prepared to accept the risks of high-rise work. At a wage of £7, more workers (40) are induced to forgo the safer job for the extra rewards. The variation in workers' attitudes towards the risk causes the relative supply curve to be upward sloping.

▨ ▩ ▪ 7.2.3 Labour supply and demand and 'compensating wage differences'

Let us now put our supply and demand curves together. Pursuing the same example, the market demand for high-rise window cleaners will be downward sloping, as for any labour. The determination of wages and employment is shown in Figure 7.3.

It is assumed in this figure that a process of free-market bidding will sooner or later lead to a market equilibrium with supply equal to demand at a level of 35, with a wage rate of £6.50 per hour. There is thus a wage premium of £1.50 or 30 per cent compared with ordinary window cleaning, which is the 'compensating wage difference', representing the market valuation of what it takes to induce workers to assume the extra risk of high-rise work.

Exercise 7.2

Show, using a demand and supply diagram, what would happen to high-rise window cleaners' wages and employment on the completion of a new high-rise office block in town.

▨ ▩ ▪ 7.2.4 Human capital

One over-simplification in the model of labour markets so far is that we have ignored the effect of differences in skill. Yet skill differences account for a good proportion of wage differences, for the simple reason that the supply of workers with specialized skills is restricted. It could be argued that a few jobs require rare abilities that can be developed

Figure 7.4
Age–wage profiles
and the investment
in human capital

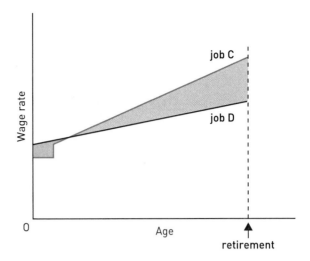

but not acquired if not already present – not everyone can acquire the skill to participate in professional tennis, for example. Nevertheless, most jobs use skills that require greater or lesser amounts of education and training. The theory of human capital states that people will have an incentive to acquire skills (or 'human capital') if it gives them access to high-paying jobs. Suppose that we consider two further jobs, C and D. Job C pays more than job D but it requires an extra year's training. The pay differential thus 'compensates' for the disadvantage of having to take an extra year's training, in a way analogous to our window cleaner example, where the high-rise worker is compensated for the extra risk.

But what is the precise disadvantage of this training? We can picture this by looking at how wages might hypothetically alter over a lifetime of work, as shown in Figure 7.4.

In job D a steady increase in wages is expected through to retirement. In job C only a low income is received in the year spent training (perhaps from a government grant). But while the starting wage for job C is the same as for job D, only a year behind, it is pictured as increasing more rapidly over the lifetime. The differentials of job C over job D increase over time. The total blue area represents the benefit of the extra training. The cost, however, is the grey area. This cost represents the lost wages during the early period. To be added to this are the fees incurred for the training and any other 'out-of-pocket' costs, and the total costs represent the 'disadvantage' of the training.

Put in this way, this is really a theory of investment, similar to any investment in physical capital. A firm buys a machine and thereby incurs costs in the present. It expects that the machine will produce extra revenues and profits in the future, these being the pay-off to the investment. Similarly, the pay-off to the individual of undergoing education or training is the extra wages to be gained later on. There will also, in the case of training, be a pay-off to the firm that provides the training for its workforce, in the form of greater productivity from that workforce. The only difference, then, between investment in physical capital and investment in human capital is that, whereas physical capital could be sold off to another user, it is difficult or impossible to sell human capital once acquired, except in a slave society.

Monetary advantage is not the only reason for education and training. The theory of human capital stresses the monetary rationale but this need not exclude other 'non-pecuniary' factors. These must include the satisfaction of studying (I hope you agree) and the potential future rewards of being more educated or trained, or perhaps a more satisfying job.

Exercise 7.3

What are the costs and benefits, as you see them, of studying on a distance-learning course, such as an Open University course? When are they likely to occur? Which of them might, in principle, be quantifiable?

In thinking of the acquisition of human capital as an investment, the particular case of training presents a problem that has proved vitally important in the UK economy and other economies. The problem is that much training, to be effective, needs to be done in and by firms rather than schools. The basic question this poses is: who pays for the training?

One way for the individual to pay for firm-based training is to work for the firm but receive lower wages during the training period. At the extreme, trainees might receive no wages, or even pay the firm for the training received. The underlying assumption here is that the trainees (or their families) own sufficient funds to cover living expenses during the training period or can gain access to funds through the capital market. You might want to judge for yourself how realistic that assumption is.

▪ ▪ ▪ 7.2.5 Summary and implications of the perfect competition model

The analysis began with five economic assumptions, A1 to A5, to which we now add another:

A6 Potential trainees have access to perfect capital markets.

Question What answers are given by the perfect competition model to the two broad questions in Section 7.1.2?

Taking the first question, wage differentials are explained as the outcome of the individual choices underlying the supply of and demand for labour. In sum, the wages of one job may be more than another's because:

1 there is a 'compensating difference' in the conditions of work (e.g. risk or unpleasantness);
2 the job requires particular skills which are costly to acquire. Workers must incur these costs through undergoing education or training. Only those that choose to do so receive the compensating rewards of better-paid jobs.

As for the second question, the only aim of government intervention in this view should be to support free-market processes. For example, within such a framework it is easy to rationalize the case that is sometimes made against minimum-wage legislation. This issue is taken up in Section 7.3.

7.3 From perfect to imperfect competition: minimum-wage legislation

In 1999 the then recently elected Labour government introduced a national minimum wage for the first time in the UK. Such legislation is an example of the institutional structures that make labour markets imperfectly competitive. This section uses the example of minimum-wage legislation to effect a transition from the perfectly competitive labour market to imperfectly competitive labour markets. Minimum-wage legislation is examined, first, from the perspective of the perfectly competitive model, and then from within an imperfectly competitive framework. The policy implications of the models are very different.

▪ ▪ ▪ 7.3.1 The perfectly competitive labour market and minimum-wage legislation

This section begins with an illustration of the general argument against intervention fore-shadowed at the end of Section 7.2. It examines the case that is made against the state attempting to raise the wages of the low-paid. In most industrialized countries there is a national minimum wage that applies to all jobs. Economists basing their arguments on the demand and supply framework have usually argued that this must reduce employment in those jobs where the minimum wage is above the market wage.

The argument is illustrated in Figure 7.5, which gives the supply and demand for labour hours in the low-pay sectors of the economy. If the government imposes a wage W_M, where the market would otherwise settle on a wage W_E, the hours of work in these jobs are restricted to L_M. The benefit to workers who keep their jobs is the increased wage rate, but $L_E - L_M$ labour hours are no longer available. The extent of this shortfall is determined by the size of the wage rise and the elasticity of labour demand.

On the basis of this analysis it is commonly argued that minimum-wage legislation is detrimental to economic efficiency even if it reduces inequality. It could also be argued that the legislation might exacerbate inequality: if large numbers of people were to be made unemployed and they all received low state benefits, this could more than outweigh any benefits to equality from raising the pay of those in work.

The development of UK government policy during the 1980s and early 1990s was con-sistent with these general conclusions. In the UK, until recently, minimum-wage legislation applied to only a minority of the workforce – those in industries thought to be unprotected by trade unions and covered instead by Wages Boards and Councils. The chief areas covered were clothing, agriculture, retail trades and catering. In 1986 protection was limited to those over 21 years of age, and holiday pay was excluded from the regulations even for adults. This was a precursor to the eventual abolition of all the councils in 1993 except the one for agricultural workers.

Figure 7.5
The effect of minimum-wage legislation on employment under perfect competition

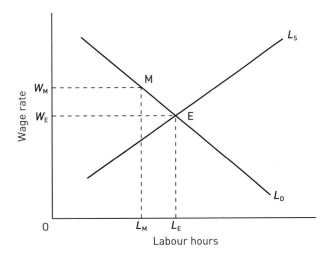

The reintroduction of minimum-wage legislation in 1999 clearly reflected policy makers' reliance upon a different economic model of the labour market.

■■■ 7.3.2 Minimum-wage legislation in imperfectly competitive labour markets

For the rest of this chapter we will dismantle the perfect competition model, by considering what happens in a number of cases when the assumptions are dropped and new ones inserted. This will bring us to a more detailed examination of the policy issues we have highlighted, starting with minimum-wage legislation.

With this issue fresh in mind from the previous section, it is appropriate to begin with assumptions A1 and A2, two assumptions that were crucial to deriving the policy conclusion that argued against intervention. In particular, we should question the proposition that firms cannot individually alter wages. This proposition is illustrated by the horizontal curve L_{S1} in Figure 7.6, which shows an infinitely elastic supply of labour hours to a firm at the going wage rate. For two related reasons this assumption may be false. Let us assume that a firm offers to employ workers at a wage less than W. Would anybody work for the firm? The answer is yes. First, there may be many workers who lack information about what jobs and wages are available elsewhere – so they accept the job or, simply, continue working for the firm if they already work there. Second, even if they have information about better-paying jobs they may face transport and other costs that make it detrimental to switch jobs. Some workers may leave the company, or fewer workers apply, so on balance the firm that offers lower wages will get some labour but less than before. In other words, the supply curve of labour to a particular firm is likely to be upward sloping. This is illustrated by the curve L_{S2} in Figure 7.6.

The fact that the labour supply curve L_{S2} slopes upwards means that we must now reconstruct the analysis of the firm's employment decision. This is done in Figure 7.7.

We start with a labour supply curve L_S which is upward sloping like the curve L_{S2} in Figure 7.6. Under perfect competition the upward-sloping labour supply curve was a *market* supply curve and the profit-maximizing level of employment was determined to be $MRP = W$. The curve L_S in Figure 7.7, on the other hand, is the supply curve for a single firm under imperfect competition, taken from Figure 7.6. The profit-maximizing level of employment is no longer where $MRP = W$.

Figure 7.6
Labour supply curves of a single firm. L_{S1}: labour supply to a firm under perfect competition; L_{S2}: labour supply to a firm under imperfect competition

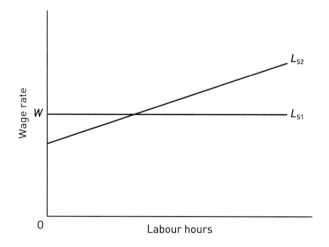

Figure 7.7
The determination
of wages and
employment under
imperfect
competition

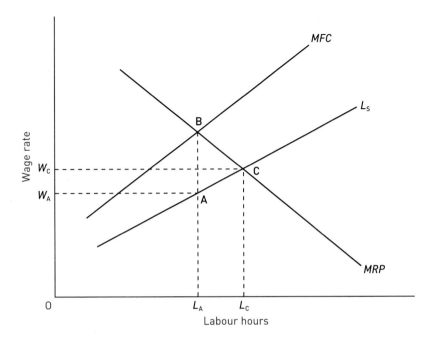

**Marginal
factor cost**

The marginal
factor cost of
labour is the extra
cost of employing
an extra unit of
labour.

The firm which aims to maximize profits would be failing to do so if it set labour hours at the point C, where $MRP = W_C$ on the supply curve. Why is this? To answer this question, we must recognize that the **marginal factor cost** (*MFC*) of labour, that is, the cost to the firm of employing one extra hour of labour, is not identical to the wage rate if the firm faces an upward-sloping labour supply curve.

In Figure 7.6 the horizontal labour supply curve to the firm under perfect competition, L_{S1}, implies that the *MFC* is equal to the wage rate (which is why we did not need to distinguish them in Section 7.3.1). Because the supply curve of labour is upward sloping for the firm under imperfect competition, the *MFC* is equal to the wage rate (the cost attributed to the one extra hour) *plus* the small change in the wage bill of all the other hours worked. That is, the *MFC* must be *above* the wage rate. A numerical example will serve to illustrate this point. Suppose a firm employs 100 hours of labour for £5 per hour. Its total wage bill is therefore £500. If it were to increase the hours to 101, it would need to raise its wage rate to, say, £5.25 in order to attract the extra hour of labour. The new wage bill is $101 \times £5.25 = £530.25$. Hence the cost of the extra hour is £30.25, greater than the wage rate for one hour's work.

Figure 7.7 shows the relationship between L_S, which traces out the wage rate the firm must offer to attract each level of labour supply, and the *MFC* curve, which traces out the marginal cost to the firm of employing successively greater amounts of labour.

We can now answer the question posed above. Why will the firm fail to maximize profits if it sets labour hours at point C in Figure 7.7? Suppose that the firm were to set employment at point C, where $W = MRP$. If it lowers labour hours by one unit, the amount of labour cost saved equals the wage rate, W_C, plus the reduction in the wage bill of its remaining workers. This is shown by the *MFC* curve, which lies above L_S. Hence the amount saved is greater than the revenue lost (*MRP*) and the firm's profits will rise.

Only when *MFC* equals *MRP* will profits be maximized – as illustrated by point B on Figure 7.7. Why? If labour hours were lower than at B, profits could be raised by increasing them, since $MRP > MFC$. Conversely, if labour hours were higher than at B, profits could be raised by lowering them, since $MFC > MRP$.

Figure 7.8
Minimum wages
under imperfect
competition

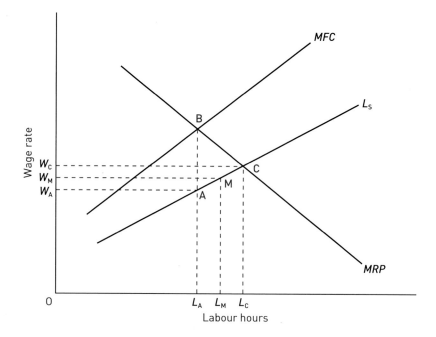

Note, however, that when hours worked are determined in this way the wage rate is W_A, given by the relevant point on the supply curve – that is, A. It is evident that both wages W_A and employment L_A are *lower* than at C, where $W = MRP$, the equilibrium position that would apply if the imperfectly competitive firm were replaced by a number of perfectly competitive firms collectively facing the market labour supply curve L_S.

Consider, now, the impact of minimum-wage legislation where the minimum wage is set at W_M, above the level W_A that the firm would otherwise choose. Figure 7.8 repeats Figure 7.7 but adds a minimum wage of W_M. In this case we can say that the firm would employ labour hours L_M, greater than L_A. Why? Because there is no advantage for the firm in employing fewer labour hours. At M the *MRP* is greater than the minimum wage rate W_M, so any cut-back in hours would lead to a fall in profits. The point is that the minimum wage prevents the employer from reducing the wage bill for the remaining workers, which would otherwise have been the reason for lowering the hours worked. To the left of point M, the *MFC* facing the employer is equal to W_M however many labour hours employed, since the existence of the minimum wage makes this section of the supply curve horizontal. On the other hand, the firm would not raise hours worked because that would mean raising wages above W_M and, the *MFC* being above *MRP* at that point and all points rightwards, this would lower profits. Hence M must be the profit-maximizing point under the minimum-wage legislation.

How does this conclusion differ from that obtained in the perfect competition model?

The conclusion is in striking contrast to that obtained in the perfect competition model. Up to the value W_C, any increase in the minimum wage brings unequivocal benefits to workers, in the form of both higher wages and greater employment levels, while removing some of the profits of the companies. Once W_C has been reached, however, any further rises in the minimum wage would lead to falls in employment, in line with the perfect competition model.

As a result of this analysis, we can only conclude that the effect of minimum-wage legislation on employment is uncertain from the point of view of economic theory. If the perfect competition model is correct, or if the minimum wage is pushed too high (above W_C), we would expect a reduction in employment. But if the imperfect competition model with an upward-sloping labour supply is correct, and the minimum wage is not pushed excessively above the free-market level W_A, we would expect an increase in employment. Only careful empirical investigation will be able to show us which effect is valid, and the conclusion could be different for different countries. Most empirical studies have been done for the US labour market, where there is currently no consensus as to the impact on employment. A number of recent studies have shown little or no effect in either direction.

Case study: Should Florida introduce a minimum wage?

On 2 November 2004, Florida voters overwhelmingly approved new minimum-wage legislation that would apply throughout the state. This meant that Florida was the thirteenth state to introduce a minimum wage that was higher than the federal minimum which applied across the United States. In a report designed to evaluate the impacts, Pollin, Brenner and Wicks-Lim (2004) suggest that the economic case in favour of the higher minimum was strong. In the first instance, the federal minimum-wage level had fallen by nearly 40 per cent, in real terms, from its peak in 1968. At a minimum wage of $5.15 per hour in 2004, a significant number of families supposedly well above the official poverty line were facing hardships such as missing meals, housing evictions and disconnection of utilities.

In their evaluation, Pollin *et al.* suggested that the overall cost to business of the increased minimum would be $406 million, which amounted to 0.04 per cent of total sales revenues. The main reaction of businesses would, the researchers argued, be to increase prices by a small amount, part of which would be offset by productivity gains as workers would be expected to become slightly more committed to their

jobs. On the other hand, their analysis showed little reason to be concerned about 'unintended' consequences. The implications for costs were small while layoffs and relocations were themselves costly suggesting that the effect on unemployment levels might be minimal. Indeed, the fact that the disposal income of low-wage workers and families would increase by $500 to $600 per household would not only bring about an opportunity to improve their own quality of life but also raise the turnover of retail stores in low-income neighbourhoods. Indexing the minimum wage to changes in the cost of living as measured by the retail price index would be an important part of making this change valuable to low-paid workers over the medium to long term.

(Source: adapted from Pollin *et al.*, 2004)

Question

Would you expect to see similar conclusions for different countries? In this case, do we need the imperfect competition model to provide an economic justification for Florida's increased minimum wage? If not, why not?

This conclusion is consistent with the recent UK experience. Following the change of government in 1997 to a Labour administration, a national minimum wage was introduced for the first time on 1 April 1999, set at an hourly rate of £3.60 for adults (with a reduced rate of £3.00 for 18–21 year olds). Roughly 1.3 million workers became eligible for wage rises, of whom 7 out of 10 were women. The nation's wage bill rose by about 0.35 per cent on average, but much more in the low-paying industries. Yet, according to the Low Pay Commission, there were no discernible effects on employment. The groups most affected saw rises in their levels of employment both before and after the introduction of the minimum wage. Reassured by the absence of adverse employment effects, the government annually revised the level of the minimum wage upwards: thus the adult rate is £5.05 (October 2005).

7.4 Imperfectly competitive labour markets: trade unions and segmentation

Two aspects of the unrealistic nature of the perfectly competitive model of labour markets are its assumption that firms and workers are independent agents (assumption A1) and its failure to correspond to the observed realities of labour markets. Assumption A1 is contradicted by the existence of trade unions in many industries. The observed reality of wages in many labour markets is that differentials seem to reflect a 'segmentation' of labour markets into 'good' and 'bad' jobs rather more than skill differences and compensating differences in work conditions.

▨ ▨ ■ 7.4.1 Trade unions and the labour market

Perhaps the most unrealistic aspect of the model of perfect competition in the labour market is the view that labour-market actors – firms and workers – all act independently and are unable to influence prices or wages (assumption A1). This may be a fair approximation in a few minor sectors of the economy, but for the most part in many countries wages and conditions are the subject of collective negotiations between trade unions and employers, or sometimes between groups of unions and employers. If wages and conditions are not the subject of collective bargaining, they are often regulated by explicit legal or implicit customary codes. In addition, many millions of people in Europe are employed by governments whose behaviour cannot simply be likened to a profit-maximizing firm. In all these cases, the simple notion of labour supply and labour demand under perfect competition, as outlined in Section 7.2, is inapplicable.

We will look here at some of the ways in which the presence of trade unions changes the picture. Table 7.3 gives an approximate idea of the potential influence of unions in some different countries. It gives the union density, defined as the number of union members as a percentage of potential union members. While it might be reasonable as a first approximation to disregard unions in the USA (it has a union density of only 16 per cent), an analysis of labour markets in most of Europe, especially in Scandinavia, would be seriously unrealistic. Nevertheless, UK unions have been substantially cut down to size in the last 20 years. The union density of 34 per cent for 1994 in Table 7.3 is actually a point on a slope, as the density has steadily fallen from over 50 per cent in 1980. This fall occurred in the context of adverse economic conditions (high unemployment) and a series of anti-union pieces of legislation, starting with the 1980 Employment Act, which successfully limited the ability of unions to recruit new members and reduced their power in relation to management.

The perfect competition theory essentially regards the impact of unions on the market as detrimental; hence the evident policy conclusion is to reduce their influence. There are two main bases for the argument. First, it is assumed that unions raise wages, thus moving the firm up its labour demand curve to point M in Figure 7.8, thereby displacing employment from the unionized to the non-unionized sector of the economy. What is

Table 7.3
Union density in
1994

Country	Union density %
Australia	35
Canada	38
France	9
Germany	29
Italy	39
Japan	24
Netherlands	26
Spain	19
Sweden	91
UK	34
USA	16

Source: *OECD Employment Outlook*, 1997, p.71

not clear is how far up the curve the unions would want to force wages. It is hardly reasonable to think of unions aiming to push wages up indefinitely. Assuming they had the power to raise wages, but assuming also that they were aware of the downward-sloping labour demand curve, they would want to limit the use of that power so as not to sacrifice too much employment. But how much is 'too much'? This is not an easy question, because it depends on what sorts of workers have power in unions – is it the older workers with relatively secure jobs who would want to raise wages substantially, or is it the more marginal younger workers whose jobs are less safe?

Empirical estimates of unions' impact on wages are hard to obtain, but what economists can find is an estimate of a union/non-union wage differential for otherwise similar workers. In Britain, the best estimates of this lie in the 10–15 per cent range for manual workers, though these are subject to quite wide margins of error.

For non-manual workers the estimated impact on wages is much lower, and arguably zero. In most countries (including Britain) the evidence is that trade unions tend to reduce wage inequalities because they are better at raising the wages of lower-paid workers. For policy makers who wish to allow market forces always to have sway, this evidence is one reason for the introduction of policies to reduce the bargaining power of unions.

Second, policy makers might want to reduce unions' influence because they may slow down innovation and lower productivity by enforcing restrictive practices within companies. Here the argument is that, in order to protect jobs, unions prevent the introduction of labour-saving innovations, and hinder the substitution of one kind of labour for another.

Set against these negative connotations for the economic effects of unions, there are also reasons to expect that unions might have a positive impact on productivity. American writers Freeman and Medoff (1984) argue that unions provide a collective 'voice' to speak to management, and that this can improve productivity. Without a union an aggrieved worker may have little choice but to remain unhappy or to quit the firm. A union helps sort out the grievance and hence lowers labour turnover. Lower labour turnover reduces the costs of hiring replacements and provides more incentives for firms to train their employees. Moreover, unions acting in co-operation with management can find ways to improve efficiency that are eventually beneficial. In so far as unions do raise wages, this can also keep up worker morale and hence worker effort (Section 7.5). Finally, it is often recognized that upward pressure on wages may stimulate efficiency gains from improved management. In the short run, higher wage demands from a newly organized union can 'shock' a sleepy management into better performance. But perhaps more important is the long-run effect attributed to unions that have been successful in keeping wages high in Germany. The result has been to force management to adopt strategies for high skills and high productivity. Arguing that managers given the choice will often opt for a low-wage route to competitiveness, the high wages that unions impose could act as a barrier to this route. Instead, management will opt for high value-added products that require high levels of ongoing research and development, sustained investment and continued training for the workforce.

For all these reasons it is theoretically possible that the presence of unions can raise the marginal physical product of labour (MPP_L) and hence the marginal revenue product, which is the basis of the demand for labour curve. A conceivable scenario is then illustrated by Figure 7.9. Our initial point is E, the intersection of the labour supply curve L_S and the marginal revenue product curve in a perfectly competitive labour market in the absence of unions. Now examine the impact of unions. On the one hand they may raise the wage rate, which in the absence of any changes in efficiency would lower employment accordingly, as shown by a movement along the MRP curve to point M. However, where unions also raise the MRP, shifting the MRP curve rightwards, this would in itself raise employment. Putting the two effects together results in an ambiguous effect. As drawn at point N the net result is no impact on employment, but depending on the extent of unions' impact on the MPP_L, the employment effect could be positive or negative.

In view of the theoretically conflicting theories about unions' impact on productivity, economists have sought to estimate the empirical effects. The results are not clear-cut, but the balance of evidence suggests that in a significant number of cases the impact on productivity is positive. That does not mean to say that it always is or will be positive: this is one of those many areas in economics when the answer cannot be predicted by theory and may differ empirically from circumstance to circumstance.

Thus far we have considered the impact of unions on wages and on productivity in companies. In addition, unions can have an effect on other aspects of the labour market. For example, it has been found quite consistently in a number of studies that unions tend to compress wage differentials. That this is so should not be too surprising, because much

Figure 7.9
Unions' impact on wages and employment

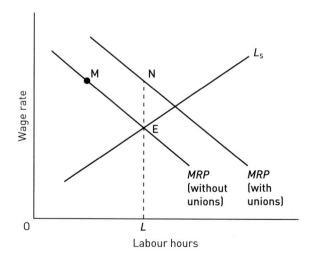

of the union movement has been historically rooted in an ideological commitment to equality. This means that a complete assessment of unions should not rest simply on the theoretical and empirical issues looked at here, even though they are important for our analysis of labour markets.

▪▪▪ 7.4.2 Segmentation and segregation in the labour market

Segmentation and wage differentials

While the perfect competition model suggests to us that wage differentials in the economy reflect skill differences or 'compensating' differences in work conditions, such a conclusion has often seemed at odds with the reality observed by empirical labour economists. Starting in the USA in the late 1960s, observers began to notice an intransigent 'segmentation' of jobs – initially a dual system of two segments. In one segment, the primary labour market, were 'good jobs' – ones with reasonably high wages, some prospects for improvement (including access to training), relative job security, high fringe benefits and long job tenure. In the secondary labour market were 'bad jobs' with the converse, that is, low pay, high turnover and relative insecurity, with few other benefits. Such segmentation has also been observed in other countries. One way of seeing this in Britain is to note the considerable differences in average wages in different industries, as shown in Table 7.4. It is apparent that jobs in, say, the energy and water supply industries pay well, while the hotel and catering industry is an area of low pay. Thus male manual workers in the former industry receive on average 81 per cent more in wages than their equivalents in the latter industry. Other wage differences are less extreme, but still substantial.

There are many empirical studies by economists which attempt to explain differences in wages. It is common for such studies to focus on differences in skill levels and on compensating factors, as suggested by the perfectly competitive model of the labour market. But although such considerations do play a role, the studies almost invariably leave

Table 7.4
Average hourly pay (excluding overtime) of full-time employees, Great Britain, 2000

Industry	Men		Women	
	manual £	non-manual £	manual £	non-manual £
Agriculture, forestry and fishing	5.62	–	5.23	6.65
Energy and water supply	10.31	15.66	–	10.22
Mining	8.01	–	–	–
Manufacture of basic metal and fabricated metal products	7.92	12.48	5.24	7.95
Manufacture of transport equipment	9.40	14.61	6.68	10.00
Other manufacturing industries	6.75	11.65	5.67	7.94
Construction	7.68	13.00	–	8.47
Hotels and catering	5.71	9.97	4.68	7.50
Transport and communications	7.60	13.08	7.66	9.14
Banking, finance, insurance, etc.	9.39	18.41	5.71	10.46
Other services (including government)	6.72	13.47	5.20	9.52

Source: *New Earnings Survey*, 2000

unexplained some of the variation in wages between industries. The remaining variation may be thought to reflect elements of segmentation, wherein there are notable barriers to entry preventing workers in less good jobs from transferring to the better ones. This implies a rejection of assumption A3: perfect labour mobility. Here are three factors preventing such mobility that economists have looked at.

1 There may be barriers to obtaining the necessary skills for a primary-sector job.
2 Groups of workers may seek to protect their privileged status by erecting artificial barriers around their occupation. Professional workers may use artificially high qualifications standards; trade unions may use industrial muscle to protect their craft status.
3 Discrimination on the grounds of sex, race or disability is sometimes associated with such barriers and is used to keep certain groups out of an occupation by rejection or, more usually, by discouragement.

Exercise 7.4

Can you think of any other factors preventing labour mobility?

Occupational segregation and male/female differentials

An enduring and striking feature of labour markets in all countries is the lower pay received by female workers. This is evident in every industry in Britain, as you can see from taking another look at Table 7.4. Table 7.5 shows that the ratio of female to male earnings is less than 100 per cent in all the countries listed. However, there is considerable variation in the extent to which women are disadvantaged: of the countries shown, female workers fare best in Australia and worst in Japan. This variation suggests that women's disadvantages in the labour market are linked to the social and economic environment, which varies from country to country.

One of the major explanations that writers have given for the low pay of women is their concentration into relatively few occupations. As women's labour is over-supplied to

Table 7.5
Ratio of female to male weekly earnings of full-time workers

Country	Ratio of female to male weekly earnings %
Australia	87
Sweden	84
Switzerland	75
Spain	71
UK	75
Japan	64
USA	76

Source: Blau, 2000, pp.75–99

Table 7.6
Proportion of
female workers,
Great Britain, 1992

Occupation	Proportion of female workers %
All workers	47
Managers and professionals	30
Intermediate non-manual workers	62
Junior non-manual workers	76
Personal service workers	82
Foremen and supervisors	17
Skilled manual workers	10
Semi-skilled manual workers	41
Unskilled manual workers	64

Source: *Labour Force Survey*, 1992

these occupations there is no market pressure for a rise in pay. This unbalanced supply of female labour comes from the exclusion of women from many high-paying occupations. This is a process I like to refer to as *horizontal segregation*. Horizontal segregation is an instance of labour market segmentation, where the host of social and economic forces limiting the access of women to the high-paying occupations constitutes the source of labour immobility. Note, however, that segmentation can occur independently of such segregation and is conceivably quite separate.

The horizontal segregation of women is supplemented by *vertical segregation*, whereby males are disproportionately found in higher grades and females in lower grades, within any particular occupation or industry. This is a most obvious source of pay inequality. The reasons for the disparity range from overt discrimination to more subtle limitations placed upon women via their role in domestic labour. Some idea of how extensive horizontal and vertical segregation is in Britain can be gleaned from looking at Table 7.6. Note the predominance of female workers among the lower-ranking occupations (in terms of expected pay levels), such as personal service workers and unskilled manual workers. Nearly three-quarters of women workers are to be found either in these occupations or among junior and intermediate non-manual workers. Moreover, these figures conceal further concentrations of women among the detailed occupations subsumed within each group of the table.

Both segmentation and segregation are contributory causes of inequality in the labour market. Moreover, artificial barriers to labour mobility and the under-use of women in many areas of the labour market are evident aspects of inefficiency. The case for government intervention, contrary to the perfect competition model, is strong. Some policies directed at these features of the labour market are:

1 To subsidize the acquisition of skills through education and training.
2 To prevent the artificial use of barriers into the professions by ensuring that qualifications used as entry criteria are justified – that is, to regulate the profession from outside.
3 To use education and training to counteract forms of socialization that support the gender-identification of jobs.
4 To proscribe acts of direct discrimination in selecting on grounds of sex or other characteristics. Into this category in Britain, for example, come the 1970 Equal Pay Act and the 1975 Discrimination Act.

▨ ▧ ■ 7.4.3 Recent changes in the UK labour market revisited

We are now in a position to use some of the ideas already developed to try to understand two of the recent changes to the UK labour market observed in Section 7.1.1. These are the increase in the relative wages of skilled workers and the rise in the proportion of skilled workers. The analysis begins with the perfectly competitive model and then introduces institutional factors.

An application of supply and demand analysis

We can begin to make analytical sense of these changes by making use of the ideas and tools we have developed in this chapter. It is useful to start with the competitive model, represented in Figure 7.3, but we are now going to change the framework to the relative supply and demand for skilled workers.

In Figure 7.10 the line L_D represents the relative demand for skilled workers. By the word 'relative' I am referring to the ratio of skilled to unskilled workers. It slopes downwards because firms want to minimize the costs of producing each unit. If skilled workers became relatively more expensive, firms would want to substitute cheaper workers where possible. L_S represents the relative supply of skilled workers. A higher wage induces more people to undergo the necessary training to become skilled. Note that we are assuming a certain time-lapse here: new skilled workers cannot be found instantaneously. Rather the line says that, following a wage rise and after time for the training and education to have taken place, there will be more skilled workers.

Suppose now that new technology leads to an increase in the relative demand for skilled workers (for any given relative wage). There will be an outward shift from L_{D1} to L_{D2}. If nothing else happens, the effect will be to raise both the relative wage (from w_1 to w_2) and the relative quantity (from n_1 to n_2). This is precisely what we have observed in Table 7.1.

The story, however, is far from complete, because we ought to ask whether changes have also been occurring in the relative supply of skilled labour. The answer is patently yes: over recent decades great efforts have been made by UK governments (and other governments) to open up access to education and training in many ways. We can represent this change by a shift in the supply curve of skilled labour from L_{S1} to L_{S2}. Note, however,

Figure 7.10
Relative supply and demand for skilled workers

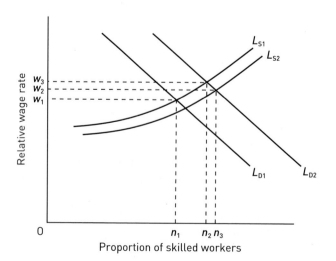

the way I have drawn the diagram: the rightward shift in the supply curve is smaller than the rightward shift in the relative demand curve. The significance of this assumption is that the resulting new equilibrium still has both higher relative wages for skilled workers and a higher relative stock of skilled workers, consistent with Table 7.1.

Institutional factors

Although a supply/demand framework has got us some way in understanding the observed directions of change, this does not mean that we are relying on a perfectly competitive model. There are several ways in which institutions are important components of a full analysis. We will now discuss two of them.

First, a crucial aspect of the above analysis is that the growth of the supply of skilled workers was seen to lag behind the growth of demand. The supply of skilled workers depends partly on the decisions of individuals (and their families) but also, fundamentally, on the decisions of governments, which control and largely fund the education and training institutions that generate the skills. If skills supply is failing to keep up with the growth in demand, this could be because government and individuals have failed to anticipate the changes and to devote sufficient resources to the necessary investment in schools and colleges. Thus the politics of education, over a long period, are important to understanding the relative shifts in skilled labour supply. A traditional accusation levied against British education was that for too long it was elitist, caring for the needs of the brightest and wealthiest but neglecting to develop the skills of the majority (by comparison with other countries). A corollary of this analysis is that, should government become more successful in accelerating the supply of skills faster than demand, an equalizing tendency could develop in the labour markets, in which the relative pay of skilled workers would fall.

Second, an institutional feature that needs to be incorporated into the analysis is the role of trade unions. However, they have been going through a period of declining density (Section 7.4.1), so their direct sphere of influence has become a smaller part of the overall economy. Declining union power helps to explain why wage inequality has increased especially fast in Britain since the 1970s. In other countries, presumably experiencing a similar increase in demand for skills, the rise in the skilled wage premium was much less than in Britain. In principle, this cross-country difference can be explained in terms of our analysis in two ways. First, in other countries governments may have been more successful in keeping the supply of skills up with the rising demand (as in the above example). Second, union power persisted longer or even grew in the other countries, modifying the competitive forces to sustain greater equality. As we saw above (Section 7.4.1), this power has traditionally been used to support a somewhat lower wage dispersion between workers.

7.5 Imperfectly competitive labour markets: efficiency wages

Section 7.5 continues the application of supply and demand analysis and institutional factors to recent changes in the UK labour market by turning to the third change: increased work intensity. This introduces the main topic of the section, which is the analysis of worker motivation and management.

Question	How could one adapt the analysis of the relative supply and demand of skilled workers (Figure 7.10) to explain the increased proportion of workers with high levels of work effort?

The answer is fairly straightforward. A similar analysis could be used to understand the increased work effort, if we were to redraw Figure 7.10 but label the axes as 'Wage rate' and 'Number of high-effort workers relative to low-effort workers'. If the technology changes lead to a demand for higher effort, we would expect to see both higher effort on average and greater relative rewards. Table 7.1 shows the higher effort, but we do not have evidence about how the relative wages of high-effort and low-effort workers have changed.

Part of the answer may lie in the reduced influence of trade unions. Trade unions have traditionally attempted to resist pressures to intensify work. However, they have been going through a period of declining density (Section 7.4.1), so their direct sphere of influence has become a smaller part of the overall economy. Moreover, even where they are present, unions are likely to be less able to influence events than they were when there were fewer restrictions on their activities, including their ability to use the strike weapon. The fact that trade unions have declined faster in Britain than elsewhere in Europe may be a factor in making Britain the place where effort has increased the most in Europe (Green and McIntosh, 2001).

This brief discussion of increasing work intensity in the UK labour market opens up the more general issue of worker motivation. An important economic approach to this issue links wages and productivity, arguing that higher wages can increase productivity.

▦ ▪ ■ 7.5.1 Efficiency wages and the worker discipline effect

Efficiency wage models

Efficiency wage models recognize that higher wages raise productivity by increasing the efficiency with which labour is managed and motivated.

We have already alluded briefly, in discussing the role of unions (Section 7.4.1), to the possible effect of higher wages in eliciting greater effort through improved 'morale' and hence motivation of workers. This effect is one example of a range of models for labour market analysis entitled, a bit misleadingly, **efficiency wage models**.

The common conclusion of efficiency wage models is that higher wages can raise productivity. In each case, we shall, in effect, be dropping assumption A4. So far in this chapter I have looked at the complications that arise when assumptions A1, A2 and A3 are replaced by various alternatives. Turning to assumption A4 shows why it too plays a crucial role in the perfect competition model. We shall address the fact that, once the labour contract has been agreed, it is impossible for employers to monitor the effort that is put in during every minute of the day. Some way of *managing and motivating labour* has to be found.

There are three such models. In the first model, it is argued that better wages may lead to improved relations between employers and workers. The 'morale' effect arises when the employer pays wages above the minimum that would be necessary to keep employees from quitting the firm, and workers respond by exceeding the production targets that management sets for them. Thus, up to a point, it pays the employer to pay a 'good' wage, above the basic minimum: the improved morale results in greater productivity that more than covers the extra expense.

A second model of how higher wages might improve productivity applies primarily in low-income countries. In fact it was here, in the context of agriculture in low-income countries, that economists first noticed the relationship between wages and productivity. The argument is that higher wages enable a better standard of living for the workforce, which leads to stronger and healthier workers. Where a firm's workforce is largely manual, keeping it healthy will increase productivity.

There are obvious limits to this model. It could not apply where there is a high turn-over of workers – it is no good from the firm's angle to create a healthy workforce for other firms. It would not apply where there is a reasonable level of welfare benefits or other sources of income that allow good nourishment independent of wages from work. For this reason it is not a model we would expect to be relevant in the industrial world, except perhaps in pockets of extreme poverty.

The worker discipline effect

A third, and more general, argument builds from the proposition that work itself is disliked by workers, and that the only reason people go to work is for the wages. This proposition underlies the approach of most economists. We can immediately object that many workers gain satisfaction from their jobs. Nevertheless, there is a large class of work which is essentially alienating or unpleasant. Moreover, it remains a reasonable starting point to suggest that if workers could have the same wages without having to put in the effort, they would frequently choose to do so.

In 1915, Henry Ford instituted a further dramatic change in his automobile factory near Detroit. I say 'further' because he had only recently introduced his revolution-ary assembly-line techniques to car production. Now he suddenly raised the wages of shop-floor workers from $3 to $5 a day. Furthermore, he maintained this would increase his profits. From the point of view of much conventional economics based on the simple perfect competition model this makes little sense. But it is possible to see Ford's reasoning in the context of the theory of efficiency wages. Part of the story was prob-ably to do with the morale effect outlined above. It may also be due to the 'worker discipline effect'.

The idea behind the worker discipline effect is that workers cannot be monitored closely every minute. They must be induced to continue supplying effort when not observed by a manager or supervisor. But if work is unpleasant and disliked, why work? In such circumstances, the 'rational' worker would choose to minimize his or her effort, except for one thing: the risk of being caught shirking and consequently dismissed. From the firm's point of view, this discipline must be sufficiently strong to motivate effort from the workforce. This necessitates the following measures.

1 There must be some chance of workers who are not working properly being caught. In other words, there must be some supervisors to direct and monitor workers in their daily tasks. These supervisors add to the costs of production.
2 The threat to dismiss shirking workers (or otherwise penalize them) must be serious.

It is in the latter point that the importance of wages comes in. Suppose that wages are low – at or not much above the income that workers would get easily from elsewhere, either from state benefits or from other easily available employment. In these circumstances, there is not much to lose from being dismissed. The 'cost of job loss' – the difference between wages and the income that could be obtained if dismissed – must be sufficient to make dismissal a real danger. Otherwise, why would workers work? The problem Henry

Ford found among his workforce prior to his raising wages was that there was a great deal of disenchantment with the work itself, and consequently a low level of effort and high turnover (either from dismissal or from workers simply leaving). By upping the stakes, Ford made the 'cost of job loss' considerable for his workforce. His confidence in the profit-increasing reason for his move lay in his expectation that at $5 a day he would have a more loyal, harder-working workforce, whose overall productivity would increase by more than the extra wage cost.

Having looked at these three models of how high wages can lead to higher productivity, we will now ask: what implications do they have for our analysis of labour markets? We will look at two answers to this question: the first leads to a modification of our analysis, while the second introduces the subject of unemployment.

▦ ▨ ▪ 7.5.2 Implications of efficiency wage models

First implication: the elasticity of demand for labour

Recall that the marginal revenue product of labour (MRP) curve is the basis of the derived demand for labour, because the profit-maximizing condition for the firm is to employ workers up to the point at which the MRP equals the wage rate. This proposition remains true. But we must now recognize that firms could change the MRP, for any value of L, by changing the wage rate. The higher the wage rate the greater the effort and productivity of the marginal worker (and, also, of the average worker). Thus the marginal physical product of labour (MPP_L) could shift when the wage is changed.

In Figure 7.11, the wage rate is initially W_0. The curve labelled MRP ($W = W_0$) is the appropriate marginal revenue productivity curve for that wage rate. Profits are therefore maximized at labour hours L_0. Notice that, in this analysis, we are working with a model in which profit maximization occurs at $W = MRP$, as in perfect competition, but dropping the assumption that firms cannot individually alter wages. The firm could choose to raise wages to W_1, but if so it would be incorrect to say that hours would fall to the point B. Rather, since at each level of hours the MPP_L is higher due to the efficiency wage effect, the whole MRP curve shifts upwards. In Figure 7.11, maximum profits would instead be obtained at point C and labour hours L_1.

Figure 7.11
Demand for labour, with efficiency wages

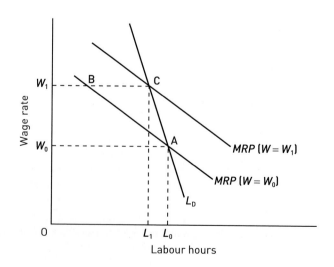

Figure 7.11 thus illustrates that the demand for labour curve in this case (joining points A and C) is less elastic than the *MRP* curve as a result of the efficiency wage effect. Indeed, if you reflect a little, you will see how the *MRP* curve could conceivably have shifted up sufficiently to ensure *no* cut in hours worked or even a rise coincident with the wage rise. Whether that would happen depends on the strength of the efficiency wage effect, which would differ according to circumstances.

Question

At this point it is worth checking your understanding of the above analysis against a possible confusion that sometimes occurs. Consider the following two statements:

1 The basic model tells us that the marginal revenue product of labour is equal to the wage.
2 The efficiency wage model tells us that the marginal revenue product of labour (as well as the marginal physical product of labour) is affected by the wage.

These two statements are both valid, but are making different propositions. Can you see how they are different?

The answer is that the first proposition is a condition that ensures the firm is maximizing its profits. It would be true, under competitive conditions, whether or not efficiency wage forces were important. The second is a causal statement about what determines marginal productivity: the fact that wages are thought to have an impact is the hallmark of efficiency wage models. The statement would be true even if the firm were not at its profit-maximizing position.

Second implication: a rationale for unemployment

For our second implication, we introduce the topic of unemployment, in order to examine an interesting conclusion that follows from efficiency wage models in contrast to the perfect competition model. Recall that, in the latter, it was assumed that labour markets cleared by means of wage adjustments which equate supply and demand. Figure 7.3 depicted one particular cleared labour market. The same arguments apply to the labour market as a whole. In the perfect competition model, then, there is no explanation of why unemployment occurs, other than to imply that if unemployment exists, wages must have failed to adjust to the market-clearing rate. In brief: unemployment could always be eliminated by lowering wages sufficiently.

Consider now the impact of the worker discipline effect. This tells us that, in a world where work is disliked and supervision less than perfect, it would be impossible to motivate workers to work if there were no unemployment. Workers would see that there is little or no cost to being dismissed, because with full employment they could immediately get a job elsewhere at the same wage. Only if there is a risk of spending some time unemployed, with a consequent reduction in income, would workers be induced to work rather than shirk.

This basic insight can be used to show that there must be a certain amount of unemployment to keep the economy at work – perhaps a rather surprising conclusion.

Figure 7.12 is an adaptation of the demand/supply framework applied to the aggregate labour market, but amended to account for the worker discipline effect.

Figure 7.12
Unemployment
from the worker
discipline effect

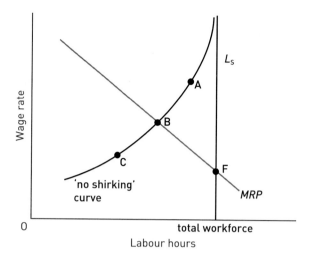

We assume for simplicity a fixed workforce, depicted by the vertical line L_S. The *MRP* is the marginal revenue product of labour curve which is drawn in the usual way, assuming that workers once employed put in the required effort. In terms of the perfect competition model, equilibrium would occur at point F with everyone employed.

However, the argument above has shown that the trouble is that *no worker would choose to work at the wages paid at point F*. Instead, we can plot a relationship between the level of wages and the level of employment as follows.

For a relatively high level of employment (for example, point A) a dismissed worker would experience a relatively short spell of unemployment. Hence a high wage level is needed to motivate workers – a low wage and workers would choose to shirk.

By contrast, at a low level of employment (for example, point C) the consequence of dismissal could be a long period out of work. Therefore a much lower wage level is needed to get people to work. Joining up points such as A and C gives us the 'no shirking curve', meaning that this gives us the wage that employers must pay to elicit proper effort from their workers for each level of employment and unemployment. There is, in other words, a trade-off between high wages and unemployment: lower one of them and it becomes necessary to raise the other in order to secure sufficient employee motivation.

Point B, the intersection of the 'no shirking curve' with the *MRP* curve, is the point at which employers will be maximizing their profits. Hence B is the equilibrium point for the economy. Firms will have no incentive to employ more (or fewer) workers since the wage equals the *MRP*.

Exercise 7.5

At point B, the equilibrium, there are unemployed workers. Why can they not offer to work for lower wages than the existing workers and so get jobs?

This equilibrium with unemployment has been arrived at without assuming that trade unions or governments or any other outside agent manipulates wages. The only departure from the perfect competition model is to drop assumption A4 and replace it with a simple model of worker motivation.

Intervention: could government eliminate unemployment?

The perfect competition model counselled no intervention, owing to its conclusion that full employment was the normal outcome from unfettered market processes. The rather striking conclusion of the model we have just looked at is that it may be counterproductive for government to attempt to reduce or eliminate unemployment, when that unemployment functions as a threat or discipline for those in work. Assume, for the moment, that government policies can alter the level of employment on Figure 7.12. Ask what would be the consequence of raising employment beyond the point B. Answer: a considerable disruption of effort. In a prescient paper written not long after the depression years of the 1930s, the Polish economist Kalecki questioned whether big businesses or the governments under their influence would ever want to eliminate unemployment entirely, even if they would try to reduce it below the levels of the depression years (Kalecki, 1943). In the middle 1960s, when the British economy seemed to operate successfully enough with only a few hundred thousand unemployed, Kalecki's fear appeared misplaced. It was widely assumed then that Keynesianism could ensure full employment. Two decades later, no one was so sure after a prolonged period of high unemployment. It seems likely that the risk of months, even years, on the dole was a motivating factor for many workers in Britain and elsewhere.

But we should not necessarily conclude that it is government's job to maintain a suitable level of unemployment in support of business enterprise, even if the model helps to explain the relaxation of the objective of full employment which no government could fail to emphasize in the 1950s and 1960s. First, there is no suggestion that the currently very high levels of unemployment across Europe are necessary for worker motivation. Nothing in the current argument speaks against aiming for a reduction in these levels. Second, it must be remembered that the model is built on an assumed world of alienating, disliked work, where motivation to work comes primarily through the fear of lost wages. But there are many lines of work where this is not the case, and there are other, more positive forms of motivation, including the provision of more challenging and satisfying work. Encouraging and enabling these other routes to worker motivation would also be a valid form of government intervention. If successful, it would open the door to macroeconomic policies aimed not just at reducing unemployment but also at genuine full employment.

7.6 Conclusion

If nothing else, this chapter will have shown how complex labour markets are in reality, far from the simple perfect competition model of supply and demand. As a general rule, though with exceptions, each time an element of complexity was introduced, questioning the assumptions of the perfect competition model, we developed an alternative model designed to capture some known feature of actual labour markets. Moreover, with each new model we arrived at a rationale for government intervention in one form or another on the grounds of economic efficiency. To take some examples, governments have a case for intervening to remove or minimize barriers to labour mobility between sectors of the labour market, or to impose a wage minimum on the labour market.

Despite the complexity, we have also seen how some far-reaching changes in the labour market can be analysed using a combination of models of supply and demand in the labour market, and an understanding of the institutional features that impinge upon and modify the forces of supply and demand.

Questions for review and discussion

Question 1 Figure 7.13 shows a firm in an imperfectly competitive labour market. Say which wage rate(s) (e.g. W_1, W_2) is/are identified by each of the following descriptions. Note that there may be more than one of the wage rates that satisfies some of the descriptions.

Note:
MFC = Marginal Factor Cost
MRP = Marginal Revenue Product

(a) The wage rate that will be set by the firm if it maximizes its profits in a free market.

$W_1 \ W_2 \ W_3 \ W_4 \ W_5 \ W_6 \ W_7$

(b) The equilibrium wage rate that would result if the imperfectly competitive firm were replaced by a number of perfectly competitive firms collectively facing the market labour supply curve L_S.

$W_1 \ W_2 \ W_3 \ W_4 \ W_5 \ W_6 \ W_7$

(c) A statutory minimum wage rate that would result in the profit-maximizing imperfectly competitive firm employing *fewer* labour hours than it would in a free market.

$W_1 \ W_2 \ W_3 \ W_4 \ W_5 \ W_6 \ W_7$

(d) A statutory minimum wage rate that would result in the profit-maximizing imperfectly competitive firm employing *more* labour hours that it would in a free market.

$W_1 \ W_2 \ W_3 \ W_4 \ W_5 \ W_6 \ W_7$

Figure 7.13
Firm in imperfectly competitive labour market

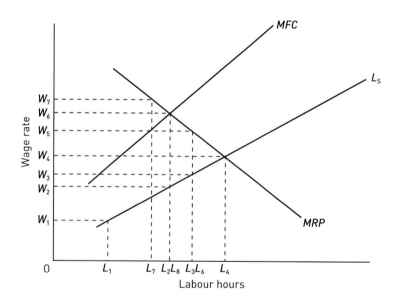

Question 2   Say which statement correctly completes this sentence:

If males are disproportionately found in higher grades and females in lower grades within an occupation, this is an example of

A ❑   labour market segmentation.
B ❑   vertical segregation.
C ❑   horizontal segregation.
D ❑   efficiency wages.

Question 3   Assume that students pay for their own tertiary education and that the market for tertiary education is perfectly competitive. Assume also that students undertake tertiary education only in order to obtain employment afterwards. We may depict such a market as in Figure 7.14 (this is the same as Figure 10.1 in Chapter 10).

(a) Make a copy of the diagram. Identify the private market equilibrium and label this equilibrium quantity as Q_p and equilibrium price as P_p. Also, label the social optimum output as Q_s and the market price required to induce suppliers to supply that quantity as P_s. Explain with the aid of the diagram the concept of positive externalities and why this might apply to the market for tertiary education. Give some examples of the positive externalities you might observe.

(b) Briefly explain how the analysis in (a) could be used to make the case that tertiary education should be subsidized by government.

(c) In 1998 the government required students to pay a flat-rate fee of £1000 a year for their university tuition. From 2006 the government will enable universities to charge top-up fees of up to £3000 a year more. In the light of your analysis of the private and social benefits of tertiary education, comment briefly on the government's policy of making students pay part of the cost of their tuition.

Figure 7.14
Private and social benefits in the market for education

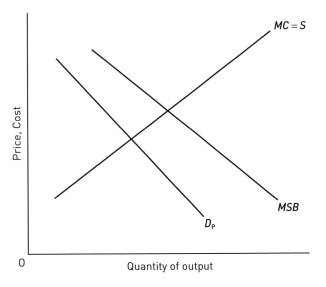

199

8

Welfare: from income to well-being

Paul Anand

<table>
<tr><td>

Concepts

- welfare economics
- national income
- indices
- circular flow (CF) model
- marginal utility and total utility
- Pareto optimality and Pareto improvements
- allocative efficiency
- capabilities

</td><td>

Objectives

After studying this chapter you should be able to:

- understand the measurement of national income, and appreciate its limits as an approach to the measurement of welfare
- understand the concept of utility as used in consumer behaviour theory and in welfare economics
- understand some concepts and evidence associated with well-being.

</td></tr>
</table>

8.1 Introduction: Socrates and the Pot Noodle

Chief: A Pot Noodle is the most beautiful thing on Earth. It is a new way of making money. A way of making money . . . *where no money existed before*: the very definition of excitement.

Philip: Look, I'm probably being thicker than a middle manager's Filofax here Chief, but I'm just not in an 'understanding you' mode at all. Uhm . . . what *is* a Pot Noodle? . . .

Chief: The most unlikely food stuff in history . . . Only the British could market Pot Noodle, because only the British would eat them . . . Anyone worth their company BMW can carve a bigger share of an existing market, but show me the person who can make a pound where there was no pound to be made. That's the fellow who's going to be sitting alongside me and the board in the executive Jacuzzi whirlpool bath.

Philip: The executive Jason Chief, that's a mightily big carrot!

Chief: Find me a Pot Noodle and you're in it Philip, what's more you can sit on one of the jets . . . Make an old man happy!!

(Ben Elton, Gasping, *1990, pp.9–11)*

| Question | What makes you happy? In what ways does the economy contribute to your welfare? Can happiness be measured or modelled? What role do markets play in providing for people's happiness? |

Throughout history, humanity has pondered these questions. Socrates, the Greek philosopher, born to a midwife and sculptor in 469 BC, thought particularly hard about them. A small man, known for his wit and conversation, he was never slow to share his thoughts with others. He gave lessons without charge, falling into poverty as a result, and he became known throughout the city of Athens for his habit of interrogating complete strangers on matters they would otherwise have taken for granted. Socrates believed he could help people improve their lives by reason alone, although enough people found his directness sufficiently threatening that he was eventually tried for corrupting the social fabric of the city and failing to worship the city's gods. 'I have neglected the things that concern most people – making money, managing an estate, gaining military or civic honours . . . I tried to persuade each of you not to think more of practical advantages than of his mental and moral well-being' (Plato, 1993).

It was the practice in Athens for major decisions to be made by a show of hands from an electorate comprising all free adult males. Of the 500-strong jury of citizens at Socrates' trial, 280 voted for conviction, to which Socrates is said to have quipped that he 'didn't think the margin would be so narrow'. Socrates seemed less concerned about his fate than the others around him were, and stated that he would hold steadfast to his views about the relative importance of philosophy and material concerns. After that, 360 of the 500 jury members voted for the death penalty.

Socrates' life and death and Ben Elton's satirical attack on the 1980s are examples of different approaches to the relationship between money and happiness.

Perhaps you are surprised that economists are even concerned with such things. They are not the sort of issues that economic journalists cover on the evening news; they seem to be questions that belong more to the realms of philosophy or psychology. You have seen in previous chapters that economics, like other social sciences, is concerned with *explanation*, *prediction* and *description*, but in this chapter and the next we are going to emphasize the importance of *normative* questions – that is, questions about what *should* be done to improve people's lives. Such judgements are central to economics. For example, whenever the government investigates anti-competitive behaviour in a particular industry, it does so largely because our models of market behaviour show that a monopoly can give rise to *inferior* outcomes. And as you will see in Chapter 9, governments are intimately involved in questions about the best distribution of income and wealth within societies. In these situations economists are concerned with welfare, that is, with the consequences of economic activity for people's lives. Welfare has been interpreted in a range of different ways, from a materialistic emphasis on access to and control over money and material goods to a wider view that encompasses physical, mental and spiritual well-being. Economics *is* intimately concerned with welfare, and it is here that we shall begin to focus on the significance of welfare in economic analysis.

So what does welfare imply for economic analysis? In this chapter we will consider three different perspectives.

In Section 8.2 we will look at income and an economic model of national income known as the 'circular flow' (CF) model. In most countries around the world, income in the form of money is vital to people's everyday existence, and the CF model provides us with a framework for understanding changes in income at a national level. In recent years, however, economists working on environmental issues and low-income countries have been critical of national income as a measure of welfare, and we will look at some of these criticisms.

Section 8.3 deals with the utility approach to welfare. Utility offers us a way of thinking about individual choice, and you will see that it helps us to understand, among other things, why the demand curves you have been using since Chapter 3 often slope downwards. This application of utility to individual choice completes the theory of consumer demand introduced in Chapter 3. Returning to the welfare implications of the utility approach, the idea of Pareto improvements, changes from which nobody loses and some gain in terms of utility, will be introduced. We will look at the argument that Pareto optimality is an appealing idea and that it plays a significant role in helping us to understand the merits of competitive market structures; but we will also see that it has some significant limitations.

Finally, in Section 8.4 we will consider a third approach, one that looks at different aspects of well-being, a topic which draws on ideas from psychology and philosophy. This section will look at empirical evidence on the relationship between happiness and income. We will then move on to explore the idea that well-being depends not only on outcomes, but also on how those outcomes are achieved, and examine Sen's capabilities theory, which has been used to develop measures of well-being based on individuals' own accounts of what matters to them. We will conclude by suggesting that Sen's theory provides, or at least implies, an interesting, and in many ways persuasive, answer to questions about the nature of individual happiness in public policy.

8.2 The economic wealth of nations

'Money doesn't talk, it shouts.'

A paraphrase of Bob Dylan (1965)

■ ■ ■ 8.2.1 The circular flow (CF) model of income

How is it that individuals and societies come to be wealthy in economic or material terms? There are various answers to this question, but an important part of the story has to do with trade. If human beings did not engage in exchange, the specialization and division of labour that Adam Smith highlighted in his famous book, *The Wealth of Nations* (first published in 1776), would not be possible. Were everyone forced to provide for all their own needs, the technological and material cultures that distinguish humanity could not have emerged and spread. Today, in most economies around the world, most exchanges depend upon the use of money.

Economists analyse such exchanges using a circular flow (CF) model of income (Figure 8.1).

The basic CF model strips the economy down to some bare essentials. We can think of the economy as comprising a set of exchanges. Firms pay wages to households in exchange for labour. Firms also pay other forms of income (dividends and interest, rent) to households in return for the supply of other factors of production (capital, land). Households pay firms for the goods and services they consume. So there are two flows. The first is a 'physical' flow of goods and services from firms to households and of the services of factors of production such as labour from households to firms. The second is a money flow in the opposite direction, from firms to households in the form of income for the factors of production they supply and from households to firms in the form of consumption expenditure for the purchase of goods and services. The physical flow

Figure 8.1
The basic CF model
of income

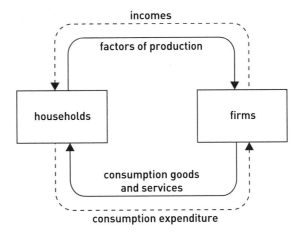

comprises all the goods and services, including the services of factors of production, involved in the different economic interactions that are made between households and firms. The financial flow records these transactions. In Figure 8.1 the dotted lines are financial flows, and the solid lines show flows of real goods and services.

This version of the CF model is sometimes referred to as the 'spendthrift' economy, because the households spend all their income. Another aspect of its being a very basic model is the omission of the government sector and international trade. We will therefore make some additions to the model, and explore how this more sophisticated model can be used to measure economic activity using the national income accounts.

▨ ▦ ■ 8.2.2 Extensions to the CF model

A more realistic version of the CF model is represented in Figure 8.2, which shows three extensions of the basic model. To keep Figure 8.2 uncluttered, we will concentrate on the *financial* flows, but you should remember that these are always balanced by physical flows of goods and services. One important extension to the basic CF model incorporates savings by households and investment by firms. Householders do not typically spend all their income; rather they save some of it. But what do they do with their savings? Unless

Figure 8.2
The CF model with
injections and
withdrawals

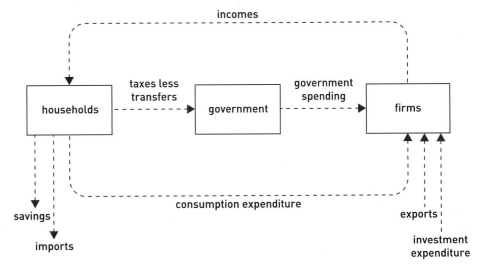

they simply keep them at home in the form of idle cash balances, they deposit them in a financial institution such as a bank or a building society. It is common usage to describe funds deposited in this way as 'investments'. In economic terms, this behaviour is known as 'financial investment'. Financial institutions play a crucial role in collecting up savings (i.e. financial investments) and lending to firms so that physical investment can take place (i.e. investment in directly productive assets). Financial institutions thus act as intermediaries between financial investment and physical investment.

In this CF model, savings reduce consumers' expenditure below their incomes, and can therefore be envisaged as a withdrawal from household spending. This creates a potential imbalance between the flow of money and the flow of goods and services around the system. If there are savings, consumption expenditure will be less than incomes and so the production of consumption goods and services cannot generate all the incomes in the economy. Some income must be generated by production for other purposes. In addition to producing consumer goods, firms produce capital goods, that is, goods such as machinery that are used in making consumer goods to purchase from each other. We can schematically picture two kinds of firm, one producing consumption goods and the other producing capital or investment goods. The firms sector as a whole purchases capital goods from itself. Purchases of these investment goods are financed in this model by borrowing from financial institutions, and this borrowing for investment can be envisaged as an 'injection' of finance into firms.

Our CF model has now become more complicated, but it is still an economy without a government sector. Typically, the most significant sources of government revenue are direct taxes such as income tax, indirect taxes levied on consumption such as value added tax (VAT), so-called 'sin' taxes on alcohol and tobacco products, and corporate taxes levied on businesses. Some of this tax revenue goes straight back to recipients of financial support in the form of pensions and social security. These payments are known as *transfer payments* and are not included in the CF model because there is no corresponding flow of goods and services. So tax revenue, minus transfers, is another withdrawal from the circular flow of income. The corresponding injection is the money that the government spends on goods and services in defence, health, education and so on.

We can also use the CF model to calculate the implications of international production and trade. Goods or services we bring into the country are known as 'imports' and goods and services we sell abroad are referred to as 'exports'. The physical flow of goods and services is always matched by a financial flow in the opposite direction when people pay for the goods and services they buy. So what happens to national income when we introduce exports and imports into the model? Any goods and services sent out of a country will be accompanied by a corresponding payment of money to factors of production in that country. This is the economic argument for believing exports to be a good thing.

The argument about imports is just the reverse of that for exports. If we increase our imports, then we have to increase the amount we pay to foreign factors of production, resulting in a withdrawal from the circular flow of income. Buying a foreign holiday results in a financial flow out of the country to pay for goods and services produced in another country, so this is an import.

▨ ▨ ■ 8.2.3 Measuring national income using the CF model

Question	Look back at Figure 8.1. How many ways of measuring income do you think it suggests?

National income

National income is the value of the goods and services available in a national economy over a given period of time, usually a year.

Even the basic CF model suggests that there might be more than one way of measuring **national income**. First, we could try to measure the values of the 'physical' flow of goods and services from firms to households, that is, national output. Second, we could try to measure the money flow moving in the opposite direction, that is, national expenditure. Third, we could try to measure the money flow from firms to households, in return for the services of factors of production, that is, in a literal sense, national income. Because of the ways in which economic transactions are recorded, these three methods are all commonly used, and all of them should give the same result. Why?

There are two reasons. The first is that the two money flows, income and expenditure, must be equal. In any transaction there is a buyer and a seller, and the buyer's expenditure *is* the seller's income. The second is that the physical flow, output, can be measured or valued in terms of either of the money flows, as expenditure incurred in producing it or as income received from selling it.

The more realistic CF model in Figure 8.2 is more complicated in two ways. First, households receive incomes as sellers of labour and other factors of production, but as potential buyers they do not spend all their incomes on the output of the national economy; some is saved, some is paid to the government in taxes and some is spent on imports. Second, these withdrawals of expenditure from the circular flow of income are balanced by injections of expenditure on national output by other sectors. Firms buy capital goods; the government buys capital goods (e.g. aircraft carriers, schools and hospitals); and consumers from overseas (as well as foreign firms and governments) buy the nation's exports.

The CF model in Figure 8.2 is more realistic than the basic model in Figure 8.1, but it is by no means a complete representation of all the transactions in an economy. For example, in the interests of simplicity we have omitted the income flow from government to households that corresponds to the labour services of public sector employees. Calculating national income is complicated, but remember that it is based on the simple identity of income and expenditure whenever money changes hands in an economic transaction.

Output measurement

The output approach involves collecting data on output through surveys of firms. To avoid double counting, economic statisticians focus only on the value added by each firm, that is, the value of each firm's output minus the value of intermediate goods, those that were used up in producing it. For example, a firm buys steel and adds value to it by using it in the manufacture of a car; double counting would occur if the national accounts included the value of both the steel and the car. Totalling up the value added by each firm in the economy gives a figure for the gross domestic product (GDP), that is, the value of all the output produced by factors of production located in the national economy. The main advantage of this method is that it provides a breakdown of the output value of each industry, which is useful if one wants to monitor the performance of specific areas of an economy.

Figure 8.3 shows the gross value added at basic prices for the main sectors of the UK economy in 1999. The term 'gross' means that no deduction has been made to reflect the fact that capital equipment depreciates, that is, that it loses value, becoming worn out or obsolete until it must be replaced. The qualification 'at basic prices' means that the figures exclude taxes on goods and services, such as value added tax (VAT), and include subsidies, in order to reflect the cost of the factors of production used in producing the goods and services.

Figure 8.3
Gross value added
at basic prices,
UK 1999

Source: Office for
National Statistics,
2001, Table 2.1,
p.109

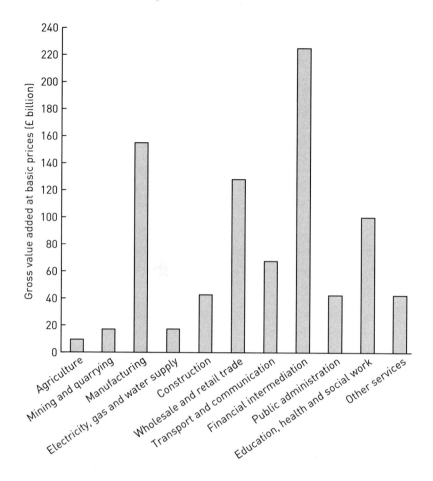

What do you think are the main features of Figure 8.3? Does anything surprise you?

Figure 8.3 underlines the status of the UK economy as a 'service economy' (Chapter 1). The largest contribution to the value added was made by financial services. Adding finance to the other major service industries – wholesale and retail, education and transport – shows that the value added by services (very approximately £490 billion) is more than three times greater than the value added by manufacturing (approximately £155 billion). This may strike you as surprising in an economy that was once renowned (not necessarily accurately) as 'the workshop of the world'. The small contribution made to value added by agriculture is also striking. The contribution of electricity, gas and water supply appears to be smaller than the impact of domestic bills might suggest.

These are the only figures we shall look at that are expressed in terms of basic prices; all the others are shown at market prices. This adjustment is necessary to prevent inconsistency between the results of the output and expenditure methods of calculating national income. Market prices are the prices consumers actually pay in the shops and supermarkets, and these prices are affected by taxes on goods and services such as VAT and subsidies such as those on agricultural produce. It is therefore necessary to add taxes on products (goods and services) to output at basic prices and to subtract subsidies from

Table 8.1
UK gross domestic product (GDP), 2000: the output approach

	£m
Gross value added, at basic prices	831 053
Value added taxes (VAT) on products	64 906
Other taxes on products	54 271
Less subsidies on products	−6 818
GDP at market prices	943 412

Source: Office for National Statistics, 2001, Table 1.2, p.39

output at basic prices in order to arrive at the gross domestic product (GDP) at market prices. Table 8.1 shows this adjustment to give UK GDP at market prices for 2000.

Expenditure measurement

Question Look back at Figure 8.2, which shows the CF model with injections and withdrawals. What are the four sources of expenditure on firms' output?

The components of aggregate (i.e. total) expenditure are consumption expenditure, investment expenditure, government spending and exports. The *expenditure* method of measuring national income relies on surveys and data collection centred on the final expenditures of the various agents in the economy engaged in expenditure. The qualification 'final' is necessary to avoid double counting, which would occur if, to adapt the example used earlier, expenditure by a car manufacturer on steel was added to consumption expenditure on the car (including the value of the steel used in making it). We should also subtract the spending on imports that forms part of each component of expenditure. It is easier in practice to subtract import expenditure as a whole and therefore just treat net exports (i.e. exports minus imports) as a component of aggregate expenditure. Household data are collected through the Household Expenditure Survey; government data through its accounts; data on investment expenditure or 'gross capital formation' from surveys of firms; and net exports or the 'external balance' through figures collected by the government for goods and services sold abroad (exports) minus goods and services bought from overseas. Adding all these final expenditures together gives a second measure of national income. As is shown in Table 8.2, GDP at current market prices measured by the

Table 8.2
UK gross domestic product (GDP) at current market prices, 2000: the expenditure approach

	£m
Consumer expenditure	617 648
General government final consumption	174 791
Gross capital formation	167 099
External balance	−15 719
Statistical discrepancy	−407
GDP at current market prices	943 412

Source: adapted from Office for National Statistics, 2001, Table 1.2, p.39

expenditure approach provides estimates of the components of aggregate expenditures in the economy. These estimates are widely used in formulating economic policy.

Income measurement

The *income* approach tries to measure incomes directly from the returns lodged with the tax-collecting branch of the government – the Inland Revenue in the UK. If economic activities were reported correctly, this method would give a third estimate of national income. The advantage of this approach is that it could provide statistics on the distribution of incomes, between different social groups or between different factors of production.

From Table 8.3 we can begin to see how the UK economy is constituted using data from the income approach. Income from employment, including self-employment, accounts for just over half of total GDP. If we look at gross trading profits, we can see that they account for just over a quarter of total GDP. This item includes the operating surpluses (excess of revenue over costs) of some governmental organizations as a rather minor component.

Table 8.3
UK gross domestic product (GDP) at current market prices, 2000: the income approach

	£m
Income from employment	521 443
Profits	237 051
Mixed income	54 442
Taxes on production and imports	137 955
Less subsidies	−7 724
Statistical discrepancy	245
GDP at current market prices	943 412

Source: adapted from Office for National Statistics, 2001, Table 1.2, p.39

So far we have focused on GDP as the measure of national income. You may also hear commentators refer to gross national income (GNY), which is the value of the final output produced by nationally owned factors of production, wherever that production takes place (Table 8.4). If a UK supermarket owns a mango plantation in Peru, then the profit from that farm's output is part of the UK's GNY (but not its GDP). Alternatively, the output produced by a Japanese car company located in Derbyshire is part of the UK's GDP, because it is output produced in the UK's domestic economy. It is not part of the UK's GNY, because the profits do not accrue to factors owned by UK companies or individuals. In sum, GNY measures income relating to factors *nationally owned* (wherever they are); GDP measures income due to factors *domestically located* (whoever owns them).

Table 8.4
UK gross national income (GNY) at current market prices, 2000

	£m
GDP at current market prices	943 412
Net income from the rest of the world	3 036
GNY at current market prices	946 448

Source: adapted from Office for National Statistics, 2001, Table 1.2, p.39

National income accounting, as we saw above, is based on an economic model, the circular flow of income. Remember that, in principle, all three approaches to national income measurement should give the same result. The practicalities of data gathering, however, mean that methods vary in their accuracy and so in practice, as you have seen in Tables 8.2 and 8.3, there are generally small discrepancies between the measures.

Like most economic models, the CF model has some important insights as well as a few significant limitations. On the positive side, it helps us to understand how the economy changes over time and to estimate the standard of living, which is one important measure of welfare.

Real and nominal income

Economic change is the guiding theme of this book, and economists use national income statistics to obtain a sense of how an economy is changing. If we were to use data expressed in '£ million', the results could be misleading. Suppose, for example, that a country's GDP increased by 25 per cent between 1990 and 2000. Were its consumers 25 per cent better off in 2000 than in 1990? Did they have 25 per cent more goods and services to buy? Not necessarily.

Question	Can you think of a reason why not?

Inflation

Inflation refers to a rise in the general level of prices in a country.

Inflation rate

The inflation rate measures the rate at which prices are rising, and is expressed as a percentage increase in the general level of prices from one year to the next.

The reason is a familiar facet of economic experience: **inflation**. Inflation refers to a rise in the general level of prices in a country, and the **inflation rate** measures the rate at which prices are rising, usually expressed per year. So the answer to my two questions above would be 'Yes, definitely' only if the inflation rate during the 1990s had been exactly 0 per cent, that is, if there had been no inflation at all, a situation known as 'price stability'. At the other extreme, if the inflation rate had been 25 per cent, the apparent increase in output would have been illusory; there would have been no increase at all in the quantity of goods and services available for consumption, only a rise in the prices at which an unchanged quantity of output was sold. In reality, the truth usually lies somewhere between these two extremes, and an increase in a country's GDP reflects both an increase in the quantity of output and the effects of inflation.

Suppose we want to compare real output in different years. If we can find a way of adjusting for inflation, or removing its influence, we would be left with the actual increase in the quantity of output, that is, real output. Nominal or money output is the value of output expressed in the prices prevailing at the time it was sold; so it can also be referred to as GDP in current market prices. In order to strip away the effect of inflation, we want output for each year to be expressed in prices that have not changed over the period, that is, GDP at constant market prices or real output. The way in which this is done can be illustrated using the UK national income accounts, which express the national income of the UK in terms of both current market prices and constant 1995 market prices (Table 8.5).

The only figures that are the same in the two rows are those for 1995. The figures in the top row – GDP measured in the prices current in the years in question – have all been adjusted for inflation in the bottom row, taking 1995 prices as the 'base year' for the adjustment.

Table 8.5
UK GDP in current market prices and constant market prices, 1985–2000

	1985 £m	1990 £m	1995 £m	2000 £m
GDP at current prices	354 952	557 300	719 176	943 412
GDP at constant 1995 prices	560 255	659 171	719 176	826 144

Source: Office for National Statistics, 2001, Table 1.2, pp.38–9 and Table 1.3, pp.40–1

Let us see how the calculation of real income works by taking a hypothetical example. Let us suppose that money GDP at market prices for Utopia in 1995 was equivalent to £400 million and it increased to £430 million in 1996. The inflation rate between 1995 and 1996 was 5 per cent. What was Utopia's real income in 1996 expressed in terms of 1995 prices? This can be calculated as follows.

1 First, we can think of the 1995 prices as equivalent to 100. These are the 'base year' prices. In effect, we are making the 1995 income represent 100 per cent, and then thinking of any change from one year to the next as a percentage change. To do this we derive an index of inflation between 1995 and 1996 expressed in terms of this figure of 100. With 5 per cent inflation the price index for 1996 will be 105.

2 We then need to 'deflate' the 1996 money GDP of £430 million using the inflation index. This is done by dividing 430 by 105 and then multiplying the result by 100.

$$\frac{430}{105} \cdot 100 = 409.5 \text{ (to one decimal place)}$$

This result is equivalent to dividing 430 by 1.05.

So, the real value of 1996 GDP is £409.5 million, which is considerably less than the nominal GDP of £430 million.

Exercise 8.1

Suppose that the inflation rate had been 7.5 per cent between 1995 and 1996. What would have been Utopia's real GDP, or GDP at constant market prices, in 1996?

The figures in the bottom row of Table 8.5 have been recalculated using this method to provide 'real' values expressed in terms of 1995 prices. Clearly, the figures for the years before 1995 have been recalculated to 'inflate' them forward to 1995 prices, but the same principles apply. In fact, the UK national income accounts provide a quick way to calculate these real changes in the national income totals by the use of the 'GDP deflator'. The GDP deflator expresses the ratio of GDP at current prices to GDP at constant prices:

$$\text{GDP deflator} = \frac{\text{GDP at current prices}}{\text{GDP at constant prices}} \cdot 100$$

Data for this index are shown in Table 8.6.

If we have the GDP deflators we can calculate real GDP from money GDP using the following formula:

$$\text{real GDP} = \frac{\text{money GDP}}{\text{GDP deflator}} \cdot 100$$

	1985	1990	1995	2000
GDP deflator	63.3	84.6	100.0	114.2

Table 8.6
GDP deflator
(1995 = 100), 1985,
1990, 1995 and 2000

Source: Office for National Statistics, 2001, Table 1.1, pp.36–7

This is a reorganization of the above definition of the GDP deflator, as you can see if you remember that money GDP is GDP at current prices and real GDP is GDP at constant prices.

Exercise 8.2

You can check the way this is done by taking the figure for 2000 UK GDP at current market prices from the top row of Table 8.5 and calculating 2000 UK GDP at constant market prices using the GDP deflator from Table 8.6. Your answer should coincide with the figure for 2000 UK GDP at constant market prices in the bottom row of Table 8.5.

Have a go at this calculation now.

Now we turn to the second application of the CF model: estimating the standard of living.

The standard of living interprets welfare in terms of access to material goods and services. GDP estimates the value of the total output of goods and services produced in an economy. It tells us how big the economy is. If we want to know the share of output available to the average person in the economy, however, we need to divide GDP by the number of people living in the economy. This adjustment yields a figure for GDP per head (of the population). From Tables 8.1, 8.2, 8.3 and 8.5 we know that UK GDP (for 2000 at current market prices) was £943 412 million. The UK population in 2000 was 59 756 000.

Question   What was GDP per head for the UK in 2000?

The answer is:

$$\frac{£943\ 412\ 000\ 000}{59\ 756\ 000} = \text{(approximately)} £15\ 788$$

This means that the average person (woman, man and child) had a share of goods and services worth £15 788. This highlights one limitation of national income accounts as a measure of welfare: GDP per head tells us nothing about the actual distribution of goods and services. Is the value of the goods and services available to most individuals approximately £15 788, just a little above or a little below? Or do the majority of people get by on substantially less than that, with relatively few individuals having access to much more? Chapter 9 discusses the distribution of income and methods of measuring it.

The CF model tells us little about other issues that might have an effect on well-being. It is not explicitly concerned with individual people's preferences, the availability of employment or the quality of the environment. But economists, and those in related disciplines, do have things to say about all of these issues, and it is to those issues that we will now turn.

▩ ▩ ■ 8.2.4   An alternative approach: sustainable economic welfare or 'green income'

National income is not a perfect measure of welfare. For many years, economists used to point out that national income would go down if a person married their housekeeper. This is because the standard measure of national income measures only output that is sold in a market transaction and so produces a money income. The presumption was that after the marriage the work would still be done but the market transaction would disappear, and the conclusion was that national income was defective as a measure of the value of output. This somewhat old-fashioned story highlights a real problem: namely, that there are many valuable activities – such as work in the home – that are simply invisible to measures of national income based on market transactions. In 2002 the Office for National Statistics started to publish a separate Household Satellite Account, which gives an estimate of the output of all unpaid work. It showed that the total value of the output of unpaid work was almost as much as that of GDP in 2002.

There are other problems too. Let us take three that illustrate the range of issues that have been discussed by critics of national income accounting. First, there are questions of distribution. We have seen that national income measures are well suited to summarizing the total amount of activity in an economy, but even GNY per head does not tell us about the distribution of income within countries. This is a serious omission if policy makers think that economic growth will alleviate poverty.

Second, as labour economists have noted, national income accounts fail to make allowance for changes in human capital. Human capital comprises the skills and abilities that people have as a result of education or experience, and its importance to individual earnings means that it will be relevant to national income (Chapter 7, Section 7.2.4). Changes in physical capital through investment and depreciation are measured in national income accounts, but changes in human capital are not. The fact that they are much harder to measure is probably the reason, but the omission is serious nonetheless.

Third, it is now widely accepted that many environmental issues are not handled well by national income accounts. For example, the current and future costs of climate change and rising sea levels are a direct consequence of previous economic activity that led to the emission of greenhouse gases. At the time of these emissions, however, no charge was made against the national income accounts to reflect these future losses. Furthermore, when we come to spend money on preventing or repairing damage done by climate change in the future, it will be entered in the national income accounts as an increase in economic activity. The problem is that the accounts are not accompanied by a statement of what is happening to the value of our national assets, such as the climate and low-lying land on the coast.

Environmental economists have attempted to deal with just these issues. One of the more influential attempts can be found in a publication by Herman Daly, a World Bank economist, and John Cobb, an academic theologian (Daly and Cobb, 1994). Their approach involves making some 20 adjustments to consumption (as measured in GDP) in order to derive an index of what they call 'sustainable economic welfare' (ISEW).

The first adjustment involves dividing consumption by a measure of inequality. The ISEW assumes that greater inequality in the distribution of income reduces welfare, because an extra $100, for example, would have no effect on the welfare of a millionaire but would be much appreciated by someone living in poverty (see Section 8.3.1 on the diminishing marginal utility of income, and Chapter 9 on measuring inequality and poverty). In Table 8.7, column B gives an index of inequality and indicates that inequality has increased since 1951, which implies that column A overstates the contribution of consumption to welfare.

Table 8.7 A simplified calculation of the index of sustainable economic welfare (ISEW) for the USA, 1990

Consumption	Distributional inequality[1]	Weighted consumption	Services[2]	Environmental impacts[3]	Other	ISEW
A	B	C (= A/B)	D	E	F	= C + D + E + F
1265.6[4]	1.087	1164.3	807.8	−1149.3	−4.6	818.2

1 Distributional inequality measured by an index set to 1 in 1951.

2 Includes services such as household labour, benefits from consumer durables and improvements in health and education that are not reflected in national income.

3 Includes environmental impacts such as car accident costs, loss of wetlands and farmland, long-term environmental damage and ozone depletion.

4 Currency: 1972 US dollars.

Source: adapted from Daly and Cobb, 1994, pp.462–3

Dividing column A by column B corrects this overstatement, as shown in column C. This constitutes a major departure from just using figures such as GNP, the US equivalent of UK GNY, which reflect only an *average* level of economic welfare, something that most people do not actually receive. There are more people who live below the average income than live above it, because a few very rich people pull the average up.

Next, Daly and Cobb add to 'weighted consumption' the value of services that are excluded from national income, including items such as the value of unpaid work done in the home. The deductions made in the next column reflect the omission from GNP of environmental impacts, including health expenditures (e.g. treatment of asthma caused by worsening air pollution), the loss of wetlands, ozone depletion and other forms of long-term environmental damage. This approach is illustrated in Table 8.7 with US data for the year 1990.

Daly and Cobb used their approach to calculate an index of SEW (ISEW) for the USA, which they then compared with per capita GNP, 'per capita' being a Latin term meaning 'per head' (see Figure 8.4).

Question	From Figure 8.4, what can you say about the relationship between GNP and 'green national income' (ISEW) over time?

Figure 8.4
A comparison of ISEW and GNP per capita for the USA

Source: Daly and Cobb, 1994, p.464

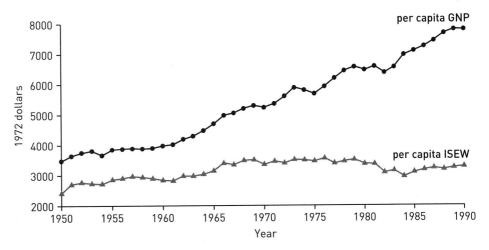

One point to note is that from 1950 to 1990 both GNP and ISEW increased in the USA, although the increase in ISEW was noticeably smaller. Perhaps a more important difference is that ISEW and GNP moved in opposite directions in the 1980s: GNP rose but ISEW declined. Looking at the reasons behind these changes, it seems that inequalities in consumption changed quite dramatically over the period. Inequalities were at their lowest in the latter half of the 1960s, after which the trend was towards greater inequality. And although efforts to reduce pollution and accidents were largely successful in the 1970s and 1980s, the impact on total ISEW was modest.

Daly and Cobb concluded their study by reflecting on the purpose and nature of such measurements:

> The purpose of an index that strives to measure economic well-being is not simply to show us how we are presently faring . . . It should also reveal the kinds of policies that would enable a nation to improve its welfare . . . Are the policies of our government going to be guided by GNP, or by ISEW or some other measure of sustainable welfare?
>
> *(1994, p.507)*

Question | To what extent do you think Daly and Cobb's ISEW is an improvement over GNP or GDP as a measure of welfare?

Let us consider three points. First, Daly and Cobb's analysis shows that environmental costs are large and growing. Because this environmental damage is not included in US GNP or GDP, one might conclude that these will be seen as increasingly flawed measures of national income. Second, while acknowledging that ISEW performs an important service by reflecting the value of environmental damage, one might ask what it is that ISEW measures. Does it really indicate how sustainable economic welfare is? It seems that just incorporating environmental costs tells us very little, if anything, about how likely it is that these levels of economic welfare can persist into the future if that is what 'sustainability' means. Third, the ISEW includes a measure of inequality. While distributional issues are important, they enter the formula for ISEW in a particular way. Other approaches are equally plausible. For instance, the weight or importance ISEW attributes to inequality appears to be arbitrary.

8.3 Utility, welfare and markets

> For money can't buy me love.
>
> *(Paul McCartney)*

You have seen, in Chapters 4 to 6, that the analysis of different kinds of market structures plays a central role in economics. In this section, we will examine in a bit more detail how the analysis of markets is related to views about what people want. Traditionally, economists have used the concept of *utility* (rather than money income) in this analysis. Utility expresses the idea that the welfare derived from consumption is a subjective concept, in the sense that the satisfaction one person gets from consuming a given amount of a particular good may be quite different from the satisfaction another person gets from

Utility

Total utility is the satisfaction derived from consuming a given amount of a good.

consuming the same amount of the same good. Think, for example, of the UK television commercials for Marmite – one person loves it, another hates it. Or think of the saying that one person's meat is another's poison. The idea of utility also captures the idea that the satisfaction from consumption varies with the amount of the good consumed: too much of good thing can make you bored, sick or drunk. And, finally, many economists have argued that if society wants to maximize welfare, it should aim to maximize the **utility** enjoyed by consumers.

■ ■ ■ 8.3.1 Consumption and diminishing marginal utility

Marginal utility

Marginal utility refers to the change in total satisfaction derived from consuming a good when the amount consumed changes by one unit.

One of the oldest ideas in utility theory is the concept of diminishing **marginal utility**, something first discussed by mathematicians in the early 1700s. The idea is that the more units of something that are consumed, the less valuable are successive units to the consumer. For instance, you might consider how much coffee you need to drink in order to complete the next essay. Perhaps one cup would help keep you awake, but two cups would make you alert as well. A third cup might have no further effect, and a fourth cup might begin to produce undesirable effects. The fact that the value of cups of coffee declines the more we consume is an example of what economists refer to as 'diminishing marginal utility'. If we could imagine the utility or satisfaction derived from each cup of coffee as a number, we might represent the coffee example as shown in Table 8.8, where utility is measured in units called 'utils'.

The first two columns of Table 8.8 show a particular cup of coffee and the utility derived from that particular cup. These figures depict the marginal utility of coffee. In this case, the first cup of coffee gives 5 utils, and the fourth cup gives −2 utils. Each successive cup provides less utility than the one before. For most goods and services we expect that, eventually, successive units of consumption will produce smaller and smaller additions to the consumer's total utility. In such cases, marginal utility is said to be diminishing. In last pair of columns, we have the total number of cups drunk and the total utility derived from drinking those cups. The total and marginal utility figures are related: in mathematical terms, marginal utility represents the change in total utility. Conversely, total utility is just the sum of all the marginal utilities. In our example, total utility increases until the third cup of coffee, but by a declining amount. Drinking the fourth cup of coffee has a negative marginal utility that reduces the total utility.

Exercise 8.3

If marginal utility is positive, does the total utility rise or fall?

Table 8.8
The utility of coffee

Cup of coffee	Marginal utility	Total number of cups drunk	Total utility
0	–	0	0
1st	5	1	5
2nd	4	2	9
3rd	0	3	9
4th	−2	4	7

Where do these marginal utility numbers come from? Historically, the idea comes from work by experimental psychologists which shows that, in many fields, our response to stimuli tails off as the intensity of the stimulus increases. For example, we might detect minor changes in volume at low levels of sound but are unable to detect similar changes at much higher sound levels. And you might find that your essays get better the more work you do, but that diminishing returns set in, until a point is reached at which further effort seems to add very little.

Question	Diminishing marginal utility has been used by economists to argue for income and wealth redistribution – that is, a tax and benefit system that redistributes income or wealth from the rich to the poor. Can you think in what way?

Economists generally assume that one person's 'utils' cannot be compared to another's. However, the argument in favour of redistribution involves making a comparison between consumers. If it is true of most consumers that the marginal utility of income declines the more one has, and people have similar levels of utility from similar levels of income, then people on low incomes will have the highest marginal utility from additional income. Redistribution from rich to poor amounts to shifting income from people for whom it produces little utility, at the margin, to people capable of using it to produce more utility, at the margin. Whatever the motive, most countries do have redistributive tax and benefit systems. Of course, income taxes are difficult to avoid, so they represent an infringement of personal liberty, one that some cultures find more acceptable than others.

▨ ▩ ■ 8.3.2 Individual equilibrium

An important use of utility theory is in describing equilibrium conditions for consumers. This application of utility theory enables us to complete the theory of consumer demand that was introduced in Chapter 3. When economists say that a consumption pattern is in equilibrium, they mean that the consumer could obtain no more utility from any other consumption pattern and therefore has no reason to deviate from that pattern. You will recall from Chapters 4 and 5 that the profit-maximizing firm, in equilibrium, sets output levels so that marginal cost equals marginal revenue ($MC = MR$). Similar insights apply to the equilibrium of the consumer. Suppose that there are two goods, videos and takeaways.

A necessary condition for equilibrium in consumption is that the marginal utility of the last £1 spent on videos equals the marginal utility of the last £1 spent on takeaways. Why? If not, that is, if the consumer is getting more utility from one good at the margin (e.g. videos), then it pays to shift consumption away from the other good (takeaways). For example, suppose the last £1 you spend on videos brings you 30 utils, while the last £1 you spend on takeaways brings you 10 utils. You would not be in equilibrium, that is, you would not be maximizing your utility, in that situation. Assuming videos and takeaways display diminishing marginal utility, suppose you buy more videos and fewer takeaways. You could continue to switch your spending in this way until the last £1 you spend on (more) videos brings you 20 utils and the last £1 you spend on (fewer) takeaways also brings you 20 utils. At this point you cannot increase your utility by changing your consumption of videos and takeaways; you get the same number of utils whether you spend your last £1 on videos or takeaways. So your consumption is in equilibrium.

We can restate the condition for equilibrium as follows:

$$\frac{\text{marginal utility of videos}}{\text{price of videos}} = \frac{\text{marginal utility of takeaways}}{\text{price of takeaways}}$$

Put informally, this equation asserts that, in equilibrium, the consumer should get the same 'bangs for their bucks' in different areas of expenditure. Economists have also used this equation to explain why demand curves slope downwards. Suppose that the utility from additional consumption of videos and takeaways is positive but declining, that is, that diminishing marginal utility applies to both goods. What happens if the price of videos goes up? The quantity on the left-hand side of the equation will be less than that on the right-hand side, indicating that the consumer is not in equilibrium. To compensate, the consumer must increase the marginal utility they receive from consuming videos, and this requires the consumption of fewer videos and more takeaways. Alternatively, if the price of videos were to fall, then the ratio on the left-hand side of the equation would be larger than that on the right-hand side. To restore equality between the two sides of the equation, the consumer would need to decrease the marginal utility of videos which, given diminishing marginal utility, means consuming more videos. So diminishing marginal utility implies that, to maximize utility, the consumer's demand curve should be downward sloping.

Let us work through a more formal derivation of the consumer's demand curve from information about utility. To see how this can be done, assume that the consumer buys one cup of coffee, at a price of £1. If one cup is the right quantity for the consumer at this price, then this price–quantity point represents equilibrium for the consumer. Using the ratio condition for equilibrium above, we can calculate that in this equilibrium the ratio of marginal utility to price must be equal to 5 (ignoring units). Furthermore, this ratio should be the same for all goods and their prices, that is, 5. As more coffee is consumed, the marginal utility is ultimately likely to fall, but we could reasonably assume that as a person's equilibrium bundle of spending moves from one to two cups of coffee, the ratio stays approximately the same – as coffee takes a rather small proportion of a person's total income. Given these assumptions, we can use information on utility to say how much the consumer is willing to pay for different quantities of coffee; in other words we can derive their demand curve.

So, if we consider the demand for two cups of coffee, we see, from Table 8.8, that the marginal utility of a second cup is 4 utils. From the equilibrium condition and the information above, 4/£price = 5, so the £price of coffee must be 4/5 (by simple algebraic rearrangement) or 80 pence. In other words, the consumer needs the price of coffee to fall by 20 pence in order to justify buying two cups. We now have two price–quantity points on the consumer's demand curve (Figure 8.5(a)); we can obtain more points by repeating this process and, where it makes sense, we might join these points together to give the familiar, continuous downward-sloping curve that is generally used to represent demand (Figure 8.5(b)). Traditionally, it has been important to economists to argue that a consumer's demand curve can be derived from their underlying preferences for goods measured by the utilities they enjoy from their consumption. So this derivation shows how the theory of consumer demand is grounded in utility theory.

We can, and do, apply the above equation well beyond its application to the analysis of consumer demand. Some of these uses seem to be more important than the application to consumption might suggest. For instance, the economist-philosopher John Broome (1993) has used this equation to argue that governments should distribute expenditure so that the marginal utility of life-saving expenditures is the same in different areas of

Figure 8.5
Deriving a demand curve from utility information

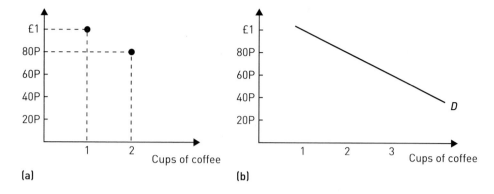

(a)   (b)

government expenditure. If it costs much less to save lives by spending money on environmental programmes than it does to save lives and thereby increase utility by spending money on health care, then we should divert resources from health to environment. Or to put it another way, we should expect to see equal value for money in different areas of expenditure on consumption.

Case study: The value of life and government policy

An interesting exercise in quantifying the different benefits in various areas of expenditure was conducted by the Harvard-based economist Kip Viscusi, who looked at the cost per life saved for risk and safety legislation in the USA.

Table 8.9 indicates a number of areas in which regulatory legislation has been passed, the sponsoring agency and the cost per life saved for each regulation. These cost figures may not be exact, but they illustrate the range of costs that different agencies impose. It is worth pointing out that we are assuming that the average cost per

life figure is closely related to the marginal cost per life figure. In practice, these figures will be different, so we should regard this assumption as an approximation.

Question

Suppose that you were in a position to make marginal changes to the expenditure decisions of the organizations in Table 8.9. Examine the data in the table and decide what changes you would make to increase utility by saving more lives.

Table 8.9
Cost of saving lives by regulation and agency

Regulation	Agency	Cost per life saved $m[1]
Unvented heaters	Consumer Product Safety Commission	0.1
Seat belts	National Highway Traffic Safety Administration	0.3
Alcohol and drugs	Federal Railroad Administration	0.5
Servicing wheel rims	Occupational Safety and Health Administration	1.2
Grain dust	Occupational Safety and Health Administration	5.3
Asbestos	Environmental Protection Agency	104.2
Land disposal	Environmental Protection Agency	3 500.0
Formaldehyde	Occupational Safety and Health Administration	72 000.0

[1] Currency unit is 1984 US dollars.
Source: adapted from Viscusi, 1998, p.98

Viscusi's analysis (see case study above) suggests that the regulations sponsored by the Environmental Protection Agency tend to have a higher cost per life saved. We might therefore say that to get more lives saved per unit of expenditure we should be moving regulatory effort and resources from issues such as formaldehyde to issues such as heater design and seat belts. If one were able to make marginal changes to the budgets of these organizations, one could use the necessary conditions for equilibrium to argue that expenditure should be shifted to those agencies and regulations that save more lives per dollar. The fact that regulations relating to formaldehyde cost a staggering $72 billion to save one life, a sum approximately equivalent to the entire national income of some low-income countries, suggests that a redirection of resources, assuming it were possible, would lead to outcomes that saved more lives and so increased utility.

▨ ▨ ▪ 8.3.3 Pareto optimality and the utility possibility frontier

Welfare economics

Welfare economics is the study of the effect on well-being of different allocations of resources among individuals.

An important use of the concept of utility arises from its application to **welfare economics**, the study of the effect on well-being of different allocations of goods and services between individuals. In this simple example, we will assume that we have a variety of goods and services that can be shared out in numerous ways between two people, Alice and Ben. We can also assume, for simplicity, that each person derives utility only from the goods they are allocated, and that both have a maximum level of utility beyond which they cannot be any happier. Under these assumptions (both of which might be challenged), we can draw what is called a utility possibility frontier for Alice and Ben (Figure 8.6).

In Figure 8.6, the horizontal and vertical axes represent the utilities of Alice and Ben respectively. At the origin, in the left-hand corner, both parties obtain zero utility. The wavy line on the right-hand side, the utility possibility frontier (UPF), represents the most utility that could be obtained by Alice and Ben from the goods and services available. The points U_{Alice}^{max} and U_{Ben}^{max} show the maximum levels of utility for Alice and Ben respectively. In this case, both parties obtain maximum utility when the other party has zero utility. (The waviness represents the difficulty of measuring the individual utilities of Alice and Ben. This being the case, one could have drawn a smoother curve, while noting that the line cannot be measured precisely in practice.)

Many economists have argued that the utilities of different people cannot be compared. This is often referred to as 'the problem of interpersonal comparisons'. Suppose there is

Figure 8.6
Utility possibility frontier for Alice and Ben

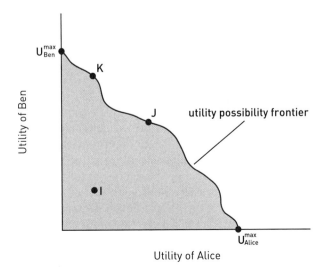

only one kidney machine to treat two patients. One might allocate the machine to the patient who would get more utility from being treated, but it is difficult to see how anyone could tell which of the two patients this would be. In some sense, most people are probably attracted to the principle that both patients have an equal right to treatment, so it is not even clear that any measure of utility differences should play a policy role in determining access to health.

These problems of interpersonal comparisons have led many economists to focus on comparisons between distributions or states of affairs in which *everyone* is better or worse off. Each possible allocation of goods will give rise to a utility level for Alice and a utility level for Ben, which we can plot as points on the two-dimensional graph in Figure 8.6. Point I is one such point, and the set of all feasible distributions of utility is given by the shaded area. If we move to points above I, Ben gets more utility; if we move to points to the right of I, Alice's utility increases. Moving to points north-east of point I, towards point J, represents increases in the utility of Alice and Ben, changes known as *Pareto improvements*. The term comes from the Italian economist, Vilfredo Pareto, who noted the importance of allocations in which the welfare of everyone improves. A weak Pareto improvement is a change in which some people are better off but no one is worse off.

All points on the north-eastern boundary of the shaded area represent allocations of utility from which no further Pareto improvements can be made. At point J, for example, it is possible to increase Ben's utility (by moving up) only by reducing the utility of Alice (moving left). This is true of all the points on this north-eastern boundary and all the points are, therefore, known as *Pareto optimal* distributions of utility.

Question Do you think there are many Pareto improvements to be made in the economy? Do you think all Pareto improvements are desirable?

When interpersonal comparisons of utility are not thought to be possible, Pareto optimality plays a central role in social choice and public policy. If we are unwilling to make comparisons between people with respect to utility we can look only for improvements in which everyone is made better off. In conventional welfare economics, this remains an important belief. And improvements in which everyone is made better off do occur. For example, suppose that there are people who are unemployed and desperately want to work. Getting them into jobs not only makes them better off but also improves the welfare of the rest of society, who can now buy the extra goods produced by the previously unemployed people. Diagrammatically, this corresponds to point I in Figure 8.6. Alice and Ben can both be made better off by moving towards the frontier and point J. Although the idea might seem unobjectionable, there are two simple but significant problems.

First, many social choices and public-policy problems involve options in which there are winners and losers. Even simple traffic schemes, for example, affect pedestrians and vehicle users, taxpayers and even local residents in ways that set up complex patterns of winners and losers. Pareto improvements apply to those situations in which everyone is no worse off and some are better off than before. A second concern emerges if we consider what happens when one moves from point I to point K. The move is a Pareto improvement as Ben's utility is increased and Alice's stays the same, but the distributional consequences appear far from satisfactory. At point K, Ben is near his maximum level of utility, but Alice is still near her lowest utility level. Furthermore, all of the improvements have benefited Ben. So it seems that although Pareto improvements apply to only a limited set of distributions, even some of those might be undesirable (or unsustainable) by virtue of their distributive consequences. Nonetheless, if there were Pareto improvements, with acceptable distributional consequences, they would be worth seeking out. So a final question to ask is about what institutional mechanisms, if any, can be used to generate such distributions.

■■■ 8.3.4 Welfare economics: perfect competition and Pareto optimality

Notwithstanding some of the limits of Pareto optimality, it seems likely that there will be situations, such as the unemployment example, in which choices that satisfy Pareto optimality will be available. So a natural question to ask is whether we can find economic mechanisms or institutions that will deliver Pareto optimal outcomes. An economy made up of markets that satisfy all the assumptions of the model of perfect competition (Chapter 5, Section 5.2.1) would be a Pareto optimal economy. The argument supporting this statement is too complex to set out in detail here, but it is possible to gain an intuitive feel for why perfect competition produces a Pareto optimal outcome from the following argument. The optimality properties of perfect competition are the main reason for the influence of this model on economic policy.

Let us first consider a single market, and begin with consumers. As we saw in Section 8.3.3, consumers are assumed to gain utility from consumption, and to seek to maximize their utility from their incomes. It was argued that a consumer who maximizes his satisfaction (or utility) will alter his purchases at the margin until he gets the same amount of satisfaction (utility) from the last pound spent on each good. In other words, the *marginal* utility – the satisfaction from the last item – of each good bought is in a sense equal to the price. If the marginal utility from a good were less than the price, it would be worth too little to the consumer and the last item would not be bought. So price equals marginal utility.

Now consider the production side. Chapter 5, Section 5.2.3 established that under perfect competition the firm will produce the level of output at which $MC = P$. This is the main distinction drawn between perfect competition and the model of monopoly in Chapter 4. Because the firm is a price-taker it maximizes its profits when price equals marginal cost.

The implication is that, under perfect competition, the common price taken by firms and consumers becomes a mediator which ensures that the worth to the consumer of the last item of each good bought is equal to the marginal cost of producing it. Marginal utility equals price equals marginal cost: $MU = P = MC$.

Once the perfectly competitive market has settled at an equilibrium where these equalities hold, no further improvement is possible by expanding or contracting output. Since marginal costs are assumed to rise, and consumers' willingness to pay falls as output increases, a production increase will mean that consumers value the last unit below its marginal cost to society. And, conversely, lower output means marginal benefit above marginal cost, suggesting that the economy should produce more.

An example of a choice between two goods may help to show that a competitive equilibrium is Pareto optimal.

Question   Suppose that the equality of marginal utility with marginal costs does not hold. On the contrary, a consumer values the last meal at twice the last pair of socks, but the last meal costs three times as much to produce. Could production and consumption be rearranged to give more total benefit?

We could certainly extract more utility here. The consumer could sacrifice a meal and be compensated fully with two pairs of socks. But the resources released allow three pairs of socks to be produced. So either the consumer, or someone else, is better off to the tune of one pair of socks. Or the spare resources from one pair of socks can be used for some other beneficial purpose.

Hence, when the equivalence of marginal utility and marginal cost does not hold, there is scope for a Pareto improvement. In the above example the ratios of the marginal costs of socks and meals (the rate at which one could be replaced with the other at the margin) did not equal the ratios of the marginal utilities to the consumer. Thus rearrangement improved welfare. Once marginal costs are equated to marginal utility, there is no scope left for this kind of rearrangement.

In this way perfectly competitive markets lead to a Pareto optimal outcome. In equilibrium in a perfectly competitive market there are no benefits in further adjusting consumption/production, because the utility lost to the consumer if a good is not bought is exactly balanced by the marginal cost saved. In maximizing their own welfare, consumers and producers make choices at the margin which ensure that there is no better outcome for one participant except at a cost to another. Such a situation is Pareto optimal.

This intuitive explanation has referred to product markets and to two-good economies. It can, however, be extended to more complex economies as a whole, with markets for factors of production as well as goods and services. It can be shown quite generally that if all markets are perfectly competitive, then the equilibrium for the economy as a whole is Pareto optimal. Another way of saying this is that a perfectly competitive economy is **allocatively efficient**: resources could not be reallocated to improve anyone's welfare without reducing the welfare of another.

This efficiency property of perfect competition has constituted a powerful argument for free markets. But you should note how strong the conditions are. All producers and consumers in product and factor markets must be perfectly informed price-takers (Chapter 5, Section 5.2.1). The essence of allocative efficiency (or Pareto optimality) in perfect competition lies in the choices which producers and consumers make – between factors of production, in how much to produce and in the allocation of incomes between goods. Unless the prices of all products reflect marginal costs, consumers' choices will be based on misleading information – and analogous conditions apply to factor markets and production.

Hence to achieve allocative efficiency the entire economy must operate under conditions of perfect competition, a condition which is likely to be impracticable in real life. It requires only one monopolist or firm operating strategically in oligopoly to put price above marginal cost (which, as we have seen in Chapters 4 and 6, they will do to maximize their profits) for these efficiency characteristics in the rest of the economy to be lost. This dependence for allocative efficiency on universal applicability throughout the economy is a harsh blow to the practical use of perfectly competitive models as a basis for policy.

Perfect competition therefore achieves Pareto optimality (allocative efficiency) only under restrictive assumptions. Another such assumption is that there are no externalities. Network externalities were introduced in Chapter 3, and externalities will be discussed in more general terms in Chapter 9. The assumption is that any utility is derived from a person's own consumption activities, but we know this not to be true as externalities abound in real economies. Every person who buys a mobile phone, for example, serves to make everyone else's mobile phone a little bit more useful at no cost to everyone else (Chapter 3). Virtually all countries in the world are producing greenhouse gases likely to contribute to global warming and the destruction of wildlife habitats and coastal cities. Externalities may be positive or negative, but if they exist perfect competition cannot be relied on to generate Pareto optimal outcomes.

Allocative efficiency

Allocative efficiency occurs when resources are allocated among consumers and producers in such a way that no reallocation could improve anyone's welfare without reducing the welfare of someone else.

A further point is that there exists the possibility that other, non-market mechanisms for allocating goods and services can also be shown to be desirable, in the sense of satisfying Pareto optimality. Central planning is one alternative to setting prices, and although this prevails in only very few parts of the world as a dominant ideology, most governments around the world do allocate funds between regions (e.g. for health, education and transport). These formulae might be based on the number of people living in a region, say, and the rationale for their use is usually that they reflect need. As they allocate resources without reference to prices, they represent an alternative to the market.

Occasionally, economics uses concepts such as Pareto optimality that appear to be unobjectionable. But I want to suggest that only some Pareto optima are desirable. To see this, consider a game, called the ultimatum game, that illustrates the point. We have $100 to divide up between us. I get to propose a division, and if you accept my proposal, that determines what we get. If you reject my proposal, we both leave with nothing. What should I propose? And how should you react?

If I propose $99 for me and $1 for you, you should accept my generous offer, because $1 is better for you than nothing. Most people don't do this. If offered a very unequal division, most people respond by rejecting the proposal, even though it seems not be in their own personal interest. People thus reject Pareto improvements if they are very unequal. Furthermore, experimental studies show that very unequal distributions are rarely proposed, perhaps because they seem to be unfair, or perhaps because people know they are unlikely to be accepted (inequality is discussed in Chapter 9). This game is usually presented as evidence that people in competitive settings are not just interested in maximizing monetary income. But the point I want to stress is that only some Pareto optimal distributions tend to be proposed and accepted, namely those that are relatively equitable.

In my view, and notwithstanding some of the really important theoretical insights and results that the concept has generated, there are problems in trying to apply the concept of utility that have not had the attention they deserve. However, economists are now beginning to take more interest in the extent to which psychological evidence can inform the development of economic models. In the next section I want to look at well-being from a viewpoint in which empirical evidence plays an important role in generating theory.

8.4 Well-being

The assertion that well-being is important to many people should not surprise anyone. But what does it mean, and how does it relate to income and utility? In this section we will examine different aspects of well-being, a concept that has both subjective and objective aspects. We shall see that what one has is not the only thing that matters; what one is free to do (the opportunities people have) and the process by which decisions are made also determine well-being.

8.4.1 Happiness and its relation to income

One approach to welfare that is beginning to attract attention from economists, particularly those working on issues to do with labour markets, health and the macro economy, concerns the role of economic factors in explaining happiness. As we have seen, there is a tendency to supplement simple financial measures of economic welfare in a variety of ways, and one way of doing this is to ask people directly how they feel. Typically, people are given a question about their mental state (which might range from happy to depressed) and are asked to say how well they normally feel, on a five- or seven-point scale. Clearly, answers to such questions do need to be interpreted with care, but there are, nevertheless, some issues that we might address using this kind of data. First, we can ask what, if anything, is correlated with happiness. (The terms 'subjective well-being' and 'experienced utility' have also been used.) Does happiness vary with measures of economic well-being, or are other, non-economic, factors more important? Second, can we develop theories that explain behaviour? It has been noted that measures of well-being do not increase much over time, despite large increases in measures of national income such as GDP. Why is this? Third, and related to the previous questions, what can we say about self-reports relating to well-being and objective measures of economic welfare?

Veenhoven (1993) collated data from subjective well-being surveys over the period from 1946 to 1990 for 55 nations. His data have been analysed by a number of researchers, and perhaps the most significant finding is positive relationships between happiness or subjective well-being (SWB), economic welfare and a small number of other variables (Table 8.10). Links of this kind between statistical data are known as 'correlations'. The idea is that finding similarities between changes in two or more variables suggests that the changes in one variable are related in some way to changes in another. For example, if every increase in SWB were accompanied by an increase in GDP per head, and every decrease in SWB were accompanied by a decrease in GDP per head, it would seem unlikely that SWB and GDP per head are completely causally unrelated.

The measure of correlation is a number between 1 (an exact positive relation – whenever one variable rises, the other rises by the same amount) and −1 (an exact negative relation – whenever one variable rises, the other falls by the same amount). A zero correlation between two variables means that there is no empirical evidence of a relation between them.

Exactly what the relation between SWB and GDP per head might be is another story. At least, a strong correlation of this kind suggests an avenue to be explored. Perhaps GPD per head exerts a powerful influence on SWB – perhaps being rich does make you happy. Or does SWB influence GDP per head – if people are 'happy in their work', do they work more effectively and so produce more GDP? Table 8.10 lists four variables that are correlated with happiness (SWB). We may not be able to draw conclusions about the direction of causality but, referring to Table 8.10, we can link SWB and GDP per head more strongly than we can link, say, SWB and human rights. All of the correlations shown in Table 8.10 are sufficiently strong for it to be unlikely that they were generated just as a matter of chance.

Schyns' (1998) analysis identified four covariates of SWB, that is, variables that are correlated with SWB. GDP per head, the measure of economic welfare, is the most strongly correlated variable, but the third and fourth variables measuring gender inequality and the individualist or collective orientation of a country respectively are not far behind. Human

Table 8.10
Variables correlated with happiness for 55 countries

Measure	Correlation with SWB
GDP per head	0.64
Human rights	0.39
UN Gender Empowerment Measure	0.52
Triandis's Measure of Individualism/Collectivism	0.51

Source: Schyns, 1998, p.15

rights, referring to measures of political and civil rights, also turns out to be statistically significant. Schyns believes all three non-economic variables relate to freedom as an aspect of a country's culture.

However, as suggested above, correlation does not prove causation. It could be that happiness *is* caused by economic prosperity and freedom, but other causal explanations are possible. One possibility is that freedom causes happiness and economic prosperity, but separately. People are happy if their human rights are respected, and a nation is productive if people are free to make economic decisions for themselves. Support for such an interpretation might be taken from the fact that job satisfaction is only weakly related to job performance.

We have seen that, in dealing with welfare, economists have used objective measures such as income as well as subjective approaches such as utility. Recently, quality of life researchers have suggested that we need both objective and subjective perspectives to understand welfare properly. The difference between subjective and objective dimensions is nicely illustrated by events following the publication of the 1981 *Places Rated Almanac* (Boyer and Savageau, 1981), which judged, using objective measures, Lawrence, Massachusetts, the least desirable town in America in which to live. Objective measures are those that are independent of the views and feelings of the respondents and include criteria such as GDP per head, air quality, health status and traffic congestion. The media interviewed residents subsequently to see if they agreed, but found instead a group of people with a positive sense of community, who emphasized family and friends and shared a genuine attachment to their town. The subjective ratings of Lawrence's denizens gave quite a different picture from the external picture that emerged from the 'objective' assessment.

But how might we combine the objective and the subjective? Robert Cummins (2000) discusses the topic using an analogy with human anatomy. Human bodies have many mechanisms for controlling variables such as temperature or blood pressure, and Cummins suggests that our experience of well-being is similarly controlled. A large proportion of survey respondents report themselves as being at the top level of SWB, and it might be that people automatically adapt their subjective experience to changes in their objective situation. For example, many people find it easy to get used to increases in income and most people do adapt, if more slowly, to decreases in income. The process is not entirely symmetrical, however, because below certain levels of objective welfare, subjective well-being declines along with objective welfare. There are limits to people's adaptability.

If Cummins (2000) is correct, we might expect to see objective and subjective measures rise and fall together at very low levels of welfare. Once a threshold has been reached, objective welfare might increase without any observed impact on subjective welfare. As it happens, evidence from a number of studies in different countries is consistent with this idea.

8.4.2 Procedural utility

Sometimes people are concerned not just about outcomes, but also about processes. When a person is subjected to a miscarriage of justice these issues often stand or fall together. For example, a person might claim that they were unfairly imprisoned (an outcome) on the procedural grounds that some of the evidence produced by the prosecuting authorities had been manufactured. Conversely, when people are happy with an outcome they may be encouraged to view the process by which the outcome was produced as adequate. Procedures and our attitudes to them have been discussed and investigated extensively by psychologists and legal scholars, and there are some interesting studies in this field.

Table 8.11
Acceptability of
decision procedures

Procedure	Respondents finding this mechanism acceptable %
Negotiations	72
Referendums	39
Expert decision	34
Lottery	32
Willingness to accept compensation	20
Willingness to pay	4

Source: Oberholzer-Gee *et al.*, 1996

A study conducted by the Swiss economist Bruno Frey and his colleagues asked voters to indicate their attitudes to different procedures for locating a medium-level nuclear waste depository. The measures they sought to evaluate included willingness to pay and willingness to accept compensation, which are economic or market-based approaches. However, they also included other approaches, such as the consultation of experts and negotiations involving community representatives. The results of this study are summarized in Table 8.11.

The market-based approaches, willingness to pay to avoid the imposition of a waste repository and willingness to accept compensation for the imposition of one, are the least popular options. It is sometimes argued that where an indivisible good (or bad) has to be allocated between different individuals, the fair method to use is randomization via a lottery. This, at least, equalizes the probability of obtaining the good/bad, even if it cannot be divided equally between all the parties. Although this is acceptable to more people than the willingness to accept compensation or willingness to pay criteria, over two-thirds of the sample still do not find it acceptable. However, the lottery is only marginally less acceptable than expert decision, a method that has played a significant, albeit changing, role over the past 50 years. Most popular are the two forms of public consultation. Referendums are conducted frequently in Switzerland, and negotiation is acceptable to approximately three-quarters of the sample, possibly because it allows for a more open-ended dialogue between the parties involved (see also Frey and Stutzer, 2002). In reality, many social choices contain aspects of more than one of these approaches, but this survey work throws into stark relief people's attitudes to different aspects of decision-making processes.

▦ ▨ ■ 8.4.3 Capabilities and well-being

Capabilities

Capabilities are abilities to do certain things, such as read, secure adequate nourishment and play a full part in the life of the community.

An approach attracting growing popularity among welfare economists, and one that draws together many of the strands in this chapter, has been developed by Amartya Sen, a Nobel laureate in economics (Sen, 1985). Instead of measuring economic development in terms of average money income, Sen argues that we should look at indicators of people's opportunities, as measured by indices such as literacy rates, nutrition and life expectancy. Such indicators are now widely used. They are also consistent with a different theoretical approach, the so-called 'basic needs' approach, which favours measuring and providing things that are fundamental to existence. As Sen has noted, however, the **capabilities** approach provides a rationale for monitoring political and civil liberties, which the 'basic needs' approach does not.

Table 8.12
Capabilities and achievements – results from a voter survey

	Capabilities	Achievements
Happiness	3rd	1st
Achievement	5th	7th
Health	2nd	3rd
Intellectual stimulation	4th	5th
Social relations	6th	4th
Environments	1st	2nd
Personal projects	7th	6th

Source: Anand and van Hees, 2001

In a number of important ways, Sen's approach is informed by and deals with the problems of earlier approaches to welfare, such as income or utility. It stresses the existence of subjective differences between people and suggests that money income measures only opulence, not well-being. But it is also consistent with the idea that there is an objective list of issues that are important to the happiness of nearly everyone. What really matters to people is the opportunity to make their own choices between valued options and that these opportunities are distributed equitably among people. People have rights to equal opportunities, and these may take precedence over maximizing utility.

We introduce you here to some empirical work that I conducted with Martin van Hees (Anand and van Hees, 2001), looking at well-being through the lens of Sen's capability–rights theory. Briefly, we noted that Sen's theory emphasizes two distinctions. The first is between *well-being*, which might include things such as health that have objective aspects, and *agency* goals, which concern things such as being a competent piano player that are more particular to an individual person. The second distinction Sen makes is between capabilities (i.e. what people are free to do) and their achievements (i.e. the outcomes of choosing between different capabilities).

Table 8.12 reports evidence from some of my own research using Sen's framework. Half the questions relate to people's opportunities and half to their corresponding achievements in seven areas of life. Respondents were asked, for instance, about the scope to seek happiness and to indicate their capacity on a seven-point scale (1 = very good, 7 = very poor). They were subsequently asked to indicate, again on a seven-point scale, the extent to which they agreed with statements about their achievements in various areas.

Happiness and health might be thought of as examples of areas related mainly to well-being, while achievement and personal projects are related more to agency. Intellectual stimulation, social relations and environments appear harder to classify, as they contribute substantially to both agency and well-being. The survey was given to a random sample of voters in England, and the analysis summarized in Table 8.12 is based on approximately 270 responses.

For our sample, the scope for being in pleasant environments was rated as most adequate, while the scope to develop personal projects was rated as least adequate. When it came to achievements, the respondents were in most agreement with the statement that their life was happy and least in agreement with a statement about satisfaction with what they were able to achieve. These findings are not necessarily what one would expect, although they appear to be consistent with related empirical research. Perhaps people are happy for reasons associated with the aspirations and adjustment argument put forward by Cummins (2000). Furthermore, when we investigated agreement with the statement

Table 8.13   Quality of life indicators for ten high-income countries

Country	Consumption (national income)[1]	Life expectancy[2]	Unemployment[3]	Suicide[4]	Education[5]	HDI rank
Canada	17 363 (8)	77.4	11.2	21	100	1
USA	20 170 (4)	76.0	7.3	20	95	2
Japan	18 918 (6)	79.5	2.2	22	77	3
Netherlands	15 693 (9)	77.4	6.8	14	88	4
Finland	19 364 (5)	75.7	13.0	45	96	5
Iceland	21 685 (2)	78.2	3.0	18	81	6
Norway	20 284 (3)	76.9	5.9	21	88	7
France	18 093 (7)	76.9	10.2	30	86	8
Spain	11 460 (10)	77.6	18.1	11	86	9
Sweden	23 389 (1)	78.2	4.8	22	78	10

[1] £ thousand per annum.

[2] Years from birth.

[3] Proportion of workforce unemployed.

[4] Annual numbers of male suicides per 0.1 million of population.

[5] Combined gross enrolment ratio.

Source: adapted from Quizilbash, 1997

'generally my life is happy', two capabilities were correlated, and of these the one with the stronger correlation was the judgement about the scope to develop personal projects. So there would seem to be some support for the idea that the achievement of happiness depends not just on the quantity of happy events in a person's life but also on their ability to develop and shape meaningful sequences of actions and events. This result seems to provide support for the emphasis on the relationship of personal projects to well-being found in the magnum opus of the philosopher Derek Parfit (1984).

A number of economists have explored the impacts of different measures of well-being. Mozaffar Quizilbash (1997), for example, has collected data that show clearly how the incorporation of different criteria changes, in some cases dramatically, how we rank countries with respect to the well-being of their populations.

The 'HDI' column in Table 8.13 requires a more extended explanation. The Human Development Index is constructed from data on a number of key indicators of well-being, including life expectancy at birth, health status, educational opportunities, employment and political rights. These indicators are expressed as an index number for each country, which makes it possible to rank countries in terms of human development.

Table 8.13 is valuable because it demonstrates how different conceptions of well-being give rise to different rankings. For example, if we measure well-being in terms of the amount spent on consumption, Sweden is ranked first and Spain last; using suicide as an indicator of well-being puts Spain first and relegates Sweden to joint last but one. It is worth noticing that HDI is a measure of well-being originally designed to aid policy makers in monitoring development in low-income countries. Most of the differences among the high-income countries in Table 8.13 are relatively small.

In short, we do have options for adopting measures of well-being that go beyond national income: the capabilities approach gives us a good indication of the kinds of things that really matter and deserve thoughtful measurement.

8.5 Conclusion

This chapter has looked at welfare from three perspectives.

The CF model focuses on money income and is the basis for three different ways of measuring national income. It provides a basis for a macroeconomic analysis. GDP per head is widely used as a measure of welfare despite its limitations.

People's preferences vary considerably, and so, reflecting this, economic theorists tend to base their analysis of individual welfare on utility, an idea that allows us to relate goods and services to their subjective value to individuals. The concept of utility has been used to characterize individual choice behaviour and, with Pareto optimality, to suggest the superiority of perfect competition.

However, welfare economics has a critical edge too. The welfare theorem establishing the desirability of perfect competition depends on a number of questionable assumptions.

The fact that environmental problems are now threatening extensive economic damage later this century provides an economic motivation for questioning the extent to which material goods and services are really what generate well-being. One theory, the capabilities approach, puts emphasis on the options people have and on what it is they achieve. If one looks around the world, or back in history, at the things people almost universally value – dignity, involvement, respect, happiness, social contact, meaning, achievement, joy, excitement and status, to name but a few – it is far from clear that these require, or are guaranteed by, the consumption of large amounts of material goods and services.

In their influential textbook, Samuelson and Nordhaus approvingly conclude their review of the limits of national income accounting by citing Arthur Okun (1970, p.124):

It should be no surprise that national prosperity does not guarantee a happy society, any more than personal prosperity ensures a happy family . . . Still, prosperity . . . is a precondition for success in achieving many of our aspirations.

(Samuelson and Nordhaus, 1989)

An alternative view is that an economic system has emerged from the private pursuit of goals and aspirations. This view implies that the causality runs in the opposite direction from that suggested by Okun (1970). For Okun, the provision of prosperity by the economy is a precondition of individual happiness, but the view underlying this chapter is that in pursuing happiness we create, almost inadvertently, an economic system. In that case, policy makers might ask, not what we should do for the economy, but what the economy can do for us.

Questions for review and discussion

Question 1 Figure 8.7 shows the circular flow of income model. Insert the labels below in their correct positions on the diagram:

Transfers exports, X savings, S imports, M investment expenditure, 1

Figure 8.7
Circular flow of
income model

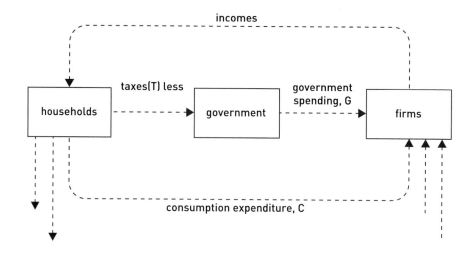

Question 2 The table shows values at GDP current prices and at constant 2000 prices for a hypothetical economy. Add the missing values in the spaces in the table.

	Year	
	2000	2001
GDP at current prices (€ million)	1500	
GDP at constant 2000 prices (€ million)	1500	1250
GDP deflator		200

Question 3 The following statements are about changes in total utility and marginal utility obtained as more of a good or service is consumed. Say which is the correct statement.

A ❏ If total utility is rising, marginal utility must be rising too.
B ❏ If total is remaining constant, marginal utility and total utility must be the same.
C ❏ If total utility is falling, marginal utility must be negative.

Question 4 Figure 8.8 shows a utility possibility frontier for Anna and Bjorn. Say which *three* statements below are correct.

Figure 8.8
Utility possibility
frontier for Anna
and Bjorn

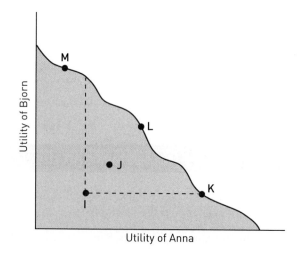

A ❑ Movement from I to J is a Pareto improvement.
B ❑ Movement from J to K is a Pareto improvement.
C ❑ L and K represent Pareto optimal distributions of utility but M does not.
D ❑ Movement from J to L is a Pareto improvement.
E ❑ Movement from I to K is not a Pareto improvement.
F ❑ K, L and M are all Pareto optimal distributions of utility.

Question 5 The table below presents data on GDP and changes in the price level for a country over a four-year period.

GDP and changes in the price level

	2000	2001	2002	2003
GDP at current prices (£ billion)	3.7	3.9	4.0	4.4
Price index	100	104	105	106

(a) Using the price index as a GDP deflator, calculate GDP at constant prices for each year.
(b) Draw a graph, plotting GDP at current prices and constant prices on the vertical axis and time along the horizontal axis.
(c) How would you describe the difference between the changes in GDP at current prices and the changes in GDP at constant prices shown in your graph?
(d) The Index of Sustainable Economic Welfare (ISEW) makes a number of adjustments to the consumption measure of income. Comment briefly on the nature of these adjustments and their rationale.

Question 6 Essay: To what extent does Sen's capabilities theory provide a persuasive account of well-being?

9

The economics of governance

Maureen Mackintosh

9.1 Markets, inequality and governance

> It is a fundamental error to imagine that capitalist economics means an absence of government intervention.
>
> *(Barr, 1994, p.29)*

> The new economy is a place of hope and fear. The hope is that policy activism can cement in potential productivity gains; the fear is that government actions will not mitigate the seemingly ineluctable pressures towards social exclusion.
>
> *(Van Reenan, 2001, p.307)*

Nicholas Barr is an economist specializing in the economics of the public services. He was writing in the early 1990s on the economic problems of the early stages of the transition in eastern Europe and the ex-Soviet countries from centrally planned economies to capitalism. In capitalist economies change is driven by private investment and market exchange. By 'capitalist economics' Barr means the economic theory of the operation of such economies: that is, the topic of this book. The transition economies initially faced rising unemployment and poverty, widening inequality, deteriorating 'social' provision such as health care, declining output and poorly functioning markets. Tackling those problems required the recognition that high-income capitalist economies both display and require high levels of government expenditure and regulation, to help markets work efficiently and to promote the access of all citizens to the economic benefits available.

The rate of technological change associated with the so-called 'new economy' at the turn of the last century, and the rising inequality and sense of insecurity this has brought with it within many high-income countries (Chapters 1 and 2), has led economists such as Van Reenan, concerned with industrial policy, to make similar arguments. Governments, particularly European governments of economies lagging behind the USA in productivity growth, need to intervene actively to promote effective innovation and import of leading-edge technologies, to support research and development, and above all to ensure that people have the skills to participate in the changing labour market (see the discussion of human capital in Chapter 7). The need is for 'smart' regulation (Van Reenan, 2001, p.331) encouraging innovation while fostering competitiveness, and at the same time for policies to avoid 'social exclusion' resulting from a lack of the capability to participate in markets.

These responses by two economists faced, several years apart, by two very different kinds of rapid economic change, illustrate a central theme of this chapter. Market-based – or capitalist – economies need governing *both* in order to promote market efficiency *and* to try to ensure the social inclusion of all citizens. Neither of these two authors sees those two broad objectives as necessarily in conflict, rather the contrary: achieving one will help support the other. And this approach reflects, I think, a real shift in economic policy debate at the beginning of the twenty-first century. While economists have long argued that greater efficiency may require the acceptance of greater inequality, there is today a more active search for policies that promote both equity and efficiency. As a result, there is a new acceptance of active government, after the political pressure of the 1980s and 1990s to restrict government activities. We seem to be leaving behind the late twentieth-century preoccupation with whether governments should be bigger or smaller, and turning instead to consider how governments can be *smarter* (Van Reenan, 2001).

Part of smarter government is a recognition that markets and economic activity are 'governed' not only by governments but also by voluntary collective action. People get together in a wide variety of associations, outside the framework of formal government, to influence aspects of our economic lives: for example, there are many charitable activities that help to support vulnerable people in capitalist economies. These associational forms of governance are sometimes summarized as 'civil society'.

By 'governance' in this chapter, we mean both government and such voluntary collective action. We begin the chapter by analysing some *efficiency* reasons why governments intervene in the economy: to make markets work better or supply goods and services markets cannot efficiently provide (Section 9.2). Section 9.3 then considers the scope for collective rather than government action to promote both efficiency and equity, using the example of local management of natural resources. In Sections 9.4 and 9.5 we turn to the 'welfare state'. To what extent does government provision of cash benefits and services such as health and education reduce inequality, and does this 'welfare' spending have costs in terms of economic efficiency? Finally, Section 9.6 considers democratic government itself, not as an independent economic agent, but as an agency to which we delegate actions too hard to achieve by voluntary collaboration. I analyse just one difficult case, where there is conflict between the interests of different voters: policies on redistribution.

9.2 Shaping market incentives and providing public goods

Markets organize the supply of many of the goods and services we consume, and our ability to buy them is therefore a key determinant of our well-being (Chapter 8). However, there are some goods and services that we wish to consume that cannot be efficiently supplied through markets. This section uses economic theory you have already learned to explore some reasons for such market failure, to see why voluntary collective action may not work either. It then develops a rationale for government intervention to improve market efficiency, both in the static sense of achieving a Pareto optimal allocation of resources (Chapter 8, Section 8.3) and in the dynamic sense of successful industrial innovation and competition (Chapters 2 and 3).

We explore the problem of market failure through an issue raised in Chapter 8, Section 8.2.4: the supply of environmental 'goods' such as clean air, or, to put the same point in another way, the supply of environmental protection from 'bads' such as pollution.

▪▪▪ 9.2.1 Externalities and public goods

Public good

A public good is a good that is *not rival*, that is, my consuming it does not reduce the amount available for you; it is also *not excludable*, that is, if I am consuming it I cannot prevent you from consuming it too.

The first step to solving a problem is to admit that you have one. For Houston, years of living in denial about its polluted air have made things even worse. This conurbation, which each year pumps 200,000 tons of nitrogen oxide (a component of smog) into the air, has recently beaten Los Angeles for the title of America's smoggiest city.

(The Economist, 8 January 2000)

The situation in Houston in Texas is an example of a worldwide problem of urban smog. Urban air pollution is generated by industrial emissions and by car exhausts. However, it can also be cleaned up: London had its last great smog in 1954. So what can economics tell us about why air pollution happens and the problems of stopping it?

We will start by analysing the problem from the point of view of the urban citizens.

> **Question**   Suppose that residents of a polluted city such as Houston all want cleaner air. Could they buy that environmental improvement individually through the market? If not why not?

You may have thought of a number of problems. An obvious one is that air moves about and cannot be divided into packets above each house for private ownership and cleaning up. To clean up your own air is to clean up the air for everyone. Economists call goods like clean air **public goods**.

> **Question**   Stop and think about that definition. Can you think of other examples of public goods, besides clean air?

The definition amounts to saying that a 'public good' is not divisible into separate bits for sale on a market. Rather, each person can use it as they choose without subtracting from the amount available for others and no one can be excluded from using it. Military forces ('defence'), street lighting and rural road networks: these goods and services, generally provided by governments, come reasonably close to the definition. Very few activities fit it precisely. As with many economic concepts, a 'public good' is an abstract idea which can be applied to explain aspects of the economic world. Street lighting, for example, benefits anyone walking down the street. Most rural and urban roads – until congested – are available for anyone who wishes to drive, cycle or walk along them. If the military deter armed aggression, everyone is defended.

Let us return to our polluted city, and consider further the problem facing citizens in search of clean air via market mechanisms.

Question	Suppose I own a firm producing a well-tried gadget that greatly reduces pollution from industrial processes, such as petrochemicals production and oil refining in Texas, that are damaging city air. Why can't I sell my gadget to those who want to breathe clean air?

Put like that the question answers itself. I am trying to sell the gadget to the wrong people. It is no use to the consumers. The producers of the pollution are the industrial firms. So why not sell the gadget to them?

Well, why should they buy it? It is just another industrial cost (and the owners may well not live in the city). For the polluting firms, such as the petrochemical and oil refining industries of Texas, the damaging emissions are a by-product: a by-product of their activity that imposes costs on others (the citizens of Houston) for which the firms are not required to pay compensation (yet). In other words, the pollution is an **externality**.

Externality

An externality occurs when one person's action affects the welfare of another in ways that the first need not take into account. An externality therefore arises in a market when a producer's, seller's or buyer's actions influence the welfare of others in ways not reflected in market prices.

You have seen the concept of externalities before. Chapter 3, Section 3.4.2 explained 'network externalities' using an example of a telephone user whose benefits from their phone rise as more people acquire phones. You can think of externalities as 'spillover effects': effects of one person's or one firm's actions on the welfare of others that do not pass through the market mechanism. So pollution is an externality because firms do not have to pay for its costs to others.

So how about the consumers who want clean air paying the producers to use the clean-up gadget? Imagine you are one of the people who cannot breathe properly, and you want to do this. What is the snag? You probably cannot afford on your own to pay all the producers to use the gadget. You need all those who want clean air to get together to pay.

However, there is a problem with this kind of collective action. Each person will think, well, if I refuse, then others will pay, and I will have clean air for free. Once the air is cleaned up, anyone can breathe it. Having access in this way to a public good you have refused to finance is called *free-riding*: you are taking a free ride on the payments of others. If each person seeks to free-ride, then no one will pay for the clean up, and the air will stay polluted.

Question	Think about free-riding. You have seen an economic problem of this form before. What is it?

The free-riding problem is an example of a prisoners' dilemma. There are lots of 'prisoners' (coughing citizens) in the polluted city, but you can model the basic problem by imagining a city of two people, as in Figure 9.1.

In this game, each citizen has a choice of paying to clean up the air, or not paying. If one agrees to pay and the other does not, then the one who pays must pay the full cost.

Figure 9.1
A prisoners' dilemma facing residents of a polluted city

		Person 2	
		pay	do not pay
Person 1	pay	1, 1	−1, 2
	do not pay	2, −1	0, 0

If both agree to pay they split the costs. The pay-offs are the net benefits: the benefits of clean air less the cost of achieving it. Each citizen has the lowest pay-off from supporting the whole cost of cleaning up; in that situation the cost to a player far outweighs the benefits of clean air (pay-off −1). To that, each player prefers not to pay and to leave the air polluted (pay-off 0). Each, however, would rather pay half the cost of clean up and breathe clean air (pay-off 1). Finally, for each player, the highest pay-off comes from 'free-riding', breathing clean air while paying nothing (pay-off 2).

Question | Work through this pay-off matrix carefully, assuming that each person makes their individual private decision. What is the dominant strategy for each person? What precisely is the dilemma?

The dominant strategy is 'do not pay'. Consider Person 1. If Person 2 does not pay, Person 1 will not pay (a pay-off of 0 is better than −1). If Person 2 pays, Person 1 will not pay (a pay-off of 2 is better than 1). So each player will decide not to pay, irrespective of the choice of the others. So the outcome is polluted air. Yet each person would prefer to pay half the cost and to clean up if only that could be organized. The dilemma is that individual decision-making results in an inferior result for each person. The attempt to free-ride is self-defeating. This two-person model can be applied to our example of a polluted city. If many players/citizens try to free-ride, then the air will remain polluted and citizens will continue to cough.

The example of environmental protection has some particular features explored further below. But the prisoners' dilemma model of free-riding applies generally to public goods. Voluntary payment for public goods provision tends to be undermined by free-riding.

▦ ▨ ■ 9.2.2 A rationale for government intervention

So how are public goods that citizens wish to consume to be produced? One method is government intervention. Suppose that a government – local, regional or national – wishes to intervene to 'produce' the public good of clean air. How might a government do that? Unlike some other public goods – such as street lighting – clean air cannot simply be produced and installed. Instead, a government needs to deal with the polluters.

To analyse the policy problem, let us start with externalities as a source of pollution and analyse their effects on the market for the products of a polluting industry such as petrochemicals. There is a cost of the air pollution that falls not on the firms in the industry but on local residents. It follows that the costs of production perceived by the firms are lower than the total costs of the production to society.

Figure 9.2
The divergence
between private and
social costs of a
polluting industry

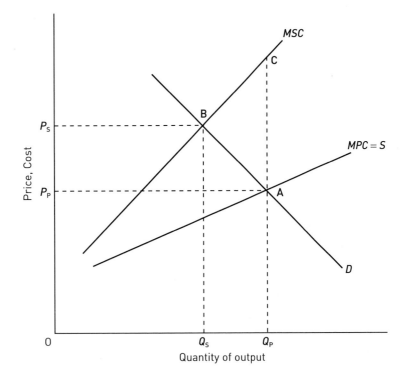

Figure 9.2 illustrates the effect of the externality on market efficiency. I assume that the polluting industry is perfectly competitive. The curve labelled $MPC = S$ is the supply curve for the industry, which is derived from the marginal cost curves of the individual firms (Chapter 5, Section 5.2). But this marginal cost curve only includes those costs which each firm actually has to pay. Hence it is the firm's marginal *private* cost (MPC) curve. The pollution is not the firms' problem (yet). So the marginal *social* costs (MSC), including the cost of pollution for residents, are higher than the marginal private costs as shown by the gap between the MSC and the MPC curves in Figure 9.2.

The private market equilibrium is at A, where firms equate their marginal private cost to marginal revenue with price P_P and output Q_P hence supply equals demand. But this is not an efficient market equilibrium.

Question   Can you explain why not, using the diagram? Look back at Chapter 8 and remind yourself of the conditions for a Pareto optimal market outcome before reading on.

A market is at a Pareto optimum – that is, no one can be made better off without also making someone worse off – when $MC = P = MU$ throughout the market. This is not the case at point A. Individuals' marginal utility – expressed in their individual demand curves (look back at Chapter 8, Section 8.3 again if that statement puzzles you) – is equated to the price they pay. But the full marginal social cost when output is Q_P (point C) is above the market price P_P.

For an allocatively efficient market outcome, the sum consumers are willing to pay for the last unit of output (indicated by the demand curve) should be equal to the full marginal cost of generating that last unit. In Figure 9.2, this would be at point B with price P_S and output Q_S. At B the marginal benefit to consumers is equal to the full marginal social cost. Where there are externalities in production of the type described, Pareto optimality requires that price be equated to the marginal *social* cost:

$$MSC = P = MU$$

Market failure

A market in which competition does not bring about a Pareto optimal outcome is said to exhibit market failure.

Externalities therefore imply **market failure**.

A market failure identifies an opportunity for intervention to improve market outcomes. Note, however, an implication of Figure 9.2: consumers do not want pollution reduced to zero; rather the optimal outcome is less output and hence less pollution. We will consider the implications in two stages. First, we will look at how governments might achieve a market equilibrium at point B in Figure 9.2. Then we will consider what (smarter) policies might break this unappealing policy dilemma of less output or more pollution.

Governments have two basic methods open to them to force output and pollution down. They can impose a tax that *internalizes the externality*, that is, it increases firms' costs to include the full costs of their output including the social costs. This will cause them to make output decisions that move the market towards the social optimum. To see how that might work, we need first to analyse how taxes in general affect competitive markets (Figure 9.3).

Figure 9.3 shows a perfectly competitive market for an unspecified good. The market equilibrium without the tax is at A with price P and output Q. Imposing a tax *t* per unit of output shifts the supply curve upwards, because each firms' costs are increased by the tax. That is, before they take their profit on each unit, they must pay the tax, which they therefore experience as a cost.

Question	How large is the tax shown in Figure 9.3?

Figure 9.3
A tax on output in a competitive market

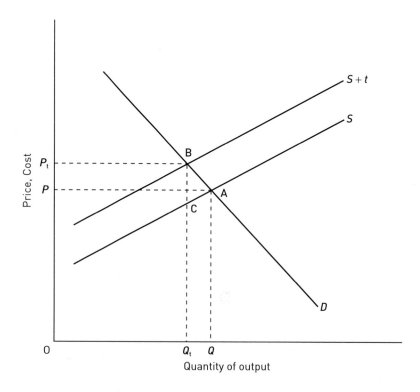

Figure 9.4
A specific tax on polluting firms' output

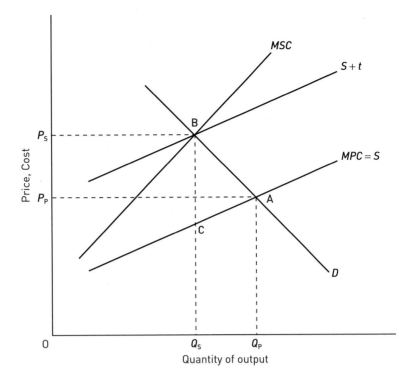

The tax *t* is measured by the vertical distance between *S* and *S + t*. This is equal to the distance BC on Figure 9.3. The market equilibrium with the tax is at point B, where the supply curve with the tax *S + t* intersects the demand curve. Price has risen to *P*t and output has fallen to *Q*t.

Exercise 9.1

How will the supply curve including the tax *S + t* change in shape if the tax is *ad valorem*, that is, if its value is a percentage of total revenue at each level of *Q*?

Now, armed with this diagrammatic analysis of taxes, we can return to the pollution problem. Figure 9.4 is based on Figure 9.2, and illustrates the use of a specific tax to force down output of the polluting industry to the optimum level.

The tax rate on Figure 9.4 is again the vertical distance between the supply curves *S* and *S + t*, equal to the distance BC. The market equilibrium without the tax is at A, with price *P*p and output *Q*p. The tax shifts the firm's supply curve to *S + t*, and the market equilibrium to B with price *P*s and quantity *Q*s. As the figure is drawn, the tax is at precisely the level to force output down to the market optimum level *Q*s. Achieving that in practice would not be easy. Government officials would need to calculate what the market optimum should be, and the precise tax needed to achieve it. There is a great deal of room for error.

Even if you managed to pull this off, however, as Environment Minister, you might feel rather dissatisfied. All that effort, and yet the air is still (rather less) polluted.

There are two key assumptions, I think. The first is that the right solution balances people's desire for output and for clean air, so we get a little less of one and more of the other – rather than completely clean air. There is no overriding priority on breathing properly; output matters too. Even more important, the analysis assumes that the technology used by firms is given. It doesn't allow for innovation, just for changes in output. Once there can be technological change and governments can support innovation, the dismal choice of less output and less pollution, or more of both, can be sidestepped.

▨ ▧ ■ 9.2.3 Government intervention in market dynamics

Look back at Figure 9.4. How could the government, instead of accepting that the only options are less pollution plus less output or the status quo, create incentives for firms to find new technology and to clean up their emissions, that is, to innovate?

There are several ways in which the government can change the incentive structure facing firms. Let us start with the circumstances described above where a gadget already exists to clean up emissions. A government could use regulation to enforce its use: firms could be told that they must clean up to stay in business. This was a strategy used in Texas, where the state required cuts in industrial emissions of pollutants ahead of federal guidelines coming into force in 2007 (*The Economist*, 8 January 2000). Alternatively, firms might be taxed, not on output, but on measured pollution. Less pollution, less tax, hence an incentive to install the clean-up equipment.

Exercise 9.2

Consider a regulation that raises firms' average and marginal costs because they have to install new equipment and use a new process to clean up emissions. This reduces pollution to zero. Assume the industry is perfectly competitive.

1 Use diagrammatic analysis drawn from Chapters 3 and 5 to show what has happened to costs and supply at the firm level.
2 Show on a diagram how this change in firms' costs affects equilibrium price and output in the market.

So far, we have been analysing pollution policy using the model of perfect competition. However, suppose that we now pose the policy problem in terms of incentives for firms to innovate, for example by developing less-polluting production methods. We then need to move away from the perfectly competitive market model, and use more appropriate models of imperfect markets, in which technology can be changed by firms, and in which firms can have diverse capabilities. In such markets, there is the interesting possibility that low pollution might be a source of market advantage for innovative firms, allowing them to operate profitably in highly regulated environments and to sell on innovative solutions to lagging firms.

In those circumstances, governments can try to offer firms incentives and opportunities to innovate, with increased market power for the leaders as the 'carrot'. Policies can include support for product development: for example, the creation of better, cheaper equipment for reducing emissions. Different outputs that are less polluting are another route to innovating out of environmental crisis: new high-tech firms moving into Houston are unconnected with the petrochemical industry and are interested in a clean environment for plant and staff. Regulations that restrict or heavily tax pollution can give a firm that finds a less-polluting solution a first-mover market advantage (Chapter 6, Section 6.5).

The more governments can create incentives to break the dilemmas imposed by current technology, the more efficient the solutions can be. Encouragement of a nascent 'green' industry supplying environmentally friendly solutions can both generate new markets and new employment and improve the environment; regulations can help to generate markets for such nascent industries; and government support for relevant research and development can get them started. The general point is that policies that create incentives for innovative methods of compliance – that tell firms what to achieve but not how to do it, and benefit those that generate new ideas – are both easier to monitor and generate more net benefits. This kind of solution is an example of what in Section 9.1 we called 'smarter' government in a period of high industrial innovation and increasing environmental pressure.

It remains possible, however, that if governments impose restrictions, firms may move, to go and pollute someone else with a less interventionist government – that's capitalism!

9.3 Governing the commons: the scope for collective action

Section 9.2 argued that free-riding posed a problem for attempts to deal with externalities or provide public goods through voluntary payment. In this section, we look at circumstances in which collective action can overcome free-riding, using the example of the management of natural resources.

Clean air is a public good of a particular sort: a *global* free-access good, or part of the global 'commons'. The concept of the 'commons' comes from common ground: from land or water or forest resources held in some sense in common for free access by all. In the village I lived in as a child we would go to play 'on the common'. Historically, in high-income countries, and today in many lower-income countries, people rely on such common resources to supplement their incomes from gathering or fishing, to provide inputs to farming such as irrigation, and to provide some fall-back when private incomes fail. The loss of local commons can increase destitution and force people to work for less than a living wage.

As environmental awareness has grown (Chapter 8, Section 8.2.4), so has awareness that high-income communities depend on the 'commons' too. The global commons include sea that is alive and full of fish, and fairly stable global weather systems. All commons require co-operation to manage, and Section 9.2 explained the free-rider problem that undermines co-operation. The global free-access resources belong to all of us and to none of us, posing a huge international policy challenge that will be discussed further in Chapter 19.

Local commons, the subject of this section, are rather different. Local forests, rivers, grazing land and irrigation pools do 'belong' to an identifiable group such as a village or area, and sometimes those common ownership rights are legally binding. However, turning that collective ownership into effective management of a resource raises dilemmas and has met with solutions that may hold lessons for the larger scale.

▨ ▥ ■ 9.3.1   The tragedy of the commons

Local common-pool resources can be accessed freely by a defined group. When used in non-damaging ways they are true public goods, in that one person can use them freely without reducing the resource available for another. Once overused, they become rival: more use by one person means less available to others. Free-riding can therefore cause them to deteriorate cumulatively. A much-cited article by Garett Hardin (1968) called 'The tragedy of the commons' is a classic statement of this problem. Hardin envisages a situation where local herdsmen are free to graze their herds on common land but its carrying capacity is limited. Each herdsman benefits from his own herd (in terms of the sale of cattle, meat and milk) and loses income when, beyond a certain number of animals on the land, overgrazing means each animal has less sustenance.

Hardin argues that, since each herder gains the whole benefit from his own herd, each wishes to increase it. However, once the point of overgrazing is past, each herder suffers only a small part of the losses from overgrazing which expansion of his own herd will cause. The rest of the losses fall on the other herdsmen, so they are *externalities*, this time in a non-market context. If all herders pursue their own interests, cumulative degradation of the land will occur. Hardin's conclusion – it reads more like a prediction – is infinitely gloomy: 'Each man is locked into a system which compels him to increase his herd without limit – in a world that is limited. Ruin is the destination towards which all men rush, each pursuing his own best interest in a society that believes in the freedom of the commons' (Hardin, 1968, p.1244). Hence the 'tragedy' of the commons.

Exercise 9.3

Hardin tells a story of a prisoners' dilemma and its consequences. Make up your own pay-off matrix to model this story. Start with two herders each of whom can follow one of two strategies: a moderate herd size, which, if chosen by both, will not cause overgrazing, or a very large herd size that will cause land degradation. Write in appropriate pay-offs and explain the herders' dilemma.

Hardin's conclusion from his prisoners' dilemma parable is similar to the conclusion from the analysis in Section 9.2: the government must prevent disaster through coercion to restrain overuse. In other words, people must voluntarily relinquish their rights over their local commons to a government which then exercises legitimate coercion to manage the commons in their collective interests. But is government really the only option? Or can communities break such prisoners' dilemmas and govern their own commons through forms of voluntary collective stewardship?

▨ ▥ ■ 9.3.2   Governing the commons

Three widespread examples of the protection and management – and of failures of management – of local 'commons' are irrigation water, forests and woodlands, and local inshore fisheries. In recent years, all have been quite extensively studied for lessons for collaborative resource management. One conclusion that stands out is that such commons generally *are* managed in the sense of being run through understood procedures voluntarily adhered to, though these arrangements may and do break down. Free-riding and 'ruin' are not the universal experience.

So how do communities successfully break the prisoners' dilemma?

Question	Look back at Chapter 6, Section 6.2. Which of the methods discussed there of achieving a co-operative outcome in prisoners' dilemma games seem relevant to overcoming the tragedy of the commons?

Two ways of achieving co-operation to resolve the prisoners' dilemma are discussed. One is reliance on shared norms and practices. In this case, the pay-offs are not all that matters to players when they decide on strategy. The second way in which co-operation can be achieved is through repeated interaction. When a game is played repeatedly, individual players consider their cumulative pay-offs into the future, as well as current pay-offs, so individual strategies are forward-looking.

Each of these solutions appear relevant to the problem of protecting local commons from degradation. In Hardin's parable, people 'play' the prisoners' dilemma game repeatedly, with the same set of other people. Yet they learn nothing, and do not anticipate the future effects of their actions for themselves, nor the likely behaviour of their neighbours in response to their own actions. However, the herders would in practice be aware of these things, and each would take them into account in deciding their own actions. In repeated games, patterns of behaviour can emerge – such as not expanding a herd beyond the point which would be sustainable if everyone did the same – and be sustained so long as people know they will continue to interact into the indefinite future. People know that, cumulatively, such collaborative behaviour is in their own interests.

Economists try to explore these kinds of situations using simulated games (Chapter 6, Section 6.3): people play out a game, with stated pay-offs, in a 'laboratory' situation. These simulations (often called experiments) consistently show that people playing a repeated prisoners' dilemma game tend to seek the mutually beneficial collaborative solution unless they feel 'suckered' by others defecting to pursue their immediate self-interest. So individual strategies are observed to depend on experience of others' behaviour, but to favour co-operation if possible. The more people experience co-operative behaviour by others – and the more that it is clear that if people don't hang together they will hang separately – the more likely is continued co-operation for mutual benefit.

Furthermore, Hardin's herders care only about their own fate, not at all for the fate of others. When modelling the behaviour of firms, this may be a reasonable assumption; it is less appropriate perhaps for the behaviour of people in small communities. The more each herder cares about their neighbours, instead of considering only their own returns, the more likely it is that co-operation can be achieved, since each will value less highly the situation where they benefit at their neighbours' expense. A concern for others may be expressed in practice in local norms or shared understandings that set reasonable limits for individual use of commons. In the extreme, if each valued their neighbours' well-being as highly as their own, externalities would vanish, internalized in the decision-making process of each herder.

Exercise 9.4

Look back at the pay-off matrix in answer to Exercise 9.3. Can you use it to show how caring about their neighbours may resolve the prisoners' dilemma the herders face?

Finally, the herders might form an organization that has rules and can punish default. You can think of this as a formally constituted voluntary association (rather like a formal cartel, as described in Chapter 6, but for different purposes). This can help to achieve co-operation by reinforcing shared norms and practices through organized collective management.

This analysis, and the evidence from 'laboratory' experiments, together suggest that certain kinds of communities may find collaboration easier than others: notably small, socially homogeneous communities with strong mutual knowledge. However, field research on common-pool resource management suggests that this is too simple a conclusion. It is not just the basic characteristics of communities that matter to effective management of common-pool resources. Rather, societies successfully *build* effective collaborative institutions over time – or fail to do so. Communities may organize to impose rotational use rules, designate managers and forms of scrutiny, set use limits per household and so on.

Research on management of forests by communities that depend upon them shows that many such communities do find methods of allowing members access to the benefits of the forest resource while maintaining it intact; other communities let forests deteriorate. Crucial variables appear to include clarity about who are the users; about the boundary of the resource they hold in common; and about the right of the users to organize use of the resource. In countries as diverse as Japan and Papua New Guinea, communities have legally protected common rights to control forests and have continued to exercise them effectively in an increasingly commercial context (McKean, 2000).

Where local common-access forests continue to exist – whether or not based on legal rights – some communities manage better than others. In Nepal, a survey found that forest reserves that were improving were those that were actively managed (Varughese, 2000). Key determinants of success seemed to be the perceived fairness (not necessarily or even usually equality, but acceptability) of the rules for use, their clarity, and the ability to monitor and punish infringement. An Indian study (Agrawal, 1994) found that the best managed forests were those where both the rules for use and the monitoring process and fines for violation were accepted as legitimate by users.

Behind these findings lie the nature of the relationships on which management systems are built. Communities with high levels of inequality can manage common-pool forest resources, but this only functions well where access is truly available to the poor. In those circumstances, common forests can benefit the poor since the better off have a high opportunity cost of labour and may leave much of the forest products to the poor. Women's organizations have successfully promoted communal forestry in India and China (Agrawal, 1985). However, deep social divisions including differences of interest between men and women, and de facto control by one social group over the benefits of supposedly communal land, have frequently destroyed co-operative forest management (Agrawal, 1994; Agrawal, 1985).

This brings us back to concern for others. Organizations such as the *Chipko* movement against commercial forest exploitation in India are sustained by a mix of self-interest and care for the fate of others, and actively develop mutual understanding through organizing (Agrawal, 1985). To understand how common-access resources can be managed, we need a more complex view of people than a view that sees us as pursuing just our own – or even our family's – interests. People's objectives and strategies also emerge from involvement in wider social relationships. We can – though we may not – *learn* to manage collective resources despite social divisions.

9.4 Inequality and redistribution

redistribution . . . an unrequited transfer of resources from one person to another

(Boadway and Keen, 2000)

Section 9.3 ended on the theme of inequality and social division, suggesting that inequality within communities could block effective management of common-pool resources. We now turn to considering more explicitly the extent of inequality and the challenge it poses. The scale of inequality we live with in the world today – within and between countries – is enormous, and the scope for reducing inequality while sustaining or, better, increasing efficiency is a focus of the debate around 'smarter' government, as Section 9.1 explained. This section examines inequality within countries – Chapter 15 examines international inequality – and considers the extent to which governments effectively redistribute resources to the poor. Section 9.5 will look at some effects of redistribution on economic efficiency.

Question	Look back at Chapter 8, Section 8.3 and try to draw out of it some reasons why economists – and other human beings too – might want to reduce inequality.

The proposition that marginal utility diminishes as consumption rises has been used to argue for redistribution of income from rich to poor. If we are prepared to assume that all people have the *same* utility function, then redistribution will increase the utility of the poor more than it decreases the utility of the rich, thereby increasing the sum of human happiness (Chapter 8, Section 8.3). This argument assumes that we *can* compare utilities of different people, or at least are willing to make suppositions about similarity or difference.

Exercise 9.5

Can you think of counter arguments? Try to do so before reading on.

The capabilities framework (Chapter 8, Section 8.4) suggests another argument for reducing inequality by redistributing income to the poor: that people have a right to a 'fair chance' or equal opportunity. Public services such as education and health care, access to public goods such as a clean environment or common-pool resources, and cash benefits such as pensions: all these can help people to achieve valued capabilities such as health, participation in social relationships, and a measure of individual choice (or 'agency') concerning what they wish to do or be. To have this effect, they must be provided in such a way that resources are redistributed towards those who would not otherwise have access to them. This does not mean, however, that all those who approve of more equal opportunities see equality in itself as a good thing, or less inequality as necessarily better. Margaret Thatcher, before she became the UK Prime Minister, put her disagreement this way:

> Opportunity means nothing unless it includes the right to be unequal. Let our children grow tall and some grow taller than others if they have it in them to do so.
> *(Margaret Thatcher, 1975, quoted in Timmins, 1995, p.508)*

■ ■ ■ 9.4.1 The welfare state and redistribution

Many government activities redistribute resources, and not always from rich to poor. The extent and nature of government activity therefore deeply influences the outcomes of the market system (as Nick Barr (1994) was arguing in the quotation in Section 9.1).

Figure 9.5
General government
expenditure as
per cent of GDP,
selected years
and countries

Source: based on
data in Tanzi and
Schuknecht, 2000,
pp.6–7

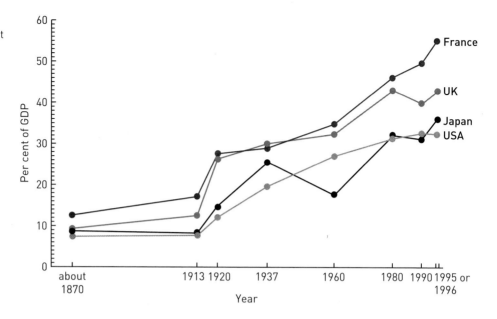

As capitalist economic development proceeds, the weight of government expenditure in the economy tends to rise, increasing this impact. Figure 9.5 shows this rise in expenditure in four countries over more than a century, starting earlier in the two European countries than the USA and Japan, with some levelling out after 1980, and a sharp drop in Japan in the aftermath of the Second World War.

Much government expenditure is *absorptive* (or *exhaustive*) *expenditure*, that is, expenditure on providing services such as health care, education and defence, that uses up (absorbs) resources such as labour and raw materials. The rest is *transfers*: shifts of spending power from one person to another, for example to provide old age pensions. Both types of expenditure may reduce inequality, or they may not. It is mainly high-income countries' governments that find the funds for transfer programmes.

Most governments in high-income countries – those in the Organization for Economic Co-operation and Development (OECD) – have an explicit commitment to the relief of poverty and to the provision of universal access to certain essential services such as health care and schooling. These services, and the cash transfers supposed to prevent destitution, are not without gaps – as the homeless sleeping on the streets of British cities testify – and the definitions of who is eligible can be narrowly drawn and discriminatory. However, only the United States among high-income countries lacks a principled governmental commitment to universalizing access to such services and benefits, known in shorthand as the **welfare state**.

There is no commonly accepted definition of the welfare state. Economics texts on the topic explicitly avoid defining it, and as the 'biographer' of the British welfare state puts it, 'Even the origin of the phrase is the subject of learned dispute' (Timmins, 1995). My working definition captures three important aspects: the mix of services and cash benefits; the mix of provision by government (i.e. the 'public sector') and ensuring provision and access by other means (e.g. contracting with private providers); and an *intention* to create a minimum level of welfare or well-being. It is not clear that a welfare state exists unless there is a real government intention to construct universal access and safety nets; hence the USA is sometimes described as the only high-income country without a welfare state, despite a high level of government spending on some relevant activities.

Welfare state

A set of
government
activities, notably
the provision
(or ensuring) of
universal access
to basic services
including health
care and
education, and
provision of cash
benefits, designed
(among other
objectives) to
ensure a minimum
level of well-being
for citizens of a
country.

▪ ▪ ▪ 9.4.2   Measuring inequality

To examine the redistributive impact of welfare spending we first need to be able to measure inequality of incomes. There are two preliminary decisions to be made. First, what is the best unit of measurement: the income of individuals or households? Some income is received and spent by individuals, other income is used for expenditure on goods and services that are shared with children, partners and other household members (not necessarily on an equal basis). We will use household income, while keeping in mind that this disguises intra-household inequality.

Second, should those incomes be adjusted to take account of the needs of the household? There is a good argument for doing so. A household consisting of one adult will have a higher standard of living than a household of two adults and four children on the same income. So, if one makes no adjustment, people in big households will seem better off than they actually are. Income distribution data are therefore generally adjusted by some 'equivalence scale' that scales down the income of large households and scales up the income of small ones. The UK Office for National Statistics (ONS), for example, treats a childless couple as equal to 1.00 (the reference household), and divides a given income by 0.61 for a single person household (increasing the income) and by 1.46 (reducing it) if a couple have two children between 8 and 10 (Goodman *et al.*, 1997, p.39). Income data in this chapter are adjusted in this way, though the precise equivalence scales used vary. In this sub-section the data are for 'disposable' income: income after income taxes are deducted and after the receipt of benefits such as pensions.

Now picture all the people in an economy lined up by 'equivalent' household income, starting with those in the poorest households and ending with the richest (Mackintosh and Mooney, 2000, p.89). Imagine yourself putting in a marker one-tenth of the way along – to mark off the 10 per cent of poorest people – then another marking off the 20 per cent poorest, and so on, until your ninth marker leaves just the 10 per cent of richest people above it. Each of these markers is at a *decile* – one-tenth of a population ranked by income.

This gives us one of the most graphic and widely used measures of income distribution: the ratio of the income at the ninth decile (P_{90}) to the income at the first decile (P_{10}), often referred to as the **decile ratio**.

Decile ratio

The ratio of income at the ninth decile to income at the first decile of the income distribution (P_{90}/P_{10}).

The decile ratio is a good indicator of inequality because it measures the 'distance' across the income distribution between a high-income and a low-income person.

The same strategy of lining up people by order of equivalent household income gives us another couple of widely used income distribution measures: the Lorenz curve and the Gini coefficient. See the case study below on disposable income.

Case study: Inequality measurement and the Lorenz curve

Column 1 of Table 9.1 ranks the population by deciles (tenths) from the poorest to the richest. Column 2 gives the percentage of total UK disposable income that goes to each tenth; the share gets larger of course as incomes rise. Columns 3 and 4 are the *cumulative* percentages of population and income. To construct cumulative income percentages, start with the percentage of income received by the poorest 10 per cent, that is, 2.9 per cent (column 2). Then add the proportion received by the next poorest 10 per cent (4.7 per cent in column 2) to give the share of the poorest 20 per cent (7.6 per cent in column 4).

Question

Check your understanding of Table 9.1 before moving on, especially the relation between columns 2 and 4.

Case study continued

Table 9.1
Data for Lorenz
curve, UK
disposable
income,
1999/2000

(1) Deciles of population	(2) Share of disposable income %	(3) Cumulative percentage of population %	(4) Cumulative percentage of disposable income %
Lowest	2.9	10	2.9
2	4.7	20	7.6
3	5.4	30	13
4	7	40	20
5	7	50	27
6	9	60	36
7	10	70	46
8	12	80	58
9	15	90	73
Highest	27	100	100

Source: Department of Social Security, 2001, p.101, based on UK Family Resources Survey

Now look carefully at Figure 9.6. This shows a Lorenz curve constructed from the data in Table 9.1.

Along the vertical axis in Figure 9.6 we measure the cumulative percentage of total disposable income, and along the horizontal axis the cumulative percentage of the population, having ranked people according to their equivalized household income. The Lorenz curve plots the relationship between these two variables.

Figure 9.6
A Lorenz
curve for UK
disposable
income,
1999/2000

Source:
Department of
Social Security,
2001, p.101,
based on UK
Family
Resources
Survey

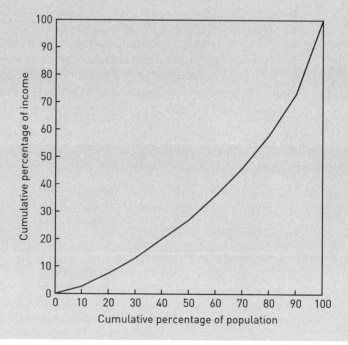

Question

Suppose that incomes were equally distributed, so each tenth of the population received a tenth of the income. What would be the shape of the Lorenz curve?

It would be a diagonal straight line. If that is not clear to you, write 10 in each row of column 2 of Table 9.1: each decile has 10 per cent of the income. Now calculate column 4 from your new column 2 and plot the curve on a figure like Figure 9.6.

Figure 9.7 adds this line of perfectly equal incomes to Figure 9.6.

Associated with the Lorenz curve is a measure of inequality known as the Gini coefficient (G). Look at Figure 9.7 again. The Gini coefficient is the ratio of the area between the diagonal and the Lorenz curve (the area marked A) to the area of the triangle beneath the diagonal (the area A + B). G varies between 0 in the case of perfect equality and 1 when all the income accrues to a single individual. The more the Lorenz curve is bowed away from the diagonal the more unequal is the distribution of income and the larger will be the value of G.

Figure 9.7
Lorenz curve and diagonal line for equal incomes

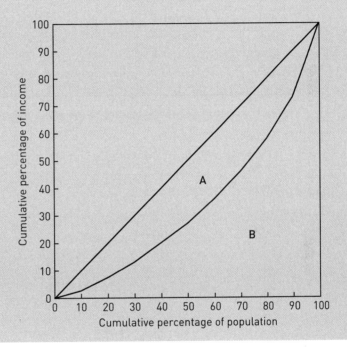

If you have understood the case study above, you should now be able to compare income distributions and to answer questions such as, to what extent are incomes in some countries more equal than in others? Here are some data for Gini coefficients and decile ratios for a number of higher income countries (Table 9.2). Figure 9.8 plots the two measures against each other, labelling the points by country. The figure shows that each measure gives similar answers to the question, which countries are the most unequal? On both measures, Mexico, Russia and the USA are the most unequal countries, having the highest Gini coefficients and decile ratios. However, the decile ratio picks up differences at the *ends* of the distribution; for example, if the rich are very rich relative to the rest this will be a large number. The Gini is a measure that particularly picks up differences in the middle income ranges. France and Canada, for example, have similar levels of inequality as measured by the Gini coefficient, but Canada has a larger decile ratio. Our choice of measure matters.

Table 9.2
Gini coefficients and decile ratios for a number of high-income and upper-middle income countries, mid 1990s

Year	Country	Gini coefficient	Decile ratio P_{90}/P_{10}
1994	Australia	0.311	4.33
1997	Canada	0.291	4.01
1996	Czech Republic	0.259	3.01
1994	France	0.288	3.54
1994	Germany	0.261	3.18
1995	Italy	0.342	4.77
1998	Mexico	0.494	11.55
1994	Netherlands	0.235	3.15
1995	Poland	0.318	4.04
1995	Russia	0.447	9.39
1995	Sweden	0.221	2.61
1995	Taiwan	0.277	3.38
1995	UK	0.344	4.57
1997	USA	0.372	5.57

Source: Luxembourg Income Study, http:\\lisweb.ceps.lu, 2 October 2001

Figure 9.8
Gini coefficients compared with decile ratios, by country, mid 1990s

Source: Luxembourg Income Study, http:\\lisweb.ceps.lu, 2 October 2001

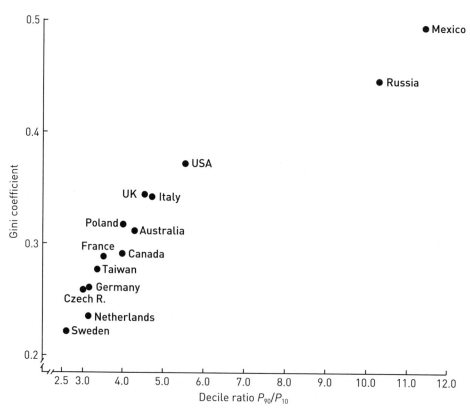

■ ■ ■ 9.4.3   Evaluating redistribution

All welfare states have emerged from a patchwork of earlier services, governmental and voluntary, and their institutional framework is very diverse. Let us judge them – in the language of our times – by their outcomes. Do they reduce inequality? Do they benefit the poorest people in high-income countries?

To answer these questions, we need to analyse the income distribution before and after government action on taxes, benefits and public service provision.

Question	Think about that last statement. Can you see a snag? Look back at Section 9.4.1 for a prompt.

Figure 9.5 showed that government spending, including both service provision and transfers, measured between 32 per cent (Japan) and 55 per cent (France) of GDP in the mid 1990s. This implies that economies cannot really be observed 'before' government activity. Individuals and markets would behave quite differently if the government and its economic activity suddenly disappeared or shrank dramatically. Indeed, some transition economies such as Russia suffered badly from this effect (Section 9.1). So we cannot strictly measure the income distribution 'before government'. Instead, economists measure the incomes of households from *market* activity (including wages paid by the government) and compare them to incomes including the effects of taxes, benefits and public services. Figure 9.9 shows how the UK Office for National Statistics explains the relation between various measures of income.

'Original', or market income, comes from wages and salaries, rent, interest payments on savings, private pensions and self-employment. The distribution of original income constitutes the **primary income distribution** that arises from the operation of the labour market and the market in financial assets and land. Private pensions, and other insurance payments, count as part of original income. As just suggested, we need to interpret the idea of 'original' income carefully: it does not represent the market outcomes we would experience were there no government.

Primary (market, original) income distribution

The primary (or market or original) income distribution is the distribution of incomes produced by factor markets and asset ownership before taxes and transfers.

The government, as part of its expenditure, pays out cash benefits such as state-provided pensions and assistance for those unable to earn an income, and deducts 'direct' taxes: taxes on income of people and firms. The result is 'disposable' income: the income data used in Section 9.4.2. We spend some of our incomes and the government levies 'indirect' taxes, such as value added tax (VAT), on those purchases: income after indirect taxes is 'post-tax' income. The government also supplies services free of charge, such as health care and education, and these 'benefits in kind' can be added to our incomes to give our 'final' income after all taxes and benefits. The distribution of final income constitutes a **secondary income distribution** which can be compared with the primary one.

Secondary (final) income distribution

The secondary (or final) income distribution is the distribution of income after taxes and benefits, including benefits in kind.

The *primary* income distribution in rich countries is very unequal, and would leave a great many people in poverty. Some people are unable to do paid work through age or disability, or because they are caring for children and do not find available options for childcare satisfactory. Some people who wish to get a job cannot find work. Figure 9.10 shows the effect of taxes and cash benefits on the UK income distribution. The data used for this are for fifths (quintiles) of the income distribution, and this time the horizontal axis shows cumulative percentages of *households* ranked by equivalized household income.

Figure 9.9
Redistribution by
government in the
UK: the relation
between different
measures of
income.

Source: based on
Lakin, 2001, p.37

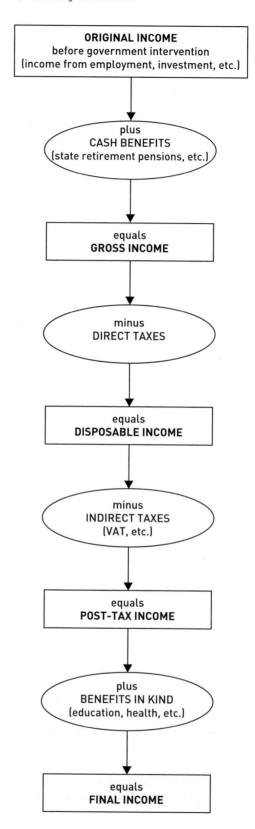

Figure 9.10
Lorenz curves for original and post-tax income for the UK, 1999/2000

Source: data in Lakin, 2001, p.66

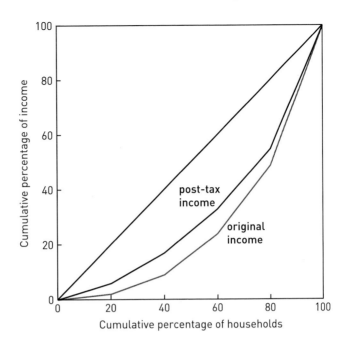

| Question | Describe the effects of taxes and benefits shown in Figure 9.10. |

The Lorenz curve for post-tax income is closer to the diagonal than that for original income. So taxes and benefits reduce inequality between households.

Adding in benefits in kind to measure final income would have further reduced measured inequality, since government-provided health care and education are distributed more equally than cash incomes. The UK ONS calculates that benefits in kind more than double the post-tax income of the lowest decile, but add only 21 per cent to the post-tax income of the top decile (Lakin, 2001, p.53).

Welfare states in high-income countries generally reduce inequality. But what of our second question above: does the redistribution lift the poor out of poverty? Figure 9.10 raises some doubts: the poorest 20 per cent of households remain a very long way short of 20 per cent of income. To look more closely, we need to identify those in poverty. To do this, we need first to define a **poverty line**, that is, a level of income below which people are living in poverty.

Poverty line

A measured level of income below which people are defined as living in poverty.

There are two ways to define a poverty line. One is to calculate the income required to obtain a 'basket' of goods and services deemed essential. This method defines an 'absolute' poverty line that will only change as prices change. The second method is to define as 'poor' people living below some fraction of average or median incomes. (The 'median' income is the income at the fifth decile: the income of the person or household halfway along the distribution.) This method gives us a 'relative' poverty line, that is, a poverty line defined relative to incomes in the country that will rise as real incomes rise.

| Question | Suppose that you take a capabilities approach to well-being. Which poverty line might you prefer? |

Table 9.3
Welfare state
redistribution and
poverty relief, mid
1990s

(1) Country	(2) Poverty rate before taxes and transfers %	(3) Poverty rate after taxes and transfers %	(4) Poverty rate relative reduction %
Australia, 1994	20.2	10.4	−49
France, 1994	22.3	8.5	−62
Germany, 1994	14.7	7.9	−46
Netherlands, 1994	19.5	9.1	−54
UK, 1995	26.2	9.8	−63
USA, 1994	21.6	18.2	−16

Source: Behrendt, 2000, p.6

Both may be relevant. You will want to ensure that the poverty line income allows access to the goods and services necessary to achieve essential capabilities. This suggests an absolute measure. But you may also recognize that essential capabilities such as participating in social relationships require different types of goods and services in different societies, so a relative measure may be useful too.

I will use a relative poverty line here. A very common one is to define as 'poor' people in households living on less than half of median income. If median incomes differ between countries, so will income at the poverty line.

Once we have defined a poverty line such as this we can calculate the proportion of the population living below it. This calculation gives the **poverty rate** for a particular country. On this basis, Table 9.3 compares the poverty-reduction effect of the welfare state in several high-income countries. In Table 9.3 the 'poverty rate' in columns 2 and 3 is the percentage of households headed by someone of 'prime age' (55 years and below) living at or below the poverty line just defined: it examines poverty relief for non-pensioner households only.

Poverty rate

The proportion of the population that is below a given poverty line.

Question | Explain what the table shows before reading on.

Table 9.3 columns 2 and 3 shows poverty rates, that is, the percentage of non-pensioner households with incomes below half of (equivalized) median disposable income in each country. The percentages are measured before taxes and transfers (i.e. original income) (column 2) and after transfers and direct taxes (i.e. disposable income) (column 3). Germany has the lowest poverty rate on the basis of original income; after taxes and transfers it is still the lowest, though the redistribution, measured as the percentage reduction in the poverty rate, is smaller than four other countries. At the other end of the scale, the table confirms that the US government redistributes very little to the poor, relative to the other countries, so ends up with by far the highest poverty rate after taxes and transfers.

One consequence of this brings us back to capabilities. Suppose that we are particularly concerned not with equality of income but of opportunity. We might then be particularly anxious that children get a fair start in life. Margaret Thatcher talked of all children growing tall. Research repeatedly shows that growing up in poverty has a negative effect on children's life chances.

Smeeding and Rainwater – two economists who specialize in income distribution issues – compared, across high-income countries, the real incomes of households with children.

Their comparison used a measure of income called 'purchasing power parity' that adjusts money incomes for differences in what money will buy in each country (e.g. housing is much cheaper in one country than another). They showed (Smeeding and Rainwater, 2001) that despite the much higher median incomes in the USA than in the other countries studied, the incomes of households with children at the lowest decile (P_{10}) in each country were *lower* in the USA than in all the other countries except the UK and Australia. Furthermore, poor children in the USA also had less access to benefits in kind than most of their peers in other high-income countries. The authors argue that:

> societies with wide income disparities across families with children have less support for public and social goods such as tax-financed health care, child care and education, because high income families can privately purchase above average levels of those goods with their higher incomes, rather than supporting high overall levels of tax-financed goods and sharing them with less well off children.
>
> *(Smeeding and Rainwater, 2001, p.24)*

We come back to this kind of political argument in Section 9.6.

9.5 The welfare state and economic efficiency

The welfare state does not only affect inequality; it also has a profound impact on the efficiency of the economy. In the 1980s and 1990s economists generally argued that the effects were negative. Policy makers saw themselves as faced with a 'trade-off': more equality meant less efficiency and policy had to choose. Now, as part of the search for 'smarter' government, economists are focusing on a search for synergy: for ways in which more equality and more efficiency might go hand in hand.

There are a number of reasons for this shift. One is the experience in Europe of the social, political and economic consequences of persistent unemployment from the mid 1970s onwards. Another is the rising perception of increased instability of employment in industries where jobs were previously expected to be long term (Chapter 1, Section 1.3.2). Economists are aware that many of the economic risks faced by individuals result from the operation of markets which – while 'imperfect' when compared with the perfect competition benchmark – have dynamic efficiency benefits such as innovation and growth. In these circumstances it is now widely argued that, if properly designed, the welfare state can help people to cope with the market risks effectively, and thereby increase the dynamic efficiency of the economy. This section aims to give you a flavour of these arguments and their critics, using the example of benefits for the unemployed.

9.5.1 Risk, market failure and social insurance

In market economies, we try to deal individually with risk by taking out insurance. We insure ourselves against burglary and car accidents. Many people in the UK pay into private pension schemes, seeking to insure themselves against destitution after retirement. 'Life' insurance is actually insurance against the consequences of our death for those who depend on us. In many countries – but few high-income countries – individual private health insurance is the only protection against the costs of treatment in illness.

The market for private insurance is, however, subject to market failure.

Question

Suppose you are employed. Can you ring up an insurance company – say the one that insures your car – and buy insurance against losing your job? If not, why not?

In the UK at present you can do this to a limited extent. For example, if you have a mortgage on your house, you may be able to insure against being unable to pay the interest, perhaps for a year. And if you are in good health, you may be able to insure part of your income against losing your job because of severe illness. But apart from that you are on your own.

However, we do not want to find ourselves destitute if we lose our job. So why is the market not providing unemployment insurance? What is the source of this market failure?

Question

Think about this. Suppose you have a job you dislike. How might unemployment insurance affect your behaviour?

Well, there are probably all kinds of ways of getting yourself sacked without the insurance company finding out that you have engineered it. The insurance company does not know the details of your individual situation; you have more information than the company. You can influence your own risk of unemployment, and the company cannot detect that – or not without major expense. The insurance policy furthermore has given you an incentive to change your behaviour – to engineer a paid break from work – to the detriment of the company's profits. This effect of insurance is called 'moral hazard'. It is a quite widespread problem in insurance markets, but particularly affects those markets where it is hard for companies to collect information about the insured.

Exercise 9.6

Think of some more examples of insurance markets affected by moral hazard.

In addition to moral hazard, companies providing private unemployment insurance also find it hard to assess the extent of individual risk because of poor information. So they cannot price their policies efficiently, by charging more for a higher risk. Worse still, companies are uncertain about the likely scale of unemployment in the future: if there is a sharp general rise in unemployment, insurance companies may fail. For all these reasons, private unemployment insurance is not generally available. Market failures have created a missing market: there is no supply of a service people would like to buy. There is thus a market efficiency problem: markets are not responding effectively to consumer needs.

So what can be done? What people want to ensure is income when unemployed. Provision of unemployment insurance in this sense has effectively been taken over by government in most high-income countries. There are two ways this can be done; they are complementary, and the mix varies between countries. Welfare state institutions are highly diverse, having grown in each country from a patchwork of local voluntary, mutual, government and private provision, but the economic *functions* those institutions fulfil are similar across countries.

Unemployment insurance can be provided through *social insurance*: compulsory contributions by all in work to a fund, to which employers also contribute and which governments may subsidize, that provides limited term benefits to those who involuntarily lose their jobs. 'Socializing' unemployment insurance in this way makes it viable, because the government has much more effective powers of investigation than a private company of reasons for leaving jobs. Furthermore, since the insurance is compulsory, it brings together those at high and low risk of unemployment, reducing the overall cost of insurance protection for those at high risk.

Social insurance of this kind is backed up, in most high-income countries, by *social assistance*: these are cash benefits which are paid on the basis of need, not on the basis of prior contributions. Social assistance is always surrounded by conditions such as evidence of actively seeking work for those able to do so, evidence of disability for those unable to, and evidence of a lack of other means to justify benefit payments. These often onerous conditions aim to reduce the effect of moral hazard on the costs of social assistance. Typically, the amount paid out in social assistance rises when long-term unemployment rises. The mix of social assistance and social insurance varies between countries, and the payments were all included in the category of cash benefits in Section 9.4. Together they respond to the missing market for unemployment insurance.

■ ■ ■ 9.5.2 Social insurance and economy-wide efficiency

Compensating for market failure in the sense of missing insurance markets is a positive efficiency effect of social insurance against unemployment. However, it has been widely argued that there are also economy-wide negative efficiency effects. The debate centres on the impact of the cash benefits on the labour market.

A central issue is the *amount* people should be paid when not in work, from a mix of social insurance and social assistance, relative to their earnings in work. This relationship is called the **replacement rate**.

Replacement rate

The ratio of income when unemployed to income (after taxes and transfers) when employed.

If replacement rates are high, people have incomes when out of work not much lower than when in work; if low, people experience a very large drop in income when they lose their jobs. 'The' replacement rate is not easy to measure. Rates differ for people with different levels of earning power, as well as varying with the structure and rules for benefits for different household members when out of work. Hence a replacement rate for a country will be an average of a number of different rates faced by people in different family and work circumstances.

Figure 9.11 shows one systematic estimate of how replacement rates changed over 40 years for a number of high-income countries. They vary enormously by country, the USA and Japan having persistently low rates. Most countries had stable or rising rates in the 1960s and 1970s. The 1980s saw rising unemployment throughout Europe, and this was accompanied by rising or stable replacement rates in most countries. The exceptions were the UK and, outside Europe, the USA.

By the 1990s, policy towards replacement rates had become contentious.

Question	Which of the two following arguments do you find most compelling and why?

1 High replacement rates increase unemployment, and reduce output, because they encourage people to remain unemployed.
2 High replacement rates improve labour market efficiency, and increase output, because they encourage people to take risks and to retrain.

This is a highly political debate and hard to resolve by the use of evidence. The fundamental problem is that the two arguments are rooted in different models of the labour market, including workers' behaviour.

Figure 9.11
Replacement rates,
1961–91, selected
OECD countries

Source: data from
OECD, 1994, p.226

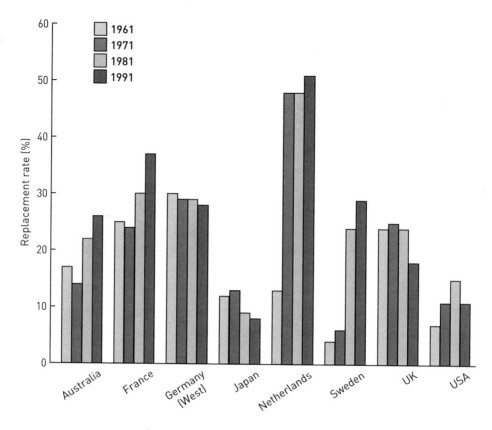

Argument 1, still the standard textbook argument, can be explained using a model of a perfectly competitive labour market (Figure 9.12). Suppose that there is a given level of benefit received by those not working, supported by a tax on employers for each worker they employ, as well as by workers' tax payments. Those benefits and the taxes that support them now fall relative to the going wage W_1. Two effects might occur in this model. Employers, paying a lower tax per worker, experience a lower total cost per worker, and labour demand shifts rightwards from L_{D1} to L_{D2}. Workers, receiving lower benefits, find that wages from employment are now higher relative to income if they stay at home. So more workers are willing to accept work at a given wage, so the labour supply shifts rightwards from L_{S1} to L_{S2}. Either effect will increase employment above L_1. The effect of the two shifts on the equilibrium wage may be to raise or lower it.

It is also argued that workers work harder if replacement rates are low because they fear the sack (Chapter 7, Section 7.5.1 similarly discussed the 'worker discipline' effect of increasing the gap between what workers could earn in, say, Ford and income they could earn elsewhere). These have been influential arguments. The OECD argued in 1994 that 'if unemployment is to be kept low, it is vital to limit entitlement to benefits' (OECD, 1994, p.213). In 1998 they complained of lack of 'progress' on this recommendation (OECD, 1998, p.15). During the 1990s, however, Germany, the Netherlands, France and the UK all reduced entitlements to benefits and/or restricted their duration.

Question   Can you think of criticisms of these arguments for lower replacement rates?

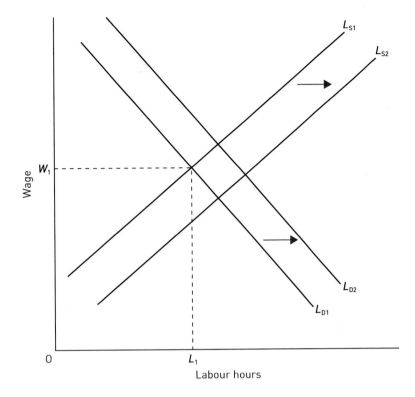

Figure 9.12
The effect of a
reduction in benefits
in a perfectly
competitive labour
market

The model in Figure 9.12 assumes a unified labour market. However, in most countries the labour market is segmented. Workers in unionized 'primary sector' jobs have rights to unemployment benefit, while 'secondary sector' workers have few unemployment benefit rights. (Chapter 7, Section 7.4.2 examined labour market segmentation into primary and secondary sectors.) Social assistance benefits are generally lower than social insurance benefits, and require stringent evidence of seeking work. A reduction in replacement rates may be brought about (as in the UK) by heavily restricting unemployment benefits, forcing more people onto social assistance.

To see why this segmentation may provide support for Argument 2, consider a person's choice between taking a low-paid 'secondary' job, or waiting for a chance to get a primary sector job. If the conditions on benefit as well as its level are generous, a feasible choice might be to wait and retrain, increasing the chances of moving to a primary job.

> For the person laid off from Joe's Café it may be the best thing that happened to him if he is subsequently taken on by a firm of catering consultants.
>
> (Atkinson, 1999, p.99)

Chapter 7, Section 7.2.4 explained the concept of human capital and analysed training as an investment decision by people and firms. If a higher replacement rate encourages retraining and thereby raises the skill levels in the economy, and particularly if that in turn attracts investment from firms looking for skilled workers, the high replacement rate will benefit, not damage, the economy.

Finally, if primary sector employers require workers not just to do what they are told, but to use their energy and imagination in their work, the security offered by high replacement rates might encourage such productive behaviour. These are arguments about dynamic efficiency benefits, which assume imperfect and segmented markets for labour. Governments used these models in the late 1990s to try to redesign benefit systems to be more 'employment friendly', helping people to cope with the changing labour market while pushing them towards paid work: trying to combine poverty relief and unemployment reduction rather than being forced (as Argument 1 proposes) to choose between them. The Netherlands has been cited as a success story along these lines, having reduced its unemployment rate sharply while maintaining generous benefit levels (Purdy, 2001).

9.6 Why do governments do what they do?

> Freedom from Want cannot be forced on a democracy or given to a democracy, it must be won by them.
>
> *(Sir William Beveridge, 1942, quoted in Timmins, 1995)*

Sections 9.4 and 9.5 argued that government activity deeply affects the operation of market economies, and discussed what governments could and should do. Now we take the step of treating government decision-making as 'endogenous' to economic modelling, by asking to what extent economic analysis might be able to *explain* what governments do. This requires us to treat politicians, civil servants and those who work in government service as individuals responding to economic incentives, just as people do in markets, and just as people in communities do in the analysis of collective action (Section 9.3); for politicians, the incentives are created in large part by the preferences of the voters who elect them. This approach to understanding government is known (confusingly) as 'public choice' economics, since voters are treated as making choices much as consumers do in a market. To give you a flavour of public choice analysis, we look at just one question: why might a democratic government redistribute income to the less well off?

■■■ 9.6.1 'Public choice' economics and redistribution

Question   Measured on the basis of disposable income the poor form a minority of the population in high-income countries. So why, in a democracy where everyone has a vote, should redistribution to the poor occur at all? Why should comfortable citizens vote to give away some of their primary income to the worst off?

We will consider answers to this question in two stages using a simplified model of how redistribution occurs. First, in a majority voting system, whose preferences expressed through voting actually 'count'? And second, what might influence those preferences?

Let us assume, initially, that in an election voters can be roughly lined up in terms of the amount of public goods and other public services they would like to see provided by government in kind and equally to all: from very few to a generous provision. And let us suppose that the distribution of voter preferences looks as in Figure 9.13: there are rather few extremists here. Most voters are moderate in their preferences, with the modal preference – the level commanding the greatest support – at the median, that is, halfway along the distribution.

Two candidates wish to be voted into office. Suppose their initial platforms are PG_S and PG_L. Now both politicians will spot an opportunity. Consider the politician proposing PG_L. Point A shows the number of voters who agree with him (measured on

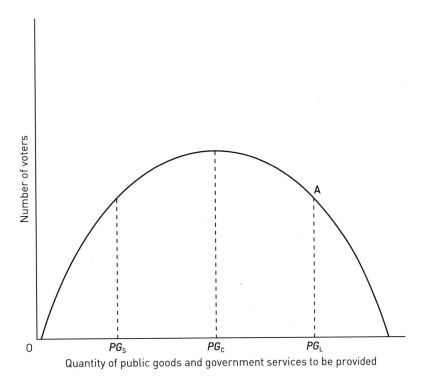

Figure 9.13
Voters' preferences
and politicians'
proposals

Number of voters

0   PG_S PG_C PG_L

A

Quantity of public goods and government services to be provided

the vertical axis). If that politician moves towards the centre, offering rather fewer goods and services but still more than his opponent, he will gain more definite votes while not losing those voters who want a lot of provision: for them, he will still be the better of the two. The politician proposing PG_S, if smart, will spot the same idea and also move towards the centre. The politician who can dominate the centre – who can gain the vote of the median voter at PG_C – will take the election.

This conclusion is called the 'median voter theorem': the argument that the median voter swings an election. So, accepting this theorem for a moment, what determines the median voter's preferences? Suppose that those on lower incomes prefer more public goods and government services and those who are better off prefer fewer. This could be explained by self-interest: the well-off pay more in total in tax and feel less need for government provision, since for health and education they can supplement government services with private supply. Those on low incomes gain more from government provision relative to their market incomes (Section 9.4).

The preferences of the median voter may then depend on the shape of the income distribution. Figure 9.14 shows the UK income distribution (disposable income) for 2000 (*Social Trends*, 2001). It shows that the median individual has an equivalized household income well below average (mean) income even after cash benefits and direct taxes. One would therefore expect a majority for some redistributive policies.

However, self-interested voters may not see the choices quite like that. Consider a rather different story. Suppose that everyone pays taxes (as we do – even the poor pay indirect taxes) and those taxes are spent on, say, the education system. Now suppose that there are three distinct sets of preferences about this. The poor prefer to avoid the tax; their priority is income over education. The middle-income voters prefer more tax and more education provision. The high-income voters prefer to buy their education privately and pay less tax. Here the median voter may not rule; instead, the two extremes may out-vote the middle.

Figure 9.14

The UK income distribution of disposable income 2000

Note: there are also 2.6 million individuals with equivalized household incomes above £700 a week. They are not included because their inclusion would extend the distribution too far to the right to be displayed on the page.

Source: Department of Social Security, 2001, Figure 2.1, p.8

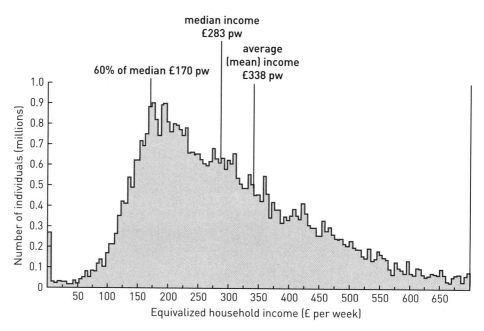

Something rather like this seems to have happened in Bristol, in the west of England, in February 2001. The local council held a referendum on council tax and education spending, and recommended more education and more tax. A majority of voters, on a 40 per cent turnout, rejected this, preferring a tax freeze and lower real education spending (*The Times Educational Supplement*, 23 February 2001). There is some evidence that the lowest- and highest-income voters tended to vote for the freeze option; one reason might be that (influencing the better off) about 20 per cent of Bristol's children were in private education in 2001, while (influencing the poorer voters) council taxes were already high by national standards.

▨ ▨ ▪ 9.6.2 Political processes and endogenous preferences

The Bristol example suggests some general problems with 'public choice' analysis. First, voters are rarely given this kind of simplified choice over policies. Instead, in most democracies, voting seems to be as much a public expression of opinion, of allegiance to a party or even an individual, and of participation in governance processes as a citizen, as it is a process of choosing specific policies.

Furthermore, there is likely to be a strong influence of experience on preferences. People may have strong preferences about institutions as well as the precise distribution of benefits. For example, they may have a preference for free access to health care on the basis of need, and may be influenced in this preference by experience of systems that proclaim that objective. There is evidence for this in comparisons of voters' preferences in the USA and western European countries. The former appear to have a stronger tolerance of inequality in health care access than European voters who are used to both the costs and the consequences of European welfare states.

Experience is also influential in another sense. People are influenced by the existence of a welfare state. If they come to rely on it, it affects their work and spending choices. Changing the system therefore has large costs. Consider, for example, a well-off Swedish voter who has no private pension provision. He or she is unlikely to vote for a smaller welfare state. Middle-income voters may rely heavily on the insurance functions of the welfare state. Such voters may indeed see redistribution itself as having an insurance aspect. People's position in the income distribution is not fixed. For example, of adults in deciles three and four of the UK income distribution in 1991, nearly a quarter had fallen into the two lowest deciles in 1997 (*Social Trends*, 2000). The existence of a redistributive welfare state insures people against destitution when things go wrong in their lives.

Finally, the better off may vote for redistributive policies for reasons other than self-interest. They may believe it to be unacceptable on ethical grounds that a country with high average incomes should tolerate severe poverty. They may fear civil unrest if a part of society is excluded from the benefits most enjoy (another version of redistribution as insurance). And, in these views, they may have been influenced by politicians themselves. People may see the political process as delegating to selected politicians the task of thinking about important issues such as the level of spending on health services and cash benefits, and of taking a public lead in arguing for what they think should be done. One Bristol resident put that point rather forcefully: 'I voted for them to lead, and not abdicate responsibility for the most challenging decision of the year, namely setting the budget.' (Letters, *The Guardian*, 17 February 2001.)

So politicians may – perhaps should – devote some time to trying to change the shape of the distribution of voters' opinions, such as those shown in Figure 9.13, as well as to changing the income distribution itself. Government seems indeed to be 'endogenous' to a wider governance process, where voters and politicians interact in a public sphere that also includes the media and the existing institutions of social provision.

9.7 Conclusion: governance with endogenous economists

A.B. Atkinson, a well-known British economist writing about inequality and welfare who also has experience of government advising, argues that:

> Calls by economists for rolling back the welfare state are themselves part of the political process; we have not just endogenous politicians but also endogenous economists, whose behaviour has to be explained.
>
> *(Atkinson, 1999, p.187)*

What Atkinson is saying here is that economic analysis does influence policy, to some extent. Furthermore, economists analyse how the political process influences policy decisions. Yet economists are much less aware that we too are influenced in our choice of model by the politics of the day – and of the consequences that may have. Atkinson's book, from which the quote is taken, is 'endogenous' in this sense: he is trying to contest the assumption that the economic literature as it stands all supports 'rolling back the welfare state', showing that plausible models can generate alternative conclusions.

Economics is thus a highly political subject. I think that is one of its pleasures. This chapter has introduced you to some of the economic analysis of government and more broadly of governance, both in the sense of collective action and in the sense of voter–politician relationships. In the language introduced in Chapter 8, Section 8.1, we have considered both 'positive' and 'normative' approaches to governance: what will or can be done, and what 'should' be done. A particular theme has been the interrelation between equity – in the sense of both greater equality of incomes and more equality of opportunities – and efficiency in both a static and a dynamic sense. The next chapter applies some of the analysis in Chapters 8 and 9 to the economics of another highly political issue: health care.

Questions for review and discussion

Question 1   Figure 9.15 shows an industry in which there is a negative externality in supply. Insert each label below to match the appropriate explanatory phrase:

Curve 1   Curve 2   Curve 3 Q_1 Q_2 AC   BE   BD

(a) .... The difference between the allocatively efficient price and the free market equilibrium price.

(b) .... The allocatively efficient quantity of output.

(c) .... The industry supply curve.

(d) .... The amount of tax per unit of output required to achieve allocative efficiency.

(e) .... The industry demand curve.

(f) .... The difference between marginal social cost and marginal private cost at the free market equilibrium output.

(g) .... The marginal social cost curve.

Figure 9.15
Industry with negative externality in supply

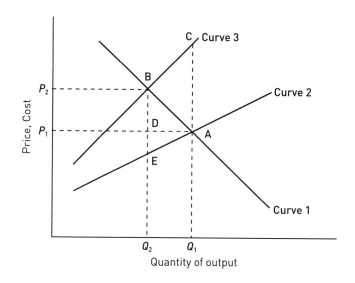

Question 2   Figure 9.16 shows two hypothetical Lorenz curves:

(a) Say which statement below is correct:

    A   Lorenz curve L_1 shows that the bottom 5 deciles receive a higher proportion of total income than L_2 shows.

    B   Lorenz curve L_2 shows that the bottom 5 deciles receive a lower proportion of total income than L_1 shows.

(b) Say which is the appropriate completion for the statement below:

    The Gini coefficient corresponding to Lorenz curve L_1

    A   is larger than that corresponding to Lorenz curve L_2.

    B   is the same as that corresponding to Lorenz curve L_2.

    C   is smaller than that corresponding to Lorenz curve L_2.

Figure 9.16
Lorenz curves

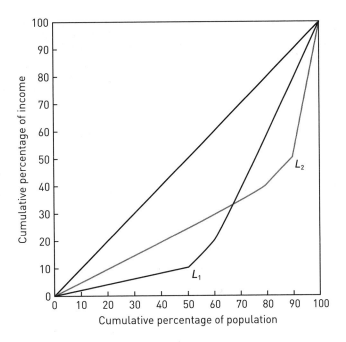

Cumulative percentage of income (y-axis)

Cumulative percentage of population (x-axis)

L_2

L_1

Question 3   Insert the correct word from the list to complete the following sentence:

Original   disposable   post-tax   final

Income from wages and salaries, rent, interest payments on savings, private pensions and self-employment *plus* cash benefits paid by the government *minus* direct taxes is known as . . . income.

Question 4   Figure 9.17 shows a perfectly competitive labour market. Suppose there is a rise in the level of benefit paid to those not working relative to the going wage. Suppose also that there is an increase in the taxes levied per employee, on employers that support these benefits. Draw a shift in the curve(s) as appropriate to show the likely impact on employment.

Figure 9.17
Perfectly
competitive
labour market

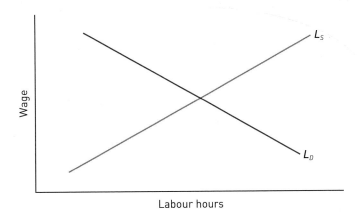

Wage (y-axis)

Labour hours (x-axis)

L_S

L_D

Question 5   Essay: In what ways, if any, can government policy both reduce income inequality and enhance economy-wide efficiency?

10

Health and health care: markets, ethics and inequality

Paul Anand and Martin Higginson

Concepts

- equity
- inequalities in health status and in access to health care
- social insurance
- private insurance
- adverse selection
- managed competition

Objectives

After studying this chapter you should be able to:

- appreciate the variety of health-care provision and finance in different countries
- apply microeconomic principles to the analysis of health care
- analyse market failure in health-care provision and finance
- understand the ethical issues raised by inequalities in health status and in access to health care.

10.1 Introduction

1 Don't be poor. If you are poor, try not to be poor for too long.
2 Don't live in a deprived area. If you do, move.
3 Don't be disabled or have a disabled child.
4 Don't work in a stressful low-paid manual job.
5 Don't live in damp, low quality housing or be homeless.
6 Be able to afford to pay for social activities and annual holidays.
7 Don't be a lone parent.
8 Claim all the benefits to which you are entitled.
9 Be able to afford to own a car.
10 Use education as an opportunity to improve your socio-economic position.

(Smith et al., *2001, p.xlviii)*

These tips were put forward ironically in an academic text as alternatives to ten tips for better health offered by the UK government's Chief Medical Officer, and they reflect the strong relationship between health and economic status. The poor tend to be ill more

Table 10.1
Income per head
and mortality rates,
by country group

Country group	Population (1999) millions	Income per head (annual average) US$	Life expectancy at birth (years)	Under five mortality (deaths per 1000 live births)
Least-developed countries	643	296	51	159
Other low-income countries	1 777	538	59	120
Lower middle-income countries	2 094	1 200	70	39
Upper middle-income countries	573	4 900	71	35
High-income countries	891	25 730	78	6

Source: adapted from Commission on Macroeconomics and Health, 2001, p.2

often and to be more severely ill than the rich. On average, those on lower incomes live shorter lives (and have a lower life expectancy at birth) and are in poorer health while alive, that is, they have higher levels of morbidity. As Dr Gro Harlem Brundtland, Director General of the World Health Organization (WHO), argued in 1999:

> First and foremost, there is a need to reduce greatly the burden of excess mortality and morbidity suffered by the poor.
>
> *(World Health Organization, 1999)*

Table 10.1 shows just how dramatic is the association between poverty and mortality across the world.

The association between poverty, mortality and ill health also holds strongly *within* countries. Health policy observers look at how health varies according to occupational group, employment status, gender, area of residence and socio-economic category. Regardless of how social position is measured, those at the bottom of the social scale in the UK have higher death rates at every stage in life, from birth until well into old age. And the poor, and their children, typically experience higher morbidity rates: 'all the major killer diseases affect the poor more than the rich' (Whitehead, 1992). There is some evidence that those in poor health move down the social scale, as one might expect, but this explains only a small part of the disparity that exists. Lifestyle and material living conditions have a substantial influence on health status. Furthermore, as income inequalities have widened, so have health inequalities.

Rags or riches on the life line

The London health observatory says that a baby boy born in the east end borough of Newham, one of the capital's poorest areas, is now likely to die at 71, almost six years earlier than a boy born in the central borough of Westminster, one of the richest.

For baby boys born in the early 1990s, the life expectancy gap between the poorest and richest boroughs was only five years.

(Carvel, 2001)

Differences in infant mortality – that is, the proportion of children who die within a year of birth – are also increasing according to the report:

> Although the London average is similar to that for England and Wales as a whole, the capital has relatively high [infant mortality] figures in its inner areas.
>
> A boy born in Hackney, next to Newham, is more than twice as likely to die in the first year of life as a boy born in Bexley, in the south-east suburbs.
>
> The London observatory is one of eight regional organisations set up last year to monitor health inequalities. Although it is the first to report, it predicts that other regions will shortly announce a similar widening of the health gap between rich and poor in their areas.
>
> *(Carvel, 2001)*

Economists have looked closely at the association between income and health, and have concluded that poverty brings with it a whole raft of influences that cause poor health. But conversely, if good health care reaches the poor, it helps to relieve poverty.

There is considerable evidence that people are more concerned about inequalities in health than they are about inequalities in income. Equality of opportunity in the workplace is widely accepted, so it is reasonable to expect a similarly widespread belief that everyone should have an approximately equal chance of a long and healthy life. In view of the observed inequalities in health status, this belief is likely to be expressed in general support for a health-care system that is redistributive, enabling individuals on low incomes to obtain more health care than they could afford to buy in a competitive health-care market. In many rich countries there is something close to equitable access to health care, in the sense of equal access for equal need. Section 10.3 discusses some of the issues concerning health care and equity and examines how economists think about these issues. In looking at the ways in which health care is redistributive (Section 10.3.1), we shall be building on some of the concepts and techniques that were introduced in Chapter 9.

A commitment to redistribution through health-care provision implies a significant degree of economic activity by the government. In the UK this commitment has taken the form of the direct provision of health care by the public sector through the National Health Service (NHS). It is often said that public sector bodies and monopolies tend to be wasteful and inefficient because they are free from the competitive pressures that might otherwise force them to reduce costs. Section 10.4 examines an attempted reform of the NHS, which was prompted in part by worries of this sort.

Before we investigate these issues, it is important to appreciate the distinctive economic characteristics of health care. In Chapter 7 it was argued that, while the model of perfect competition can throw some light on labour market issues, the insights it provides are limited by the extent to which the assumptions of perfect competition fail to capture the particular characteristics of labour markets. This chapter follows a somewhat similar strategy: it introduces the distinctive features of health care by comparing markets in health care with the assumptions of the model of perfect competition (Section 10.2). However, while Chapter 7 saw the model of perfect competition as a partial explanation of labour market phenomena (e.g. wage differentials), this chapter invokes perfect competition in a different way. Given certain assumptions, the model of perfect competition may be used as a benchmark for allocating resources among people in a way that maximizes their welfare (Chapters 5 and 8). But the particular characteristics of markets in health care are significantly different from the assumptions about markets made in the model of perfect competition. This line of thought casts doubt on the suitability of a market relatively free from government intervention for the delivery and finance of health care.

It seems appropriate for the last chapter in this book to review some of the contents of the previous chapters. This chapter applies some concepts and techniques concerning equity and redistribution that were introduced in Chapters 8 and 9. It also focuses on the ways in which the analysis of monopoly and perfect competition in Chapters 4, 5 and 8 can illuminate health-care issues. In this way this final chapter of the book looks back over aspects of the economic analysis in earlier chapters and applies them to the topic of health care.

10.2 Market failure in health-care finance and delivery

Why is health care different from many other aspects of economic activity? Why is it not an appealing prospect to pay for health care in the way that we pay for, say, biscuits? Why do most people feel that it would be wrong to leave the delivery (or production or provision) of health care to Sainsbury's and its rival supermarkets? This section will address these questions.

The first step is to notice that, in the finance and delivery of health care, the diversity across countries suggests that there is no 'right answer'. This considerable diversity in the methods of health-care finance and provision is reported in Section 10.2.1. Section 10.2.2 examines the features of health-care delivery in hospitals, clinics and doctors' surgeries that distinguish it from the delivery of many other goods and services. Section 10.2.3 investigates the special problems surrounding the finance of health care. Why, even if it is agreed that some form of insurance is essential, does it seem unwise to leave people to insure their health on the commercial insurance market in the same way that they insure their houses or their cars?

▒ ▨ ▪ 10.2.1 The diversity of health-care finance and delivery

In rich countries, people gain access to health care mainly through insurance or taxation. The need for health care is very hard to predict: in any year an individual may or may not fall ill; in a lifetime, some people need more care and treatment than others. Insurance, in principle, allows individuals to pay a predetermined amount and receive treatment if they need it. Paying taxes that support a public health-care system, such as those in the UK and Sweden, has the same effect: you pay a sum of money and receive treatment determined by clinical need, not by the amount you pay. Neither taxes nor insurance guarantees that you will receive all you need in practice. They do, however, allow people to receive expensive treatment – such as major surgery – that they could not afford if they had to pay for it at the time from their incomes.

Question	What is meant by 'social insurance'? Look back at Chapter 9, Section 9.5.1 to check your understanding.

Social insurance is insurance that is compulsory for all who can pay. The term generally refers to a system whereby employers as well as employees pay on a compulsory basis into insurance funds, and these funds provide access to a range of benefits, including health care.

Even in high-income countries, quite a lot of direct 'out of pocket' payments remain: for example, prescription charges in the UK, and 'co-payments' whereby a share of the

Table 10.2
Health-care
financing mix
in high-income
countries (as a
percentage of
total health-care
spending)

Country and year	Taxes %	Social insurance %	Private insurance %	Direct payments %
Denmark, 1987	84.7	0.0	1.5	13.8
France, 1989	0.0	73.6	6.3	20.1
Germany, 1989	17.7	65.0	7.1	10.2
Ireland, 1987	67.8	7.3	10.0	14.9
Netherlands, 1992	11.3	64.6	16.3	7.7
Spain, 1990	56.3	22.0	2.4	19.3
Sweden, 1990	71.9	17.8	0.0	10.3
Switzerland, 1992	28.7	6.9	40.5	23.9
UK, 1993	64.0	20.0	7.0	9.0
USA, 1987	35.5	13.3	29.2	22.1

Note: The totals for some countries may not sum to 100 due to rounding.
Source: Wagstaff *et al.*, 1999, Table 2, p.268

cost of treatment is paid by the patient in many social insurance systems. In many low-income countries, however, over half of the costs of health care are paid for 'out of pocket', by paying the fee demanded for each episode of treatment. This dependence on individual payment restricts access to health care in low- and middle-income countries.

Table 10.2 shows how health care is financed in some high-income countries. The table divides financing into four categories: taxation, social insurance, private insurance and direct 'out of pocket' payments. As you can see, the mix varies greatly. Only in the USA and Switzerland does more than half of health-care finance come from private insurance or direct payments. In Scandinavia, Ireland, Spain and the UK, taxes are the main source of finance. And in Germany, France and the Netherlands, social insurance provides most of the health care. The 'social insurance' element for the UK refers to National Insurance payments, some of which go to fund the NHS. Where efforts have been made to achieve universal access to health care, as in most of the countries in Table 10.2, cover for those who cannot pay is subsidized by the state. (The dates of the data sets reflect the time taken to compile comparable data sets from a wide range of sources.)

Tax-based financing of health care does not necessarily imply public sector provision. In the UK, the NHS was designed, at its inception in 1948, to use mainly tax-based finance to fund public sector provision. Internationally, however, countries vary considerably in their mix of providers, a mix determined by the history of the health services in each country, as well as by competition and political in-fighting. Tax funds can be and are used to buy health care from 'voluntary' (or non-profit) and private ('for-profit') facilities. Indeed, this is an issue arousing considerable political passion in the UK as we write, and we shall come back to it in Section 10.4. But first we shall look at how the variety of forms of health-care delivery and finance can be explained.

■ ■ ■ 10.2.2 Market failure in health-care delivery

There is such diversity in the ways in which health care is delivered because governments have, on the whole, been reluctant to leave the delivery of health care to the market. You have seen, in Chapters 5 and 8, that under conditions of perfect competition the market should deliver an efficient allocation of all goods. However, as this section will show, an unregulated market in health care is unlikely to fulfil the assumptions of perfect competition, and so would fail to be allocatively efficient.

Question Look back at Chapter 5, Section 5.2.1. What assumptions underlie the model of perfect competition? What further condition necessary for perfect competition to yield a Pareto optimal outcome is explained in Chapter 8, Section 8.3.4?

The model of perfect competition is based on four assumptions. Perfect competition assumes that all firms and consumers are price-takers, that all firms and consumers are well informed, that the goods and services supplied are homogeneous, and that firms and consumers are free to enter and exit the market. The further condition is that, for perfect competition to be allocatively efficient, or yield a Pareto optimal outcome, there must be no externalities in the market. Economists have identified a number of reasons for believing that a free market in health-care delivery would fail to satisfy three of these conditions.

Informational asymmetry

It was explained in Chapter 5, Section 5.2.1, that a local fruit and vegetable market might approximate to the informational requirements of the model of perfect competition because consumers can easily discover the different prices and qualities available. For a market in health-care delivery, however, it is clear that most 'consumers' (i.e. patients) will not be experts in either the range of health-care services or the impact of these services on their own health. The need for diagnosis is a principal reason for seeking medical help. The fact that consumers do not know what is wrong with them, or what is needed to put it right, prevents them from shopping around in the way they might if buying a kilo of tomatoes. 'Informational asymmetry' is the term given to such a situation, in which one party to a market exchange – in this case, the health-care provider – has more information than the other – in this case, the patient as a consumer of health care.

Product variability

In the model of perfect competition, the products supplied by one firm are indistinguishable from those supplied by another. But health-care services resemble 'customized' rather than 'generic' or homogeneous products. You may have heard of Savile Row, a street in London in which tailors still make clothes to measure, by hand. Such tailoring is extremely expensive, and it illustrates an important feature of health-care services, which often have to be tailored to the needs of the patient. Not everyone needs to have the same tests done if they have a rash on their arm; not everyone needs the same amount of time to recuperate from an operation. If a free market were allowed to handle these transactions, it might be necessary for consumers to negotiate a separate price for every service delivered. Again, this means that it is difficult for patients to shop around and, therefore, difficult for competitive pressures to operate.

271

Externalities

Chapter 8 noted that externalities are an important source of market failure, and externalities play a role in the analysis of health care. For many treatments, the patient is the main beneficiary, so the external effects might be minimal. In fact health care is, in economic terms, largely a private rather than a public good (Chapter 9, Section 9.2.1). For example, hospital beds are rival goods, in that one patient's consumption reduces the number available for others, as waiting lists in the UK NHS testify. Most treatments are also excludable, in that providing health care for one patient does not benefit the others; your filling does not stop my toothache. Some public health interventions, however, do involve externalities. Vaccination against infectious disease, for example, benefits both the person treated and the many other people with whom that individual comes into contact. So vaccination produces positive externalities (Chapters 3, 8 and 9), in the form of a reduced risk of infection for people coming into contact with the vaccinated person. The benefits to society are greater than the benefits to the vaccinated person.

As Maureen Mackintosh explained in Chapter 9, Section 9.2, externalities can lead to a divergence between private and social costs. The analysis showed that in a perfectly competitive market, negative externalities generated in production, that is, externalities that impose costs on others, imply that equilibrium output in the market is too high, since output decisions take into account only private costs of production, and not full social costs.

Question	Can you think of an example of a production process that generates *positive* externalities for other producers?

A classic if homely example is beekeeping: the bees pollinate nearby apple orchards, creating 'external' benefits for apple producers, that is, a useful input for which they do not pay.

Vaccinations also generate positive externalities and these too can be analysed in a market framework. However, these externalities affect *demand* decisions and hence consumption, not the costs of production. If vaccinations are supplied in a market, people's demand for vaccinations depends only on the benefits for themselves, and they do not take account of the benefits for others. Hence total demand for vaccinations will be below the market optimum.

Figure 10.1 illustrates this point, on the assumption that vaccinations are sold on a perfectly competitive market. In the figure, the line labelled D_p is the private demand curve for vaccinations. The curve labelled *MSB* is the marginal social benefit curve: it traces the total benefits – for both the consumer of the vaccination and others – of the last vaccination purchased. The *MSB* curve lies to the right of the private demand curve because there are external benefits produced by each quantity of vaccinations purchased.

Exercise 10.1

1 Mark on Figure 10.1 the private market equilibrium price and quantity demanded. Then identify the social optimum output, and the market price that would have to be set to sell that output.
2 Comment briefly on the policies that might move the market to the social optimum quantity of vaccinations.

Figure 10.1
A positive consumption externality in a market for vaccinations

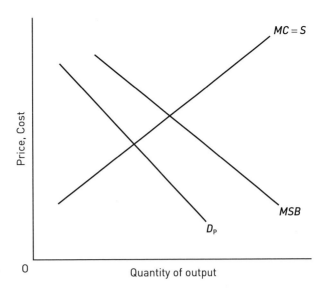

For these three reasons, a free market in health-care delivery would not be allocatively efficient.

10.2.3 Market failure in health-care finance and insurance

But what about the financing of health care? Even if the market cannot deliver health care efficiently, a market solution might be an efficient way to pay for health care. Since the need for health care is uneven and unpredictable for individuals, people who have to finance their health care themselves often take out insurance rather than paying for health care as they need it. So the market for health-care finance involves considerations that are specific to insurance markets. Once again, we shall find that the assumptions of the model of perfect competition do not hold in the market for health insurance.

Insurance can help people to cope with the uncertainties of life. An individual's future health status is uncertain in that the health outcomes associated with future courses of action are not known. Will jogging in an urban area protect someone from coronary heart disease, provoke an asthma attack, cause irreparable damage to the knees or lead to serious injury in a traffic accident? What is the *risk* of each of the adverse outcomes? In a risky activity such as jogging on busy roads, the individual does not know the outcome with any certainty but can assess the probability of each possible outcome. This is the basis of insurance, and private insurance offers protection against many contingencies.

Arrow (1963), however, has argued that the market fails to offer individuals health-care insurance in many situations where it would clearly be desirable for such insurance to be available. This section analyses the strengths and limitations of private insurance.

Probability and private insurance

Insurance works on probabilities. Private insurance companies spend large sums of money trying to work out the probabilities of various calamities occurring to identifiable groups of people. The probabilities of particular occurrences can become rather stable and predictable for large groups of people. No individual knows whether they will fall ill and be unable to work next year, but it is possible to work out with reasonable precision what percentage of a large group of people, who are similar in age and general health, will become ill over the period.

So insurance works by identifying groups with predictable probabilities of incurring a given problem, and then charging them all a sum that allows the unlucky ones to receive compensation. Let us take the example of sickness benefit insurance payments, which are made if you fall ill while working. Suppose that a private insurance company knows that there is a 0.5 per cent chance of someone like you being off work in any month, and pays you £800 if you are off work. The premium that the insurance company will charge will be 0.5 per cent × £800 plus a mark-up to cover its administrative costs and profits.

Exercise 10.2

Suppose a group of people that includes you has a 1 in a 100 chance of being ill in any year, and that the average cost to the insurance company is £2500 per illness episode, plus £5 per person for administration and to make a profit. What annual premium will the insurance company charge?

Formally, if the probability of requiring a given compensation Z is p, and the administrative costs plus profit are A, the premium is:

$$pZ + A$$

You will pay if you can afford it and are sufficiently worried about the possibility. The insurance company will accept your premium if they think that, on average, they will make a profit. That is the principle of private insurance. To make it work, several conditions are essential.

First, enough people have to be insured to make the calculated probabilities reliable. This condition is called the 'law of large numbers'. In small groups of people, the proportion that will be ill at any time will vary greatly from year to year. But with very large groups, the average sickness rate becomes much more predictable. As a result, risks can be pooled efficiently.

Second, the probability that any one individual needs compensation has to be independent of the probability of the same problem for others. If your friend becomes ill it must not influence your state of health. Otherwise, the insurance company might have to pay out to a large number of people simultaneously, and so the amounts it will have to pay out will not be stable. Infectious diseases are obviously a problem here.

Third, the probability of the insured disaster must be less than one. If $p = 1$ the problem is certain to happen. If you are already sick or disabled, health insurance to cover the condition would cost at least as much as the treatment. This means the most vulnerable people in society can find it difficult to buy certain forms of insurance.

Fourth, people must not be able to influence the probability of the insured event occurring. Hence pregnancy is hard to insure against, and so is unemployment. You have seen this source of market failure before in Chapter 9, Section 9.5.1. It is called 'moral hazard'. The market fails to work efficiently in this case because the insurance company lacks good information on the actions of the insured person, which can influence the sums paid out.

Fifth, the insurer also needs good information about the risks attached to each individual. Otherwise, some high-risk people may represent themselves as low risks and so pay insufficient premiums. This in turn pushes up the costs for others. If the result is that truly low-risk individuals find average premiums rising to a point at which insuring themselves is no longer worth while, they will drop out, further raising the costs for others. This form of market failure is called 'adverse selection'.

Question	What does this analysis suggest about the likely boundaries of private health-care insurance?

The conditions for efficient private insurance are stringent. Taken together, they suggest that private health-care insurers are likely to avoid or charge very big premiums to high-risk individuals or individuals wanting insurance against new and unpredictable health risks.

The dynamics of the private insurance industry further undermine the prospects for allocative efficiency in private health-care insurance. Risk pooling means that there is substantial scope for insurance companies to benefit from economies of scale. Larger companies will, by pooling more risks, have more predictable outgoings. In principle, there is no limit to the benefits of pooling, and there are substantial economies of scale to be had in processing the collection of premiums and the payment of claims. It is likely, therefore, that an unregulated market for health-care insurance will become highly concentrated, creating monopoly power and hence another source of market failure.

The conditions for efficient private insurance also imply distributional problems. The highest premiums may be demanded of those on low incomes. Some people will be unable to acquire private health-care insurance however much they want or need it. If others in society want these people to be insured, some form of redistribution will be necessary.

Social insurance

So, private health-care insurance is problematic and is unlikely to be sufficient if society – however defined – wishes all its members to be insured to cover the costs of health care. Some people will be excluded by a lack of income, others by the nature of the risks themselves – given the market failures in private insurance – or by their own particular probability of succumbing to these risks.

These problems can be used to explain the spread of social insurance in health care, as in other areas of concern (Chapter 9, Section 9.5.1). Have a careful look at the definitions of **social insurance** and **private insurance**. On these definitions, the state could in principle provide 'private' insurance. But social insurance would not be viable for a private insurer because it covers what are (privately) uninsurable risks.

So how can the state insure the uninsurable? The state has two major advantages over private insurers: its capacities for investigation and compulsion. By compelling universal coverage, the state can prevent low-risk people from refusing to enter a pooled system and hence reduce the costs of universal coverage.

So, one explanation from economic theory for the rise and persistence of social insurance in health care is that it represents a response to insurance market failures. The boundaries between social and private insurance are contested in theory and are shifting in practice as the insurance industry develops. You should note, however, that social insurance schemes in practice combine risk pooling – true insurance – and redistribution from rich to poor. Risk pooling requires only that people make a common flat-rate payment, based on the average costs of the scheme. Social insurance payments, however, are

Social insurance

Social insurance is compulsory and universal.

Private insurance

Private insurance, in contrast, is not universal: access to it is based on actuarial calculations of risk and the acceptance of individual applications.

often income-related, which implies that there is some redistribution between the better-off and the poorer in terms of the costs of access to the scheme, as well as redistribution towards those who fall ill (Section 10.3.1).

So the persistence of social insurance may be explained by its capacity to combine efficient insurance with rich-to-poor redistribution. It can be 'sold' as both an efficient safety net and an ethical system, and it has the additional advantage that, as contributors, people have rights to the benefits: there is none of the stigma attached to charity.

10.3 Ethics, rationing and redistribution

Section 10.2 suggested that health-care systems financed by social insurance are likely to be shaped by two principles: first, a commitment to redistribution and, second, the principle that everyone has a right to adequate health care. The aim of this section is to explore the implications of these two principles. First, we shall ask whether health care is in fact redistributive, in delivering to low-income people far more health care than they could buy from their incomes. Evidence from Europe and the USA strongly suggests that it is. Second, we shall discuss some of the issues arising out of the idea that people have rights to health care. Equity might be thought to require that these rights should be respected, but there are also reasons for believing that there may be limits to the rights that people have.

▪▪▪ 10.3.1 Is health care redistributive?

If poverty and ill health are associated, one way to weaken that link is to improve the health services that the poor receive. In the UK, as in many high-income countries, it is a widely accepted view that health care should be provided on the basis of *need* not income. Commitments of this kind are likely to be statements of principle rather than reality. In the UK, those with private medical insurance in addition to their right to publicly provided health care are the better-off, and articulate middle-class people may manage to extract more from the public system as well. However, if health-care systems in rich countries get anywhere close to distributing health care in response to need, then they are very redistributive indeed, in that they deliver to low-income people far more health care than they could ever buy from their incomes. This section looks briefly at whether this is the case.

There are two aspects to redistribution in health care: who pays for it and who gets it. In analysing both we can use the techniques you met in Chapter 9. Let us start with finance. Look at Figure 10.2.

This should look quite familiar to you. (Look back at Chapter 9 to check your understanding of Lorenz curves if necessary.) The gap between the curve labelled 'Lorenz curve for pre-tax income' and the diagonal line shows the inequality in pre-tax incomes. The new element is the line labelled 'health finance concentration curve'. This plots the cumulative proportion of total health-care financing (public and private) that is paid for by different cumulative proportions of the population, ranked by (equivalized) pre-tax income.

In interpreting Figure 10.2, take care not to think of the health finance concentration curve as indicating the distribution of *income*, as in the other Lorenz curves you have studied. Figure 10.2 is not comparing the distributions of original and post-tax incomes, as Figure 9.10 did. Instead Figure 10.2 shows the distribution of income and, with the health finance concentration curve, the distribution of the burden of payments for health care.

Figure 10.2

Analysing the progressiveness of health-care finance

Source: based on van Doorslaer and Wagstaff, 1993, Figures 3.5, 3.6

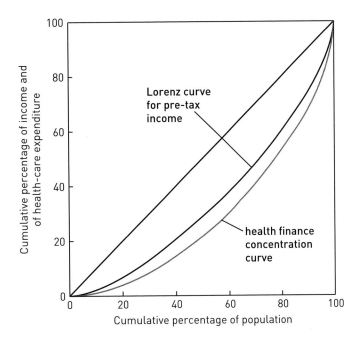

If the health finance concentration curve lies *outside* the Lorenz curve for pre-tax income, health-care finance is *progressive*: this means that lower-income groups pay a smaller proportion of their income for health care than do higher-income groups. If the health finance concentration curve lies *inside* the Lorenz curve for pre-tax income, health-care finance is *regressive*: this means that the burden falls more heavily on the poor in relative terms. If the two curves coincide, health finance is proportional: this means that the proportion of income used to pay for health care is the same for both lower- and higher-income groups.

Using this sort of analysis, researchers studied health-care financing in high-income countries in the early 1990s. They concluded (Wagstaff *et al.*, 1999) that the countries that rely most on private insurance – the USA and Switzerland – have *regressive* health-care financing systems overall, that is, health-care finance is more unequal than pre-tax incomes. It is easy to see why this is likely to be so. Private insurance payments depend on the extent of the insurance cover purchased, not on one's ability to pay. Those on low incomes purchase less, or no, medical insurance, but nevertheless tend to pay on average a higher proportion of their income for it.

The social insurance-based countries differ: in Germany and the Netherlands, the health finance system is also more unequal than pre-tax incomes, while in France it is *progressive*, that is, health-care finance is more equal than pre-tax incomes. Finally, in the largely tax-financed systems, health-care finance is either *proportional* – that is, distributed in a way similar to pre-tax incomes – or mildly progressive (more equal). The UK has progressive health-care finance, in part because private insurance is bought by the better-off but they are not permitted to opt out of tax payments.

That last point brings us to the provision of health care. Does health care go equally to rich and poor, or do those on lower incomes receive less care? To answer this question, we need to know how much care people *need*. As you would expect from the discussion in Section 10.1.1, poor people generally need more care than the better-off because they are ill more often and more severely. So health care is distributed *equally* only if those in equal need get equal care. But do they?

Figure 10.3
Concentration curves for actual and expected health-care utilization

Source: based on van Doorslaer *et al.*, 2000, p.556

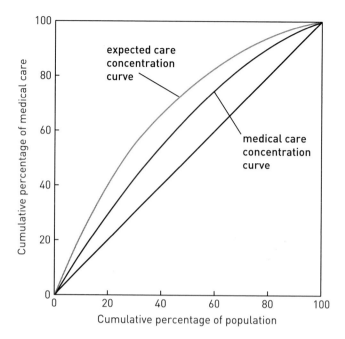

Economists have worked hard at analysing this question with reference to high-income countries. (The question is much less well explored for low-income countries.) In most cases the answer is no: that is, health care is distributed unequally in relation to need. Look at Figure 10.3. This is based on the Lorenz curve analysis but looks slightly different.

Look first at the curve labelled 'medical care concentration curve'. This shows the cumulative proportion of total medical care going to each cumulative proportion of the population, ranked by income (in this case, disposable income). Medical care is measured as the reported use of general practitioners (GPs), specialists and hospital care, valued on a comparable basis. As is typical in high-income countries, the poor use more health care. And so they should, they need more.

But is it enough? Are the poor getting their fair share? The curve labelled 'expected care concentration curve' is a measure of need. It is based on sample survey data that ask questions about self-reported levels of illness, including both general health and specific chronic conditions (which are particularly likely to be more prevalent among lower-income respondents). The answers are used to predict how much health care each individual needs, valued on the same basis as actual use.

| **Question** | What does it mean if the concentration curve for expected health care lies above the concentration curve for actual care received, as is the case in Figure 10.3? |

The implication is that those on lower incomes receive a lower proportion of the total care provided than they should do, were care provided on the basis of need. If the two curves coincide there is (estimated to be) equity in the distribution of health care in relation to need.

Estimates on this basis for high-income countries gave the following results. In all countries the lower-income groups received more care than the better-off: the medical care concentration curve was above the diagonal, as shown in Figure 10.3. The results differed, however, in terms of the type of care provided. If visits to a general practitioner

(GP) or primary doctor alone can be distinguished from specialist care (not all surveys distinguish the two, and not all countries have GPs), the distribution of primary (GP) care is close to the measure of need: that is, there is little evidence of inequity. (The countries surveyed included Denmark, Finland, Ireland, the Netherlands and the UK.) For a combination of GP and specialist care, however, half of the countries studied showed inequity in favour of the rich (the situation shown in Figure 10.3), including Finland, Sweden, the Netherlands and the USA. The greatest inequity was in the USA. Where specialist care could be separated from GP care, the provision was estimated to be biased towards the better-off in Denmark, Finland and the Netherlands, but not in the UK and Ireland.

These data have many limitations. For example, they assume that all care is of equal quality. If the quality of care for the more articulate and for those able to pay more is better, there is more inequity than is shown here; and this is likely to be particularly true where private medical insurance forms an important element of the financing.

Nevertheless, we can draw an important conclusion. The health-care systems of most of these countries, including the UK, are redistributive. To see this, consider financing and provision in the UK together. The financing is slightly progressive: that is, somewhat more equal than pre-tax income. The provision is also more equal than pre-tax income. Even when we allow for the ability of the better-off to buy more rapid or higher-quality care – not picked up here – those on low incomes are still receiving, on average, much more health care than they pay for. The association between poverty and ill health would be even stronger in the UK, and in many other rich countries, were it not for the health-care system. In the USA many millions of people lack insurance coverage, health finance is regressive and the indicators of care are inequitable in favour of the rich. But health-care systems that come close to including all citizens equitably, including those of most rich countries except the USA, strongly redistribute resources in the form of health care towards those on lower incomes.

■■■ 10.3.2 The integration of claims

Resources are scarce, medical technology is developing all the time, life expectancy continues to rise, and in rich countries governments and voters could, if they chose to do so, spend more on health care through higher taxes and social insurance contributions. So should we allow public sector health systems to fund cosmetic plastic surgery – or is this a luxury that people should pay for out of their own pockets? Should we fund expensive heart operations that leave patients with low life expectancies?

Question	Before you read on, we would like you to imagine a situation in which there are two patients, Sita and Tim, who both need kidney transplants. However, there is only enough capacity to treat one of them, even though both will die quickly if untreated. You have to decide which patient is treated. What information would you ask for before making a decision about whom to treat?

One approach to allocating health care has been suggested by health economists working on non-market systems that try to allocate resources in response to need. It is based on making choices that result in the maximization of health across a population. To implement this approach, it is necessary to find out the benefits and costs of different treatments. A benefit–cost ratio can be constructed to express the benefits of a course of treatment as a percentage return on the costs of that treatment. Some treatments, such as hip replacements, might not cost very much and lead to a good quality of life for a long time (measured in quality-adjusted life years or QALYs). These treatments would have high benefit–cost ratios. Other treatments, such as heart operations, might lead to smaller increases in life expectancy and cost more, and so they would have lower benefit–cost ratios. To maximize the QALYs produced by the health-care system, we could try to rank all health-care treatments according to their benefit–cost ratios. One could then select the treatment with the highest benefit–cost ratio and work on down the list until the health-care budget runs out.

This idea has been much discussed in the context of European health-care systems, but it was the government of Oregon, a state in the USA, that was noted for implementing the QALY ranking procedure in the early 1990s. Government officials set priorities using information on QALYs and costs, and then consulted representatives of the citizens. They found that a few treatments needed to be moved up or down in the rankings, but the set of priorities that had emerged from the QALY maximization approach was accepted for the most part. This popular support is slightly surprising because the QALY has attracted much criticism from academics outside economics, especially medical experts and health philosophers (Anand and Wailoo, 2000). In what follows, we shall look at some of the objections that have been raised.

Rights and basic needs

We didn't tell you the ages of Sita or Tim. Is this relevant information? Suppose both are expected to live into their 70s if treated, but that Sita is 45 and Tim is 40. To whom would you give the transplant now? QALY maximization requires that the treatment goes to Tim, assuming that either patient would have a similar quality of life afterwards. But it is not clear that we *must* give Tim priority. You might think that Sita has a legitimate claim.

If you do not agree with the QALY approach in this case, it might be because you feel that basing the treatment decision on a five-year age difference for people who could have a life span of nearly 80 years seems somewhat arbitrary. In a sense, both Sita and Tim have something substantial to gain from the transplant – the rest of their lives; so some might say that both patients are equally entitled to the treatment. Many people have argued that everyone has a right to be as healthy as possible, and some economists have gone on to suggest that where these equal rights cannot be recognized because of resource constraints, people should be given equal *chances* of having their needs met.

For instance, one might flip a coin to determine who should be treated. In that case, they would be treated equally *ex ante* (a Latin phrase economists use to mean 'before the event'). Actually flipping a coin might be unacceptable, but other arbitrary rules could be, and have been, devised. One could set a budget each year and operate on all new cases until the funding runs out. This still leaves people untreated, but some might find it an acceptable if pragmatic approach, as it is based on the idea that people have the same rights to health care. But there are some arguments that suggest limits to the rights that people should have.

Responsibilities

With rights go responsibilities, or so we are told. People should be free to do certain things so long as they respect the rights of others. The sociologist Amitai Etzioni has been prominent in advocating this position through a social philosophy that came to be called 'communitarianism' (Etzioni, 1988). Communitarians believe that we should emphasize our duties to give to, and participate in, the local society. In North America at least, the push for rights has gone too far, they say, and Etzioni has proposed a ten-year moratorium on the creation of new rights. But what do responsibilities mean in health care? If a person's liver fails because of heavy drinking, have they fulfilled their responsibilities to themselves or others? The treatment of such patients might be given less priority.

The 'fair innings' argument

How would you feel if Sita were 25 and Tim were 70? If you felt that the claims were evenly balanced before, perhaps you now think Sita has a stronger claim. Tim has nearly matched the life expectancy of a man in a high-income country, while Sita may have over two-thirds of her life left. As the philosopher John Harris puts it, Tim has had a 'fair innings' but Sita has not. The transplant should be given to Sita so that she can have a fair innings too. The cost of the kidney transplant will be the same regardless of whom we treat, but Sita is expected to live much longer so the benefits are expected to be greater if she receives the treatment. This is how an advocate of QALY maximization would see things.

Contractual views

The idea that there might be a social contract between the governed and the rulers first came to prominence in the writings of the philosopher Jean Jacques Rousseau (1712–78) and was rejuvenated in 1972 with the publication of *A Theory of Justice* by the US philosopher John Rawls. To work out what a fair society would mean, Rawls invites us to consider a situation in which we negotiate with each other about what society will look like. But we do so from behind a *veil of ignorance*. We know what the lot of all the members of the society will be, but we don't know which particular slot any one individual will take up. So you would be invited to agree, for example, what the salaries or wages would be for all jobs, without knowing whether you would be the director of a multinational company or a waste removal operative. Rawls claims that one of the principles that would emerge from behind this veil of ignorance is the 'maximin' principle. This states that:

> Social and economic inequalities are to be arranged so that they are . . . to the greatest benefit of the least advantaged.
>
> *(Rawls, 1972, p.83)*

Rawls argues that people negotiating future social and economic arrangements would choose the 'maximin' principle because they would not know whether they would be among the most or the least advantaged members of the future society. Assuming that people are averse to risk, that is, that they want to 'play safe', they would be anxious, from behind the veil of ignorance, to ensure that the worst position in which they might find themselves would be as good as possible. Rawls interprets this idea of 'maximizing the minimum' condition of life in terms of primary goods, including health care and education, that no one would be willing to risk being without. In this view, health care goes to people because they need it, in that its provision is an essential component of an acceptable condition of life for the least advantaged members of society. It follows that, for Rawls, health care does *not* go to people because they will live longer and happier lives than others as a result, as is the case in the QALY approach.

Another strand of thought, related to but distinct from the contractual view, can be found in work that argues for the importance of public deliberation. As Chapter 8 noted, there is evidence of support for what some economists have called 'procedural utility', that is, the view that we derive intrinsic value from being involved in decision-making regardless of the outcome. In the UK, some health authorities have commissioned public consultations, although support for the idea is somewhat reduced by the fact that most lay people are not sufficiently informed about the options and issues. This is not to say that public consultation is not viable in the long run – the BBC has been doing it for years with some success – but doing it properly is an expensive process. More importantly, it leaves unanswered the question of what sort of views should be reflected in the determination of entitlements. There are clearly some views that we would not expect a national health service to listen to, which brings us full circle to the problem of what kinds of claims should count.

In this section we have seen that the health-care systems of most high-income countries are redistributive, redistributing resources in the form of health care towards lower-income groups. We have also examined several approaches to the issue of integrating competing claims on resources in public sector health-care systems. There is no simple answer to the question of which claims should count. In Section 10.4 we shall analyse a putative solution to another issue that has featured in debates about public sector health-care systems. This is the question of whether they are wasteful in their use of resources.

Case study: Managed competition in the NHS

This extended case study critically examines a specific attempt to reform a public sector health-care system. The reform discussed is one that took place in the UK National Health Service (NHS), but it is illustrative of the economic reforms that have sought to bring competition into previously monopolistic public sector social provision. Increasingly, the distinction between public and private sectors is blurring, largely because governments are looking for ways of bringing private sector incentives, mechanisms and funds into the provision of public services. This NHS reform was known as the 'internal market' but, as we shall see, its lessons may be relevant to other uses of market exchange in the NHS, including buying health care from overseas. This particular case study illustrates those lessons in the context of a major health-care reform. It also serves to show how you might apply and combine some of the general principles of microeconomic analysis you have been studying throughout this book.

Aneurin Bevan, Minister of Health in the 1946–51 Labour Government, established the National Health Service (NHS) on 5 July 1948. Before that date hospitals in the UK were either voluntary, that is, funded by benefactors and fees, or managed by the local authority and financed in part by local taxes. By the 1930s over half the income of voluntary hospitals came from patients' fees, GPs charged fees and municipal hospitals raised a small part of their income from fees. The aim of the NHS was to ensure that equally good health-care services were available to everyone, including those who had previously been unable to pay. Central government brought under its control all the voluntary and local authority hospitals it needed for the NHS, to be financed out of general taxation. GPs became private contractors to the NHS. GP and hospital services were to be provided free at the point of delivery. When charges were introduced for spectacles and dentures, Bevan resigned in protest at this early departure from the principle of making health care available to the whole population free at the point of delivery.

The expectation was that demand for health-care services and hence expenditure on them would decline as the health of the population improved. The reality was rather different (Peden, 1985, pp.155–6, 190–1). Freed from expenditure constraints imposed by the limited resources of benefactors and political resistance to local tax increases, hospitals set out to achieve the best possible standards of care and to introduce new technologies (drugs, equipment and surgical procedures) when they had the resources to do so.

The expansion and improvement of health care under the NHS encountered two main difficulties. First, central government funding was necessarily limited and the financial constraints imposed on the NHS led to the appearance of waiting lists, even though expenditure on the NHS as a percentage of GPD rose in the 1960s (Peden, 1985, p.191). With no fees to raise to curtail demand, and with technological progress providing more and more expensive new treatments, hospitals used waiting lists to balance competing claims on their resources. Politicians and commentators who favoured free markets accused the NHS of inefficiency, as the monopoly provider of health care free at the point of delivery. Second, in the absence of any other information, the initial allocation of resources among the NHS hospitals and GPs was based on the resources each hospital and GP had been using before 1948 (a procedure sometimes known as 'grandfathering'). The effect was to perpetuate to some extent pre-NHS inequalities in the provision of health care among different regions and social groups (Peden, 1985, p.190).

Little could be done about these problems under the initial NHS management structure. Hospitals and GPs were administered separately and central government lacked the information necessary to reallocate resources more equally (Klein, 1983, Chapter 2). In 1974 the NHS was reorganized to allow greater centralization in the allocation of resources. The intention was to implement the original guiding principle of providing equally good health care everywhere, by allocating resources according to need. The RAWP (Resource Allocation Working Party) formula measured need in terms of the population served by a hospital or GP, with adjustments made for factors such as the proportion of children and old people and indicators of poverty, given the association between poverty and ill health

(Section 10.1). The perception remained among policy makers impressed by the efficiency gains provided by competition in free or lightly regulated markets that the NHS was wasteful of resources.

Let us now examine some of the issues surrounding the introduction of managed competition into the NHS in 1991.

What economists said about plans for managed competition

In the 1980s, Alan Enthoven, an American economist and long-time observer of the UK health scene, was invited to provide some ideas for what was to be one of the most radical and, in some ways, innovative economic reforms of the Thatcher era. His main proposal was that competition should be introduced into the NHS while leaving intact much of its public sector status. Enthoven's proposals were not for a free market, but to bring the essential benefits of competition into the public sector in a controlled manner by creating market-like relationships within the NHS (an 'internal market'). As he wrote:

> The markets for health insurance and health care are not naturally competitive like the markets for transportation, financial services, automobiles or jogging shoes. 'Deregulation' will not make them competitive. In a 'free market' made up of health plans on the supply side and individual consumers on the demand side, without carefully drawn rules and without active management by sponsors, the health plans would be free to pursue profits or survival by using numerous competitive strategies that would destroy efficiency and equity, and that individual consumers would be powerless to counteract.
>
> *(Enthoven, 1988, p.87)*

Enthoven discussed a number of issues that would be critical to the functioning of markets within the NHS. In particular, he noted that 'a competitive market will not automatically produce high quality care; especially to the extent the market is characterized

Case study continued

by poor information about quality' (Enthoven, 1988, p.108). He emphasized the importance of information about quality (of health care and outcomes), if quality was to be maintained. And he noted the importance of encouraging new entrants into health-care provision as a way of maintaining competitive behaviour. Well-informed, sophisticated buyers who could pool risks adequately and monitor quality would be central to the successful application of market principles to health.

Akehurst *et al.* (undated) provided a useful summary of some of the issues that economists raised prior to the implementation of the NHS internal market. We can divide them into two categories: efficiency and equity.

First, government-run organizations are frequently accused of failing to produce output at the lowest possible cost for a particular level of output. Competition between hospitals and other health-care providers should encourage both to drive costs down towards the minimum possible costs identified by the marginal and average cost curves (Chapter 4, Section 4.3.1 and Chapter 5, Section 5.3).

Second, it was felt that there could be improvements at the level of capacity planning. Because money would follow patients, providers would have an incentive to provide specialized services to patients outside their own geographical regions. It might then be possible to benefit from economies of scale. Furthermore, it was felt that a number of teaching hospitals had capacity that was under-utilized. Such hospitals would be able to generate extra revenue by using this surplus capacity.

On the question of equity, it was felt that the risks might outweigh the opportunities. A public health-care system in which access is free at the point of delivery is likely to produce results that are equitable, in the sense of not discriminating against those who are unwilling or unable to pay. But against this, there was a concern that specialization of service provision would mean that many patients would have to travel further for treatment. Those on low incomes might find the costs difficult to meet. Others argued that competition would also succeed in driving down wages in a sector of the economy in which wages were already perceived to be low.

The ability of patients or their doctors to choose health-care providers on their behalf was felt to offer an element of consumer choice that would favour patients and facilitate competition.

Implementation and results

Managed competition in the NHS, or the 'internal market', was an attempt to introduce competitive pressures into the NHS, while seeking to preserve its commitments to free health care at the point of delivery and to ensure the availability of equally good health care everywhere in the UK. A competitive market requires buyers and sellers, so an 'internal market' was created by dividing the institutions of the NHS into purchasers and providers. Health authorities as purchasers would use their allocation of funds from central government to buy services for their patients from hospitals, with the allocation of funds continuing to reflect the calculation of need. Incentives were put in place to encourage GPs to become budget holders, purchasing services for their patients directly from hospitals and seeking to secure the greatest amount of services with the budget at their disposal by 'shopping around'. Hospitals could opt to become 'hospital trusts', with incentives to generate extra income by winning new business by supplying services at a lower cost than their competitors.

Before the changes, there was much lobbying, particularly by the medical profession, to have the internal market dropped. For a while after the changes were implemented, very little happened. Health authorities and hospitals dealt with each other via block contracts – and these contracts were much like the old budgets, amounting to a single payment for all the services previously provided by the health-care provider. Health-care providers were supposed to make a surplus of 6 per cent (the word 'profit' was not used), which could then be ploughed back into the hospital's activities.

After the election of the Labour government in 1997, the experiment officially ended, just when some might say it was about to get going. Nonetheless, there are some very important general lessons about the operation of markets to be learnt, and a number of researchers in economics and other disciplines have evaluated aspects of the reforms. Appropriate data are not available to evaluate all the changes, but researchers at the King's Fund, a health-policy think-tank based in London, noted a number of outcomes (Le Grand *et al.*, 1998).

Equity

Two of the most important ethical issues raised by the NHS internal market are 'cream-skimming' and 'two-tierism'. Cream-skimming is the practice, evident in parts of the US health-care system that are in some ways similar to GP budget-holders, of discriminating against high-cost patients such as the elderly and the infirm in favour of low-cost patients. The internal market seemed to give GP budget-holders a financial incentive towards cream-skimming, which would help to avoid over-spending their budget. However, Goodwin (1998) found, after reviewing the research, that GP budget-holders 'have not undertaken cream-skimming despite the theoretical financial incentives to do so' (p.58). The explanation is threefold: budgets were generous, there was no personal financial penalty incurred by GPs who overspent and the government reimbursed GP budget-holders for the costs of treating an individual patient if they exceeded £5000 (Goodwin, 1998, p.58).

The term 'two-tierism' expresses the fear that the NHS internal market would create a two-tier system of GPs, with the patients of budget-holding GPs enjoying better access to health care than those of other GPs. Hospitals would favour patients from budget-holding GPs whose money they could spend on reducing waiting lists. Since it was expected that GPs serving disadvantaged urban areas would lack the administrative support that budget-holding required, this would reinforce existing inequalities in NHS health care. Goodwin (1998) found that 'most commentators accept that fundholding [budget-holding] has exacerbated two-tierism' (p.56). For example, patients of budget-holding GPs faced significantly shorter times for elective surgery. It is important to note that the two-tier issue 'arose not because of the intrinsic nature of an internal market,

but because this particular internal market had two kinds of purchaser [GP budget-holders and GP non-budget-holders]' (Le Grand *et al.*, 1998, p.124).

Efficiency

There is some evidence that cost per unit of activity (a measure of average cost) in the NHS fell more rapidly after 1991 than before and newly created hospital trusts had lower costs than other hospitals (Le Grand *et al.*, 1998, pp.120–1). Whether the superior cost performance of trusts can be attributed to the internal market is a controversial issue. Perhaps hospitals opting for trust status were able to do so in part because they already had lower unit costs. It is also possible that, insofar as falling costs reflected advances in medical technology, they would have been secured without the internal market.

A major issue in the public debate about the NHS reforms was the increase in management costs that the internal market was expected to cause. The decrease in cost per unit of activity implies that, if there was an increase in management costs that can be attributed to the internal market, it was outweighed by cost savings in other areas. It is not certain that management costs did rise, because there was some reclassification of senior nursing and health-care professional posts as managerial (Hamblin, 1998, p.105).

Market structure

On the supply side, between 25 per cent of hospitals and 38 per cent of patient episodes were conducted in situations in which there was some degree of monopoly power. So in terms of market structure there were reasons to suppose that competition would not be widespread. When it came to demand-side issues, the evidence was mixed. There was some evidence that providers and purchasers developed agreements lasting beyond a year to provide a secure market that could justify investment in new low-cost techniques, such as non-invasive ('keyhole') surgery. Contracts appeared to evolve and did not change radically every year. In part this cut down on negotiation costs, but it allowed providers some security of demand, on which they could plan investment.

An essential element for competition in practice is that customers can switch between suppliers with relative ease. There are a number of reasons why people do not change the brand of soap powder they use or the financial institution at which they bank. When GPs were asked about their willingness to refer patients to different hospitals, those who held their own budgets were much more willing to refer to hospitals that involved the patient travelling relatively long distances. In densely populated urban areas, and for relatively common ailments, travel probably played a relatively minor role in inhibiting competition. But one can see that competition in these markets depends on the willingness of patients to travel, as well as the referral behaviour of GPs, and that in rural areas, or for rarer conditions, both factors could serve to reduce the competitive pressures faced by hospitals.

Information

We have noted that information about service quality and outcomes is essential to the successful operation of markets, but there were serious problems with the information in the 'internal market'. The information systems were poor: there was a lack of data about current service provision and doubts about the accuracy of the data that was available; there was poor information about health needs and only crude information about costs and activity. The rise of information and communication technologies and pressures to reform have, in recent years, resulted in some improvements to these information systems.

However, these remarks apply to the large information systems operated by health regions and hospitals. GPs have access to more immediate before and after information about the health of their patients. For many conditions, GPs refer on a regular basis and so are well placed to monitor and evaluate service quality. But changes in the relationship between GPs and providers went beyond the flow of information. One anecdotal indicator, taken seriously nonetheless, was found in a reversal of the direction in which Christmas cards were sent. GPs had sent cards to consultants but, as the market turned the consultants into competitors looking for business, they began to send cards to GPs.

Questions

1 When introducing market mechanisms into a public service like the NHS, it is not always easy to predict what the impacts on efficiency are going to be: Do you agree or not agree? Why?

2 'Market mechanisms are likely to be produce unfair outcomes.' Does the case support this view? Discuss the evidence for your view.

Health service reform will remain on the political agenda for many years to come. This case study has highlighted the difficulty of achieving a balance between equity and efficiency, of preserving the distinctive values of the NHS while introducing competition into its operation. In the future it is likely that NHS reform will continue to pivot on dilemmas of this kind. However, it also seems likely that the infusion of competition will take a different form.

Redefining the National Health Service

The NHS will be decentralized with a plurality of providers operating within a framework of clear national standards regulated independently . . .

Changing it from a monolithic, centrally run, monopoly provider of services to a values-based system where health care providers – in the public, private and voluntary sectors – provide comprehensive services to NHS patients with a common ethos: free at the point of use, based on patient need and informed choice and not on their ability to pay . . .

NHS care does not have to be delivered exclusively by line-managed NHS organizations but by a range of organizations working with the national framework of standards and inspection.

(Alan Milburn, Secretary of State for Health, 2002)

Look back to Section 10.2.1. How would you interpret Alan Milburn's 'redefinition' of the NHS in the light of our comments on health-care delivery in an international context?

There will be no change to the core values that have informed the NHS from its inception: the goal of health care free at the point of delivery or use and the goal of equally good health care for everyone everywhere. However, the much more recent introduction of market-based methods of delivering that health care seems likely to remain in the forefront of NHS reform, although in a rather different form. The aim of NHS reform for the foreseeable future seems likely to lie in a more straightforward style of privatization than that exemplified by the '*internal market*'. Instead the emphasis will be placed upon *external* contracting, buying in health-care services from public, private and voluntary sector providers. In this way there seems to be a prospect of the UK losing some aspects of its distinctive system of health care and moving towards the mixed systems of health-care provision to be found in many other countries.

10.4 Conclusion

The economic analysis of health status and health care tells us something about a particular market, the generality and applicability of microeconomic principles, the normative nature of economics, and the extent to which economics can be enriched and tested by empirical applications. You might want to draw up a list of points that are reinforced or changed by some of the issues raised in this chapter, but let us conclude with a few notes of our own.

Perhaps the fundamental point is that health status is closely linked to economic status: the poor have a lower life expectancy and a greater likelihood of illness than the rich. In view of this link, it is important to remember that health care is often redistributive, in that it enables the poor to secure more health care than they would be able to purchase from their incomes. The fact that health care is redistributive reflects the extensive role of the state in most health-care systems, even though there is great diversity. This in turn is a response to the existence of market failures in both the delivery and the finance of health care. It is also a reflection of widespread views in society about equity, inequality and rights.

Health-care systems need to change, and the medical technologies with which the health professionals respond evolve on a continual basis. The managed competition experiment is just one example of the innovation and change that are features of health-care systems the world over. New drugs and equipment often embody the results of impressive scientific research, but their cost may leave those at the bottom end of the economic spectrum excluded from an ever-increasing set of opportunities. Balancing the hot pursuit of market opportunities against the protection of basic human rights and the promotion of human health is a dilemma that all modern economies now seem to face.

Questions for review and discussion

Question 1 Figure 10.4 shows the market for a particular vaccination. The industry is perfectly competitive but, in this market, there are positive externalities affecting consumption. Insert labels from the list below so as to label the diagram correctly.

Figure 10.4
Market for a
particular
vaccination

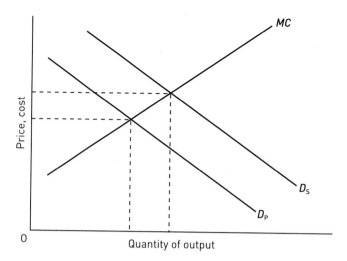

Q_P the free market equilibrium output
Q_S the allocatively efficient output
P_P the free market equilibrium price
P_S the allocatively efficient price
MC the marginal cost curve
D_P the free market demand curve
D_S the social demand curve

Question 2   Suppose that an insurance company quotes you a premium of £25 per month to insure you against loss of earnings if you are off work through sickness. The company will pay you £1000 per month if you are off work through sickness. This premium includes £5 for administration and profit mark-up. What is the insurance company's assessment of your probability of missing work through sickness in any month?

....

....

Question 3   Say which statement from the list below best explains what is meant by 'adverse selection' in an insurance market:

A ❏ The person insured has an incentive to change their behaviour so as to receive compensation to the detriment of the insurance company's profits.

B ❏ High- and low-risk people are both insured at an average premium. Low-risk people will feel this to be expensive and will drop out of the market.

C ❏ Asymmetric information leads people to be under-insured because they select unsuitable policies to cover their particular risks.

Question 4   Figure 10.5(a) shows the Lorenz curve for the pre-tax income and the health finance concentration curve for a hypothetical country called Erewhon.

Figure 10.5(b) shows the medical care concentration curve and the expected care concentration curve for Erewhon over the same period of time.

Say which statement correctly describes health care finance and provision in Erewhon.

Figure 10.5
(a) Lorenz curve for pre-tax income and health finance concentration curve for Erewhon
(b) Medical care concentration curve and expected care concentration curve for Erewhon over the same period

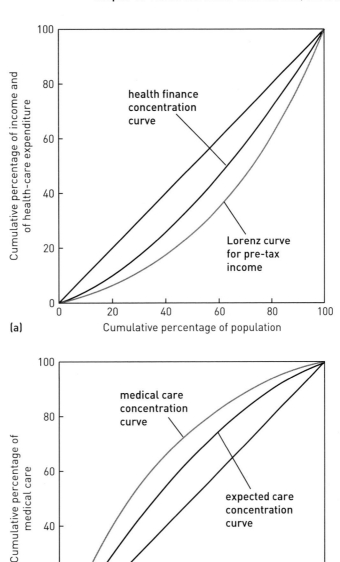

A ❑ Health-care finance is progressive; lower-income groups receive a higher proportion of total care than they would on the basis of need.
B ❑ Health-care finance is progressive; lower-income groups receive a lower proportion of total care than they would on the basis of need.
C ❑ Health-care finance is regressive; lower-income groups receive a lower proportion of total care than they would on the basis of need.
D ❑ Health-care finance is regressive; lower-income groups receive a higher proportion of total care than they would on the basis of need.

Answers to exercises

Chapter 2

Exercise 2.1 $15\ 000 - 12\ 000 = 3000$

$$\frac{3000}{12\ 000} \cdot 100 = 25.\ \text{The increase in 25\%.}$$

Exercise 2.2   A period of technological change that transforms the way that goods are produced and distributed is known as an 'industrial revolution'. A general purpose technology such as electricity, which stimulates constant improvements and is used widely across the economy, may initiate improvements in productivity or the efficiency of production. A further elaboration of the division of labour within the economy, exemplified by the factory system, is also likely. The result is an increase in the total output of the economy known as 'economic growth' and, usually, an increase in the wealth of producers and consumers.

Exercise 2.3   Three things that could happen in industrialized economies in the future that would go some way towards settling the debate between optimists and pessimists on the impact of IT on productivity in favour of the optimists/pessimists are:

1 the US economy endures a recession and productivity growth remains unusually high/ falls back to its historical average
2 other industrialized economies with relatively inflexible labour markets experience/ fail to experience a surge in productivity led by IT
3 a permanent trend rise in productivity begins/is not observed a few years after PCs reach 50 per cent market saturation in successive economies.

Exercise 2.4   **Table 2.2 (completed)**

Year	Actual price of product €	Price index (base 2003)
2003	12.00	100
2004	16.00	133
2005	19.00	158
2006	21.00	175

Chapter 3

Exercise 3.1   **Table 3.1 (completed)** Shifts in the market demand curve for electronic personal organizers

Change in variable	Effect on demand curve
Decrease in income	Decrease in quantity demanded at all prices Demand curve shifts to the left
Increase in income	Increase in quantity demanded at all prices Demand curve shifts to the right
Rise in price of a substitute	Demand curve shifts to the right
Fall in price of a substitute	Demand curve shifts to the left
Rise in price of a complementary good	Demand curve shifts to the left
Fall in price of a complementary good	Demand curve shifts to the right
Change in socio-economic influences in favour of electronic personal organizers	Demand curve shifts to the right
Change in socio-economic influences away from electronic personal organizers	Demand curve shifts to the left

Exercise 3.2   1 (a) Increasing returns to a factor of production occur when output increases faster than the input of a variable factor; decreasing returns to a factor of production refers to the opposite situation, in which output increases more slowly than the input of a variable factor.
(b) Economies of scale and increasing returns to scale are used interchangeably; both refer to a decrease in long-run average costs as output increases.
(c) Decreasing returns to scale and diseconomies of scale are used interchangeably; both refer to an increase in long-run average costs as output increases.
2 Short-run average costs differ from long-run average costs because in the short run at least one factor of production is fixed in quantity, resulting in diminishing returns to each variable factor of production above some level of output.

Chapter 4

Exercise 4.1   See Table 4.1 completed. The output numbers were of course kept unrealistically small to simplify the arithmetic.

Table 4.1 (completed)

Price (P) = average revenue (AR) €	Quantity (Q) of computers demanded	Total revenue (TR) €	Marginal revenue (MR) €
1000	1	1000	–
950	2	1900	900
900	3	2700	800
850	4	3400	700
800	5	4000	600

Exercise 4.2 1 The percentage decline in price is calculated by first working out the change in price. Subtract the old price from the new one:

$$€600 − €800 = −€200$$

The change in price is negative, since the price fell. Then calculate the percentage change. Divide the change in price by the original price and multiply by 100:

$$\frac{−€200}{€800} \cdot 100 = −\frac{1}{4} \cdot 100 = −25\%$$

2 Quantity sold rises from 5 to 9. The percentage change in quantity demanded is:

$$\frac{4}{5} \cdot 100 = 80\%$$

The change is positive since output rises.

3 The price elasticity of demand is then calculated by dividing the percentage change in quantity by the percentage change in price:

$$\text{price elasticity of demand} = \frac{80}{−25} = −3.2$$

Exercise 4.3 Figure 4.16 graphs columns 2 and 4 of Table 4.2 (completed).

Figure 4.16
Average and marginal cost curves from data in Table 4.2

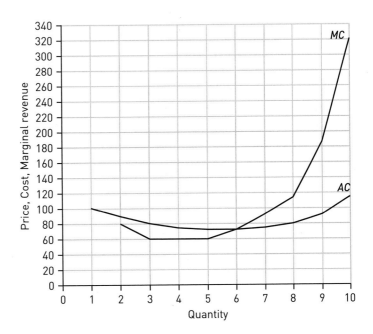

Table 4.2 (completed)

Units of output (Q)	Average cost (AC)	Total cost (TC)	Marginal cost (MC)
1	100	100	–
2	90	180	80
3	80	240	60
4	75	300	60
5	72	360	60
6	72	432	72
7	75	525	93
8	80	640	115
9	92	828	188
10	115	1150	322

Exercise 4.4   See Figure 4.17. The monopolist will now charge price P_2 and sell quantity Q_2. The firm's supernormal profits after the innovation are shown by the shaded rectangle.

Figure 4.17
A monopolist's profit-maximizing price and quantity after a process innovation

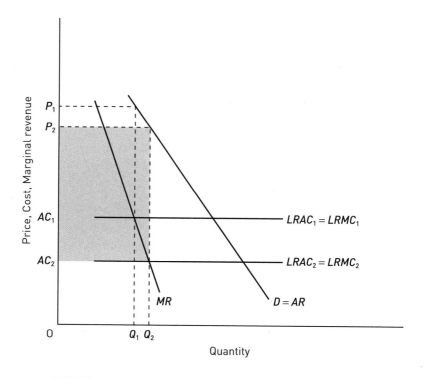

Chapter 5

Exercise 5.1   1   See Table 5.3 for marginal costs.

Table 5.3   Output, total cost and marginal cost of a shirt manufacturer

Quantity (shirts/day)	Total cost £	Marginal cost £
0	12	–
1	17	5
2	20	3
3	21	1
4	24	3
5	29	5
6	36	7
7	45	9
8	56	11

2   6 shirts per day.

Exercise 5.2   See Table 5.4.

Table 5.4   Short-run average variable cost and average total cost of a shirt manufacturer

Quantity (shirts/day)	Short-run average total cost (*SRAC*) £	Short-run average variable cost (*SRAVC*) £
0	–	–
1	17	5
2	10	4
3	7	3
4	6	3
5	5.8	3.4
6	6	4
7	6.4	4.7
8	7	5.5

See Figure 5.20. Note that the short-run *MC* curve cuts the short-run *AC* curve only approximately at its lowest point, since curves drawn from discrete points only approximate the relationships between smooth curves such as those shown on Figure 5.4.

Figure 5.20
Short-run marginal
cost, average
variable cost and
average total cost
curves from data in
Tables 5.3 and 5.4

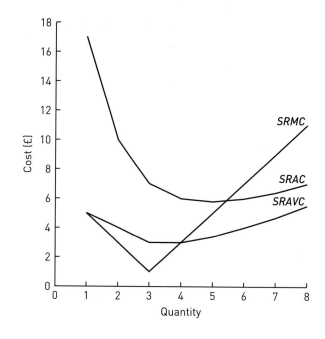

Exercise 5.3   Figure 5.21 shows the downward shift of the marginal cost curve from MC_1 to MC_2 as a result of the decline in unit costs. (The firm's average cost curves – not shown – would also shift downwards.) The profit-maximizing output of the firm at price P rises from Q_1 to Q_2. The firm's supply curve has shifted rightwards.

Figure 5.21
The effect of cost-
reducing technology
on equilibrium
output of a perfectly
competitive firm

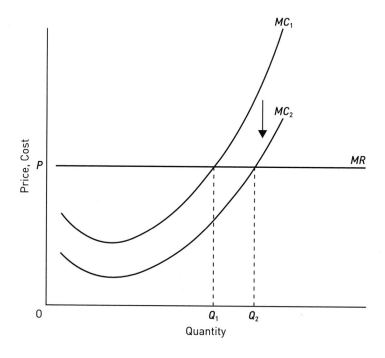

Figure 5.22
A shift to the right in
the supply curve for
orange juice

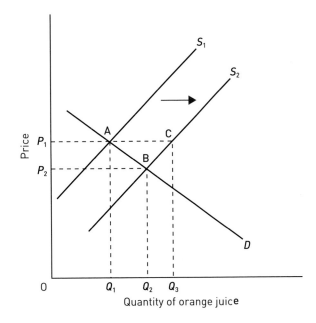

Exercise 5.4 Figure 5.22 shows the change in the equilibrium market price. The initial market equilibrium is at point A with price P_1. Unexpectedly warm weather increases the supply of orange juice at each price, hence the supply curve moves to the right from S_1 to S_2. The new market equilibrium at B will be at a lower price with a higher quantity sold. Consumers will move along their demand curve to the new price P_2 and quantity Q_2. It may help to envisage unsold orange juice piling up at the old price P_1 where supply now exceeds demand. That is, there is excess supply at P_1 measured by the distance AC. If some suppliers reduce price to clear their warehouses, others will have to follow, and demand will increase as price falls until the new equilibrium is reached. But the model only really tells us how the two equilibria A and B differ. It is a comparative static model.

Chapter 6

Exercise 6.1 If B co-operates, A does not co-operate (4 > 3). If B does not co-operate, A does not co-operate (2 > 1). Therefore, whatever B does, A does not co-operate. (Note that the sign '>' means 'greater than' and the sign '<' means 'less than'.)

If A co-operates, B does not co-operate (6 > 5). If A does not co-operate, B does not co-operate (4 > 3). Therefore, whatever A does, B does not co-operate.

The dominant strategy for each is not to co-operate, so the outcome is that neither co-operates with a pay-off of 2 for A and 4 for B. If each one co-operates, however, A would have 3 and B would have 5.

Exercise 6.2

Figure 6.15
General form of the
one-shot prisoners'
dilemma game

		Player B	
		co-operate	not co-operate
Player A	co-operate	P_3, P_3	P_1, P_4
	not co-operate	P_4, P_1	P_2, P_2

The structure of pay-offs takes the form $P_1 < P_2 < P_3 < P_4$. The outcome is that neither player co-operates, with pay-offs of P_2, P_2. If the players were to co-operate, the pay-offs would be P_3, P_3.

Exercise 6.3

Figure 6.16
Pay-off matrix
showing cartel
firms' pay-off

		Firm 2	
		increase output	reduce output
Firm 1	increase output	300, 300	600, 200
	reduce output	200, 600	500, 500

Although the strategy 'reduce output' would yield higher pay-offs (500 for each of the firms), collusion to reduce output would not succeed. The reason for this is that the dominant strategy for each firm is 'increase output'. For Firm 1, the pay-off is 300 to 'increase output' and 200 to 'reduce output' if Firm 2 increases output, and it is 600 to 'increase output' and 500 to 'reduce output' if Firm 2 reduces output. Thus, whatever Firm 2's strategy, Firm 1's pay-off is greater if it increases output. The same holds for Firm 2. The outcome is that each firm increases output with a pay-off of 300.

Exercise 6.4

Figure 6.17
A pay-off matrix
illustrating price
competition

		HighFlights	
		standard fare	discounted fare
FlyingHigh	standard fare	60, 60	30, 80
	discounted fare	80, 30	40, 40

The dominant strategy for each airline is to charge the discounted fare, so each one has a profit of £40 million. If HighFlights charges the standard fare, FlyingHigh has a profit of £60 million if it charges the standard fare and £80 million if it charges the discounted fare. If HighFlights charges the discounted fare, FlyingHigh has a profit of £30 million if it charges the standard fare and £40 million if it charges the discounted fare. Thus, whatever HighFlights' strategy, FlyingHigh has a better pay-off to 'discounted fare'. FlyingHigh's dominant strategy is therefore to discount its fares. The same applies to HighFlights. If both had charged the standard fare, the pay-offs would have been £60 million each.

Exercise 6.5   The 'meet competition' promise eliminates the strategy combinations in which just one airline cuts the price. This implies that the bottom-left and top-right strategy combinations are eliminated. The dominant strategy now is for each airline to charge the standard fare with a profit of £60 million.

Figure 6.18
A pay-off matrix illustrating 'meet competition'

HighFlights

		standard fare	discounted fare
FlyingHigh	standard fare	60, 60	
	discounted fare		40, 40

Exercise 6.6

Figure 6.19
A pay-off matrix illustrating an R&D investment decision

FastForward

		no R&D project	R&D project
LeadTheWay	no R&D project	100, 100	10, 180
	R&D project	180, 10	80, 80

The dominant strategy for each firm is to go for the new R&D with a pay-off of £80 million. If neither does so, the pay-off would be £100 million each. This game illustrates the risk involved in extensive innovation, as well as the potentially enormous gains for the firm that successfully innovates ahead of rivals. Strategic alliances – which help to spread the risks for firms trying to invest in R&D ahead of their rivals – are discussed in Section 6.6.

Chapter 7

Exercise 7.1   The demand for labour is derived demand, which means that it is valued for what it can be used to produce, rather than for its own sake. The marginal revenue product (MRP) is the extra revenue obtained by the firm from employing an extra unit of labour.

$$MRP = P \cdot MPP_L$$

Where MPP_L is the marginal physical product of labour. Diminishing marginal returns causes the MPP_L to decline, and because it is assumed that a perfectly competitive firm is a price-taker, the MRP is also declining. Profit maximization ensures that firms will employ labour up to the point where:

$$W = MRP$$

Hence (with labour as the only variable factor of production) the demand curve for labour is the same as the MRP curve, and is therefore declining as labour increases. Accordingly, a fall in wages leads a profit-maximizing firm to employ more labour.

Exercise 7.2   After the completion of the new office block, the demand curve for high-rise window cleaners shifts outwards from L_{D1} to L_{D2}, as shown in Figure 7.15, resulting in an increase in both wages and employment.

Figure 7.15
An increase in the demand for high-rise window cleaning

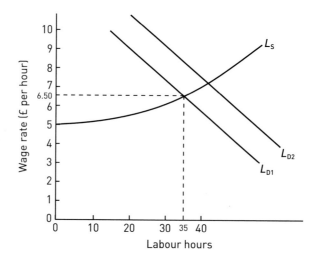

Exercise 7.3   My brief list of costs would include the following.

■ Time spent studying means less potential work time and accordingly perhaps less current income. There will also be a sacrifice of domestic labour time, with, for example, less time for household responsibilities or leisure.
■ There will be direct costs such as fees, stationery items and perhaps books. In addition, there may be other costs associated with the need to have somewhere quiet to study.

Perhaps we should add the mental anguish involved in having to tackle difficult material or in completing assessments – and the possible strain on family life!
     My list of benefits would include the following.

- Improved future job prospects, in terms of a reduced chance of future unemployment.
- A future potential to earn higher wages.
- A future potential to do a more intrinsically satisfying job.
- In the present there is the intellectual satisfaction of studying.

One could, in principle, estimate the future wage benefits and employment prospects obtained as a result of doing the course. Perhaps you will be pleased to learn that economic research generally indicates a considerable economic return from obtaining degrees, with evidence of some increase through the 1980s compared with the 1970s. You could also estimate reasonably well the costs to you in terms of the time taken up by studying. On the other hand, it is hard to quantify the consumption benefits and costs of doing courses, even if your judgement as to whether to start the course cannot avoid taking them into account.

Exercise 7.4 Other factors sometimes preventing mobility include:

- difficulties involved in moving house (including buying and selling houses), or in travelling to where the jobs are
- family and social ties
- language and social barriers.

Exercise 7.5 If some workers offered to work for wages below the equilibrium point B on Figure 7.12, the employer would deduce that it would not be worthwhile for workers to work properly once employed. The employers would expect the workers to shirk and take the chance of being caught, since the cost of being caught is not so great with such low wages. Even if the workers would prefer to work at these wages, rather than remain unemployed indefinitely, they would find it impossible to convince the prospective employers of their intentions as, with imperfect monitoring of the workplace, the promise of 'good' behaviour could not be guaranteed. Any such promise would have to be disregarded if the employer is rational and if it is recognized that the workers are rational. All this, of course, applies strictly to a world of alienating and unsatisfying work, where unemployment is the prime disciplinary measure against shirking.

Chapter 8

Exercise 8.1 $\dfrac{£430 \text{ million}}{107.5} \cdot 100 = £400 \text{ million}$

Thus there would have been no change in real GDP. The apparent (nominal) increase would have been purely the result of inflation.

Exercise 8.2 $\dfrac{£943\,412 \text{ million}}{114.2} \cdot 100 = £826\,105 \text{ million (approximately)}$

This is not the same figure as in Table 8.5; it is about £39 million out because of rounding errors.

Exercise 8.3 Total utility rises. Total utility will always rise if marginal utility is strictly positive, that is, greater than zero.

Chapter 9

Exercise 9.1

Figure 9.18
An *ad valorem* tax on output in a competitive market

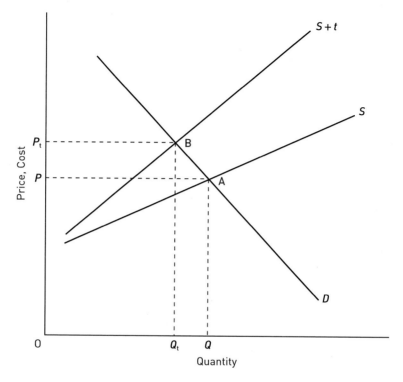

See Figure 9.18. The distance between the supply curve without the tax S and the supply curve with the tax $S + t$ will increase as output rises, instead of being constant as in Figure 9.3. The market equilibrium with the tax is again at B, with price P_t and output Q_t.

Exercise 9.2

1 See Figure 9.19. The new equipment shifts each firm's average and marginal cost curves upwards. Each firm's marginal cost curve is also its supply curve. Firms are now making a loss and some firms will leave the industry.

Figure 9.19
The effect of new
clean-up equipment
on a competitive
firm's costs

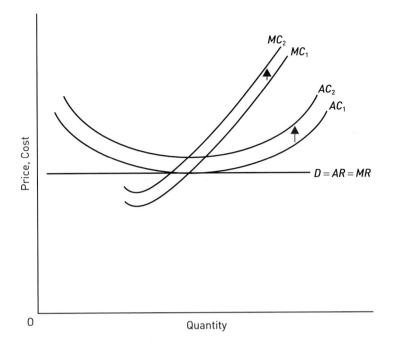

2 On Figure 9.20, the $MPC_1 = S_1$ curve is the industry supply curve before the regulations. (To simplify the diagram I have omitted the MSC curve.) After the installation of new equipment, the industry supply curve shifts to $MPC_2 = S_2$. Equilibrium output has fallen, and price is higher. If the equipment has reduced pollution to zero, there will be no separate MSC curve after the installation, since the externality will have disappeared: the marginal social cost and marginal private cost curves now coincide.

Figure 9.20
The effect of a rise
in costs on the
industry supply
curve

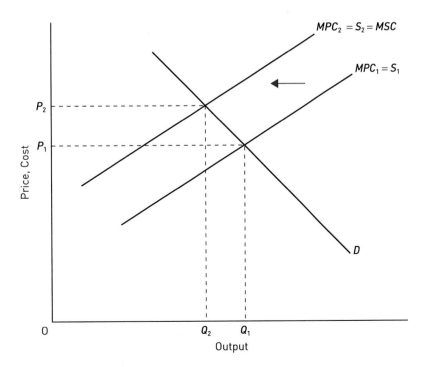

Exercise 9.3

		Herder 2	
		moderate herd	very large herd
Herder 1	moderate herd	3, 3	1, 4
	very large herd	4, 1	2, 2

See Figure 9.21. You will probably have chosen different numbers. What matters is that the relationship between the pay-offs must be as shown in the answer to Exercise 6.2 in Chapter 6. In Figure 9.18, if Herder 2 has a very large herd, Herder 1 will have a very large herd ($2 > 1$). If Herder 2 has a moderate herd, Herder 1 will have a very large herd ($4 > 3$). So Herder 1's dominant strategy is a very large herd. The same is true for Herder 2. Each herder's dominant strategy is to maintain their herd at a level that degrades the land, with pay-offs 2, 2. The dilemma is that each herder would have preferred that both should have moderate herds, causing no overgrazing, with pay-offs 3, 3.

Exercise 9.4 There are two ways to think about this, drawing on Chapter 6. Consider Figure 9.21 (my answer). If each herder values their neighbours' benefits – and suffers from their hurts – then we might argue that in the two-person game shown it is no longer only the pay-offs that matter. Each herder will take into account the needs of the other, in addition to his own pay-off, and choose a moderate herd, rejecting the dominant strategy. Alternatively, we might amend the pay-offs themselves, to incorporate the effect of caring for neighbours. There are many ways this could be done: for example, the pay-off of 3 to having a moderate herd when the other herder does too might be increased – say to 5 – by pleasure at the benefit to the other of this outcome; similarly the pay-off of 2 to having a very large herd when the other does too might be reduced – say to 0.5 – by sadness at the other's losses. Change 3 to 5 and 2 to 0.5 in Figure 9.21 and check that the dominant strategy for each herder is now a moderate herd: the dilemma has been overcome.

Exercise 9.5 If you think that the poor are inured to their poverty while the rich feel passionately about holding on to every last penny, then you might disagree with the proposition that marginal utility declines as income rises. The conclusion concerning redistribution also depends on the assumption that people get the same utility from the same income. You might disagree that this is likely, arguing instead that people are very different. Alternatively, you might disagree with the idea of comparing utilities at all, arguing that the concept is a subjective one so people's utilities cannot be compared.

Exercise 9.6 Health-care insurance suffers from moral hazard, since insurers cannot know what treatment people need. There is more discussion of health insurance in Chapter 10. Life insurance is another example: policies do not pay out if the insurance company discovers that the policy holder committed suicide. Buildings insurance too: a company will try to establish that you have not burned down a property yourself, to claim the insurance, before paying out. As these examples show, a private insurance market may still exist in the face of moral hazard: it depends on the severity of the problem and the cost of investigation.

Chapter 10

Exercise 10.1

Figure 10.6
Market equilibrium
with a positive
consumption
externality

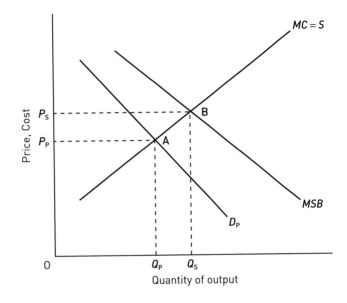

See Figure 10.6. The market equilibrium that results from private decision-making is at A, with price P_P and quantity of vaccinations purchased Q_P. The social optimum quantity of vaccinations is at B, where the marginal social benefit of the vaccinations MSB is equal to the marginal cost of producing them MC. Price would have to be higher, at P_S, to induce suppliers to supply the optimum quantity of vaccinations Q_S.

To raise the quantity of vaccinations purchased towards the social optimum, the government could subsidize the consumption of vaccinations, in order to reduce the price facing consumers at each level of output. Or the government could campaign to make people aware, through public health education, of the social benefits from vaccinations, in the hope that they might increase their own demand as they start to take into account the needs of others as well as themselves.

Exercise 10.2

Your premium is 1 per cent of £2500 = £25, plus £5 = £30 per year.

References

Serials

Annual Abstract of Statistics, London, The Stationery Office for Office for National Statistics (annual).

Economic Trends, London, The Stationery Office for Office for National Statistics (monthly).

Labour Force Survey, London, The Stationery Office for Office for National Statistics (quarterly).

Labour Market Statistics, London, The Stationery Office for Office for National Statistics (monthly).

New Earnings Survey, London, The Stationery Office for Office for National Statistics (annual).

OECD Economic Outlook, Paris, Organization for Economic Co-operation and Development (twice yearly).

OECD Employment Outlook, Paris, Organization for Economic Co-operation and Development (annual).

Social Trends, London, The Stationery Office for Office for National Statistics (annual).

United Kingdom National Accounts (The Blue Book), London, The Stationery Office for Office for National Statistics (annual).

Other references

Abernathy, W.J., Clark, K. and Kantrow, A. (1983) *Industrial Renaissance: Producing a Competitive Future for America*, Basic Books, New York.

Agarwal, B. (1985) *Cold Hearths and Barren Slopes: The Woodfuel Crisis in the Third World*, London, Zed Press.

Agrawal, A. (1994) 'Rules, rule making and rule breaking: examining the fit between rule systems and resource use' in Ostrom, E., Gardner, R. and Walker, J. (eds) (1994) *Rules, Games and Common-Pool Resources*, Ann Arbor, University of Michigan Press.

Akehurst, R., Brazier, J. and Normand, C. (undated) *Internal Markets in the National Health Service: A Review of the Economic Issues*, York, University of York Centre for Health Economics, Discussion Paper No.40.

Anand, P. and van Hees, M. (2001) 'Capabilities and achievements: logistic models of survey evidence', Milton Keynes, The Open University Economics Discipline, discussion paper.

Anand, P. and Wailoo, A. (2000) 'Utilities versus rights to publicly provided goods', *Economica*, vol.67, no.268, pp.543–77.

Arrow, K.J. (1963) 'Uncertainty and the welfare economics of medical care', *American Economic Review*, vol.53, pp.941–73.

Atkinson, A.B. (1999) *The Economic Consequences of Rolling Back the Welfare State*, Cambridge, Mass., MIT Press.

Axelrod, R.M. (1990) *The Evolution of Co-operation*, Harmondsworth, Penguin.

Barr, N. (ed.) (1994) *Labor Markets and Social Policy in Central and Eastern Europe: The Transition and Beyond*, Oxford, Oxford University Press.

Beck, U. (2000) *The Brave New World of Work*, Cambridge, Polity Press.

Behrendt, C. (2000) 'Holes in the safety net? Social security and the alleviation of poverty in comparative perspective', *Luxembourg Income Study Working Paper*, no.259, December.

Berndt, E.R. and Rappaport, N. (2000) 'Price and quality of desktop and mobile personal computers: a quarter century of history', paper presented at the National Bureau of Economic Research's Summer Institute 2000 session on 'Price, Output and Productivity Measurement', Cambridge, Mass.

Blau, F.D. (2000) 'Gender differences in pay', *Journal of Economic Perspectives*, vol.14, no.4, pp.75–99.

Boadway, R. and Keen, M. (2000) 'Redistribution' in Atkinson, A.B. and Bourguignon, F. (eds) (2000) *Handbook of Income Distribution, Volume I*, Amsterdam, Elsevier.

Bonacich, E. and Appelbaum, R. (2000) *Behind the Label: Inequality in the Los Angeles Apparel Industry*, Los Angeles, University of California Press.

Borenstein, S. and Saloner, G. (2001) 'Economics and electronic commerce', *Journal of Economic Perspectives*, vol.15, no.1, pp.3–12.

Boyd, M., Mulvihill, M. and Myles, J. (1995) 'Gender power and postindustrialism' in Jacobs, J.A. (ed.) *Gender Inequality at Work*, Thousand Oaks, Calif., Sage.

Boyer, R. and Savageau, D. (1981) *Places Rated Almanac: Your Guide to Finding the Best Places to Live in America*, Skokie, Ill., Rand McNally.

Bresnahan, T.F. (1998) 'The changing structure of innovation in computing: sources of threats to the dominant US position', in Mowery, D. *et al.* (eds) *America's Industrial Resurgence*, Washington, DC, National Research Council.

Broome, J. (1993) 'Qalys', *Journal of Public Economics*, vol.50, no.2, pp.149–67.

Bureau of Economic Analysis (2000) *Survey of Current Business*, Washington, US Department of Commerce.

Carroll, G. and Hannon, M. (2000) *The Demography of Corporations and Industries*, Princeton, NJ, Princeton University Press.

Carvel, J. (2001) 'Rags or riches on the life line', *The Guardian, Society*, 10 October, p.4.

Castells, M. (2001) *The Internet Galaxy: Reflections on the Internet, Business and Society*, Oxford, Oxford University Press.

Colecchia, A. and Schreyer, P. (2002) 'ICT investment and economic growth in the '90s: is the US a unique case? A comparative study of 10 OECD countries', *Review of Economic Dynamics*, vol.5.

Commission on Macroeconomics and Health (2001) *Macroeconomics and Health: Investing in Health for Economics and Development*, report presented to the World Health Organization, December, Geneva, WHO.

Cummins, R.A. (2000) 'Objective and subjective quality of life: an interactive model', *Social Indicators Research*, vol.52, pp.55–72.

Daly, H.E. and Cobb, J.B. (1994) *For the Common Good*, Boston, Mass., Beacon Press.

David, P. and Wright, G. (1999) 'General purpose technologies and surges in productivity: historical reflections on the future of the IT revolution', *University of Oxford Discussion Papers in Economic and Social History*, no.31, September.

Department of Social Security (DSS) (2001) *Households Below Average Incomes*, London, The Stationery Office.

Dixit, A.K. and Nalebuff, B.J. (1991) *Thinking Strategically: The Competitive Edge in Business, Politics, and Everyday Life*, New York, W.W. Norton.

Economides, N. (2001) 'The Microsoft antitrust case', *Journal of Competition and Trade*, at www.stern.nyu.edu (accessed September 2001).

Economist, The (2000) 'Supplement: The new economy: untangling e-conomics', 23 September.

Economist, The (2001a) 'Renault's alliance with Nissan: halfway down a long road', *The Economist*, 18 August, p.59.

Economist, The (2001b) 'Corporate alliances: just good friends', Leader article, *The Economist*, 18 August, p.12.

Elton, B. (1990) *Gasping*, London, Sphere Books.

Enthoven, A.C. (1988) *Reflections on the Management of the National Health Service*, London, Nuffield Provincial Hospitals Trust.

Epstein, R. (1928) *The Automobile Industry: Its Economic and Commercial Development*, New York, Arno Press.

Etzioni, A. (1988) *The Moral Dimension: Towards a New Economics*, New York, Free Press.

Eunjung Cha, A. (2001) 'Former Sotheby's chairman could get up to three years in prison', *Washington Post*, 6 December, p.E1.

Filson, D. (2001) 'The nature and effects of technological change on the industry life-cycle, *Review of Economic Dynamics*, vol.4, pp.460–94.

Financial Times (2001) 'The Lex Column: picking and choosing', *Financial Times*, 26 June, p.22.

Finch, J. (2001) 'On the markets: laughing stock', *The Guardian*, 3 October, p.25.

Fisher, F. and Rubinfeld, D. (2000) 'United States v. Microsoft: an economic analysis', *Public Law and Legal Theory Working Paper No.30*, UC Berkeley School of Law, Calif., at http://papers.ssrn.com (accessed September 2001).

Flores, F. and Gray, J. (2000) *Entrepreneurship and the Wired Life: Work in the Wake of Careers*, London, Demos.

Fortune International (1993) 'Toshiba pioneers new alliances with American and European partners', Advertising section: 'Global alliances', vol.128, no.4, 23 August, p.S5.

Freeman, R.B. and Medoff, J.L. (1984) *What Do Unions Do?*, New York, Basic Books.

Frey, B.S. and Stutzer, A. (2002) *Happiness and Economics*, Princeton, NJ, Princeton University Press.

Gibson, C., McKean, M. and Ostrom, E. (eds) (2000) *People and Forests: Communities, Institutions and Governance*, Cambridge, Mass., MIT Press.

Gilbert, R. and Katz, M. (2001) 'An economist's guide to US v. Microsoft', *Journal of Economic Perspectives*, vol.15, no.2, pp.25–44.

Goodman, A., Johnson, P. and Webb, S. (1997) *Inequality in the UK*, Oxford, Oxford University Press.

Goodwin, N. (1998) 'GP fund holding' in Le Grand *et al.* (1998).

Gordon, R.J. (2000) 'Does the new economy measure up to the great inventions of the past?', *Journal of Economic Perspectives*, vol.4, no.14, pp.49–74.

Graham, A. (2001) 'The assessment: economics of the Internet', *Oxford Review of Economic Policy*, vol.17, no.2, pp.145–58.

Green, F. (2001) 'It's been a hard day's night: the concentration and intensification of work in late twentieth-century Britain', *British Journal of Industrial Relations*, vol.39, no.1, pp.53–80.

Green, F. and McIntosh, S. (2001) 'The intensification of work in Europe', *Labour Economics*, vol.8, no.2, pp.291–308.

Greenspan, A. (1998) 'Is there a new economy?', *California Management Review*, vol.41, no.1, pp.74–85.

Gregg, P. and Wadsworth, J. (1999) 'Job tenure 1975–98' in Gregg, P. and Wadsworth, J. (eds) *The State of Working Britain*, Manchester, Manchester University Press, pp.109–26.

Guerrera, F. (2001) 'Hectic year for Monti in his crusade against "cancers" ', *Financial Times*, 28 December.

Hamblin, R. (1998) 'Trusts' in Le Grand *et al.* (1998).

Hardin, G. (1968) 'The tragedy of the commons', *Science*, vol.162, 13 December.

Harrison, B. and Bluestone, B. (1990) 'Wage polarisation in the US and the "flexibility" debate', *Cambridge Journal of Economics*, vol.14, no.3, pp.351–73.

Hay, D.A. and Morris, D.J. (1991) *Industrial Economics and Organization: Theory and Evidence*, Oxford, Oxford University Press.

Hayek, F. (1976, first published 1948) 'The meaning of competition' in *Individualism and Economic Order*, Chicago, University of Chicago Press.

Hicks, J.R. (1935) 'Annual survey of economic theory: the theory of monopoly', *Econometrica*, vol.3, no.1, pp.1–20.

Hochschild, A. (1997) *The Time Bind*, New York, Metropolitan Books.

Incomes Data Services (2001) *Pay and Conditions in Call Centres*, IDS Research Report, September, London, IDS, at http://www.incomesdata.co.uk (accessed January 2002).

IPPR (2000) *Future of Work*, findings of a series of focus groups with people in low-paid jobs, funded by the Reed Academy of Enterprise, London, Institute for Public Policy Research.

Kabeer, N. (2000) *The Power to Choose: Bangladeshi Women and Labour Market Decisions in London and Dhaka*, London, Verso.

Kalecki, M. (1943) 'Political aspects of full employment' in Kalecki, M. (ed.) *Selected Essays on the Dynamics of the Capitalist Economy, 1933–1970*, Cambridge, Cambridge University Press, pp.138–45.

Kehoe, L. (2001) 'PC shipments suffer fall', *Financial Times*, 21 July, p.6.

Keynes, J.M. (1936) *The General Theory of Employment, Interest and Money*, London, Macmillan.

Klein, B. (2001) 'The Microsoft case: what can a dominant firm do to defend its position?', *Journal of Economic Perspectives*, vol.15, no.2, pp.45–62.

Klein, N. (1999) *No Logo: Taking Aim at the Brand Bullies*, New York, Picador.

Klein, R. (1983) *The Politics of the National Health Service*, London, Longman.

Lakin, C. (2001) 'The effects of taxes and benefits on household income, 1999–2000', *Economic Trends*, no.569, April.

Landes, D. (1972) *The Unbound Prometheus: Technological Change and Industrial Development in Western Europe from 1750 to the Present*, Cambridge, Cambridge University Press.

Le Grand, J., Mays, N. and Mulligan, J. (eds) (1998) *Evaluating the NHS Reforms*, London, King's Fund Institute.

Lewis, S. and Brannen, J. (2000) 'Forever young? Generation X's views on gender, work and family issues' in Wilkinson, H. (ed.) *Family Business*, London, Demos.

Lipsey, R., Bekar, C. and Carlaw, K. (1998) 'General purpose technologies and economic growth', in Helpman, E. (ed.) *General Purpose Technologies and Economic Growth*, Cambridge, Mass., MIT Press, pp.38–43.

Lutz, M. (1999) *The Economics of the Common Good*, London, Routledge.

Machin, S. (1999) 'Wage inequality in the 1970s, 1980s and 1990s' in Gregg, P. and Wadsworth, J. (eds) *The State of Working Britain*, Manchester, Manchester University Press, pp.185–205.

McKean, M. (2000) 'Common property: what is it, what is it good for and what makes it work?' in Gibson *et al.* (2000).

Mackintosh, M. and Mooney, G. (2000) 'Identity, inequality and social class' in Woodward, K. (ed.) *Questioning Identity: Gender, Class, Nation*, London, Routledge/The Open University.

Makowski, L. and Ostroy, J.M. (2001) 'Perfect competition and the creativity of the market', *Journal of Economic Literature*, vol.XXXIX, no.2, pp.479–535.

Marshall, A. (1925) *Principles of Economics*, Book IV (8th edn), London, Macmillan.

Milburn, A. (2002) 'Redefining the National Health Service', speech to New Health Network, 15 January, *Guardian Unlimited*, http://www.guardian.co.uk/Archive/Article/0,4273,4336093,00.html (accessed May 2002).

Mokyr, J. (1997) 'Are we living in the middle of an Industrial Revolution?', *Federal Reserve Bank of Kansas City Economic Review*, Second Quarter, pp.31–43.

Nelson, R.R. and Winter, S.G. (1982) *An Evolutionary Theory of Economic Change*, Cambridge, Mass., The Belknap Press of Harvard University Press.

Oberholzer-Gee, F., Frey, B.S., Pommerehne, W.W. and Hart, A. (1996) 'Panik Protest und Paralyse: Eine Empirische Untersuchung Uber Nukleare Endlager in der Schweiz', *Scweiserische Zeitschrift fur Volkswirtschaft und Statistik*, vol.131, pp.147–77.

OECD (1994) *The OECD Jobs Study: Evidence and Explanations Part II*, Paris, Organization for Economic Co-operation and Development.

OECD (1998) 'The OECD Jobs Strategy: progress report on implementation of country-specific recommendations', *Economics Department Working Paper*, no.196, May.

OECD (2000) 'E-commerce: impacts and policy challenges' in *Economic Outlook No.67*, Paris, Organization for Economic Co-operation and Development.

Okun, A. (1970) *The Political Economy of Prosperity*, New York, Norton.

Osborn, A. (2001) 'Banks pay heavy fine for price-fixing', *The Guardian*, 12 December, p.22.

Parfit, D. (1984) *Reasons and Persons*, Oxford, Oxford University Press.

Peden, G.C. (1985) *British Economic and Social Policy: Lloyd George to Margaret Thatcher*, Oxford, Philip Allan.

Perrons, D. (2001) 'The new economy and the work–life balance: a case study of the new media sector in Brighton and Hove', *Research Papers in Environmental and Spatial Analysis No.67*, Department of Geography and Environment, London School of Economics.

Plato (1993) *The Last Days of Socrates*, Harmondsworth, Penguin Books (translated by H. Tredennick and H. Tarrant).

Pollin, R., Brenner, M. and Wicks-Lim, J. (2004) *Economic Analysis of the Florida Minimum Wage Proposal*, PERI (Political Economy Research Institute)/Center for American Progress.

Popovich, K. (2001) 'Dell predicts industry shakeout', *Eweek*, 22 January.

Purdy, D. (2001) 'Social policy' in Artis, M. and Nixson, F. (eds) *The Economics of the European Union*, Oxford, Oxford University Press.

Quah, D. (1996) *The Invisible Hand and the Weightless Economy*, Centre for Economic Performance Occasional Paper No.12, London, London School of Economics.

Quah, D. (1999) *The Weightless Economy in Economic Development*, Centre for Economic Performance Discussion Paper No.417, London, London School of Economics.

Quah, D. (2001) 'Technology dissemination and economic growth: some lessons for the new economy', public lecture at the University of Hong Kong, at http://econ.lse.ac.uk/staff/dquah/ (accessed January 2002).

Quizilbash, M. (1997) 'Pluralism and well-being indices', *World Development*, vol.25, pp.2009–26.

Raff, D.M.G. and Trajtenberg, M. (1997) 'Quality-adjusted prices for the American automobile industry: 1906–1940' in Bresnahan, T.F. and Gordon, R.J. (eds) *The Economics of New Goods: NBER Studies in Income and Wealth: Vol.58*, Chicago, University of Chicago Press, pp.71–107.

Rawls, J. (1972) *A Theory of Justice*, Oxford, Oxford University Press.

Reich, R. (2001) *The Future of Success: Work and Life in the New Economy*, London, Heinemann.

Samuelson, P.A. and Nordhaus, W.D. (1989) *Economics* (13th edn), Singapore, McGraw-Hill.

Schofield, J. (2000) 'Trouble at the top for PC giants', *The Guardian* online, 13 September, pp.1–3.

Schumpeter, J. (1942) *Capitalism, Socialism and Democracy*, New York, Harper.

Schyns, P. (1998) 'Cross-national differences in happiness: economic and cultural factors explored', *Social Indicators Research*, vol.43, pp.3–26.

Sen, A.K. (1985) *Capabilities and Commodities*, Amsterdam, North-Holland.

Sennett, R. (1998) *The Corrosion of Character*, London, W.W. Norton.

Shipman, A. (2001) 'Privatized production, socialized consumption? Old producer power behind the new consumer sovereignty', *Review of Social Economy*, vol.LIX, pp.331–52.

Shy, O. (2001) *The Economics of Network Industries*, Cambridge, Cambridge University Press.

Smeeding, T. and Rainwater, L. (2001) 'Comparing living standards across nations: real incomes at the top, the bottom and the middle', *Luxembourg Income Study Working Paper*, no.266, May.

Smith, A. (1937, first published 1776) *The Wealth of Nations*, The Cannan Edition, New York, Modern Library.

Smith, G.D., Dorling, D. and Shaw, M. (2001) *Poverty, Inequality and Health in Britain 1800–2000: A Reader*, London, Policy Press.

Solow, R.M. (1987) 'We'd better watch out', *New York Times Book Review*, 12 July, p.36.

Sutliff, T.J. (1901) 'Revival in all industries exceeds most sanguine hopes', *New York Herald Tribune*, 6 April, p.3.

Tanzi, V. and Schuknecht, L. (2000) *Public Spending in the Twentieth Century*, Cambridge, Cambridge University Press.

Thompson, G. (2000) 'Economic globalization?' in Held, D. (ed.) *A Globalizing World? Culture, Economics, Politics*, London, Routledge/The Open University.

Timmins, N. (1995) *The Five Giants: A Biography of the Welfare State*, London, HarperCollins.

Toffler, A. (1980) *The Third Wave*, New York, William Morrow.

Tushman, M. and Anderson, P. (1986) 'Technological discontinuities and organizational environments', *Administrative Science Quarterly*, vol.31, pp.439–65.

van Doorslaer, E. and Wagstaff, A. (1993) 'Equity in the finance of health care: methods and findings' in van Doorslaer, E., Wagstaff, A. and Rutten, F. (eds) *Equity and Finance in the Delivery of Health Care: An International Perspective*, Oxford, Oxford University Press.

van Doorslaer, E. *et al.* (2000) 'Equity in the delivery of health care in Europe and the US', *Journal of Health Economics*, vol.19, no.5, pp.553–83.

Van Reenan, J. (2001) 'The new economy: reality and policy', *Fiscal Studies*, vol.22, no.3, pp.307–36.

Varughese, G. (2000) 'Population and forest dynamics in the hills of Nepal: institutional remedies by rural communities' in Gibson *et al.* (2000).

Veblen, T. (1912) *The Theory of the Leisure Class*, London, Macmillan.

Veenhoven, R. (1993) *Happiness in Nations: Subjective Appreciation of Life in 56 Nations*, Rotterdam, RISBO.

Viscusi, K. (1998) *Rational Risk Policy*, Oxford, Clarendon Press.

Voyle, S. and Edgecliffe-Johnson, A. (2001) 'Tesco exports online trading to US', *Financial Times*, 26 June, p.23.

Wagstaff, A. *et al.* (1999) 'Equity in the finance of health care: some further international comparisons', *Journal of Health Economics*, vol.18, no.3, pp.263–90.

Whitehead, M. (1992) 'The Health Divide' in Townsend, P., Whitehead, M. and Davidson, N. (eds) *Inequalities in Health: The Black Report and the Health Divide*, Harmondsworth, Penguin.

Women's Unit (2000) *More Choice for Women in the New Economy: The Facts*, London, Cabinet Office.

World Health Organization (1999) *The World Health Report*, Geneva, WHO.

Acknowledgements

Grateful acknowledgement is made to the following sources for permission to reproduce material in this book.

Introduction

Photo p.xi: Copyright © Ronald J. Thomas.

Chapter 1

Text

Extract on p.18: Jewson, N. (2003) 'Work changes us as people', *The Sunday Times*, 18 May 2003. Copyright © Nick Jewson.

Chapter 2

Figures

Figure 2.1: Copyright © 1997 Wasserman, *Boston Globe*, LA Times Syndicate; *Figure 2.3*: taken from www.obsoletecomputermuseum.org.

Chapter 3

Text

Extract on p.69: 'BMW wants to make internal-combustion engines that run on hydrogen', *The Economist*, 21 July 2001. Copyright © The Economist Newspaper Limited, London.

Figures

Figure 3.1: Copyright © Citroën UK Ltd; *Figure 3.2*: Copyright © IPC Media Ltd; *Figure 3.9*: Copyright © IPC Media Ltd.

Chapter 4

Text

Extract on p.76: Samuelson, R.J. (2000) 'The mystifying Microsoft case', *Washington Post*, 11 April 2000. Copyright © 2001 The Washington Post Writers Group. Reprinted with permission; *Extract on p.101*: Spiegel, P. and Abrahams, P. (2001) 'Appeals court rules against Microsoft break-up', *Financial Times*, 28 June 2001. Copyright © 2001 Financial Times Syndication.

Figures

Figure 4.1: Copyright © The New Yorker Collection from cartoonbank.com. All Rights Reserved; *Figure 4.10*: Klein, B. (2001) 'The Microsoft case: what can a dominant firm do to defend its position?', *Journal of Economic Perspectives*, Spring 2001, vol.15, issue 2, American Economic Association.

Chapter 5

Text

Extract on p.123: adapted from Finch, J. (2001) 'Body Shop buyers line up', *The Guardian*, 3 October 2001. Copyright © The Guardian.

Figures

Figure 5.14: Copyright © Fat Free Ltd/Miramax/The Kobal Collection.

Chapter 6

Text

Extract on p.167: O'Donnell, J. (2003) 'Price fixers face jail, fines and disqualification in crackdown', *The Sunday Times*, 23 February 2003. Reproduced by permission of News International Syndication Ltd.

Figures

Figure 6.10 (left): Courtesy of Mark Chilvers; *Figure 6.10 (right)*: Copyright © David Ashdown, The Independent.

Chapter 7

Tables

Table 7.1: From *The State of Working Britain*, by Paul Gregg and Jonathan Wadsworth, 1999, Manchester University Press, Manchester, UK; *Table 7.3*: OECD *Employment Outlook*, July 1997. Copyright © OECD.

Chapter 8

Figures

Figure 8.3: Office for National Statistics, 2001, Table 2.1, p.109. Crown copyright material is reproduced under Class Licence Number C01W0000065 with the permission of the Controller of HMSO and the Queen's Printer for Scotland.

Tables

Table 8.1: Office for National Statistics, 2001, Table 1.2, p.39. Crown copyright material is reproduced under Class Licence Number C01W0000065 with the permission of the Controller of HMSO and the Queen's Printer for Scotland; *Table 8.5*: Office for National Statistics, 2001, Table 1.2, pp.38–9 and Table 1.3, pp.40–1. Crown copyright material is reproduced under Class Licence Number C01W0000065 with the permission of the Controller of HMSO and the Queen's Printer for Scotland; *Table 8.6*: Office for National Statistics, 2001, Table 1.1, pp.36–7. Crown copyright material is reproduced under Class Licence Number C01W0000065 with the permission of the Controller of HMSO and the Queen's Printer for Scotland; *Table 8.9*: Viscusi, K. (1998) *Rational Risk Policy*, Oxford University Press, Inc.; *Table 8.11*: Oberholzer-Gee *et al.* (1996) *Schweiserische Zeitschrift fur Volkswirtschaft und Statistik*, no.131, Helbring und Lichtenhaln Verlag; *Table 8.13*: Reprinted from *World Development*, vol.25, no.12, Mozaffar Quizilbash (1997) 'Pluralism and well-being indices', pp.2009–26, Copyright © 1997, with permission from Elsevier Science.

Chapter 9

Figures

Figure 9.5: based on Tanzi, V. and Schuknecht, L. (2000) *Public Spending in the Twentieth Century: A Global Perspective*. Copyright © Vito Tanzi, Ludger Schuknecht, published by Cambridge University Press; *Figure 9.8*: *Luxembourg Income Study*, 10 October 2001, Copyright © LIS 2001; *Figure 9.9*: Lakin, C. (2001) *Economic Trends*, no.569, April 2001. Crown copyright material is reproduced under Class Licence Number C01W0000065 with the permission of the Controller of HMSO and the Queen's Printer for Scotland; *Figure 9.11*: adapted from *The OECD Jobs Study: Evidence and Explanations*, Part II, 1994; *Figure 9.14*: DSS (2001) *Households Below Average Income 1999/00*, p.8. Crown copyright material is reproduced under Class Licence Number C01W0000065 with the permission of the Controller of HMSO and the Queen's Printer for Scotland.

Tables

Table 9.1: DSS (2001) *Households Below Average Income 1999/00*, p.101. Crown copyright material is reproduced under Class Licence Number C01W0000065 with the permission of the Controller of HMSO and the Queen's Printer for Scotland; *Table 9.2*: *Luxembourg Income Study*, 10 October 2001, Copyright © LIS 2001; *Table 9.3*: Behrendt, C. (2000) 'Holes in the safety net? Social security and the alleviation of poverty in comparative perspective', December 2000. Copyright © Christina Behrendt, University of Konstanz.

Chapter 10

Text

Extracts on p.267: Carvel, J. (2001) 'Rags or riches on the life line: London reveals a widening gap in the fight against health inequalities', *The Guardian*, 10 October 2001. Copyright © 2001 Guardian Newspapers Limited.

Figures

Figure 10.2: van Doorslaer, E. and Wagstaff, A. (1993) 'Equity in the finance of health care: methods of dealings' in van Doorslaer, E., Wagstaff, A. and Rutten, F. (eds) *Equity in the Finance and Delivery of Health Care: An International Perspective*, Commission of European Communities; *Figure 10.3*: reprinted from *Journal of Health Economics*, vol.19, van Doorslaer, E. *et al.* (2000) 'Equity in the delivery of health care in Europe', p.556. Copyright © 2000, with permission from Elsevier Science.

Tables

Table 10.2: reprinted from *Journal of Health Economics*, vol.18, Wagstaff, A. *et al.* (1999) 'Equity in the finance of health care', p.268. Copyright © 1999, with permission from Elsevier Science.

Every effort has been made to trace all copyright owners, but if any has been inadvertently overlooked, the publishers will be pleased to make the necessary arrangements at the first opportunity.

Index